D0195785

THE CAMBRIDGE
COMPANION TO

AMERICAN REALISM AND NATURALISM

This Companion offers a look at a number of issues related to the terms *realism* and *naturalism,* which have long served to designate major late-nineteenth-century American fiction. The Introduction seeks both to discuss the problems inherent in the use of these two terms in relation to late-nineteenth-century fiction and to describe the history of previous efforts to make them expressive of American writing of this period. The Companion includes eleven essays that fall into three categories: the historical context of realism and naturalism (Louis J. Budd and Richard Lehan); critical approaches to the movements since the early 1970s (Michael Anesko and Elizabeth Ammons); and a full-scale discussion of twelve major texts, from William Dean Howells's *The Rise of Silas Lapham* to James Weldon Johnson's *The Autobiography of an Ex-Colored Man.*

Cambridge Companions to Literature

Continued on page following Index

813.09
C178c

THE CAMBRIDGE
COMPANION TO

AMERICAN REALISM AND NATURALISM

Howells to London

EDITED BY

DONALD PIZER

Tulane University

CAMBRIDGE
UNIVERSITY PRESS

PUBLISHED BY THE PRESS SYNDICATE OF THE UNIVERSITY OF CAMBRIDGE
The Pitt Building, Trumpington Street, Cambridge, United Kingdom

CAMBRIDGE UNIVERSITY PRESS
The Edinburgh Building, Cambridge CB2 2RU, UK   http://www.cup.cam.ac.uk
40 West 20th Street, New York, NY 10011-4211, USA   http://www.cup.org
10 Stamford Road, Oakleigh, Melbourne 3166, Australia
Ruiz de Alarcón 13, 28014 Madrid, Spain

© Cambridge University Press 1995

This book is in copyright. Subject to statutory exception
and to the provisions of relevant collective licensing agreements,
no reproduction of any part may take place without
the written permission of Cambridge University Press.

First published 1995
Reprinted 1996, 1999

Typeset in Sabon

A catalog record for this book is available from the British Library

Library of Congress Cataloging in Publication Data is available

ISBN 0 521 43876 4 paperback

Transferred to digital printing 2002

CONTENTS

CONTRIBUTORS

ELIZABETH AMMONS is Professor of English and American Studies and Dean of Humanities and Arts at Tufts University. She is the author of *Edith Wharton's Argument with America* (1980) and *Conflicting Stories: American Women Writers at the Turn into the Twentieth Century* (1991). She is a coeditor of the forthcoming *Oxford Companion to Women's Writing in the United States*.

MICHAEL ANESKO is Associate Professor of English at Pennsylvania State University, University Park. He has published *"Friction with the Market": Henry James and the Profession of Authorship* (1986) and an edition of Horatio Alger's *Ragged Dick* (1993).

LOUIS J. BUDD is James B. Duke Professor of English at Duke University. Among his books are *Mark Twain: Social Philosopher* (1962), *Robert Herrick* (1971), and *Our Mark Twain: The Making of His Public Personality* (1983).

JOHN W. CROWLEY is Professor of English at Syracuse University. His books include *George Cabot Lodge* (1976), *The Black Heart's Truth: The Early Career of W. D. Howells* (1985), *The Mask of Fiction: Essays on W. D. Howells* (1989), and *The White Logic: Alcoholism and Gender in American Modernist Fiction* (1994).

BLANCHE H. GELFANT is the Robert E. Maxwell '23 Professor at Dartmouth College. She has published *The American City Novel* (1954), *Women Writing in America: Voices in Collage* (1984), and *Cross-Cultural Reckonings: A Triptych of Russian, American, and Canadian Texts*.

BARBARA HOCHMAN is Lecturer in English at Tel Aviv University. As well as essays on Edith Wharton and Theodore Dreiser, she has published *The Art of Frank Norris, Storyteller* (1988).

RICHARD LEHAN is Professor of English at the University of California, Los Angeles. He is the author of *F. Scott Fitzgerald and the Craft of Fiction*

(1966), *Theodore Dreiser: His World and His Novels* (1969), *A Dangerous Crossing: French Literary Existentialism and the Modern American Novel* (1973), and *The Great Gatsby: The Limits of Wonder* (1990).

J. C. LEVENSON is Professor of English at the University of Virginia. He is the author of *The Mind and Art of Henry Adams* (1957), coeditor of *The Letters of Henry Adams* (1982), and editor of Stephen Crane's *Prose and Poetry* (1984) in the Library of America.

DONALD PIZER is the Pierce Butler Professor of English at Tulane University. Among his books are *Realism and Naturalism in Nineteenth-Century American Literature* (1966; rev. ed., 1984), *Twentieth-Century American Literary Naturalism: An Interpretation* (1982), *The Theory and Practice of American Literary Naturalism: Selected Essays and Reviews* (1993), and studies of the fiction of Frank Norris, Theodore Dreiser, and John Dos Passos.

TOM QUIRK is Professor of English at the University of Missouri, Columbia. He is the author of *Bergson and American Culture: The Worlds of Willa Cather and Wallace Stevens* (1990) and *Coming to Grips with Huckleberry Finn: Essays on a Book, a Boy, and a Man* (1993) and is coeditor of *Writing the American Classics* (1990).

JACQUELINE TAVERNIER-COURBIN is Professor of English at the University of Ottawa. She is the author of *Ernest Hemingway's "A Moveable Feast": The Making of Myth* (1991) and is editor of *Critical Essays on Jack London* (1983) and the journal *Thalia: Studies in Literary Humor.*

KENNETH W. WARREN is Associate Professor of English at the University of Chicago. He has published *Black and White Strangers: Race and American Literary Realism* (1993).

1865   Thirteenth Amendment abolishes slavery; Lee surrenders at Appomattox; Lincoln assassinated, Andrew Johnson succeeds (president to 1869).
Mark Twain, "The Celebrated Jumping Frog of Calaveras County."
Walt Whitman, *Drum-Taps*.

1866   Atlantic cable completed; Ku Klux Klan founded. Fyodor Dostoeveski, *Crime and Punishment*.
John Greenleaf Whittier, *Snow-Bound*.

1867   Reconstruction Act; Alfred Nobel perfects dynamite.
John W. De Forest, *Miss Ravenel's Conversion from Secession to Loyalty*.
George Washington Harris, *Sut Lovingood Yarns*.

1868   Effort to impeach President Johnson narrowly fails; Fourteenth Amendment guaranteeing civil rights.

1869   Ulysses S. Grant, president 1869–77; Suez Canal opens; Union Pacific-Central Pacific transcontinental railroad completed; Wyoming passes first woman's suffrage act in the United States.
Matthew Arnold, *Culture and Anarchy*; John Stuart Mill, *The Subjection of Women*.
Harriet Beecher Stowe, *Oldtown Folks*.
Mark Twain, *The Innocents Abroad*.

1870   Franco-Prussian War (France capitulates in 1871); John D. Rockefeller founds the Standard Oil Company; death of Charles Dickens.
Bret Harte, *The Luck of Roaring Camp and Other Sketches*.

1871   Chicago destroyed by fire; Smith College founded. Emile Zola publishes the first novel in his Rougon-Macquart series (completed in 1893). Charles Darwin, *The Descent of Man*.
Edward Eggleston, *The Hoosier Schoolmaster*.

William Dean Howells, *Their Wedding Journey.*
Walt Whitman, *Democratic Vistas.*

1872 John W. De Forest, *Kate Beaumont.*
Mark Twain, *Roughing It.*

1873 *Crédit Mobilier* scandal implicates many in federal government; failure of Jay Cooke & Co. precipitates Panic of 1873. Herbert Spencer, *The Study of Sociology;* Leo Tolstoy, *Anna Karenina.*
William Dean Howells, *A Chance Acquaintance.*
Mark Twain and Charles Dudley Warner, *The Gilded Age.*

1874 Woman's Christian Temperance Union founded; first impressionist exhibition in Paris.
Rebecca Harding Davis, *John Andross.*
Edward Eggleston, *The Circuit Rider.*
John Fiske, *The Outlines of Cosmic Philosophy.*

1875 John W. De Forest, *Honest Jane Vane.*
Bret Harte, *Tales of the Argonauts.*
William Dean Howells, *A Foregone Conclusion.*
Henry James, *A Passionate Pilgrim and Other Tales.*

1876 Disputed election of 1876 between Samuel J. Tilden and Rutherford B. Hayes, with Hayes declared president (1877–81) by the Electoral Commission; Alexander Graham Bell invents the telephone; Centennial Exposition in Philadelphia; Custer defeated at the Battle of Little Big Horn.
Henry James, *Roderick Hudson.*
Mark Twain, *The Adventures of Tom Sawyer.*

1877 End of Reconstruction.
Henry James, *The American.*
Sarah Orne Jewett, *Deephaven.*

1878 Thomas Hardy, *The Return of the Native.*
Henry James, *French Poets and Novelists.*

1879 Edison patents the incandescent lamp. Henrik Ibsen, *A Doll's House.*
George Washington Cable, *Old Creole Days.*
Henry George, *Progress and Poverty.*
Henry James, *Daisy Miller.*
Albion W. Tourgée, *A Fool's Errand.*

1880 Death of George Eliot.
Henry Adams, *Democracy.*
George Washington Cable, *The Grandissimes.*

William Dean Howells, *The Undiscovered Country.*
Lew Wallace, *Ben-Hur.*

1881　James A. Garfield, president in 1881, is assassinated; succeeded by Chester A. Arthur, 1881–5; Booker T. Washington establishes Tuskegee Institute; American Federation of Labor founded.
Joel Chandler Harris, *Uncle Remus.*
Henry James, *The Portrait of a Lady* and *Washington Square.*

1882　Chinese exclusion act; deaths of Ralph Waldo Emerson and Henry Wadsworth Longfellow.
William Dean Howells, *A Modern Instance.*

1883　Pendleton Act, establishing Civil Service; Northern Pacific transcontinental railroad completed; Brooklyn Bridge opens; first Chicago skyscraper.
E. W. Howe, *The Story of a Country Town.*
Mark Twain, *Life on the Mississippi.*

1884　Mugwump liberal wing of Republican party contributes to defeat of James G. Blaine by Grover Cleveland, president 1885–9, 1893–7, the only Democratic president from the Civil War to the election of Woodrow Wilson in 1912.
John Hay, *The Bread-Winners.*
Mary Noailles Murfree, *In The Tennessee Mountains.*
Mark Twain, *Adventures of Huckleberry Finn.*

1885　Leopold II, king of Belgium, takes personal possession of the Congo; internal combustion engine patented.
Ulysses S. Grant, *Personal Memoirs.*
William Dean Howells, *The Rise of Silas Lapham.*

1886　Haymarket Riot in Chicago, anarchists blamed. Karl Marx, *Capital* (first appearance in English).
Andrew Carnegie, *Triumphant Democracy.*
William Dean Howells, *Indian Summer* and the "Editor's Study" (to 1892), *Harper's Monthly Magazine.*
Henry James, *The Bostonians.*
Sarah Orne Jewett, *A White Heron.*
Constance Fenimore Woolson, *East Angels.*

1887　Interstate Commerce Act; first electric streetcars.
Mary Wilkins Freeman, *A Humble Romance and Other Stories.*
Harold Frederic, *Seth's Brother's Wife.*
William Dean Howells, *The Minister's Charge.*
Joseph Kirkland, *Zury: The Meanest Man in Spring County.*

1888   Nicholas Tesla invents the first electric motor; George Eastman perfects the box camera. Rudyard Kipling, *Plain Tales from the Hills*.

Edward Bellamy, *Looking Backward*.

Henry James, *The Aspern Papers* and *Partial Portraits*.

1889   Benjamin Harrison, president 1889–93.

Lafcadio Hearn, *Chita*.

William Dean Howells, *Annie Kilburn*.

Theodore Roosevelt, *The Winning of the West* (completed 1896).

Mark Twain, *A Connecticut Yankee in King Arthur's Court*.

1890   Sherman Anti-Trust Act. J. G. Frazer, *The Golden Bough* (completed 1915); Henrik Ibsen, *Hedda Gabler*.

Emily Dickinson, *Poems*.

James A. Herne, *Margaret Fleming*.

William Dean Howells, *A Hazard of New Fortunes*.

William James, *The Principles of Psychology*.

Jacob Riis, *How the Other Half Lives*.

1891   First International Copyright Law; deaths of Herman Melville and James Russell Lowell. Thomas Hardy, *Tess of the D'Urbervilles*.

Ambrose Bierce, *Tales of Soldiers and Civilians*.

H. H. Boyesen, *The Mammon of Unrighteousness*.

Mary Wilkins Freeman, *A New England Nun and Other Stories*.

Hamlin Garland, *Main-Travelled Roads*.

William Dean Howells, *Criticism and Fiction*.

1892   Strike riots at Carnegie Steel Company, Homestead; formation of the People's party (Populists) to press for farmers' reforms; deaths of Walt Whitman and John Greenleaf Whittier.

Charlotte Perkins Gilman, "The Yellow Wallpaper."

William Dean Howells, *The Quality of Mercy*.

1893   Grover Cleveland, president 1893–7; Wall Street Panic of 1893 begins depression (to 1897); Anti-Saloon League formed; World's Columbian Exposition in Chicago.

Stephen Crane, *Maggie: A Girl of the Streets*.

Henry B. Fuller, *The Cliff-Dwellers*.

Frederick Jackson Turner, "The Significance of the Frontier in American History."

1894   Pullman Company strike and violence in Chicago followed by nationwide rail strike; Coxey's Army marches on Washington; first kinetoscope (motion picture) opens in New York.

George Washington Cable, *John March, Southerner.*
Kate Chopin, *Bayou Folk.*
Hamlin Garland, *Crumbling Idols.*
William Dean Howells, *A Traveller from Altruria.*
Mark Twain, *The Tragedy of Pudd'nhead Wilson.*

1895   Marconi invents radio telegraphy; Röntgen discovers x-rays; death of Frederick Douglass. Joseph Conrad, *Almayer's Folly;* H. G. Wells, *The Time Machine.*
Stephen Crane, *The Black Riders* and *The Red Badge of Courage.*
Henry B. Fuller, *With the Procession.*
Hamlin Garland, *Rose of Dutcher's Coolly.*

1896   William Jennings Bryan's "Cross of Gold" speech at Democratic Convention; beginning of Klondike Gold Rush; first modern Olympic Games; Nobel Prizes established; death of Harriet Beecher Stowe.
James Lane Allen, *A Summer in Arcady.*
Abraham Cahan, *Yekl: A Tale of the New York Ghetto.*
Paul Laurence Dunbar, *Lyrics of a Lowly Life.*
Harold Frederic, *The Damnation of Theron Ware.*
Sarah Orne Jewett, *The Country of the Pointed Firs.*
Charles M. Sheldon, *In His Steps.*

1897   William McKinley, president 1897–1901; Greco-Turkish War.
Richard Harding Davis, *Soldiers of Fortune.*
William Dean Howells, *The Landlord at Lion's Head.*
Henry James, *What Maisie Knew* and *The Spoils of Poynton.*
Edwin Arlington Robinson, *The Children of the Night.*

1898   Spanish-American War, 25 April–12 August; defeat of Spanish forces at Manila Bay, Cuba, and Puerto Rico; United States ceded the Philippines and Puerto Rico; Dreyfus case turmoil in France; death of Harold Frederic.
Stephen Crane, *The Open Boat and Other Tales of Adventure.*
Finley Peter Dunne, *Mr. Dooley in Peace and War.*

1899   Beginning of Philippine insurrection (to 1902) and the Boer War in South Africa (to 1902).
George Ade, *Fables in Slang.*
Charles W. Chesnutt, *The Conjure Woman.*
Kate Chopin, *The Awakening.*
Stephen Crane, *The Monster and Other Stories.*
John Dewey, *The School and Society.*

Harold Frederic, *The Market Place.*
Edwin Markham, *The Man with the Hoe and Other Poems.*
Frank Norris, *McTeague.*
Booth Tarkington, *The Gentleman from Indiana.*
Thorstein Veblen, *The Theory of the Leisure Class.*

1900 Paris International Exhibition; death of Stephen Crane. Joseph Conrad, *Lord Jim;* Sigmund Freud, *The Interpretation of Dreams.*
Charles W. Chesnutt, *The House Behind the Cedars.*
Theodore Dreiser, *Sister Carrie.*
Robert Herrick, *The Web of Life.*
Jack London, *The Son of the Wolf.*
Theodore Roosevelt, *The Strenuous Life.*
Mark Twain, *The Man That Corrupted Hadleyburg.*

1901 William McKinley reelected (1900) and assassinated; succeeded by Theodore Roosevelt, president 1901–9; death of Queen Victoria, succeeded by Edward VII; J. P. Morgan organizes United States Steel Corporation.
Winston Churchill, *The Crisis.*
Frank Norris, *The Octopus.*
Booker T. Washington, *Up From Slavery.*

1902 Deaths of Frank Norris and Emile Zola. Arnold Bennett, *Anna of the Five Towns;* Maxim Gorki, *The Lower Depths.*
Ellen Glasgow, *The Battle-Ground.*
Henry James, *The Wings of the Dove.*
William James, *The Varieties of Religious Experience.*
Owen Wister, *The Virginian.*

1903 Wright Brothers' first flight; founding of the Ford Motor Company; death of Herbert Spencer. Samuel Butler, *The Way of All Flesh.*
W. E. B. DuBois, *The Souls of Black Folk.*
Henry James, *The Ambassadors.*
Jack London, *The Call of the Wild.*
Frank Norris, *The Pit* and *The Responsibilities of the Novelist.*

1904 Russo-Japanese War (to 1905); Saint Louis Exposition; American Academy of Arts and Letters founded; death of Kate Chopin.
Henry Adams, *Mont-Saint-Michel and Chartres.*
Ellen Glasgow, *The Deliverance.*
Robert Herrick, *The Common Lot.*
Henry James, *The Golden Bowl.*
Jack London, *The Sea-Wolf.*

Lincoln Steffens, *The Shame of the Cities.*
Ida Tarbell, *The History of the Standard Oil Company.*

1905   Revolutionary violence in Russia; International Workers of the World (IWW) founded; Einstein formulates special theory of relativity. Sigmund Freud, *Three Essays on the Theory of Sexuality.*
Thomas Dixon, *The Clansman.*
Robert Herrick, *The Memoirs of an American Citizen.*
David Graham Phillips, *The Plum Tree.*
Edith Wharton, *The House of Mirth.*

1906   San Francisco earthquake and fire; Pure Food and Drug Act.
O. Henry, *The Four Million.*
Jack London, *White Fang.*
Upton Sinclair, *The Jungle.*
Mark Twain, *What Is Man?*

1907   Financial Panic of 1907.
Henry Adams, *The Education of Henry Adams.*
Henry James, *The American Scene.*
William James, *Pragmatism.*

1908   Arnold Bennett, *The Old Wives' Tale;* E. M. Forster, *A Room with a View.*
Jack London, *The Iron Heel.*
H. L. Mencken, *The Philosophy of Friedrich Nietzsche.*

1909   William Howard Taft, president 1909–13; Henry Ford begins mass production of Model T; Robert E. Peary reaches the North Pole; W. E. B. DuBois helps found the National Association for the Advancement of Colored People (NAACP); Sigmund Freud lectures in the United States.
Jack London, *Martin Eden.*
Ezra Pound, *Personae.*
Gertrude Stein, *Three Lives.*
William Allen White, *A Certain Rich Man.*
William Carlos Williams, *Poems.*

1910   Death of Edward VII, succeeded by George V; deaths of William James, Florence Nightingale, Leo Tolstoy, and Mark Twain.
Jane Addams, *Twenty Years at Hull House.*
Edwin Arlington Robinson, *The Town Down the River.*

1911   Supreme Court orders dissolution of the Standard Oil Company and the American Tobacco Company; Roald Amundsen reaches the South Pole.
Theodore Dreiser, *Jennie Gerhardt.*

Edith Wharton, *Ethan Frome.*

1912 Three-way presidential election, with Woodrow Wilson (president 1913–21) defeating William Howard Taft and Theodore Roosevelt; American marines occupy Nicaragua; *Titanic* sinks on maiden voyage; *Poetry* magazine founded in Chicago.
Theodore Dreiser, *The Financier.*
James Weldon Johnson, *The Autobiography of an Ex-Colored Man.*

1913 Sixteenth Amendment authorizes federal income tax; Armory Show on modern art in New York. D. H. Lawrence, *Sons and Lovers;* Thomas Mann, *Death in Venice;* Marcel Proust, *Swann's Way.*
Willa Cather, *O Pioneers!*
Robert Frost, *A Boy's Will.*
Ellen Glasgow, *Virginia.*
Vachel Lindsay, *General William Booth Enters into Heaven.*
Edith Wharton, *The Custom of the Country.*

1914 World War I begins following the assassination of Archduke Ferdinand in June; Panama Canal opens; United States marines land at Vera Cruz, Mexico.
Theodore Dreiser, *The Titan.*
Robert Frost, *North of Boston.*
Robert Herrick, *Clark's Field.*

DONALD PIZER

Introduction: The Problem of Definition

Anyone seeking, as are the contributors to this volume, to write about American literature between the Civil War and World War I in relation to the literary movements known as realism and naturalism faces a twofold initial difficulty. First, there exists a traditional suspicion, often arising from the very attempt to write literary history, of large-scale classifying rubrics. Is there any advantage, one might ask, in conceptualizing the richly diverse expression of this period in terms of such inherent simplification as realism and naturalism? A second problem derives from the recent theorizing of literary study. The attraction, for many theorists, of a deconstructive stance has bred skepticism toward interpretive enterprises that posit such communities of belief and expression as those subsumed under the headings of realism and naturalism. And, from a somewhat different theoretical viewpoint, recent scholars of a New Historicist bent have tended to discount traditional historical divisions in the study of American literature on the ground that they obscure underlying ideological similarities present in all American writing since the Civil War.

Yet, as this volume testifies, the effort to describe and understand a historical phase of American writing in terms of major shared characteristics of that writing continues. At its deepest and probably most significant level of implication, this attempt derives from the same reservoir of humanistic faith which feeds the act of creative expression itself. The artist, putting pen to paper, is expressing a belief in the human capacity to overcome such obstacles to understanding as the existence in all communication acts of unconscious motive and value in both writer and reader, the inherent ambiguity of the symbolic expression which is language, and the heartbreaking distinction in human utterance between intent and effect. He or she does so, despite these difficulties, because of faith in the value of striving to create threads of shared experience and meaning out of the inchoate mix of life. The literary historian, in his or her own way, also functions within this charged field of doubt and faith. Indeed, the literary historian can profit from the increased appreciation in recent decades of the difficulties inherent in the effort to interpret. An awareness of the hazards and complexities of textual and historical analysis can lead, not to abandonment of the attempt to understand the past, but rather to a refining of that undertaking.

As a minor reflection of this awareness, I would like briefly to describe the assumptions that underlie the contents and organization of this collection of essays devoted to late-nineteenth- and early-twentieth-century American writing. The general notion of the volume is that of an exercise in literary history in which various conflicting impulses in the writing of literary history are paired off against each other – a method, in other words, that dramatizes some of the opposing pulls in the construction of history rather than one which assumes that they are somehow resolved within a single seamless narrative. One such opposition is social and intellectual history versus the close reading of texts. Another is the older modes of critical and historical analysis versus those currently in fashion. And a third is the traditional canon versus an emerging alternative canon. The first pair of tendencies is represented by the opening essays on American and European intellectual and social background and by the studies devoted to specific works of the period. The next is found in the review of earlier criticism of the period undertaken later in this introduction and in the essay on recent critical approaches. And the last is reflected in the traditional texts examined at length and in the essay on expanding the canon as well as in the final case studies on works by Johnson and Du Bois. The controlling strategy of this book, in brief, is that of dialectic. It is hoped that this approach suggests something of the dynamic nature of literary history, that it is an interpretive act in process, and (more specifically) that it will contribute to an understanding of some of the distinctive characteristics of late-nineteenth- and early-twentieth-century American literature.

Michael Anesko, in his essay "Recent Critical Approaches," will be discussing basic tendencies in the study of American realism and naturalism since approximately the early 1970s. It remains for me, therefore, to describe several areas of interest in earlier efforts to come to grips with the nature of late-nineteenth- and early-twentieth-century American fiction. One is the always troublesome issue of whether *realism* and *naturalism* are indeed satisfactory critical and historical terms in relation to the writing of the period. Another is the presence of distinctive phases in the critical interpretation of realism and naturalism since the emergence of the movements in the late nineteenth century. In addition, although this volume is devoted to discussions of fiction written between the Civil War and World War I, it

2

may be useful to comment briefly on critical attempts to describe the existence of naturalistic strains in American literature since 1918.

A major problem inherent in the use of the terms *realism* and *naturalism* in discussions of literature is the fact that both words also have distinctive meanings in philosophical discourse that can spill over into literary analysis, with awkward consequences. For example, metaphysical and epistemological inquiries as to what is real, or the ethical implications of what is natural, can be used to undermine almost any act of literary historiography or criticism. This destabilization arises, not from the efforts of scholars who seek a meaningful engagement with the possible philosophical implications of a literary work, but rather from the attempts of various writers from the mid-nineteenth century onward to ridicule the pretensions of works purporting to be realistic or naturalistic by noting the emptiness, in relation to philosophical usage, of any such claims. As a result of this conventional stance of critics instinctively hostile to realistic or naturalistic expression, it has become common to preface serious discussions of the literary dimensions of realism or naturalism with statements disclaiming any relationship between the literary and philosophical usages of the terms.[1]

Another, somewhat related, problem is that the terms bear social and moral valences that are frequently attached to any work designated as realistic or naturalistic, whatever the specific character of that work. The real and natural, on the one hand, suggest the genuine and actual shorn of pretension and subterfuge. The real, especially in America, has therefore also had a positive political inflection, as is revealed by several generations of Howells scholars who have related his literary beliefs and practices to democratic values.[2] On the other hand, realism and naturalism imply, through their association with the concrete immediacies of experience, a literature unmediated by the intellect or spirit, and therefore lacking in those qualities necessary to sustain the mind or soul of man. Naturalism in particular is thus held to be morally culpable because it appears to concentrate on the physical in man's nature and experience.[3] (Theodore Dreiser's naturalism, Stuart P. Sherman stated in a famous pronouncement, derived from an animal theory of human conduct.)[4] Thus, it is assumed by critics seeking to exploit the negative associations conjured up by the terms *realism* and *naturalism* that any literature so designated proclaims the shallowness of mind and spirit of its creator.

Realism and *naturalism* have therefore often served as shibboleths in social and literary controversy – comparable to *liberal* and *reactionary* in present-day political affairs – at various moments in American cultural history. The terms played a central role during late-nineteenth-century debates on the value of the ideal versus the commonplace in experience, and they recurred in 1920s arguments about whether the writer should depict the rational or the irrational as central to human behavior. They reappeared in 1930s discussions about the need for literature to serve a social purpose rather than fulfill an aesthetic need, as well as in disputes during the 1960s and 1970s over whether or not the romance or novel is the distinctive form of American fiction.[5] Each of these controversies has usually cast more light on the polemical preoccupations of the moment than the literature under discussion. Of course, it can be maintained that the inseparability of subject from object, of the knower from what he wishes to know, is inherent in the act of seeking to know, and can therefore no more be avoided in the effort to "know" realism and naturalism than it can in any similar enterprise. The issue in this instance, however, is the blatant irrelevancy of much that has been imposed on *realism* and *naturalism* as terms by critics preoccupied with polemical ends. In other words, given this history in the use of the terms, can we have any faith in the possibility of a more "objective" use?

A final major problem in the use of *realism* and *naturalism* as key terms in American literary historiography arises from several significant differences in the way the terms have been used in European literary history. It has often been remarked that realism and naturalism occurred earlier in Europe than in America (from the late 1850s to the late 1880s in France); that they contained – in the pronouncements of Flaubert and Zola, for example – self-conscious and full-scale ideologies; and that they functioned within a coherent network of personal relationships for much of their existence. In America, on the other hand, it is noted that the boundaries of the period are the Civil War and World War I, which suggests a substitution of historical event for ideology as the significant basis for understanding literary production; that critical discussion, as characterized by Howells's definition of realism as "the truthful treatment of material,"[6] lacks depth; and that the movements also lacked a social base or center. For some critics, the inescapable conclusion to be drawn from these differences is that it is inappropriate and poor criticism to attempt to apply terms with a body of specific meaning derived from the specific characteristics of their European origin to a very different set of circumstances in American literary history.[7]

George J. Becker, who took the lead during the 1960s in this effort to dismiss the credibility of *realism* and *naturalism* as terms in American literary history, also noted another troublesome issue in their varying European and American usage. In Europe the terms were used interchangeably in the late nineteenth century and often still are, while in America they have served to distinguish between the fiction of the generation of Howells and James (the 1870s and 1880s) and that of Norris and Dreiser (the 1890s). To Becker, a reliance on this distinction is further evidence that both terms have been distorted in their application to American literary conditions and should therefore be discarded by American literary historians.[8]

Becker's objections, however, have not prevented the continued use of the terms *realism* and *naturalism* in American literary historiography. They are too deeply implanted to be dislodged, and their removal would leave unanswered the question of what would replace them. But Becker's attempt, as well as those made by such scholars as Harry Levin and René Wellek,[9] to describe Continental realism and naturalism as a body of belief and practice has clarified both the difference between the movements in Europe and America and what is distinctive in the American movements. In short, it is now generally held that American realism and naturalism are not similar to the European varieties, but that the differences between them should lead, not to a rejection of the use of the terms in America, but rather to studies that will exploit an understanding of these differences in order to help us interpret the American literary phenomena designated by the terms.

Thus, in the long debate on the advantages and disadvantages of using the terms *realism* and *naturalism,* a rough operative (rather than fully articulated) consensus has emerged. (Not to say that there are not vigorous dissenters to this consensus.) Efforts to dispose of the terms because of the various semantic confusions that have adhered to them over the last hundred years have been rejected. Whatever the philosophical, moral, and social baggage that encumbers them, they will have to do; including, indeed, this baggage itself as a profitable object of study. In addition, efforts to confine the meaning of the terms to normative definitions derived from European expression have also been rejected. Rather, it is now generally accepted that the terms can be used to historical and critical advantage to designate a body of writing produced during a distinctive phase of American expression. Or, to put it another way, that the historian can accept the premise that whatever was being produced in fiction during the 1870s and 1880s that was new, interesting, and roughly similar in a number of ways can be designated as *realism,* and that an equally new, interesting, and roughly similar body of writing produced at the turn of the century can be designated as *naturalism.* This is not, of course, an entirely satisfactory "solution" to the various problems inherent in the use of the terms *realism* and *naturalism* in American literary history. But when the evidence provided both by the texts themselves and by a complex cultural and intellectual history (as will be seen) cannot itself produce precise and uniform definitions, we must accept the fact that the definitions must be adapted to the evidence, and that an amorphous, flexible, and ultimately "undefinable" terminology is in itself a contribution to the understanding of what occurred.[10]

Literary historians of the 1920s and 1930s, following the lead of V. L. Parrington, tended to describe realism as a new phenomenon unleashed upon the American scene during the 1870s and 1880s by the rapid industrialization and urbanization of America in the post–Civil War period. But as Robert Falk and others have demonstrated, no such swift and complete rejection of earlier nineteenth-century literary beliefs and practices occurred. In particular, critical pronouncements during this period about the new writing were firmly Victorian in their basic assumptions about life and literature.[11]

One of the most important of these assumptions is closely identified with the critical views of W. D. Howells during the late 1880s, though it appears as well in the literary journalism of a number of other writers seeking to defend and promote the new fiction. Literature, Howells argued in his "Editor's Study" columns in *Harper's Monthly,* ought to reflect and play a major role in encouraging the social and political progress that characterized nineteenth-century life, progress that had received its fullest expression in the American effort to unite scientific inquiry and political democracy into a means for a better life for all men. Howells and such figures as Hamlin Garland, T. S. Perry, and H. H. Boyesen thus accepted wholeheartedly the central evolutionary premise of much nineteenth-century thought that loosely joined social, material, and intellectual life into a triumphant forward march.[12] The function of literature in this universal progress was to reject the outworn values of the past in favor of those of the present. Or, in more literary terms, the writer was to reject the romantic material and formulas of earlier fiction, as these derived from the limited beliefs and social life of their moment of origin, in favor of a realistic aesthetic which demanded that the subject matter of contemporary life be objectively depicted, no matter how "unliterary" the product of this aesthetic might seem to be. "Nothing is stable," Garland wrote in 1882, "nothing absolute, all changes, all is relative. Poetry, painting, the drama, these too are always being modified or left behind by the changes in society from which they spring."[13]

Garland's pronouncement, and many like it, appears to require a radical dismissal of traditional literary belief and practice. (The title of his 1894 collection of essays, *Crumbling Idols,* reflects a similar radical aura.) But in fact, when separated from its polemic posturing and examined for its specific proposals about fiction, criticism of this kind discloses a far less revolutionary cast than its rhetoric suggests. Howells's famous grasshopper analogy, in his 1891 collection of "Editor's Study" columns, *Criticism and Fiction,* is revealing in this context. All is to be true and honest in fiction, Howells states, within a realistic aesthetic in which the writer, like a scientist with democratic values, discards the old heroic and ideal, and therefore false, cardboard model of a grasshopper and depicts the commonplace activities of a commonplace grasshopper. This engaging plea, however, disguises the tameness, and indeed often the superficiality, of much fiction subsumed under the notion of the commonplace or realistic. For Howells and others, the "progressive realism of American fiction" (to use H. H. Boyesen's language) lay principally in portraying "the widely divergent phases of our American civilization,"[14] that is, a local-color literature. In addition, these "phases" were to be depicted normatively in the negative sense of omitting areas of human nature and social life that were "barbaric" in nature. The new literature, Garland announced in *Crumbling Idols,* "will not deal with crime and abnormalities, nor with diseased persons. It will deal . . . with the wholesome love of honest men for honest women, with the heroism of labor . . . , a drama of average types of character. . . ."[15]

In short, the underlying beliefs of this first generation of critics of realism were firmly middle-class. Literature had a job of work to do: to make us known to each other in our common political and social progress (and also, in Howells's later modification of his views, our defects). It was to serve social ends as these ends were defined by the socially responsible. It is therefore not surprising to find a disparity between the radical implications of the realists' ideal of change and the actual themes and forms of the literature proposed as meeting this ideal. We have a realistic fiction that "every year [grows] more virile, independent, and significant," announced Boyesen, who cited as examples of this expression the work of such thin and pastiche local colorists as Thomas Nelson Page, H. C. Bunner, and Edgar Fawcett.[16]

To put this distinction between critical pronouncement and literary production in somewhat different terms, Howells, Garland, Boyesen, and others appeared to have confused the proliferation and acceptance of local color, a literature expressive above all of middle-class taste and values, with their call for a fiction reflective of the radical changes occurring in American life. Something new and exciting was indeed happening in fiction, but it was happening principally in the work of the major novelists of the day, Henry James, Twain, and Howells, who, except for Howells, were writing outside the parameters of the commonplace, as well as in the largely neglected work of women and minority authors. In slighting these forms of expression in favor of the "positive" social work performed by a normative local color, Howells and others were misfiring in ways that had a permanent effect on the conception of American realism.

Realism, because of Howells's prominence as critic and novelist and because of its widespread public acceptance in the form of local color, attracted a considerable body of critical commentary during the late nineteenth century. But naturalism, as it emerged as a major new form of expression at the turn of the century, was often ignored, or, when not ignored, condemned out of hand. Socially and morally suspect because of its subject matter, and handicapped as well by the early deaths of Stephen Crane and Frank Norris and the long silence of Dreiser after the "suppression" of *Sister Carrie* in 1900, naturalism was for the most part slighted as a general topic except for Norris's miscellaneous comments in various essays and reviews. Less a profound thinker than a defender of his own work and a popularizer of "ideas in the air," Norris's conception of naturalism is nevertheless significant both for what it contains and what it omits. Naturalism, Norris declares, must abjure the "teacup tragedies"[17] of Howellsian realism and explore instead the irrational and primitive in human nature – "the unplumbed depths of the human heart, and the mystery of sex, and the problems of life, and the black, unsearched penetralia of the soul of man"[18] – and it should do so within the large canvas and allegorical framework that permit the expression of abstract ideas about the human condition.

So far so good. Norris is here describing not only *McTeague* and *The Octopus,* his best novels, as two poles of naturalistic inquiry (a chaotic inner life and a panoramic social world) but also suggestively revealing the appeal of this conception of literature for a large number of twentieth-century American writers ranging from Faulkner to Mailer. But Norris's idea of naturalism is also remarkably silent in a key area. For despite his close familiarity with the work of Zola and other French naturalists, nowhere in his criticism does he identify naturalism with a deterministic ideology. Naturalism, to Norris, is a method and a product, but it does not prescribe a specific philosophical base. Norris was thus identifying, in his criticism, the attraction of naturalism in its character as a sensationalistic novel of ideas flexible enough in ideology to absorb the specific ideas of individual writers – and this despite the efforts of several generations of later critics to attach an unyielding deterministic core to the movement.

A basic paradox characterizes much of the criticism of late-nineteenth-century realism produced between the two world wars. On the one hand, the writing of the period is often applauded for its depiction of the new actualities of post–Civil War America. This celebratory stance is revealed most obviously in the metaphors of progress and success present in the sectional titles of literary histories containing accounts of the period – "The Triumph of Realism" and the like.[19] On the other, critics also wished to register their disapproval of the restraints in choice of subject matter and manner of treatment imposed on writers by the literary and social conventions of late Victorian American life. In this connection, the terms *puritanism* and *genteel tradition* were heavily employed. Writers of the time, in short, were described as seeking to be free but as still largely bound.

This view is closely related, of course, to the prevailing winds of 1920s and 1930s social and literary discourse. During the twenties, when the act of rejection of American cultural codes and economic values (a rejection most clearly enacted by the expatriates' self-exile) was almost a requirement for serious consideration as an artist, it is no wonder that those late-nineteenth-century figures who sought to live out roles of personal and literary alienation – a Mark Twain at his bitterest or a Stephen Crane – were centers of attention,[20] while those who were seemingly willing to accept codes of gentility or cultural elitism, a Howells or a James, were relegated, in general accounts of the period, to the role of symbolic reflectors of these limitations. Thus, an entire generation of literary journalists, led by H. L. Mencken, but including such prominent and well-respected figures as John Macy, Van Wyck Brooks, Ludwig Lewisohn, Carl Van Doren, Randolph Bourne, Lewis Mumford, and Henry Seidel Canby, fed off the critical commonplace of a literature attempting to be free to depict American life fully and honestly but deeply flawed by the limitations placed upon this effort by its own time.

This broad-based attitude, because it served contemporary polemic purposes, tended toward the absolute dichotomy as a critical tool. One such polarization, as noted earlier, was that of distinguishing sharply between ante- and postbellum writing in order to dramatize the dramatic differences between a pre- and postindustrial America. Another, as in V. L. Parrington's *The Beginnings of Critical Realism in America* (1930), was to bifurcate American life into those forces contributing either to plutocracy or freedom. But despite the prevalence of these and a number of other widely shared beliefs and strategies, criticism of realism and naturalism during this period was neither monolithic nor static. A significant illustration of one of the shifting perspectives of the time is present in estimations of the work of Howells. To a Mencken, writing in the literary climate of the late teens and early twenties, Howellsian realism epitomized all that must be avoided by the writer seeking to be a meaningful critic of his own time and life.[21]

Mencken thus did not so much attempt to understand Howells as to use him as a negative touchstone. But as economic issues became paramount in the minds of many literary historians and critics, beginning in the late 1920s, Howells's conversion to socialism served the very different role of dramatizing the response of a sensitive and thoughtful writer to the conditions of his day. For Parrington in 1930, and for Granville Hicks somewhat later, Howells assumed almost heroic stature. In Hicks's militant terminology, he was one of those who "marched out upon the field of battle" to struggle against the forces of economic oppression.[22]

Discussions of naturalism between the world wars, and especially of the work of Norris and the early Dreiser, were also deeply influenced by the polemic dynamics of the age. Initially, it was the naturalists' choice of material, in particular its more open sexuality, which led to their high standing as "trailblazers" of freedom. But gradually, with the greater prominence given economic and social issues in the 1930s, the naturalists of the 1890s became less valued as exemplars of freedom of expression than as reflectors of the closed and destructive mechanistic and Darwinian world of struggle in which it was assumed most Americans functioned.[23] It was during this stage in the criticism of naturalism that it became obligatory for the critic to spell out the relationship of American naturalism to Zolaesque determinism and firmly to equate the two. Since it was believed that American life at the turn of the century imprisoned the average American in a "moving box" of economic and social deprivation, naturalism (with its deterministic center) was a writer's appropriate, and indeed inevitable, response to this condition. Thus, while it might be acknowledged that Norris and Dreiser were often crude and formless and that their work appeared to be confined to the depiction of man as victim, it was believed as well that naturalism of this kind was an apt expression of late-nineteenth-century American social reality.

From the end of World War II to the watershed years of the late 1960s and early 1970s, realism fared far better on the critical scene than did naturalism. Realistic fiction, whatever its degree of social criticism, was more readily reconcilable than naturalistic writing to the postwar emphasis on the role of American literary expression in affirming democratic values. In addition, with the exception of the work of Stephen Crane, naturalistic fiction, with its assumed defects of form and style, was largely ignored as a result of the New Criticism stress on close reading that dominated much criticism of the period.

Both the war and its Cold War aftermath generated a commitment on the part of most literary historians to demonstrate the vital presence of the

American democratic tradition in all phases of American expression. Thus, the work of Howells and his contemporaries was discovered to be deeply impregnated with such democratic beliefs as trust in the common vision and in pragmatic values. In addition, as Henry Nash Smith put it in his chapter on realism in the *Literary History of the United States,* by identifying and dramatizing the "problem areas" of American social life, realists were playing a role in the solution of those problems.[24] This point of view, with an emphasis on the importance of Howells's beliefs and practices, characterizes Everett Carter's *Howells and the Age of Realism* (1954) and E. H. Cady's work culminating in his *The Light of Common Day* (1971). Much criticism of the period, however, was also increasingly devoted to the fiction of Twain and James, finding in *Huckleberry Finn* and in James's major novels a rich source of formalistic analysis. Striking patterns of symbolic imagery and structure and suggestive currents of irony and ambiguity, it was discovered, could be found in these works as well as in those by Melville and Hawthorne.[25] These two strains – a stress on the functional value system underlying realistic portrayals and a revelation of the subtlety and complexity of realistic fictional aesthetics – joined triumphantly in Harold H. Kolb's *The Illusion of Life: American Realism as a Literary Form* (1969). Kolb accepted almost as proven the democratic underpinning of the three novels he concentrated on – *Huckleberry Finn, The Rise of Silas Lapham,* and *The Bostonians* – and devoted most of his attention to the ways in which such formal characteristics of the novels as point of view technique and imagery successfully express these foundations of belief.

Everett Carter's landmark study of Howells and his age, in addition to stressing Howells's democratic beliefs, is also noteworthy for its delineation of various stages in his ideas. So, for example, Carter locates the sources of Howells's concept of realism in Comte and Taine and then traces the permutations of the concept in Howells's career and in those of his major contemporaries. Realism, in short, was not a static entity but rather consisted of ideas in motion.[26] This appealing notion of the dynamic nature of the beliefs of the period – of writers responding to changing ideas and social life by rethinking their own beliefs – characterizes such major literary histories of the period as Robert Falk's essay in *Transitions in American Literary History* (1953) and (as is suggested by their titles) Warner Berthoff's *The Ferment of Realism* (1965) and Jay Martin's *Harvests of Change* (1967).[27]

These various threads of criticism – the celebratory democratic, the New Critical, and the dynamic – are related in their common affirmative view of realism as a significant moment in American literary history. No longer was the movement marginalized, as had been true of much criticism of the previous generation, because of its gentility or imperception. Its importance, centrality, and worth had, in the minds of most scholars, been firmly established.

Naturalism, however, suffered either dismissal or critical neglect for much of the postwar period. The assumed crudity and stylistic incompetence of Norris or Dreiser of course rendered their work suspect within a critical climate deeply affected by New Critical beliefs and methods. Also telling as a negative factor in the estimation of naturalism was the disillusionment, beginning in the mid-1930s, of American intellectuals with what they held to be the mindless authoritarianism of communist ideology. Many writers of the 1930s who had been identified with a resurgence of naturalism – Steinbeck, Dos Passos, and Farrell, for example – were also on the Left, an association confirmed above all by Dreiser's full endorsement of the Communist party and its goals from the early 1930s to his death in 1945. Discussions of naturalism, because of the movement's origins in Zola's beliefs and practice, had always contained a tendency toward considering it a foreign incursion with little relationship to American values and experience. This tendency, as well as other threads in the negative conception of naturalism, received full and influential expression in Oscar Cargill's *Intellectual America* (1941), in which Cargill disposed of naturalism as a crude and thinly derivative fiction with fascistic inclinations.[28] By the postwar years, with the revulsion against communism deepened by the Cold War, a powerful antinaturalism stance characterized the criticism of such major voices of the day as Lionel Trilling, Malcolm Cowley, and Philip Rahv.[29] As Irving Howe later noted, during the 1940s and 1950s Dreiser's work was "a symbol of everything a superior intelligence was supposed to avoid."[30]

Despite this hostile critical convention, a counterflow of more sympathetic inquiry into the nature of American naturalism also emerged during the 1950s and 1960s. Willard Thorp and Alfred Kazin, for example, asked the question begged by the rejection of naturalism: If naturalism is inept, intellectually impoverished, and foreign to American values, why has it persisted as a major element in all phases of twentieth-century American fiction?[31] A number of scholars accepted the challenge implicit in this question and began to examine the relationship between naturalism and American life on a deeper level than the obvious association between naturalistic factuality and American materialism. One influential effort was that by Richard Chase, who in his *The American Novel and Its Tradition* (1957) located naturalism within the American romance tradition because of its union of sensationalism and ideas. On the other hand, Charles C. Walcutt, in his *American Literary Naturalism, A Divided Stream* (1956), rejected the notion that the naturalistic novel had achieved formal coherence in favor of the concept of naturalism's unsuccessful search for an expressive form because of its divided roots in transcendental faith and scientific skepticism. And Donald Pizer, in his *Realism and Naturalism in Nineteenth-Century American Literature* (1966), as well as in later works,[32] sought not only to locate the American roots of naturalistic belief in a close reading of the works themselves (as had Walcutt) but also to establish the fictional complexity and worth of the naturalistic novel at its best. By the early 1970s, therefore, led by a number of major studies of Dreiser (Robert Penn Warren's *Homage to Theodore Dreiser* [1971] is symptomatic), it had become possible to discuss the movement outside of the a priori assumptions of inadequacy established by the New Critical and anticommunist critical contexts of the previous generation.

This more receptive critical climate for the study of naturalism has also contributed to the effort to describe its enduring presence in twentieth-century American fiction. While realism, as defined and practiced by Howells, has been confined in modern American fiction to a relatively minor role, naturalism, in its various interests and strategies, has continued to flourish. This is not to say that naturalism has been the principal force in American fiction since the turn of the century. Since the 1920s, the novel of social realism has had as a constant complement a fiction of the fantastic or fabulistic, whether as expressed by the sophisticated cleverness of a group of 1920s writers led by James Branch Cabell or by the more intellectualized allegories of such 1960s and 1970s figures as John Barth, Thomas Pynchon, and Donald Barthelme. Nor has American naturalism been static or monolithic in theme and form since its origin in the 1890s. Indeed, one of the striking characteristics of the movement has been its adaptability to fresh currents of idea and expression in each generation while maintaining a core of naturalistic preoccupations. The nature of this core is not easy to describe, given the dynamic flexibility and amorphousness of naturalism as a whole in America, but it appears to rest on the relationship between a restrictive social and intellectual environment and the consequent impoverishment both of social opportunity and of the inner life. This is the common theme of such major writers of the 1930s as John Steinbeck, John Dos Passos, and James T. Farrell, whether the theme is worked out in narratives of group defeat or of personal emptiness and collapse. It continues into the generation of the 1940s and 1950s in the early work of Saul Bellow, William Styron, and Norman Mailer, though now often combined with the existential theme of the need for a quest for meaning in the face of the inadequacy of social life and belief. And it persists in the partial recovery of the naturalistic themes of political constraint and urban blight in the work of such contemporary novelists as Robert Stone, Joyce Carol Oates (in her early novels), and William Kennedy. Naturalism thus seems to appeal to each generation of American writers as a means of dramatizing "hard times" in America – hard times in the sense both of economic decline and of spiritual malaise, with each generation also incorporating into this continuing impulse or tradition of naturalism the social and intellectual concerns of that age: Freudianism and Marxism in the 1930s, for example, or the Viet Nam War in more recent years.[33]

In addition to the writers already mentioned, it is also possible and useful to note the powerful naturalistic impulse in the fiction of such literary giants as Hemingway and Faulkner, as well as in that of a large number of relatively minor figures. Faulkner's major theme of the burden of the past as expressed through regional and family destiny strikes a firm naturalistic note, as does Hemingway's preoccupation with the behavioristic interplay between temperament and setting. Entire subgenres of modern American writing – the novel of urban decay, for example (Richard Wright and Nelson Algren), or the fiction of World War II (Norman Mailer and James Jones) – lend themselves to analysis in relation to naturalistic themes. Even a figure such as Edith Wharton is increasingly viewed in naturalistic terms, despite the upper-class milieu of much of her fiction, because of her central theme of the entrapment of women within social codes and taboos. Indeed, a great deal of fiction by women about women, from Wharton and Kate Chopin onward, can be said to reflect this naturalistic theme. Naturalism thus truly "refuses to die" in America. And it therefore especially behooves us, as students of American life, to reexamine its late-nineteenth-century roots, as this book in part seeks to do.

Although the contributors to this book were of course free to discuss their subjects in whatever ways they thought appropriate, a number of common threads of approach and attitude run through the volume, threads which thereby suggest several areas of consensus or synthesis in the dialectical plan of the volume that I noted at the opening of this introduction.

One such area is the tendency of most of the essayists to adopt one of two basic strategies toward the issue of modal definitions. Some, such as Richard Lehan, John Crowley, Blanche Gelfant, and Jacqueline Tavernier-Courbin, accept the usefulness of discussing specific literary tendencies or works within general definitions of realism and naturalism. Others, most notably Elizabeth Ammons, find the notion of a normative mode undescriptive of the rich variety of expression occurring within the period and thus, either openly or implicitly, argue for definitions of realism and naturalism that are historical in the absolute sense. In other words, they believe that all writing between the Civil War and World War I constitutes, in Ammons's phrase, various "realisms."

Moreover, even those critics who believe that modal definitions can serve an important function in literary history agree that such definitions should not play the largely negative roles often assigned to them in the past. No longer is it possible, in short, to use a modal definition to demonstrate the inferiority of a specific work, or to use the characteristics of a specific work to demonstrate the inadequacy of the definition. Rather, as the essays by Tom Quirk, J. C. Levenson, and Barbara Hochman reveal, the critic's awareness of the ways in which modal analysis in the past was often a means to plead special causes, and his or her greater appreciation of the possible advantageous uses of modal commentary, have resulted in a more responsible and sophisticated modal-based literary criticism.

Another significant common element in many of the essays is their responsiveness to the present emphasis in literary studies on the social basis of literary expression, a tendency characterized by Michael Anesko as "literary sociology." Significant phases of this interest are found in Louis Budd's comments on the roots of literary values in the commonality of late nineteenth-century American experience, in Barbara Hochman's analysis of the role of the literary marketplace in the work of Wharton and Chopin, in Richard Lehan's close attention to the role of the city in the rise of a naturalistic ethos, and in Kenneth W. Warren's discussion of black expression at the turn of the century.

Indeed, if the collection as a whole has a describable theoretical leaning, it resides in the assumption of most of the essayists that realism and naturalism constitute a critical response to the conditions of late-nineteenth-century American life. The inclination to reassert this traditional belief does not arise, I believe, out of a predeliction for a return to a conventional position but rather out of a reexamination of the basic cast of mind of the period, stimulated by the recent polar extremes in criticism of the period represented by Eric Sundquist's introduction to *American Realism: New Essays* (1982), on the one hand, and Walter Benn Michaels's *The Gold Standard and the Logic of Naturalism* (1987) and Michael Davitt Bell's *The Problem of American Realism* (1993), on the other. Sundquist posits an American social, economic, and political world so corrupt and dismaying that the only adequate response by the writer of integrity is to seek escape into the farthest reaches of his imagination, as do James and Crane. And

Michaels and Bell posit two generations of writers so imprisoned within the popular values of their day that they are rendered impotent as critics of their age. The burden of most the essays in this volume, however, is to reaffirm – through a variety of approaches and emphases – the belief that realism and naturalism arose in large part as responses to what Louis Budd calls the "disjunctures" between rhetoric and actuality in American life – between the language of hope in America's civil religion and the actuality of the world encountered.

NOTES

1 See, for example, René Wellek, "The Concept of Realism in Literary Scholarship," *Concepts of Criticism* (New Haven and London: Yale University Press, 1963), pp. 222–55, and George Levine, "Realism Reconsidered," *The Theory of the Novel: New Essays,* ed. John Halperin (New York: Oxford University Press, 1974), pp. 233–56.

2 See Everett Carter, *Howells and the Age of Realism* (Philadelphia: Lippincott, 1954), pp. 265–75, and Edwin H. Cady, *The Light of Common Day: Realism in American Fiction* (Bloomington: Indiana University Press, 1971), pp. 3–22.

3 Criticism reflecting this position is too plentiful to cite fully. For some blatant examples, however, see Paul Elmer More, "Modern Currents in American Fiction," *The Demon of the Absolute* (Princeton, N.J.: Princeton University Press, 1928); Floyd Stovall, *American Idealism* (Norman: University of Oklahoma Press, 1943); and Randall Stewart, *American Literature and Christian Doctrine* (Baton Rouge: Louisiana State University Press, 1958).

4 Stuart P. Sherman, "The Barbaric Naturalism of Mr. Dreiser," *On Contemporary Literature* (New York: Holt, 1917), pp. 93–4.

5 These various critical attitudes are discussed later in this introduction.

6 W. D. Howells, *Selected Literary Criticism, Vol. II: 1886–1897,* ed. Donald Pizer (Bloomington: Indiana University Press, 1993), p. 133.

7 This position is most fully expressed by George J. Becker in his "Introduction: Modern Realism as a Literary Movement," *Documents of Modern Literary Realism* (Princeton, N.J.: Princeton University Press, 1963), pp. 3–38, and *Realism in Modern Literature* (New York: Ungar, 1980), pp. 179–83. See also Lilian R. Furst and Peter N. Skrine, *Naturalism* (London: Methuen, 1971), pp. 33–6.

8 See Becker's "Introduction: Modern Realism as a Literary Movement," pp. 35–6, and his review of Donald Pizer's *Realism and Naturalism in Nineteenth-Century American Literature* (1966), in *Nineteenth-Century Fiction* 21 (1966): 196–9.

9 Harry Levin, *The Gates of Horn: A Study of Five French Realists* (New York: Oxford University Press, 1963), pp. 24–83, and René Wellek, "The Concept of Realism in Literary Scholarship."

10 Martin Kanes – in a review of Yves Chevrel's *Le Naturalisme* in *Comparative Literature* 36 (1984): 373 – notes Chevrel's effort to resolve this dilemma by

assuming "that naturalism [in France] is that series of texts perceived by contemporary readers as being naturalistic."

11 See, in particular, Falk's *The Victorian Mode in American Fiction: 1865–1885* (East Lansing: Michigan State University Press, 1964). In his recent *The Problem of American Realism: Studies in the Cultural History of a Literary Idea* (Chicago: University of Chicago Press, 1993), Michael Davitt Bell recapitulates much of Falk's discussion of the Victorian character of American realism.

12 See Donald Pizer, "The Evolutionary Foundation of W. D. Howells's *Criticism and Fiction*" and "Evolutionary Ideas in Late Nineteenth-Century English and American Literary Criticism," *Realism and Naturalism in Nineteenth-Century American Literature*, 2d rev. ed (Carbondale: Southern Illinois University Press, 1984), pp. 70–95.

13 Garland's unpublished essay "The Evolution of American Thought," quoted in Donald Pizer, *Hamlin Garland's Early Work and Career* (Berkeley and Los Angeles: University of California Press, 1960), pp. 17–18.

14 Boyesen, "The Progressive Realism of American Fiction," *Literary and Social Silhouettes* (New York: Harper's, 1894), p. 73.

15 Garland, *Crumbling Idols* (Chicago: Stone and Kimball, 1894), p. 28.

16 Boyesen, "Progressive Realism," p. 78.

17 Norris, "Zola as a Romantic Writer" (1896), *The Literary Criticism of Frank Norris*, ed. Donald Pizer (Austin: University of Texas Press, 1964), p. 72.

18 Norris, "A Plea for Romantic Fiction" (1901), in Pizer, *Literary Criticism of Frank Norris*, p. 78.

19 Russell Blankenship, "The Triumph of Realism," *American Literature as an Expression of the National Mind* (New York: Holt, 1931).

20 Two characteristic biographies of the 1920s that stress the theme of alienation in late-nineteenth-century writers are Van Wyck Brooks, *The Ordeal of Mark Twain* (1920) and Thomas Beer, *Stephen Crane* (1923).

21 Mencken, for example, tended to spice his attacks on American puritanism with offhand popshots at Howells, as in *A Book of Prefaces* (New York: Knopf, 1917), p. 218: "Of the great questions that agitated the minds of men in Howells' time one gets no more than a faint and far-away echo in his novels. His investigations, one may say, are carried out *in vacuo*; his discoveries are not expressed in terms of passion, but in terms of giggles."

22 Hicks, *The Great Tradition: An Interpretation of American Literature Since the Civil War* (New York: Macmillan, 1933), p. 301. A frequent corollary of this emphasis was the dismissal of James's fiction as irrelevant to an understanding of American life, as in V. L. Parrington's brief comments on James in his *The Beginnings of Critical Realism in America* (New York: Harcourt, Brace, 1930), pp. 239–41, under the heading "Henry James and the Nostalgia of Culture."

23 V. L. Parrington states this position succinctly in notes for a lecture on naturalism (Parrington, *The Beginnings of Critical Realism*, p. 327): "Machine industrialism. The bigness of the economic machine dwarfs the individual and creates a sense of impotency."

24 Smith, "The Second Discovery of America," *Literary History of the United States*, ed. Robert E. Spiller et al. (New York: Macmillan, 1948), 2:790.

25 Also reflecting this shift in attitude is the fact that Jay Martin, in his *Harvests of*

Change: American Literature, 1865–1914 (Englewood Cliffs, N.J.: Prentice-Hall, 1967), devotes his longest chapter to the work of Henry James.

26 Carter, *Howells and the Age of Realism*, pp. 80–169.

27 Falk, "The Rise of Realism," *Transitions in American Literary History*, ed. Harry, H. Clark (Durham: Duke University Press, 1953), pp. 379–442; Berthoff, *The Ferment of Realism: American Literature, 1884–1919* (New York: Free Press, 1965); Martin, *Harvests of Change* (1967).

28 Cargill remarks, for example (*Intellectual America: Ideas on the March* [New York: Macmillan, 1941] p. 175), that "The only possibility of Fascism in this country lies, not in the popularity of the doctrines of Fascism, but rather in the debility of the public will through wide acceptance of the philosophy of Naturalism."

29 The key documents are Trilling's "Reality in America," *The Liberal Imagination* (New York: Viking, 1950), pp. 3–21; Cowley's 'Not Men': A Natural History of American Naturalism," *Kenyon Review* 9 (1947): 414–35; and Rahv's "Notes on the Decline of Naturalism," *Image and Idea* (Norfolk, Conn.: New Directions, 1949), pp. 128–38.

30 Howe, "The Stature of Theodore Dreiser," *New Republic*, July 25, 1964, p. 19.

31 Thorp, "The Persistence of Naturalism in the Novel," *American Writing in the Twentieth Century* (Cambridge, Mass.: Harvard University Press, 1960), pp. 143–95, and Kazin, "American Naturalism: Reflections from Another Era," *The American Writer and the European Tradition*, ed. Margaret Denny and William H. Gilman (Minneapolis: University of Minnesota Press, 1950), pp. 121–31.

32 See, in particular, the essays added to the second edition (1984) of this study and Pizer's *The Theory and Practice of American Literary Naturalism: Selected Essays and Reviews* (Carbondale: Southern Illinois University Press, 1993).

33 Summarized here is the central argument in Donald Pizer, *Twentieth-Century American Literary Naturalism: An Interpretation* (Carbondale: Southern Illinois University Press, 1982). Other significant attempts to describe twentieth-century American naturalism are the chapters on Anderson, Farrell, Steinbeck, Hemingway, and Dos Passos in Walcutt, *American Literary Naturalism, A Divided Stream* (1956); Thorp, "The Persistence of Naturalism in the Novel," *American Writing in the Twentieth Century* (1960); essays on Steinbeck, Wright, Farrell, and Algren in *American Literary Naturalism: A Reassessment*, ed. Yoshinobu Hakutani and Lewis Fried (Heidelberg: Carl Winter, 1975); and Don Graham, "Naturalism in American Fiction: A Status Report," *Studies in American Fiction* 10 (1982): 1–16.

PART ONE

Historical contexts

I

LOUIS J. BUDD

The American Background

INTRODUCTION

Although realism and naturalism could have sprung up independently in the United States, the historical fact is that they flourished earlier in the European countries all the way eastward to Russia and that American writers were especially stimulated by British and French models. On the other hand, though a still provincial, moralizing culture might have rejected realism and naturalism as alien or profane or harmful, nevertheless they did become established in the postbellum United States. Even Richard Chase, whose *The American Novel and Its Tradition* (1957) had argued that the romance was the quintessential mode of fiction in the United States, felt compelled to declare:

> After all, realism, although it was there from the beginning, *did* "rise," or at least became conscious of itself as a significant, liberalizing and forward-looking literary program. Whole areas of the American novel, both classic and modern, are closed to any reader who . . . thinks that it contains no meaningful element of realism. The great writers, classic and modern, did not devote themselves exclusively to translating everything into symbols, myths, and archetypes, thus removing literature from the hazards of experience and the vicissitudes of change. These writers functioned in the real world, or tried to; they reported significant aspects of the real world in their fictions, and often they had, besides archetypes, *ideas* – political, cultural, religious, historical.[1]

American realism did and does matter importantly.

My essay will treat realism and naturalism as joined sequentially rather than as disjunctive, though either approach has good foundations. More specifically, though naturalism could have arisen only after absorbing the insights of realism, it insisted on subjects, attitudes, and techniques that bewildered and often offended its forerunners. Some literary historians feel obliged to work out an essentially unique rationale for it. Still, like the realists, the naturalists saw sentimental and adventurous fantasy and, behind that, the genteel tradition as the main source of miasma.

Critics favorable toward realism, through hindsight, can explain its rise as triumphantly irresistible. In fact there was no "movement" as any careful historian would define that word – no clubs, much less marches or any other group action. From various starting points a few writers worked toward a practice that we can class as realistic. After William Dean Howells's series of monthly essays that were stitched together as *Criticism and Fiction* (1891), he attracted letters and visits from admirers. But the realist ranks stayed thin and – in the opinion of some Europeans – stunted politically. In 1888, Edward and Eleanor Marx Aveling's *The Working-Class Movement in America* asked accusingly: "Where are the American writers of fiction?" Karl Marx's daughter and her husband meant to emphasize that no novelist (Garland, Crane, and Dreiser were still apprentices) had looked penetratingly at the small farmers and the urban proletariat squeezed by the corporations, financiers, and speculators. Even rightist Europeans thought that the Old World realists and naturalists had plumbed far more deeply. Inclined to feature innovation, literary historians of the New World have exaggerated the success of realism in the 1880s and 1890s. It met with fierce resistance in the marketplace, which preferred the gospel of positive thinking confirmed by progress – actual or imagined.

THE INTELLECTUAL BACKGROUND

The sequence with which an analysis takes up ideas inescapably implies judgments about their relative importance. More problematically, the history of ideas implies some degree of autonomy for ideas, though they always interact with their sociohistorical context. Still, there's heuristic gain in analyzing them as a self-contained system even if novelists are drawn by temperament toward narrative rather than philosophy. A narrow use of that temperament could be to extrapolate the origins of the American realists/ naturalists from the Continental masters they admired. But besides blurring national differences that would treat literature hermetically.

Domestically, the origins of realism can be traced back through famous passages of Ralph Waldo Emerson (such as "What would we really know the meaning of? The meal in the firkin; the milk in the pan; the ballad in the street . . .") and Joel Barlow's "Hasty Pudding," arriving ultimately at 1620 or 1607 (if we settle for English-language sources). But even adding side-trail sources like Sarah Kemble Knight would leave such an analysis not just provincial but too literate, as well as literary. Like everybody else, writers swim in the ocean of their society, studying (perhaps) its few metaphysicians and hearing regularly its spokespersons (politicians, editors, and ministers), yet interacting, at some level of awareness, with the spottily educated classes.

Although the illiterate leave no formal record (before the arrival of "oral history"), Lewis O. Saum has accumulated a convincing body of evidence about them rather than balancing an inverted pyramid of inference.[2] The antebellum sources he synthesizes – primarily the letters and diaries of the barely educated, who spell more by sound than rule – resist high-level abstractions, but they expressed (during the childhood of Howells, John William De Forest, or Mary Catherwood) three attitudes that could encourage realism. First, they pulsed with an earned feeling that the lifecycle was far harsher than political rhetoric or literary sentimentalism admitted; such a feeling, however patient, could welcome the relief of seeing easy optimism challenged. Second, they recorded a growing egalitarian self-respect fed by taking election-time bombast seriously; without soaring into Whitmanic gigantism, a subsistence farmer or a housewife could feel that his or her story deserved a more authentic telling. Third, they understandably saw that society and its values were changing, a fact that could open the mind to new approaches. Of course, countercurrents to these attitudes ran strong, drawing on a sturdy Christian religiosity that was de facto the official dogma.

Although Henry James grew up more remote from the sweaty masses than any other writer of his time, teeming Manhattan did surround Washington Square. Although the father of Sarah P. Willis tried hard to block her off from low people and sights, "Fanny Fern's" readers would wonder at how closely she knew life down to its grittiest. (Anybody who read the big-city newspapers imaginatively could intuit the entire spectrum.) Painfully observant Samuel Clemens matured in a bustling rivertown; as a steamboat pilot he saw an underside of antebellum glamour that he pretended to ignore; out in the mining West he prospered much less but endured much more than he had counted on. Perhaps overstating out of humility, Howells remembered an earnest and idealistic family that could never reach minimum security. None of these future novelists needed four years of civil war, with its festering casualties and its waves of frustrated hope, to learn that the day-to-day routine in the United States entailed painful problems, that the larger-scaled society emerging while at least the first-line defenses of a caste/class system crumbled was bringing changes in deep structure as well as street manners.

Fred Lewis Pattee stressed the trans-Appalachian roots of Mary H. Catherwood's fresh, honest fiction. More grandly, literary historians of his era celebrated the effects of frontiering as vital to the rise of realism, but, if pushed hard, this would imply that realism could arise only in the United

States (or similar countries). Furthermore, Saum's documents show that the push westward more often registered as an ordeal under the threat of accidents, sickness, and malign weather than as a path to innovative self-reliance. Early realistic fiction was midwestern rather than western: Edward Eggleston's *Roxy* (1878), Catherwood's "Serena" (1882), and Hamlin Garland's stories collected as *Main-Traveled Roads* (1891). Farmers, closer to the despised city, had more quickly soured on the forces sweeping the industrial Northeast.

Their urbanized counterparts, however skimpily educated, were also learning that the factory and the banks behind it directed, as best they could, the flow of power. That ethereal Truth so obvious to the antebellum spokespersons, North and South, that Truth assumed yet lovingly explicated, that certainty of transcendent order in a God-guided universe functioning down to the microlevel, had clouded over, had started to look gilded rather than solid.[3] Extending his research to the later nineteenth century, Saum discovered that *"natural,"* understood as based in observable practice, "was swiftly becoming a synonym for *good,* a change that borders on transmogrification." Just as ominous for the cozily eternal certainties, the "confined" sense of "society" as *"companion* and things partaking directly of companionship" was capitulating to a "self-centered self" that felt embedded in a broad, puzzling framework.[4]

Stephen Crane, who prided himself on avoiding pride of status, learned quickly from exploring the lower depths, concluding that the Truth proclaimed from denominational and secular pulpits had to be unmasked, especially for the masses who tried to live up to pious dogma while fuzzily suspecting they were being misled. Dreiser, who started out at the bottom of the white social ladder, believed utterly – or so he later claimed – in transcendent values that blessed his immediate world; but when he trudged into disbelief, he thought he was expressing the vague but deep doubts of his originary class. Such are the mysteries of biography that Mary E. Wilkins, rather than ridiculing what she perceived as a dying breed of small-acreage farmers further constricted by religiosity, found cause to respect their quirkiness and to memorialize the sturdy yet insightfully skeptical women. In ways that cannot be "proven," Crane, Dreiser, and Wilkins (later Freeman) drew much of their strength as realists/naturalists from their interaction with the anxieties permeating the millions rather than from sequenced discourse with intellectuals.

The attempt to demonstrate that mass-democratic attitudes also fed into realism is both inviting and elusive. Some believers have always received Christianity as egalitarian if not communitarian; Howells kept his family's fondness for such a reading, which he fleshed out with a semimodern socialism during the 1890s. Of course, the United States rested literally – through its founding documents – on the principles of liberty, equality, and impartial justice. The shrewd conservative, the schoolteacher, the editorialist, and the politician kept the catchphrases familiar and ready – ironically – for the reformers to invoke. They could invoke stronger passages from Tom Paine or the abolitionists or Whitman if they knew *Leaves of Grass* and, better still, *Democratic Vistas*. However, Karl Marx, known at second or third hand, became anathema; his shadow so melodramatically darkens two early novels about unionizing – Thomas Bailey Aldrich's *The Stillwater Tragedy* (1880) and John Hay's *The Bread-Winners* (1884) – that they are seldom instanced as realistic. But egalitarian ideas, partly as held and exemplified from below, surely encouraged Howells or Wilkins to present the bottom classes more empathetically.

Although "serious" writers naturally lived among the literate classes, realists got little help from them. The American variety of Victorianism certainly matched its model in believing that sober uplift served the community better than probing into its failures. Whereas Howells's David Sewell attacked only sentimental romances at the dinner party in *The Rise of Silas Lapham,* rank-and-file ministers were likely to carry on their tradition of warning against all fiction as sin-inducing frivolity; more importantly, they were increasingly rounding off their sermons – after the expected scourging – with a chord of hope that included worldly redemption. Without much retooling, some ministers doubled as academics, though an overworked professoriate was emerging. Professors of English who taught any literature at all favored the classics (Greek and Roman more than British) and accepted as their mission molding character rather than challenging the inherited ideology. While H. H. Boyesen spoke out for realism during his fifteen years at Columbia University, none of his colleagues joined him.

Among the other emerging professions, realists might have expected support from lawyers, who in the 1870s made the crucial passage to defending, without loss of caste, (high-paying) clients who reeked ethically; the antebellum mold of the gentleman/attorney/belletrist had crumbled. While a thin layer of *raisonneurs* was developing a new academic specialty, courses such as "mental" or "moral philosophy" were typically taught by theologians, were mandatory for all seniors, and were designed to send them out convinced that virtue was triumphant. "From the pre-eminent mental philosopher of the 1860s and the 1870s, Professor Noah Porter, Yale students learned that knowing was possible because 'the *rational methods of the divine and human intellect* are similar.'" Porter "assumed that God was beneficent and that He had arranged human and natural life according to certain uniform principles."[5] Such confidence sanctioned current principles of behavior and belief, though the intelligentsia also preached the gospel of progress – progress that would make everyday life immensely more civilized, not just more comfortable, yet would not erode the underlying Truth.

The most evident proof of progress was the accelerating success of technology. Both the sophisticate and the bumpkin marveled at the showy manipulations of a reality that, significantly, had to be uncovered by expert techniques rather than magic or prayers. Electricity was the most obviously impressive find. All along it had lurked there somewhere; once the technical mind found it, it worked for everybody's use and pleasure – the telegraph, the telephone, the light bulb, and the phonograph. A farmer who had only heard about these wonders might see a locomotive pulling an immense load. If the first electric motors seemed less mighty, they did confirm the benefits of technology. During the nineteenth century these benefits steadily evolved toward anti-supernatural or merely secular attitudes, eager to accept the treasures of this earth. Once John Stuart Mill published his *Utilitarianism* in 1861, the principle of the greatest good for the greatest number soothed many consciences. Careful, objective thought would discover new facts, from which induction derived "laws" for the laboratory and also for ethical choices. In 1866 Robert E. Lee counseled his daughter: "Read history, works of truth, not novels and romances. Get correct views of life and learn to see the world in its true light. It will enable you to live pleasantly, to do good, and, when summoned away, to leave without regret."[6] This advice could stand as a reprise of Scottish "commonsense" philosophy – the favored antebellum metaphysics – but it could also sound up-to-date during the decades ahead.

At the self-consciously intellectual level, scientific thinking, labeled as such, won supporters for its coherence and rationality, reinforced by usable results. As the century began, a coordinated universe, planned by a divine creator, was already revealing manipulable patterns; problem-solving instead of wishful thinking (or the wishful feeling encouraged by sentimental romances) produced answers beneficial ever after for this world. Closure-prone historians of ideas tend to make Darwinian biology displace mechanical physics, but even today many lay admirers of science as the path into functioning reality are fundamentally Newtonian.[7]

With the return to peacetime discourse, interest in the scientific approach jumped sharply. Examples so abound as to recall Charles Darwin's astonishment at how nature fills every crack and any crevice. In Boston the Radical Club started up in 1867 to suit the "desire of certain ministers and laymen for larger liberty of faith, fellowship, and communion . . . for the freest investigation of all forms of religious thought and inquiry." But by the time the club dissolved in 1880, its meetings had centered "generally upon scientific and educational problems."[8] As early as 1873, when Whitelaw Reid – already in control of the *New York Tribune* – delivered a widely praised speech at Dartmouth College, he could assert: "Ten or fifteen years ago, the staple subject here for reading and talk, outside study hours, was English poetry and fiction. Now it is English science. Herbert Spencer, John Stuart Mill, Huxley, Darwin, Tyndall, have usurped the places of Tennyson and Browning, and Matthew Arnold and Dickens."[9] Reid, who would have icily resented the label of philistine, was pleased that "we are no longer sentimental" but firmly quizzical instead. Although he primarily belabored "sentimentalists" about politics, he also cared about literature. To many intellectuals, science taught objectivity, defined both as the patient screening out not just of prejudices but also useless truisms and as the springboard to further insights. With a counterbalance of irony, the basis for Howellsian realism was in place.

Darwin's *On the Origin of Species* would prove more important for naturalism, though it came out as early as 1859. Not that it played to the stereotype of the epoch-making theory that inches toward notice. When *On the Origin* was soon republished in the United States, the *New York Times* ran a very long review that begins: "Mr. Darwin, as the fruit of a quarter-century of patient observation and experiment, throws out, in a book whose title at least by this time has become familiar to the reading public, a series of arguments and inferences so revolutionary as, if established, to necessitate a radical reconstruction of the fundamental doctrines of natural history."[10] But that revolutionary thrust was soon blunted by a "soft" Darwinism, partly cosmetic and partly optimistic. Like his father a Congregational minister and long a professor of moral philosophy and metaphysics at Yale University, Noah Porter, along with his peers, rejected a nature red in tooth and claw as manifestly false; more crucially, they argued that evolution was simply God's intricate, patient way of bringing humankind to its almost perfected state. Ridicule at all levels of print down to filler-jokes and cartoons doubtless discouraged other minds from bending Darwin's way. Most viscerally, there was reluctance to abdicate the throne of the chain of being or to slide from the center of the universe into the animal kingdom – moves harder to take because Thomas H. Huxley, Darwin's "bulldog," insisted on facing the brute facts.

Although "hard" Darwinism had to cut across the grain in the United States, it did spread soon. Enough proof abounds to have delighted Darwin, who liked to pile up examples stupefyingly.[11] Before the monthly *Galaxy*, Mark Twain's chief outlet, gave a rich survey, it predicted:

The Taine of the twentieth century who shall study the literature of the nineteenth will note an epochal earmark. He will discover a universal drenching of belles-lettres with science and sociology, while the ultimate, dominant tinge in our era he will observe to be Darwinism. Not only does all physical research take color from the new theory, but the doctrine sends its pervasive hues through poetry, novels, history. A brisk reaction betrays its disturbing presence in theology. Journalism is dyed so deep with it that the favorite logic of the leading article is "survival of the fittest," and the favorite jest is "sexual selection." In the last new book, in the next new book, you will detect it.[12]

The *Galaxy*'s particulars included: "At New Orleans, last Mardi Gras, what did the 'Mistick Krewe of Comus' choose for their sport but the 'Missing Links' of Darwin." Although playfulness more than anxiety must have motivated that sport, the members of Boston's Radical Club were perturbed by a lecture on "Evolution," which pointed out that the skulls of some extinct human species "did exactly resemble the corresponding features of our monkey." Discussion drifted on into "the relations of human nature to that of the lower animals."

The questions that Darwin stimulated were far-reaching yet intensely personal, gritty yet exciting, obvious to wits and journalists yet profound to philosophers of science. He "established a theoretical framework for integrating biological thought with the mechanistic structure of physical thought," thus supplying "grounds for a unified system of knowledge."[13] Lay thinkers, including novelists, absorbed Darwinism more painfully. Even those who stood immovably on religious faith had to cope harder with the possibility that science and religion are not compatible. Before Darwin, the lecturer in moral philosophy might rhapsodize that the physical world keeps offering up evidence of how the Creator had designed it to serve His flock, or still cozier evidence of how the physical and human worlds serve each other. The literal accuracy of the Bible – already clouded by the textual "higher criticism" and the comparative study of religions – grew dimmer; Heaven as both goal and endpoint also dimmed while secular values made for a better wager than in Pascal's time. As increasingly understood just before Darwin, God's design had incorporated moral order, which no longer meant predestination but a freedom of will within mutual benevolence. Huxleyan humankind competed to survive for – arguably – no demonstrable purpose beyond producing members of the species who would repeat the process.

Although basic Darwinism proposed a coordinated pair of principles, it implied consequences so wrenching that individual acceptance varied dizzy-ingly. Still, the stance of realists and naturalists differed fundamentally from that of Jane Austen, often made the exemplar of how the Newtonian world-view could shape a novel. They tried to discipline themselves to a stricter level of objectivity, even that of the scientist poised to consider any reason-able idea – such as that the ancestors of Homo sapiens may include simians but not angels, that Homo may act far less from sapience than from instinct, that physical needs may override the conscience, that life is a chancy process rather than a path toward redemption, that nurture within an inescapably specific environment shapes organisms in fascinating but sometimes grim ways. In the pre-Darwinian United States the boldest novelists, and espe-cially Herman Melville, had sensed most of these ideas, but nobody could combine such loomings into an integrated vision and technique.

Melville came close because he resonated to some of the same ideas that educated Darwin. When the other sciences get a fair hearing, *On the Origin* blurs as the massive turning point. Once mostly a hobby, geology as prac-ticed by Charles Lyell established the principle of uniformity, that is, the consistency of earth-shaping processes over aeons, over "deep" time. Like-wise, chemistry was discovering other underlying processes or structures, showily demonstrable in the kitchen or the factory or, in ten seconds, at a popular lecture. More crucial at first than any metaphysical iconoclasms was the impact on general knowledge. Sciences of the nineteenth century were of course less abstruse than today, and their leaders wrote for the weekly and monthly magazines. By 1871, when Howells took over as chief editor, the *Atlantic Monthly* carried the subtitle "A Magazine of Literature, Science, Art, and Politics." Furthermore, readers eagerly labored to keep pace, and *Popular Science Monthly*, featuring articles that now look dully formidable, reached a print run of eleven thousand soon after 1872. Its publisher had already started an "International Scientific Library" that would grow to over fifty volumes through offering the leading thinkers, not their interpreters.

E. L. Youmans (1821–87), the organizer behind those two enterprises, zealously promoted Herbert Spencer into one of the most spacious intellects since humankind began to reason – though his books are now ignored as wordy, opaque, and free-floating. His disciples took him as proving that a system of interrelated "forces" guides an evolutionary sweep upward. Building the symmetrical mansion of certainties that they yearned for, he supplied more of an emotional than a logical experience. Whereas Howells and Crane were indifferent, Dreiser and Norris realized that they had been groping to find his "universe of force." Norris's grandiosity causes later readers to skim without recognizing that *The Octopus* could not have been written without Spencer. He would help lead less ebullient minds such as Henry Adams to what Herbert Schneider, in a history of American philosophy, labels a "desperate naturalism."

Intellectuals willing to consider the scientific approach could feel that they were discovering how their world is put together, could feel proud of exploring caves that stand-fast religionists shunned, and could grow eager to apply empiricism everywhere. Getting up from armchair introspection or from prayer for a humankind that had in Adam's fall sinned all, they started to observe how individuals develop, to record how consciousness actually works, and so to move toward William James's functionalism. Gordon O. Taylor has concluded succinctly:

> Roughly between 1870 and 1900 fictive psychology in the American novel undergoes a fundamental shift. . . . The basic view of the mind underlying the representation of consciousness in fiction moves away from a notion of static, discrete mental states requiring representational emphasis on the conventional nature of particular states, toward a concept of organically linked mental states requiring representational emphasis on the nature of the sequential process itself.[14]

Although biographers profitably debate the influence of William James as psychologist on his brother Henry's novels – and possible reciprocity – other writers doubtless learned from the essays commissioned by the magazines that considered themselves conduits of the latest expertise and kept increasing their audience in the decades after the Civil War.

By the 1880s James and Howells were berated for cutting, as coldly as a scientist, into the mind of the girl-woman, endangering her ideals along with those of her admirers. We have to wonder whether that stopped James and Howells from cutting deeper, down to the libido, and whether their critics felt threatened more by biology than by current psychology. In 1871 Darwin had released *The Descent of Man,* bothersome enough with its pictures comparing the facial emoting of simians and humans. But when read carefully, it confronted the effects of pairing for reproduction, which *On the Origin of Species* had discussed inconclusively. The public was uneasily fascinated, according to the *Galaxy* essayist who complained that "the favorite jest is 'sexual selection.'" Although hit-and-run historians overstate Victorian prudery, literary realists, and much more naturalists, felt charged on behalf of objective fact to scrutinize the professed standards for sexuality and, most egregiously, for courtship and marriage.

Less traumatically, post-Darwin biology, by supporting the principle that all experience operates under "laws," contributed to the rise of sociology, already proposed by Auguste Comte as a science for codifying a fresh concept, which appropriated the term *society*. "The older disciplines had failed fully to explain human conduct, not only because of their reliance on ideal, rather than observed, categories but also because they were limited in what they investigated. In 'society,' the new intellectuals of the later nineteenth century hit upon a concept that described a space between the State as described in political theory and Man as understood in philosophy." This "recognition of society as a rule-bound entity that was greater than the sum of its individual parts" lay behind the founding in 1865 of the American Social Science Foundation, which stressed reform but increasingly debated theories of development.[15] The so-called genetic method began tracking the individual within the shaping context that might be changing too. While psychologists groped for the discrete individual, the sociologists discovered typicality. As Jerome J. McGann encapsulates the matter: " . . . it came to be believed that if one wanted to understand 'human nature' in general, one had to proceed along two dialectically related paths: along the path of a thorough sociohistorical set of observations and along the path of the, now so-called, sciences of the artificial. For 'human nature' was not (is not) 'made' by God, it was (and continues to be) artfully, artificially constructed by human beings, within certain given limits, in the course of their social development."[16] The realistic writers' dilemma had arrived, though they saw it as an invigorating challenge: how to create unique characters who nevertheless stand for more than themselves, stand for an occupation, a class, a "type."

Some, if not most, of the mainline spokespersons during the 1890s chortled at the dilemma. William Roscoe Thayer, then eminent as an editor, historian, and biographer, jeered at the novelist who pretended to "scientific impartiality," precision, and also breadth.[17] Others professed to accept current science yet insisted on a God enthroned just behind its laws, a step from where He had reigned at mid-century. Edith Wharton's slyly titled short story "The Descent of Man" (1904) sympathized with a biologist who, irritated by "soft" uses of science, tried to "avenge his goddess by satirising her false interpreters" and their "hazy transcendentalism"; but his book, which heaped "platitude on platitude, fallacy on fallacy, false analogy on false analogy," was welcomed seriously into bestsellerdom. Although acclaimed painters like F. E. Church absorbed the geologists' concept of uniformitarian process within deep time, their landscapes depended on a "natural theology"; Darwinism only sharpened their sense of the intricate variety of the Nature planned by the Creator.[18] Taking our own lesson from evolutionary thought, we must focus on how novelists behaved both individually and typically within their particular ambiance.

THE HISTORICAL BACKGROUND

Major shifts of ideas occur within broad, visible processes. Still, it sharpens insight to distinguish the historical from the intellectual sources of realism, to specify the events and groupings that elicited or else supported it. Getting specific must start, however, from the recognition that attitudes toward history itself were changing. Collectively, nineteenth-century science undercut the ancient theories that humankind moves in recurring cycles; instead, the doctrine or myth of progress sprang into many-faceted dominance. In even minimal terms this scotched any harking back to some golden age. The field marshals of progress orated with positive gestures that embraced all viable troops, including novelists. In 1870 Thomas Wentworth Higginson, now remembered mainly for his interchange with Emily Dickinson, predicted an "advance along the whole line of literary labor, like the elevation which we have seen in the whole quality of scientific work in America, within the past twenty years"; soon after, he joined the chorus anticipating the "Great American Novel" that such an advance would surely produce.[19] Progress also meant discarding the outmoded as much as it demanded openness to the new. While scientists used some facts discovered in the past, it was essentially prehistory for the bustling, superior present.

A fortified thesis holds that the modern novel, inherently mimetic, arose along with the middle class of a commercial, industrializing society. That middle class began craving to be presented respectfully and encouraged that end by buying the obliging novels. In turn, it encouraged middle-class secularism, which found that practical economics can pay off at a rising rate. Otherworldliness faded before the pleasures of consumerism and reaching shorter-term goals.

The middle class professed religious (synonymous with Christian) values. However, the realistic classics of the later nineteenth century would rarely show such values as happily directing the mainstream of experience. In fact, the genteelist critics attacked those classics as impious or actively destructive of idealism, and romances about faith that conquers all, usually through a woman's tenacity, far outsold those classics. Especially in the United States, the middle class had entered into its schizophrenia: its split between laissez-faire economics and a rationalizing denial of the brutalities entailed. As one result, men – the "breadwinners" competing head to head – belittled fiction as a toy for sheltered women, while realists tried to win respect for what they considered the highest potential of the novel, its "fidelity to experience and probability of motive," according to Howells. Since the middle class had built its success upon practicality, H. H. Boyesen, a would-be peer of Howells, argued craftily, in "The Great Realists and Empty Story-Tellers" (1895), that their mode of fiction helped toward "survival and success in life."

Although the middle class was more powerful in the United States than elsewhere, it was less self-conscious than in England or France. With some sincerity, its rhetoric for onshore politics ignored or minimized the sorting by income in a New World of equality. "I affirm," wrote Higginson in "Americanism in Literature," "that democratic society, the society of the future, enriches and does not impoverish human life, and gives more, not less, material for literary art. Distributing culture throughout all classes, it diminishes class-distinction and develops distinctions of personal character"(62). Early admirers of Howells declared Silas Lapham the embodiment of Higginson's vision, especially as he elaborated it: "To analyze combinations of character that only our national life produces, to portray dramatic situations that belong to a clearer social atmosphere, – this is the higher Americanism." But Higginson's future could not later welcome Carrie Meeber (of Columbia City) as a product of "our national life" nor the Bowery as part of our "social atmosphere"; it had retained too much of his antebellum world.

The Civil War, we now recognize, ended in victory for Northern capitalism and its centralizing bureaucracy, its network of railroads, and – most important at the time – its factories. Its captains trumpeted the visible changes, certified as Progress, and for the Centennial played loud Te Deums. The festivities of 1876 presented American history as a quickening march, a sequenced narrative. In actual demography, postwar industrialism lured people from farm to town and then to pell-mell cities, inviting yet mysterious to outsiders. Editors saw an urgent need as well as profitable opportunity to document the new social contexts – the city more than the factory – and the way that Americans were adapting to assembly lines and horsecars, electric lights and apartment houses. The competing, burgeoning metropolitan newspapers featured the twists of daily survival or success; periodicals featured breathless essays on changing facts and attitudes. Ephemeral fiction also exploited such approaches, though it more often played up to nostalgia.

Serious novelists likewise felt the impulse to explain, or at least to record, the onrushing changes. But any documentation is selective and therefore implicitly judgmental. The realistic temperament turned toward the disjunctures between optimistic rhetoric and what was actually happening. Its next phase – "critical" realism – emphasized the mismatches between the boastings of laissez-faire industry and the workers ground up in the dark satanic mills; Rebecca Harding Davis's still familiar short story had already moved in 1861 beyond documentation to pained protest. Little known today are some texts of countercritical realism that showed factory "hands" resisting their own best interests. But by the 1890s its genial foremen and owners appeared seldom. The realists we still respect, Howells especially, would increasingly indict either the logic of Manchester Liberalism or those who carried it into a practice that refused a livable wage and a safe workplace.

The Jeffersonian-agrarian ideal collapsed so slowly that, into the twentieth century, farmers attracted wider sympathy than factory workers. Their troubles had differentiated them from the quirky trailblazers, ennobled in 1893 as Frederick Jackson Turner's "pioneers," and the get-rich-quick prospectors of Mark Twain's *Roughing It*. They battled nature to function as productive units of the nation but were exploited by bankers, railroads, and "trusts" (industrial monopolies). Although the farmers producing for the commodities market were in fact gambling, they had no chance against the speculators in Omaha, Kansas City, Saint Louis, or Chicago – who looked to Manhattan for the bank of last resort. Although the Grangers and the Populists protested the farmers' entrapment sooner than did the intellectuals, by the later 1880s Hamlin Garland was writing short stories that still resonate. Historians also honor E. W. Howe's *Story of a Country Town* (1883) and Joseph Kirkland's *Zury: The Meanest Man in Spring County* (1887).

Before the Civil War the major novels had ignored current affairs. While *Uncle Tom's Cabin* (1852) made a sensation, neither chattel nor wage slavery inspired a genre of social-justice fiction. The promise of romantic democracy to set all wrong matters right for whites still sounded believable. After the Civil War, however, many of those matters not only looked but felt different; the age of Henry Clay, Daniel Webster, and even Abraham Lincoln seemed almost quaint. Overriding a chaotic increase in population, modernization crunched onward without a pause. However, historians agree on its exclamation points. Grantism, the deep corruption in federal affairs, upset revered symbols: the chief hero of the war had degenerated into a President conned by his cronies. In 1873 a depression ended the dream that the postwar prosperity would go on expanding forever. Too soon after the Centennial, the railroad riots of 1877 proved that American workers – perhaps even the native-born – could destroy property, could defy the regular army called in to rescue the police. Violence punctuated the 1880s more regularly, as the Knights of Labor led strikes and the Populist militants stirred. A judicial lynching after the Haymarket Affair astounded Howells. The bloody Homestead strike of 1892 horrified several differing constituencies; the Panic of 1893 reminded those who had prospered lately that the economic machine had structural flaws; labor unions and their allies concluded during the Pullman strike of 1894 that the wealthy made up law and order to suit themselves. If the campaign against the Filipinos in 1900 had inspired memorable fiction, that would have seemed the climax of the education that middle-class liberals had accumulated during the last thirty-five years. Instead, economic history had compiled a more dangerous liability: in Dreiser and Jack London the city's victims were starting to produce their own writers, mordantly skeptical toward what the ruling elites told them to believe.

Between 1865 and the First World War, three movements that never built to a famous crisis disturbed, nevertheless, the hymns to progress. The freed slaves themselves began contrasting the promises made (and sometimes proclaimed as kept) and the reality that was eroding the ground won during Reconstruction. White women began joining organizations that campaigned for their legal and political rights; more illuminating for novelists, the bravest women announced that the genteel version of their character and desires hid the facts. Finally, immigration, growing exponentially, flooded in a melange of humankind whose values and behavior shook WASP complacencies. Moreover, those immigrants who had believed democracy's promises began resisting their mistreatment; a few – numerous by comparison with homegrown reformers – imported a leftist critique of capitalism.

A novelist could perceive such movements as an opportunity, a challenge, or even a responsibility. At first Howells, like others, talked about the duty of literature to help heal the wounds of the war. Next, he urged middle-class readers to enter empathetically the maze of religions, ethnic enclaves, jobs, and regional mores. Pushed programatically, this added up to a wholly fresh way of looking at American society, not just through literature; minimally, it called for an objective, accurate picture of who and what was out there. Cultural historians have documented the lightning spread and deep popularity of photography, of taking and looking at pictures.[20] During the last decades of the century the trompe-l'oeil precision of William Michael Harnett and his school fascinated public taste; portrait painters, alert to the rampant diversity, understood the "anxious *need*" of Americans "to know what was going on beneath the masks of those strange others with whom they were bafflingly yet inextricably bound."[21] In newspapers and magazines, fresh targets of humor emerged: mystics, ethereal poets, hermits, fortune-tellers, and gallants looked spurious in a steam, steel, and stock-market age.

During the 1880s the realist dynamic pushed beyond the ideal of perceptive accuracy toward a criticism of the dominating consensus – criticism for its failures not only of vision but also of motives that had blinded it to its harmful results. Howells, responsive to the evolving political-economic struggle, solidified into a gentle force for social justice.[22] Among the ongoing coinages the term *liberal realism* fits his later fiction best. It exemplified his faith in achieving a shared referentiality that can function humanely and correctively. Such a faith was historically conditioned, but it continued to condition history.

THE MARKETPLACE

Although the term *marketplace* is still common, it was already an anachronism for the publishing business in the later nineteenth century. Technology, finance capital (in 1899 the venerable Harper & Brothers fell into the House of Morgan's net), and advertising (aggressive, grand-scale "marketing") would often determine what readers bought and so what got published next. That a diagram for these interactions comes harder than one for science or social conflict does not impugn their power. Of course, while publishing as a business shaped the literary realists more subtly than they could be expected to perceive, they would agree that we must consider its effects on the fiction preferred by successful editors and their customers.

However manipulated in their choices, readers ultimately exerted their own effects among the many tiers of taste available during the postbellum decades, as technologies of manufacture and distribution made more kinds of materials affordable.[23] But no technocrat has proved whether or why they will prefer one book over another. Since genuinely enthralled readers of a novel engage with it subliminally, they themselves cannot explain their preferences. Furthermore, postbellum readers, as always, switched from one clientele to another as their moods or needs oscillated.

It is clear how the realists envisioned the audience they hoped to reach. Respecting fiction as a potentially constructive discourse with social as well as private consequences, they aspired to encourage a "common culture in which all classes could partake."[24] Doubtless calculating royalties too, they aimed for a readability that would win and hold a following against fierce competition and developed a professionalism that analyzed more coldly than had the antebellum writers the dialectic of supply and demand.[25] More specifically, they felt a mission to displace fiction that inspired destructive fantasy through paragons of courage, honesty, or chaste courtship.

Because the novel offered much more room for detail, carried higher prestige, and could pay better, the realists aimed primarily at the book trade. Their desired publishers were the firms with an ongoing list for the educated general reader, who supposedly detested pulp fiction or near pornography; such a list included cutting-edge books that would bring status along with passable sales. But sentimental romance in its several varieties sold by far the best. As *Scribner's Monthly* reminded Boyesen, his breathless, exotic *Gunnar* (1874) continued to attract more buyers than novels darkened by "the objectionable influences allied to the so-called realistic school."[26] Not yet labeled by George Santayana, the genteel tradition gained strength throughout the last decades of the century. The mainstream firms resisted fiction that clearly questioned the reigning code or just lacked the élan of ideality. Quite consciously, they supported the principle that social institutions – very much including the print-agencies – are interdependent, and that each must instill the basic truths that empower a progressing humankind.

Boyesen gave the boldest analysis of how the unofficial censorship worked. "The average American has no time to read anything but newspapers, while his daughters have an abundance of time at their disposal, and a general disposition to employ it in anything that is amusing. The novelist who has begun to realize that these young persons constitute his public, naturally endeavors to amuse them."[27] Boyesen was constantly aware that editors of the "paying magazines" mediated between him and those daughters; they acted for "that inexorable force called public taste." Still, behind them loomed "the young American girl. She is the Iron Madonna who strangles in her fond embrace the American novelist. . . ." Boyesen also came closest to stating a related complaint: literature was being emasculated because its determining readers were women. More calmly, Howells pondered how to reeducate rather than dethrone the Iron Madonna; furthermore, he thought her less influential than the hardening pattern of the wife-mother as the docent of fine culture. Although recent analysis agrees that realistic fiction sold to both genders,[28] publishers doubtlessly worried about the reviewers who invoked feminine tastes, and Howells tried for a more masculine appeal.

In fusing the magazine and book business Boyesen's analysis fit the facts. Novelists with any leverage first sold the serial rights; moreover, short stories paid well and quicker as the monthlies reached their peak of prosperity. They earned it by fashioning a "family" magazine, whose contents kept up with major trends and with advice for positive thinking. Alert to their moral superiority over the *National Police Gazette* and its ilk, they rejected ads for improper merchandise, including such books. Of course they favored up-beat fiction, as Edith Wharton learned young when *Scribner's* turned down her novella "Bunner Sisters" because it did not have a cheerful episode at the break between installments.[29] Writers held back a gloomy story for a collection that might include it as counterpoint; when an editor asked for a "holiday" piece, they knew what chords to play. Boyesen grew sardonic: "The editor, being anxious to keep all his old subscribers and secure new ones, requires of his contributor that he shall offend no one. He must not expose a social or religious sham . . . he must steer carefully, so as to step on nobody's toes. . . . However much he may rebel against it, he is forced to chew the cud of old ideas, and avoid espousing any cause which lacks the element of popularity." Even so, this indictment understated how quickly subscribers protested that a story or essay had violated some point of propriety.[30]

Richard Watson Gilder could have proved that Boyesen had also oversimplified. His *Century Magazine,* the leading monthly, published stories and novels that are still respected; in the 1880s it serialized *A Modern Instance* and *The Rise of Silas Lapham* – and Henry James's *The Bostonians* to noticeably light applause – and in the next generation, Jack London's *The Sea-Wolf.* After Howells had made his staunch liberalism clear, *Harper's Monthly* renewed his contract for "Editor's Study." Although firmly preferring ideality, the dominant magazines printed essays that lifted the torch for realism. More importantly, because they sold continuous freshness, they wanted fiction that broke through predictable stereotypes. An interplay developed: realists probed the limits while watching their income; editors strained to predict subscribers' tastes and to outshine competitors while holding on to some margin of principle; readers expected fiction that suited their values but were liable to cry cliché! On the edges, latecomers probed for a share-grabbing distinctiveness. In the early 1890s the new owner of *Cosmopolitan* tried to climb along a reformist route; crusading editors of second- and third-rate magazines, most notably B. O. Flower of the *Arena,* sought out young dissenters like Hamlin Garland; a band of livelier, lower-priced monthlies inched toward the muckraking of the early 1900s that encouraged franker, more probing fiction.

Historians of realism identify journalism as the common road of apprenticeship.[31] The pattern works well enough for Howells, E. W. Howe, Ambrose Bierce, Crane, Harold Frederic, Dreiser, and Willa Cather, among others. Certainly, reporters routinely see and hear facts that contradict official morality. Just turned twenty, Howells found the sordidness of his stint on the *Cincinnati Gazette* unbearable. Dreiser recalled a ghastlier trauma: "I went into newspaper work" at the age of twenty "and from that time dates my real contact with life – murders, arson, rape, sodomy, bribery, corruption, trickery and false witness in every conceivable form."[32] But, raised two generations later, Dreiser could add, "Finally I got used to the game and rather liked it."

Less sensationally, newspapers once gave much space to reviewing books. In playing to a mass audience they were likelier than the magazines to praise native writers; calling for, predicting, the Great American Novel made the term a catchphrase, and realism was potentially the most indigenous mode.[33] Far more influential, probably, were the so-called literary comedians. Between 1870 or so and 1920 many a newspaper had its own humorist-columnist groping for the angle needed daily. Furthermore, literary burlesque had a popularity that strikes us as idiosyncratic, and drab realism made an inviting target. In the *Chicago Daily News,* Eugene Field poked fun at Hamlin Garland's heroes who "sweat and do not wear socks" and heroines who "eat cold huckleberry pie and are so unfeminine as not to call a cow 'he.'" However, sentimental or historical romances overreached worse, with characters and rhetoric that struck cynical journalists as demanding ridicule.[34] Aside from such burlesque, the literary comedians featured an honestly colloquial language seldom used elsewhere in respectable print. Boyesen's "average American" who "has no time to read anything but newspapers" was absorbing a protorealism, not just from the crime stories but also the columns meant to be amusing.

THE MOVEMENT

In any argument on whether nineteenth-century realism was concerted enough to rate as a "movement" both the positive and the negative are easily attacked. Many intelligent polemicists assumed that "realism" signified a clear and present breakthrough or else danger.[35] On the other hand, the roster of novelists who explicitly endorsed that catchword is short and conspicuously lacks the names of Mark Twain and Henry James.

The "realism war," as Howells called it, first grew sharp during the 1880s. Because art for art's sake showed no American panache until the 1890s, the debate posed realism against "ideality." While it never reached the sophistication or intensity of its earlier climax in France, it had a far stronger moral-ethical tone. For the historian, to highlight particular debaters itself turns into a test of objectivity, because either side could sound naive. Gilder's record as editor of *Century Magazine* makes his "Certain Tendencies in Current Literature" the fairest exhibit: Since "realism is, in fact, something in the air . . . the Time-Spirit . . . the state of mind of the nineteenth century," it "is at this moment vitalizing American literature and attracting to it the attention of the world." Having overstated generously, Gilder orated onward to a compromise: "The pronounced realist is a useful fellow-creature, but so also is the pronounced idealist – stouten his work though you will with a tincture of reality."[36] At the least Gilder shows that the opposing terms operated then as intrinsically significant.

Deepest down, Gilder sided with the idealists, some of whom debated far more testily. Thomas Bailey Aldrich, who kept rising in prestige from the 1860s until after 1900, sniped away. His "An Untold Story" ended provocatively: "A gloss of grim fact might have spoiled the finer text"; "At the Funeral of a Minor Poet" condemned the "Zolaistic Movement" for its "miasmatic breath." In the magazines, satiric verse consistently favored the side of ideality. Because of Boyesen's temperament and European training he emerged as realism's fiercest champion in a string of essays that his death cut short in 1895.

Besides his polemics, younger novelists could draw enough strength from the essays collected by Howells as *Criticism and Fiction*, by Garland as *Crumbling Idols* (1894), and by Norris as *The Responsibilities of the Novelist* (1903)[37] to believe that they lived in the age of realism.[38] Kate Chopin, Harold Frederic, and Edith Wharton could stand on what seemed a liberated rationale, though today we see them as having been conditioned by the same society they urged their audience to judge objectively. That society taught the dignity of self-support along with sincerity and altruism but awarded fame for strenuous personal achievement; while advising the masses to nurture themselves on "good" literature, it shaped tastes toward immediate profits, on which authors had to live. The realists, who never came close to dominating sales or critical opinion, struggled with problems they sometimes could not define, much less master. For instance, Howells puzzled over the dilemma of how to improve best-sellers by belittling them without reinforcing elitism.

Historians who hold that a movement did coalesce have to stretch when inscribing its honor roll, especially if they exclude native American humor and the larger school of local color. Some would include Harriet Beecher Stowe's turn into a household-centered "domestic" realism that they find already active by the 1850s; her *Oldtown Folks* (1869) opens with a memorable manifesto for plain-folks mimesis. Others would resuscitate Oliver Wendell Holmes's three "medicated" novels, particularly *Elsie Venner*

(1861). Historians posted on Southern literature reach back further to William Gilmore Simms, for the raw, lusty detail of his works set on the "Border" – the frontier of the antebellum Southwest.

Nevertheless, when John W. De Forest surveyed current fiction in 1868 he found no major movement in sight.[39] Actually, he could have puffed his own *Miss Ravenel's Conversion from Secession to Loyalty* (1867) for its war scenes, fitfully natural dialogue, and ironic undertone. His *Kate Beaumont* (1872) and *Playing the Mischief* (1875) moved further toward a quizzicality and self-discipline that would have improved Edward Eggleston's novels. Although the sentimentalism runs too deep for surgery in the once famous *Hoosier Schoolmaster* (1871), *Roxy* (1878) boldly accepts a Darwinian descent; its narrator comments on village folk enjoying the antics of caged monkeys that they "were not conscious that there might be aught of family affection in this attraction" and laughed "without a sense of gamboling rudely over the graves" of "their ancestors" (chap. 20). Working toward its climax, *Roxy* explodes a steamboat: a "young Baptist minister, who with his bride had just come aboard, stood . . . waving his handkerchief to the friends on shore, when in an instant the boat flew into a thousand pieces. . . . The bar-keeper alighted on the inverted roof of his bar, away in the stream, and was saved. The young Baptist minister and his wife were never found. A mile away . . . in a tree-top, there was found a coat-collar, which his friends thought belonged to him" (chap. 57). More crucially, the future of the worthy heroine, who married for love, looks troubled rather than happy.

By the 1880s the realistically persuaded were focusing on complexity of motive. S. Weir Mitchell, better known as a clinician and medical psychologist, kept readers of *In War Time* (1884) unsure how to judge the protagonist; deservedly, he ends up "broken" in mind and spirit, but that result was not predictable and was constructed with enough empathy to block any effect of a villain. For a while Henry Blake Fuller, in *The Cliff-Dwellers* (1893) and *With the Procession* (1895), promised to outdo Howells. Admirers of Boyesen's polemics had yet stronger hopes, supported less by the qualities of *The Mammon of Unrighteousness* (1891) than by its preface, which pledged to avoid "sensational incidents": "I have disregarded all romantic traditions, and simply asked myself in every instance, not whether it was amusing, but whether it was true to the logic of reality – true in color and tone to the American sky, the American soil, the American character." Although Boyesen's star dimmed quickly, Robert Herrick, another professor of literature, was soon impressing reviewers with intellectually ambitious novels, known today only to scholars. Harold Frederic's *The Damnation of*

Theron Ware (1896), which also has only such readers now, deserves better for its low-key, tolerant, slow defrocking of a Methodist preacher.

Lately, historians have been rediscovering writers such as Charles Chesnutt and Frances E. W. Harper – for *Iola Leroy; or Shadows Uplifted* (1892). However, postbellum Afro-Americans fought for other such vital causes as to leave realism secondary. Primary enrichment has come through the latest wave of feminism, which has analyzed Kate Chopin's *The Awakening* (1899) up to canonical status and has shown that Sarah Orne Jewett's *Country of the Pointed Firs* (1896) and short stories deserve a roomier, better respected category than local-color or regionalism. Overall, Josephine Donovan contends that postbellum women were marginalized in both ambition and subject, that local color was their self-censored realism.[40]

NATURALISM IN THE TWENTIETH CENTURY

Realism became an integral source of naturalism without, however, losing its own vitality. Although the post-Howells generation almost inevitably thought they were rejecting their mentors, they continued in practice to take sentimental romance as the chief, long-lived enemy in literature. The most productive questions are (1) what sources led beyond realism? and (2) how did the two ism's differ?[41]

The naturalists were the first cohort to consider without surprise the processes the Civil War had made dominant. They recognized that industrialism and urbanism, now clearly irreversible, were accelerating; iron mills had expanded into steel mills run by corporations scheming toward monopoly; not just the fitful pains of growing up, the conflict between capital and labor was getting bloodier at the seams of a hardened class structure; in 1894 Coxey's Army looked like formidable guerrillas. Naturalists framed politics in economics-oriented, more systematic and explicit terms than the reformism implied by the realists. They also recognized that science had cornered Homo sapiens by tracing his animal heritage and chemical mechanisms. More willingly than grudgingly, the business of publishing had changed as drastically. Garish facts peddled in the mushrooming tabloids had punched gaps in the reticence that the public supposedly demanded of novelists; though his enemies had shown Howells the foolishness of a static mind, he received *Maggie* gingerly as the next stage of iconoclasm, which he could not mount. Publishers and editors, competing for a readership expanding in diversity and boldness of taste, accepted brighter colors, louder tones, grubbier characters, and more brutal action; Norris felt born in the nick of time.

Because critics disagree sharply, the sane conclusion is that the naturalists wrote out of a loose gestalt of values and techniques rather than a coordinated metaphysic or aesthetic. They surpassed the realists qualitatively in exploring humankind's animal sides; their approach to psychology could let instinct overpower conscious will. Most distinctively, they pushed further toward determinism – economic or biological or cosmic – than American novelists had cared or dared to go before.[42] In method – secondary to content insofar as the choice could or had to be made – they intensified the ideal of objectivity; at documentary length, tabooed attitudes got not merely a hearing but a self-justification. Although the naturalists' rhetoric turned back toward intensity of tone and metaphor, readers were now manipulated to regret the fate of a working-class dentist or accept the rise of fallen women. Illiterate characters suffered as consciously as the rich and fluent, and struggled with guilt as painfully as a Puritan minister, though naturalistic closure brought pessimism instead of redemption. Within the protean genre of the novel, a sympathetic reader easily distinguishes a naturalistic from a realistic work, and either, through method as well as attitude, from any other mode.

No American novelist moved from realism to naturalism, leaving a neat exhibit for taxonomy. Nor did naturalism fit the metaphor of a gathering stream. The shift was not accretive but qualitative. Naturalism burst out with Crane, and then Norris and Dreiser, all more indebted literarily to foreign than to native masters. Along with realism, it merged into the permanent background for the art of the novel.[43] Likewise, it has kept its own ongoing vitality. It is the foreground for John Dos Passos, Ernest Hemingway, William Faulkner (arguably), John Steinbeck, James T. Farrell, Richard Wright, Norman Mailer, Toni Morrison, Joyce Carol Oates, and John Updike's "Rabbit" tetralogy.

NOTES

1 "Leslie Fiedler and American Culture," *Chicago Review* 14 (1960): 17–8.
2 *The Popular Mood of Pre-Civil War America* (Westport, Conn.: Greenwood, 1980). Another path to in-depth materials is through local history, as in the richly excellent Jean Bradley Anderson, *Durham County* (Durham, N.C.: Duke University Press, 1990).
3 Janet Gabler-Hover, *Truth in American Fiction: The Legacy of Rhetorical Idealism* (Athens: University of Georgia Press, 1990), recapitulates the reigning optimism before it wavered. In a broader context, the same attitude is sketched by Louise L. Stevenson, *The Victorian Homefront: American Thought and Culture, 1860–1880* (New York: Twayne, 1991), p. 139.

4 *The Popular Mood of America, 1860–1890* (Lincoln: University of Nebraska Press, 1990), pp. 169–71.

5 Stevenson, p. 108; the italics are Porter's.

6 Quoted in Burton J. Hendrick, *The Lees of Virginia* (Boston: Little, Brown, 1935), p. 413.

7 A deeply informed exposition of the differences between the early and late nineteenth-century western philosophy of science is David B. Wilson, "Concepts of Physical Nature: John Herschel to Karl Pearson," in U.C. Knoepflmacher and G. B. Tennyson, eds., *Nature and the Victorian Imagination* (Berkeley and Los Angeles: University of California Press, 1977).

8 Mary Elizabeth (Fiske) Sargent, ed., *Sketches and Reminiscences of the Radical Club of Chestnut Street, Boston* (Boston: James R. Osgood, 1880), p. [1].

9 "The Scholar in Politics," *Scribner's Monthly* 6 (1873): 608.

10 Quoted in Sender Garlin, "John Swinton, Crusading Editor," in his *Three American Radicals* (Boulder, Colo.: Westview Press, 1991), p. 9.

11 The best overall analysis is Cynthia Eagle Russett, *Darwin in America: The Intellectual Response 1865–1912* (San Francisco: W. H. Freeman, 1976). Particularly relevant here is "Evolutionary Ideas in Late Nineteenth-Century English and American Literary Criticism," chap. 7 of Donald Pizer, *Realism and Naturalism in Nineteenth-Century American Literature*, rev. ed. (Carbondale: Southern Illinois University Press, 1984).

12 Philip Quilibet, "Darwinism in Literature," *Galaxy* 15 (1873): 695–8. Quilibet wrote a regular "Department" headed "Driftwood." Each issue of the *Galaxy* also carried "Scientific Miscellany."

13 Roger Smith, "The Human Significance of Biology: Carpenter, Darwin, and the *vera causa*," in Knoepflmacher and Tennyson, p. 217. In "Charles Darwin's Reluctant Revolution," *South Atlantic Quarterly* 91 (1992): 525–55, George Levine, who has been pondering the subject for decades, explicates the humanistic implications of Darwin's work.

14 *The Passages of Thought: Psychological Representation in the American Novel 1870–1900* (New York: Oxford University Press, 1969), pp. 5–6.

15 Daniel H. Borus, *Writing Realism: Howells, James, and Norris in the Mass Market* (Chapel Hill: University of North Carolina Press, 1989), p. 13. See also Stevenson, pp. 175–80, and Susan Mizruchi, "Fiction and the Sense of Society," in Emory Elliott, ed., *The Columbia History of the American Novel* (New York: Columbia University Press, 1991).

16 *Social Values and Poetic Acts: The Historical Judgment of Literary Work* (Cambridge, Mass.: Harvard University Press, 1988), pp. 127–8.

17 "The New Story-Tellers and the Doom of Realism," *Forum* 18 (1894): 470–80.

18 See especially pp. 76–7, 133–4, and 189 of Barbara Novak, *Nature and Culture: American Landscape Painting, 1825–1875* (New York: Oxford University Press, 1980).

19 "Americanism in Literature," *Atlantic Monthly* 25 (1870): 63; "American Novels," *North American Review* 115 (1872): 366–78.

20 Most recent is Alan Trachtenberg, *Reading American Photographs: Images as History: Mathew Brady to Walker Evans* (New York: Hill and Wang, 1989); Miles Orvell, *The Real Thing: Imitation and Authenticity in American Culture,*

1880–1940 (Chapel Hill: University of North Carolina Press, 1989), pp. 25–30, discusses the literary realists' drive for photograph-like detail. More generally, see Borus, *Writing Realism*, p. 4.

21 On the school of Harnett, see Barry Maine, "Late-Nineteenth-Century *Trompe L'Oeil* and Other Performances of the Real," Prospects 16 (1991): 281–95. David M. Lubin, *Act of Portrayal: Eakins, Sargent, James* (New Haven and London: Yale University Press, 1985), p. 9, comments on other painters.

22 William Alexander, *William Dean Howells: The Realist as Humanist* (New York: Burt Franklin, 1981), best states the case for the depth of Howells's social or liberal conscience.

23 Borus, *Writing Realism*, pp. 38–9, 109, and elsewhere, develops this point convincingly. Michael Denning's *Mechanic Accents: Dime Novels and Working-Class Culture in America* (London: Verso, 1987) demonstrates that when analysis proceeds beyond the mainline books, publishers, and periodicals it encounters still more intricate problems and imponderables.

24 Borus, *Writing Realism*, pp. 4, 138–9, 172–3, 187–8.

25 Christopher P. Wilson, *The Labor of Words: Literary Professionalism in the Progressive Era* (Athens: University of Georgia Press, 1985), develops this last point, especially as it applies to the 1890s and later.

26 Quoted in Clarence A. Glasrud, *Hjalmar Hjorth Boyesen* (Northfield, Minn.: Norwegian-American Historical Association, 1963), p. 59.

27 Boyesen's essay "Why We Have No Great Novelists," *Forum* 2 (1887): 615–22, was reprinted in his *Literary and Social Silhouettes* (New York: Harper, 1894) as "The American Novelist and His Public."

28 Borus, *Writing Realism*, p. 111.

29 Elizabeth Ammons, *Edith Wharton's Argument with America* (Athens: University of Georgia Press, 1980), pp. 12–13.

30 Arthur John, *The Best Years of the "Century": Richard Watson Gilder, "Scribner's Monthly," and the "Century Magazine," 1870–1909* (Urbana: University of Illinois Press, 1981), pp. 154–66. A superintendent of schools would complain that the *Century's* already expurgated episodes from *Adventures of Huckleberry Finn* were "destitute of a single redeeming quality."

31 Shelley Fisher Fishkin, *From Fact to Fiction: Journalism and Imaginative Writing in America* (Baltimore: The Johns Hopkins University Press, 1985), covers this approach, though she prefers to describe the emerging "contours" of a "distinctively American aesthetic."

32 Robert H. Elias, ed., *The Letters of Theodore Dreiser* (Philadelphia: University of Pennsylvania Press, 1959), 1:211.

33 Benjamin T. Spencer, "The New Realism and a National Literature," *PMLA* 56 (1941): 1116–31, develops this line of analysis with more sophistication than is needed here.

34 Despite the title of William R. Linneman's "Satires of American Realism," *American Literature* 34 (1962): 80–93, he begins with fine examples of burlesques of sensationalist, sentimental, or morally pretentious fiction.

35 The chapter on "critical realism" in John W. Rathbun and Harry Hayden Clark, *American Literary Criticism, 1860–1905* (Boston: G. K. Hall, 1979), sums up the matter judiciously. Among the many other relevant articles and

books, the most insightful, as well as interesting, is Edwin H. Cady, ed., *William Dean Howells as Critic* (London: Routledge & Kegan Paul, 1973).

36 *New Princeton Review,* n.s. 4 (1887): 1–13. In "The Realism War," chap. 2 of *The Realist at War: The Mature Years, 1885–1920, of William Dean Howells* (Syracuse, N.Y.: Syracuse University Press, 1958), Edwin H. Cady critiques the debate convincingly.

37 Pizer, *Realism and Naturalism in Nineteenth-Century American Literature,* pp. 70–85, 97–102, 107–11, expounds their critical principles lucidly.

38 Robert P. Falk, "The Rise of Realism 1871–1891," in Harry Hayden Clark, ed., *Transitions in American Literary History* (Durham, N.C.: Duke University Press, 1953), best states the case for realism as a movement. Likewise, Falk's *The Victorian Mode in American Fiction, 1865–1885* (East Lansing: Michigan State University Press, 1965) makes the best approach to realism as a "period" in American literature.

39 "The Great American Novel," *Nation* 6 (1868): 27–9.

40 *New England Local Color Literature: A Women's Tradition* (New York: F. Ungar, 1983). Elsie Miller, "The Feminization of American Realist Theory," *American Literary Realism 1870–1910* 23 (1990): 20–41, argues that Howells and others increasingly accepted women as potential realists.

41 Donald Pizer has analyzed incisively the ongoing controversy; see especially chap. 3 of his *Realism and Naturalism in Nineteenth-Century American Literature.*

42 Chap. 2 of June Howard's *Form and History in American Literary Naturalism* (Chapel Hill: University of North Carolina Press, 1985) deals capably with determinism in the fiction.

43 Donald Pizer's *Twentieth-Century American Literary Naturalism: An Interpretation* (Carbondale: Southern Illinois University Press, 1982) extends into the 1930s and later. In his "Realists, Naturalists, and Novelists of Manners," in *Harvard Guide to Contemporary American Writing,* ed. Daniel Hoffman (Cambridge, Mass.: Harvard University Press, 1979), Leo Braudy, without pursuing definitions, lists many prominent living novelists as naturalists.

2

RICHARD LEHAN

The European Background

I

Literary naturalism derives mainly from a biological model. Its origin owes much to Charles Darwin and his theory of evolution, based in turn on his theory of natural selection. Darwin created a context that made naturalism – with its emphasis upon theories of heredity and environment – a convincing way to explain the nature of reality for the late nineteenth century. But before Darwin's ideas were available in literary form, they had to be transformed by Emile Zola in his *Le Roman expérimental* (1880). Zola, in turn, based his theories of heredity and environment on Prosper Lucas's *Traité . . . de l'hérédité naturelle* (1850) and especially Claude Bernard's *Introduction à l'étude de la médecine expérimentale* (1865). Zola believed that the literary imagination could make use of the ideas in these books so long as the novelist functioned like a scientist, observing nature and social data, rejecting supernatural and transhistorical explanations of the physical world, rejecting absolute standards of morality and free will, and depicting nature and human experience as a deterministic and mechanistic process. All reality could be explained by a biological understanding of matter, subject to natural laws, available in scientific terms. Controlled by heredity and environment, man was the product of his temperament in a social context. "I wanted to study temperaments and not character," Zola wrote. "I chose beings powerfully dominated by their nerves and their blood, devoid of free will, carried away by the fatalities of their flesh" (quoted by Knapp, 21).

Zola gave his contemporaries a totally new way of thinking about the novel. Temperament was more important than character; setting could not be separated from a naturalistic theory of environment, nor plot from theories of evolution. Man was in a halfway house between the realm of the animals and some more perfect realm of being which future development would reveal. While the naturalistic novel often deals with a static moment in time, it also presupposes an atavistic past or a futuristic ideal toward

47

which characters can be drawn. The futuristic plots move toward forms of science fiction and utopian fantasy; the atavistic, toward dystopia and the animalistic, often the monstrous, although in some naturalistic narratives (for example, Jack London) this pull away from civilization and decadence toward the more savage sometimes brings with it a lost vitality. But, on the whole, such movement toward a more primitive self is destructive, as we see in Frank Norris's *McTeague*. Thus, while the naturalistic novel presumes the reality of evolution, it often works in terms of devolution: degeneration and personal decline are embedded in most naturalistic fiction. And such decay finds its equivalence on the social level, where the fate of the individual is often inseparable from a declining family or the new urbanized crowd. The crowd, more than just an aggregate of individuals, has a reality of its own and is capable of bestial and violent behavior, mindlessly following a leader, whose own fate at the hands of the mob can be extremely tenuous. (Contained in this aspect of literary naturalism is an anticipation of fascism and forms of totalitarianism.) We see these elements at work in such Zola novels as *Nana* and *Germinal,* where the corruption of the individual finds a natural correspondence in the corruption of the family and society itself. Everything is corrupt and capable of degeneration and debasement, from the highest orders of government and the salon to the workers in the mines and the people in the street.

And yet naturalism, while admittedly pessimistic, seems to have an optimistic element built into it. This stems from the usually unexpressed belief that whereas the fate of the individual is circumscribed and destined to end in sickness and death, the fate of the species is to move ever onward and upward in an evolutionary march toward greater perfection. Although these ideas are implicit in Darwin, they were made explicit by Herbert Spencer, one of Darwin's most influential interpreters. Literary naturalism thus had two images of man competing within it. A good many of the later naturalists projected a more highly evolved man in our future (for example, H. G. Wells's *Invisible Man*) at the same time as they showed how debased man could become if moved back in evolutionary time (Wells's *The Island of Dr. Moreau*).

One of the major differences between literary naturalism and the romance fiction which preceded it is that naturalism moved us away from the distant historical past to the more immediate historical present. More contemporary problems were foregrounded in naturalism. Zola, for example, whose writing career spanned the years 1870–90, concentrated on the years of the Second Empire (1851–70). Every one of his novels dealt with a topical issue of these times: the greed for land of the peasantry, the movement of the peasantry from the land to the city, the fate of the urban worker, the corruption of the high-society prostitute, the rise of the department store, the function of the urban market, the fate of the new industrial worker, the rise of the steam engine and railroad system, the fate of a degenerating France as it prepared for war with Germany. Zola's influence on his contemporaries was pronounced, perhaps more so in America than in Europe. Although Theodor Fontane and Gerhart Hauptmann wrote naturalistic novels in Germany, and George Moore and George Gissing in England, the real inheritors of the method were American writers like Frank Norris, Theodore Dreiser, and Jack London. This, in turn, has raised the question of how precise is the connection between French and American literary naturalism.

The first wave of contemporary critics tended to see an exact correspondence between American and French literary naturalism. In one of the most early influential books, Lars Ahnebrink argued for a fairly close correspondence between the works of Zola and those of Hamlin Garland, Stephen Crane, and Frank Norris.[1] Such a reading brought about a diverse reaction from critics like Charles Child Walcutt and Donald Pizer. Although both Walcutt and Pizer were sensitive to the philosophical elements of literary naturalism, they tended to stress its indigenous nature in America: Walcutt believed that American naturalism was heavily influenced by transcendentalism; Pizer saw it more as a by-product of American realism. More important, both Pizer and Walcutt stressed the formal aspects of naturalism – the way the literary imagination shaped individual works of art. Their work tended to undermine the idea of naturalism as an international literary movement, saw American realism as having a distinct character of its own, and emphasized the artistic sensibility and the individual formal distinctions which shaped these novels. These assumptions controlled the major way in which these novels were read for almost a generation.[2]

More recently, we have been offered a third way of reading literary naturalism. Walter Benn Michaels, in *The Gold Standard and the Logic of Naturalism,* has given us a new historicist or Foucauldian reading of such texts. Put simply, Michaels sees each culture as producing a set of fictions, so that the economic processes behind naturalism are as much a fiction as the texts that emerge from this literary movement. By rejecting the idea that the text is "fiction" and the culture "real" and insisting that both the literary and economic products of the culture are constructs, Michaels claims that he is working "within" culture, while earlier critics were not. This, of course, belies the fact that Michaels's approach to naturalism is just as much his own construct as Pizer's or Walcutt's, a privileging of his own way of reading. Whereas Pizer has given primary attention to the way the artistic imagination has shaped a text, Michaels has given it to seeing connections between divergent aspects of the same culture. In order to do this, Michaels has to bring those connections into being. Whereas Pizer stresses the writing process behind naturalism, Michaels stresses the reading process. Whereas Pizer stresses the way the individual imagination divergently uses the idea of naturalism, Michaels does away with the idea of naturalism altogether and collapses it into cultural forms held together by institutional (primarily economic) forms of power. From reading Michaels, one would never know that there was a biological aspect to literary naturalism.[3]

Within the last decade there has been a movement back to the idea of literary naturalism. Yves Chevrel (1982) and David Baguley (1990) have both given us an extended definition of European and French literary naturalism. And in a 1985 essay, I tried to reconnect American and French literary naturalism. My attempt was not to take us back to Lars Ahnebrink and other "originist" theories, but to help us see in what way literary naturalism can work as a narrative mode – that is, as a kind of philosophical reality that both precedes the writing of the text (Pizer) and the reading of the text (Michaels). I can agree with such recent theorists of the novel as Roland Barthes that there is no such thing as literary Realism – only literary realisms. Each narrative mode has its own literary conventions, and I believe that these conventions are dependent upon a way of seeing reality. Each mode of fiction thus creates its own narrative reality, and the comic realism of Dickens is as different from the modernistic realism of Joyce as is the naturalistic realism of Zola from both. I can also concur with the formalist critics who see important distinctions between (say) the novels of Zola and Dreiser. I would argue, however, that these differences take place along a spectrum of shared meaning that leads to a difference of emphasis between texts but not a difference in narrative ontology. A theory of modes helps us to see the limits within which the literary imagination works: it moves the focus away from the idea of creative genius and the total subjectivity of the critic to the idea of a literary "reality" which precedes the text. Such an effort, I believe, cannot be transhistorical (as is the structuralist's emphasis upon synchronic time) but must be firmly historical, showing precisely how literary naturalism emerged from its culture as an idea and became one of the shared assumptions of the time. It must show what cultural needs brought it into being and what changing cultural needs allowed it to die. My purpose here is thus to go back to the beginnings of the novel in Europe, to see how realism gave way to naturalism, and how these ideas had influence on a generation of American writers. I want finally to come back to the problem of what is gained and lost by looking at naturalism as a narrative mode – as a set of philosophical and literary ideas that preexisted their textualization.

II

The novel, as we know, had its origins in the middle class. The old romance was the narrative of the medieval aristocracy, celebrating the world of the manor and the heroics and love rituals of a knightly class. The bourgeoisie wanted a fiction of its own, and the novel gave expression to the fate of the individual in a very new world. The novel was thus the end product of the Enlightenment: the Enlightenment rested upon the belief that life could best be lived through the power of reason and the empirical processes that best explained nature. Such an understanding allowed a control over nature and was suited to the commercial and later industrial exploitation that created new forms of wealth. The Enlightenment provided the ideology that accompanied the shift from an agrarian to an urban world, from the realm of the estate to a new-money order, from a belief in birth rights to an insistence upon natural rights, from the authority of the divine-right king to forms of parliamentary and democratic government, from landed wealth to commercial and later industrial wealth processed through such new institutions as the national bank and the stock exchange. The Puritan Revolution, the French Revolution, and the American Civil War – despite the differences in time – mark breaks with the feudal and aristocratic past and were all expressions of this same historical moment.

A new reading class came into being that was interested in the rituals of courtship, marriage, family, commerce and exchange, and the conflicts built into the new pursuits of money and success. In England, the novels of Daniel Defoe made currency out of this transition. The story of Robinson Crusoe replicates the story of man's transition from the primitive wilderness to toolmaker, to farmer, to lord of his manor, to finally being a member of a social order based upon the new commercial process. Whereas Henry Fielding and Jane Austen dealt with those who still found the good life on the estate, the gothic novel depicted the estate in a process of decline, the world of the old father transformed into the mutant forms we find in novels like Walpole's *The Castle of Otranto* (1764), Radcliffe's *The Mysteries of Udolpho* (1794), and Godwin's *Caleb Williams* (1794). In all of these novels, the threat to the estate and the origin of evil come from the new city. When the world of the father is disrupted, a curse is often put upon the land which disrupts the natural processes in a mysterious, sometimes supernatural, way. The victim of this sequence of events is usually a young woman who has been used as a pawn to acquire claim to the estate or to perpetuate its growth. In this context, Richardson's *Clarissa* (1747–8) is a prototypical gothic novel; and Brontë's *Wuthering Heights* (1847) and Dickens's *Bleak House* (1853) carry on this narrative tradition. Where the gothic novel ended, the young-man-from-the-provinces novel began. Whereas the gothic novel depicted the historical end of feudalism, the journey-to-the-city novel depicted the beginning of urbanism. Dickens's *Great Expectations* (1860–1) is the natural sequel to *Bleak House,* and indeed Pip comes to London once he departs the gothic realm of Satis House.

Modern realism takes much of its meaning from the rise of the new city, and this is as true in France as it is in England. Medieval Paris lasted well into the nineteenth century. In the seventeenth century, the medieval walls were torn down and turned into boulevards lined with trees from the Madeleine almost to the Bastille. In 1797 a far-sighted plan, known as the Artists' Plan, was drawn up under Napoleon and served in great part for the city that Haussmann would later bring into being. This plan, in turn, owed much to that of Christopher Wren, who in 1666 projected a plan to rebuild the London that had just burned to the ground. Wren's brilliant conception was to be a construct that reflected the new commercial functions of the city, with the Royal Exchange instead of St. Paul's occupying the physical center. Because the land costs made Wren's plan unfeasible, it died aborning; but it does reveal how the city, like the literary text, takes its meaning from the changing nature of the culture itself. And indeed, as France moved from an agrarian to an urban base, the function of Paris changed as well. By 1824 the Bourse was as much a monument as Notre Dame or the Louvre. By the time of the July revolution of 1830 and the reign of Louis Philippe, the seeds for a new Paris were already planted. Perhaps most instrumental in the change was the invention of new sources of power, especially the steam engine, which freed the factory from a rural source of water power and allowed it to come into the city, bringing with it the proletariat that would make up a major source of the new urban population and become the major concern of people like Sue and Hugo, as well as Karl Marx and Friedrich Engels. It was also at this time that Louis Philippe drove the workers' movement underground and made little provision for absorbing their rapidly expanding numbers.

It is exactly this world that Eugène Sue (1804–57) addresses in his monumental novel, *The Mysteries of Paris.* Sue's novel is ten volumes long and comes to over a thousand pages. It was published in the newspapers in serial form in 1842–3 and became a sensation in its time. The time of the plot is

1838, or eight years into the rule of Louis Philippe. The story involves Rodolph, Grand Duke of Gerolstein, a small German state, who is exiled when he has a child by the evil Lady Sarah Macgregor, who delivers the child to the even more evil lawyer, Jacques Ferrand, who sells her into a kind of white slavery system, all the while letting Lady Sarah and Rodolph believe that the child is dead – traditional characteristics of the melodramatic plot from Oedipus to Tom Jones.

A number of aspects of this novel are clear from the outset. Sue sets up a purely melodramatic world in which good and evil separate themselves. Rodolph, the exiled prince, becomes the embodiment of good; Ferrand, the lawyer, or minister of the new commercial order, becomes the embodiment of evil. The greatest influence on Sue was, strangely, James Fenimore Cooper. What Sue did was to take the sequential plot structure of the Natty Bumppo novels and simply move it to the city, the city replacing the forest, the underworld gang replacing the evil Indians, all inscribed within a competency that Rodolph shares with Natty. As contrived as this plot may seem, the novel was immensely popular in the nineteenth century and became at one point a kind of classic. It received so much attention, in fact, that it attracted the interest of an unlikely reader, Karl Marx, whose discussion of it in *The Holy Family* is the most extended critique of this novel that we have. Marx uses this novel, among other works of the time, to attack the Young Hegelians, who, he felt, advocated too idealist a notion of reality. Marx believed that Sue, in that tradition, debased the idea of mystery, turning it into a form of caricature. Marx insisted that Sue had established a transcendent rather than a human basis for relationships, and thus turned Fleur-de-Marie, Rodolph's daughter and the novel's heroine, into a grotesque form of life (*The Holy Family*, 230–4).

What Marx is dealing with specifically in *The Holy Family*, subtitled *A Critique of Critical Critique*, is that sort of idealized consciousness, here Christian in form and embodied by Rodolph, that positions itself ideally within the social matrix. Marx's point is that the social conditions of Paris under Louis Philippe had changed radically, but that the consciousness that informed the city was still medieval. As a result, instead of liberating Fleur-de-Marie, Sue only imprisons her more deeply within her environment. Sue not only holds on to the image of medieval Paris, he holds on to the consciousness – the very ideology – that keeps medieval Paris in place. Thus, by failing to see that a new consciousness is necessary to explain and account for the new economic evils that have kept the slums of Paris in place, Sue only reifies the evil that he mistakenly thinks he is opposing. Despite the sympathy that Sue created for the Paris poor, Marx believed that he held them ideologically in place by failing to come to terms with a new, evolving Paris, where commercialism was beginning to replace feudalism, and by failing to see that a new and less idealized form of consciousness must be accounted for.

Hugo's *Les Misérables* brings us a step closer to the world that Marx had in mind. This is not to say that Hugo is any less melodramatic than Sue. Hugo's novel also turns on a multitude of coincidences. Given the number and variety of characters he is dealing with and the distances that often separate them, Hugo nevertheless brings all of his principal characters together in the compressed space of a Paris slum. Good and evil are as easily divided in Hugo's world as Sue's, although by the time we get to the end, a character like Javert moves from a simple to a complex understanding of this world – so complex, in fact, that it costs him his very sense of identity, and ultimately his life. The biggest difference between Hugo's and Sue's novels, however, is that *Les Misérables* is compellingly told against the unfolding of history itself. Hugo completed the novel in 1862 after spending fourteen years totally revising an earlier draft. The novel covers the twenty years from 1815 to 1835 – that is, from the defeat of Napoleon at Waterloo until after the revolution of 1830 and the reign of Louis Philippe, ending almost at the point where Sue began. Hugo was thus looking back on events that had occurred almost forty years earlier; and he was doing it from exile, having been forced out of France in 1852 by Louis Napoleon, whom Hugo had attacked for betraying the idea of the republic.

As in most novels involving romantic realism, Hugo superimposes an extended religious trope onto the city itself, and *Les Misérables* describes a climb out of hell toward a secular kind of redemption. Jean Valjean thus becomes a secular Christ functioning toward this end. At one point in the novel he is literally buried alive and then resurrected from the grave. When he enters the gigantic Parisian sewer system, carrying the wounded Marius like a cross, he is entering a Dantean nether world. And when he crosses a River Styx, through which he is freed from this underworld by the gate-keeper Thenardier, the symbolism paralleling Christ's redemption is all too clear. The descent into the secular hell of the city seems inseparable from the political resolution of the novel, which is in turn inseparable from the union of Cossette and Marius, and their reconciliation with Valjean, who, like Javert, his opposite, must die so that another form of reality can come into being.

Hugo takes us to the very edge of the modern city – but only to the edge. We are still very much in a kind of Hegelian realm. Hegel told us that it is through logic that we superimpose categories that give meaning to the chaos of reality. That reality, in turn, is part of a transcendent process involving romantic history working through us. The oppositions of life – such as Jean Valjean and Javert – thus find their synthesis in the person of a Marius – and history moves idealistically onward.

Waterloo, Hugo tells us, was a temporary detour on the path of progress. But even Waterloo and a restored Louis XVIII could not recapture the past or hold back history, and a new spirit of liberalism worked its will, finally expressing itself in 1830. Hugo felt that his story of Jean Valjean, Javert, and Marius was inseparable from that historical process, that the contradictions which would cancel the lives of both Valjean and Javert were the contradictions of history, and that the spirit of a higher will was working through Marius, a spirit that would redeem Paris, both as the capital of France and as the container of the poor. Hegel could not have expressed it any better.

The novels that take us substantially beyond the political ideology of Sue and Hugo are Balzac's *Lost Illusions* and *The Splendors and Miseries of Courtesans,* both a part of Balzac's famous *Human Comedy.* (Balzac intentionally altered the title of Dante's *Divine Comedy* in order to emphasize that he was dealing with human and not religious matters.) Balzac was writing about roughly the same narrative time span as Hugo; *Lost Illusions* begins after the defeat at Waterloo and ends around 1822, when the narrative is picked up in *Splendors and Miseries.* Like Hugo, Balzac set his story against the history of the times, although his emphasis is far more on the way institutions work than on the fate of such larger-than-life heroes as Napoleon. His central character in *Lost Illusions* is Lucien Chardon, the son of a provincial pharmacist, who takes his mother's maiden name of de Rubempré when he leaves the provinces to make his fortune in Paris.

Like Eugène de Rastignac, Lucien comes to think of Paris as a battlefield, and it is these words that he now takes into the battle which Balzac recounts in the sequel to *Lost Illusions, The Splendors and Miseries of Courtesans.* The story here begins in 1824 and treats the last six years of the Restoration, concluding just before the July revolution in 1830. After having signed a kind of Faustian pact with Vautrin, the two travel on to Paris, where Vautrin concocts a grand scheme to marry Lucien into royalty. This scheme eventually leads to Lucien's suicide, an event that moves Vautrin to perhaps the first genuine grief he has ever experienced. Vautrin's iron nature allows him to triumph over his enemies, but not without some cost. The rest of the novel involves the story of Vautrin, who first becomes a police collaborator and eventually a police magistrate. By the end of *Splendors and Miseries,* the arch criminal is running the police.

At this point, Balzac moves us beyond premodern Paris. No longer are we in a world where good and evil are mechanically separated. Embedded in Balzac's novels are narrative elements that will become dominant in the modern era. In fact, what we find are two ways of experiencing the modern city. No longer are we in the worlds of Sue and Hugo, where a transcendent reason divides the world in two. Balzac gives us two very different kinds of urban prototypes in Vautrin and Daniel d'Arthez – one the man of power, the other the committed artist. And if Sue and Hugo can be conjoined to Hegel, the moderns find company with Nietzsche. Nietzsche, in fact, begins by questioning the assumptions that often dominate the novels of Sue and Hugo; he attacks first the Christian legacy that allows the Apollonian to suppress the Dionysian; and he attacks the Enlightenment legacy that raises reason, science, and technology to positions of dominance. Nietzsche wants to return to the world of Rousseau, but he does not want Rousseau's creator. What he postulates instead is a universe separate from its creation, and he places the emphasis upon man's consciousness confronting an unmade universe. In the modern novel the embodiments of this can be found in Zola, where we see men of power transforming the city of Paris in the Second Empire. Balzac was the link between comic and romantic realism and literary naturalism. He transformed the novel so that it would never be the same, and Emile Zola was the inheritor of that literary legacy.

III

Darwinism was both a continuation of and a challenge to Enlightenment assumptions. As a theory of evolution, it revealed the physical process of the universe, matter unfolding in time. But as a theory of natural selection – that species change through a process of adaptation to their immediate environment – Darwinism emphasized the accidental rather than a necessary unfolding, seriously challenging the notion of design. Darwin's theory of evolution contained the idea of devolution and degeneration. Natural selection argues that the best in the species are attracted to and mate with each other. This leaves the worst in the species to mate and generate their own offspring. Literary naturalism gave far more attention to such evolutionary throwbacks than to its forward progress – a fact easily seen in the *Rougon-Macquart* novels of Zola.

The *Rougon-Macquart* novels cover French history from the eve of the Second Empire (1851) to the French defeat at Sedan during the Franco-Prussian War (1870) or, as Zola put it, "from the perfidy of the coup d'état to the treason of the Sedan" (*La Fortune des Rougon*, vi).[4] Zola's sequence begins with *La Fortune des Rougon* (1871), which describes the origins of two families, the Rougons and the Macquarts, both springing from the defective blood of Adelaide Fouque, Aunt Dide, who is born in 1768 and dies 105 years later. She marries a respectable gardener, Rougon, in 1786 and bears him a son a year later. When he dies in 1788, she takes as a lover the unstable Macquart, an alcoholic, mentally defective smuggler and bears him a son in 1789 and a daughter in 1791. The son, Antoine Macquart, a soldier and later a basket-maker, dies in 1873 from alcoholism, the same year Adelaide Rougon dies in an insane asylum. His daughter, Gervaise Macquart, is born in 1828 and becomes the lover of Auguste Lantier, by whom she has the three children who become central to the *Rougon-Macquart* sequence. The story of Gervaise and Auguste becomes the basis for *L'Assommoir*. In that novel, Auguste runs away with a laundry maid named Adèle, with whom he lives for several years, before returning to Gervaise and her new husband, Coupeau, where he lives as a boarder before the arrangement degenerates into a *ménage à trois*. After he is severely injured in a fall from a roof, Coupeau becomes an alcoholic, his degeneration eventually dragging Gervaise down with him. In *La Fortune des Rougon* (1871), *L'Assommoir* (1877), *Germinal* (1885), and *L'Oeuvre* (1886) we are told that Gervaise and Lantier had two sons, Claude and Étienne, but in *La Bête humaine* (1890) the central character, Jacques Lantier, is also linked to their parentage.

Claude Lantier is Zola's artist. In Paris, he paints urban scenes, such as Les Halles Centrales, the central marketplace. His work involves a stark repudiation of romanticism and commitment to the new realism; but his paintings are ridiculed by the public, a situation that leads to doubt, depression, and finally his suicide. In the story of Claude, Zola shows how a hereditary disease eventually works its destructive influence. Both Claude's artistic genius and his fatal depressive nature are ingrained matters of temperament. In *L'Oeuvre*, Zola is able to reveal the insensitive intolerance of the public (another version of the "crowd" theme that runs throughout naturalism) as well as to depict the artist as a by-product of failed genius and a failure of character, both of which are a matter of inherited degenerative traits. The biological basis of art is clearly in focus throughout his telling of Claude Lantier's story.

The youngest son of Auguste Lantier and Gervaise Macquart is Étienne, born in 1846. He is sent to Lille, where he becomes a stoker on a train. Quick to anger, he is dismissed from this job when he strikes his boss. He then tramps through the region and eventually turns up at Montsou, the setting of *Germinal*. His love for Catherine and hatred for Chaval both stem from the bestiality of his nature. This conflict comes to a crisis when he is caught in a mine accident with Catherine and Chaval, and the two men – like savage animals – fight until Chaval is dead. Despite his desire to become a part of the working-class world, Étienne can never overcome his temperament, his physical tendency toward violence, and this hereditary lapse guarantees that he will be an outcast wherever he goes. Zola rewrites the wandering Jew theme as a proletariat story, grounded totally in biological determinism. The murderous nature of Étienne in *Germinal* takes us close to Zola's belief in the atavistic, and grounds the industrial conflict between mine owners and workers in a kind of animalistic struggle, a theme that is clearly established when the brutal crowd is described as an uncontrollable animal. The crowd itself seems to be only the larger embodiment of Étienne's own physical savagery. Once again, the degenerative blood of the Macquart-Lantier line works its destructive effects.

The middle child of Lantier and Gervaise is Jacques Lantier. As a child, he suffered from headaches and melancholy. This ailment is transformed in adolescence into an acute form of insanity wherein he is overcome by the desire to murder any woman with whom he is sexually involved. This defect shares a kind of animal savagery with Étienne's murderous outbursts, but seems archetypal in nature when Zola connects it to the blood rage of tribal memory to avenge "the harm women had done to his race." His liaison with Séverine, who has committed a political murder, seemingly unites two common psychological types, and they plan the murder of Séverine's husband. But before that murder takes place, he is sexually aroused by Séverine, whom he brutally murders. Thinking her murder has cured him of this blood lust, Jacques makes love to Philoméne Savagnaut, the wife of Pecqueux, his stoker on the train, which leads to a savage fight between Jacques and Pecqueux in which both men die beneath the wheels. In *La Bête humaine*, Zola suggests that the pathology which controls sexuality and violence can find its counterpart in the force of the train, carrying soldiers to the fatal Franco-Prussian War, running on its own, headless and out of control, like the French nation itself. The train becomes the symbol of a power that connects the workings of biology and those of society, a connection (as we shall see) that is the basis for the way literary naturalism depicted history and culture.

Gervaise Macquart's fourth child is perhaps the most famous character in the *Rougon-Macquart* series. This is Anna, known as Nana, born in 1852 when Gervaise was married to Coupeau. Nana, a product of the Parisian streets, has a child by an unknown father when she is sixteen. At eighteen, she is the mistress of a wealthy Russian merchant who spends the winters in

Paris. All of this is prelude to Nana's eventual success in the Théâtre des Variétés. Here she comes to the attention of men in high government and high society, all of whom literally destroy themselves financially and physically over their obsession for her. Nana later conquers the East as she had conquered Paris. When she returns to Paris in 1870, her sickly son, Louiset, is dying of smallpox, a disease she contracts from him. Nana's death, coming on the eve of the Franco-Prussian War, her body covered with suppurating sores, symbolizes the corruption of the Second Empire. Her own degenerate nature and the degenerate nature of the body politic are one. And the death of her sickly son marks the end of one of the Macquart lines, now totally played out in mental and physical degeneration. The death of the imbecile and/or sickly child will become a literary insignia in the naturalistic story of personal and cultural decline – an insignia written into nature itself and manifest on every page of Zola's *Rougon-Macquart* novels.[5]

Zola believed that the same forces which determined the individual were at work in society. The naturalist's view of the individual, the family, and the crowd had a logical correspondence in culture and in history itself. It oversimplifies to say that Zola believed that the life lived closest to nature was good, the life lived closest to society bad, although at times this would seem to be the case. What Zola was suggesting was something slightly different – namely, that modern man had been displaced from anything like a natural environment, had lost contact with his instincts and a more rudimentary and basic sense of self, and had become more and more distanced from the rhythms of the natural life. Money and bureaucracy had replaced the workings of nature and natural feelings.

Ironically, as civilization became more and more pronounced, society became more and more corrupt. Zola believed that beneath all the trappings society was a festering mass of infected sores. At the center of this situation was Louis Napoleon and the Second Empire. In 1848 Napoleon replaced Louis Philippe as president of France, betrayed that office on 2 December 1851 when his troops took control of Paris, and abandoned the idea of the republic a year later when he became Napoleon III, emperor of the Second Empire, with a new constitution of 14 January 1853 codifying his powers. On the surface, this event was not without benefits: canals and rivers were dug and widened, giving France one of the best transportation systems in Europe. Baron Georges-Eugène Haussmann (1809–91) was hired to remove medieval and build modern Paris. Haussmann demolished 20,000 slum dwellings and built 43,777 new homes, lengthened the rue de Rivoli from the Bastille to the Concorde, and built the boulevards Saint-Michel, Sébastopol, Strasbourg, and Magenta. The Saint-Martin canal was covered and turned into a boulevard. The Bois de Boulogne and Vincennes were made into public parks, and a new symmetry made such buildings as the Louvre, the Hôtel de Ville, the Palais Royal, the National Library, Notre Dame, and the Opéra into monuments. Paris became the center of Europe, with six great railroad lines converging on the capital. Under Napoleon III new credit lines were established by two lending institutions: the Crédit Mobilier handled mainly industrial loans; the Crédit Financier, mostly agrarian ones. Money transformed the new city from within and without; Paris and other cities became a magnet for those in the provinces. In the time of Napoleon's reign, Paris almost doubled in population, while such cities as Lyons, Marseilles, Bordeaux, and Lille became urban centers.

La Curée (1872) is Zola's first Rougon-Macquart novel to establish the meaning of Paris as the center both of France and of Zola's narrative world. Aristide Rougon comes to France from the provincial town of Plassans to hunt la curée (the quarry). In Paris he joins his brother Eugène, a minister in the emperor's government, and his sister, Madame Sidonie, a courtesan. Early in the novel, Aristide looks down upon Paris from a restaurant window on the Butte Montmartre and sees Paris much as Eugène de Rastignac saw it at the end of Le Père Goriot, as a world to be conquered. Conquer he does, making a fortune out of Haussmann's rebuilding (that is, out of the ruins) of Paris. Like Balzac, Zola depicts a city that creates its own reality, built upon a greed and material desire that sunders familial and human relationships. Having changed his name to Saccard – which suggests both money (sac d'écus) and ruin (saccage) – Aristide is at the center of the banking world in L'Argent (1891), financing investments all over the world. Money is a force greater than military and political power. Even when his plan fails, Saccard's monetary schemes have built new cities and brought remote lands into the grip of the modern world. The biological process of life and death has been transformed, moved from the realm of nature to that of the city. In Le Ventre de Paris (1873) and Au bonheur des dames (1883) Zola analyzes this idea in some detail, describing two kinds of marketplace: Les Halles Centrales, which supplies food, and the modern department store, which supplies material goods. The city now organizes the means to satisfy biological needs and desires. The modern city has taken the place of the primitive jungle, re-presenting the old natural struggle in new urban terms. The corrupting effect of the city becomes a major theme in novels like L'Assommoir (1877), Nana (1880), Germinal (1885), La Bête humaine (1890), La Débâcle (1892), and even La Terre (1887).

Although Zola depicts opposite worlds in *Nana* and *Germinal,* he also makes it clear that these worlds are really one – that the workers who produce the wealth that allows the luxury of Nana are also the means of transforming the system. Almost everything in Zola's world comes back to the nobility of work, which no longer is connected to the rhythms of nature. Instead, miners debase themselves underground to produce the wealth that in turn produces the corrupt social system within which they and their leaders are entrapped. In *La Terre* this process has reached the peasant world and transformed the land. Zola once said, "I should like to do for the peasant in *La Terre* what I did for the working man in *Germinal*" (quoted in King, 219). What Zola reveals in this novel is that the feudal world has passed away forever; the land has been bought up by the new bourgeoisie like Hourdequin or absorbed by greedy peasants like Fouan and his brutal son, Buteau. Zola depicts the land as a counterforce with its life-giving rhythms. But the city has reached out and acquired the land, destroying the natural rhythms and creating a network of its own, which has absorbed the peasants, who have become brutal in their desire to keep the land, and who participate in their own destructive process. By the end of the novel, life has given way to death – a new season upon the land takes its being from death: "Here were the Dead, there was the seed" (*La Terre,* 500). The corruption of the empire, radiating from Paris outward, has infected every limb of the society, from the aristocracy, separated for generations from the land, to the high bourgeoisie in their banks and offices of exchange, to the peasants and mine workers whose greed and strife have debased the sacred office of work. The loss of 17,000 French soldiers in Sedan becomes a great sacrificial act of bureaucratic and military incompetence – and even more so to a society that has produced wealth and luxury by exploiting the land and its people. In *La Débâcle,* Zola tells us that the center must be purged, and in the final scene Paris is burning – "burning like some huge sacrificial fire" (*La Débâcle,* 508). The novel closes with the hope of a new Paris that will somehow become reconnected to the earth and draw its strength from the land – from good, simple people with natural instincts and a capacity for work. On the level of the individual, Zola's frame of reference was biological; on the level of society, his frame of reference was the land. Although all realists do not start from the same assumptions, realism/naturalism as a literary movement depended upon showing how a new commercial/ industrial process had interrupted the old rhythms of the land and put in motion a social process that was more often than not culturally destructive.

IV

The question that now confronts us is that of whether or not European realism/naturalism had an American equivalent. No one can deny a connection between (say) Zola and Norris and Balzac and Dreiser, but what is the nature of this connection? What often goes unnoticed in this discussion is the fact that Norris and Dreiser shared a historical moment with Balzac and Zola: all these novelists were setting their novels in a world growing more and more industrial. In fact, one could argue that the aftermath of the Civil War in America paralleled the kind of historical change taking place in France between 1848 and 1870, as both economies moved from a landed to a commercial/industrial world. In America, this period witnessed the rapid growth of cities, the rise of corporate businesses, the influx of immigrant labor, and the practice of wretched working conditions. As in Zola, we can move, in the American postbellum novels, from the boardrooms of power and wealth to the salons where the wealth is displayed, to the legislative forums that the wealth controls, to the mills, factories, and mines that produce the wealth at great human sacrifice and suffering. The question of cultural conditioning, however, can take the discussion only so far. And the question of direct literary influence is even more limiting in the discourse of recent criticism: literary works are too complex to "derive" from any one source. But Zola did more than write several dozen novels: he also gave rise to a narrative methodology, a way of seeing reality, that left its mark on both sides of the Atlantic.

And, like those of Zola, Frank Norris's and Theodore Dreiser's novels (in different ways) take their being from a naturalistic biology. Characters like McTeague and Vandover are very much a product of an animality that leads to decline and degeneration, especially when their more debased instincts are stimulated by alcohol and profligacy. McTeague tries to fight off the beast within him: his resolve wavers for a moment when he has Trina helpless under the influence of gas in his dentist chair. But it is not until his office is shut down and he is thrown onto the street that he falls under the destructive influence of alcohol, which accelerates the degenerative process. Poverty has the same erosive affect on Trina and McTeague that it has on Gervaise and Coupeau in *L'Assommoir*, and it brings to the surface the same homicidal tendencies that we see in Jacques Lantier in *La Bête humaine*. What we see in Norris is the biology of greed, a desire for money and gold so extreme that it can create an illusionary reality and pathology of murder.

The same kind of extreme pathology also applies to Vandover. A graduate of Harvard University, he is protected by the money and social status his father provides. When his father dies and he is being sued for his part in the death of Ida Wade, he begins to drink more intemperately and to gamble with reckless abandon. Vandover's decline involves physical and mental sickness, a form of lycanthropy, in which he feels that he is becoming a wolf. As in Zola, the animal condition exists in us as a potential state to be aroused at moments of physical and emotional crisis, and the rise of this animality is always followed by a process of degeneration. The last we see of Vandover, he is destitute, derelict, and sick, cleaning the muck out of one of Charles Geary's rental homes. Such debris is the equivalent of the junk we see in Zerkow's junk shop in *McTeague*. Society is continuously breaking down, throwing away its waste, rubbish, and junk, including the human jetsam that makes up this world. There is always an ongoing process of death and renewal, a life force driving ahead of us, carrying the Charles Gearys to greater heights and the Vandovers and McTeagues to their deaths.

Norris's unfinished trilogy involving the story of wheat was his attempt to show how capitalism had created a world city based upon the principles of biology. While Norris's sympathy in *The Octopus* was clearly against the railroad and with the ranchers, he showed how the ranchers were also corrupted by money, how they exploited the land for immediate gain, and how they were also leaving a legacy of greed, bribery, and deceitful influence. There were no innocents in this economic process – only the working of the wheat, embodying the great force of nature itself. What used to be a symbiotic relationship between city and countryside has broken down; the city feeds off the land and depletes without restoring. Like Zola, Norris depicted the movement away from the land to the city, the wheat as a force in itself, now handled as an abstraction, being funneled through the city to markets all over the world. In his next novel, *The Pit* (1903), Norris further developed this theme, convincingly showing Chicago as a center into and out of which energy flowed: Chicago was a "force" that "turned the wheels of a harvester and seeder a thousand miles distant in Iowa and Kansas," the "heart of America," a force of empire that determined "how much the peasant [in Europe] shall pay for his loaf of bread" (*The Pit*, 62, 120). But as central as Chicago and wheat speculation are to Norris's story, the wheat is an even greater force, larger than both. Norris depicts a world of limits, and when Jadwin tries to raise the price of wheat beyond its limit, the market breaks and he is a ruined man. Every man and every social institution has its limit, and even abstract matters like wheat speculation are governed by laws that ultimately come back to nature – the land, the wheat, and the forces out of which life germinates – a theme Norris shared with Zola. Norris never finished the third volume of his story about wheat, never got to

Europe where the consumption of wheat would be the final step in the cycle of life. But thematically a third volume was unnecessary: Norris had already shown how the growing and selling of wheat touches the lives of everyone worldwide, and he had clearly documented the biological basis of economics and the process of degeneration that can occur when one is no longer in touch with the rhythms of the land.

A process of degeneration is also central to the novels of Theodore Dreiser. His novels make use of the cycle of life, the rise and fall of human energies. The story of Hurstwood's decline is counterpointed by the story of Carrie's rise. Throughout, life is combat. Beneath the calm appearance of civilized life is a struggle as deadly as that of the jungle. The metaphor of animals at war runs through his novels. Dreiser begins his *The Financier* with the famous description of the lobster consuming the squid. Men devour the lobster in turn. But who preys on men? Cowperwood puzzles before the answer comes: they prey on each other. Self-interest and self-aggrandizement belie the institutions of law and justice. The ultimate truth is biological: the battle is to the cunning and the strong. As Dreiser begins *The Financier* with a metaphor, he also ends it with one: that of the Black Grouper, a fish of 250 pounds which can adapt perfectly to its surroundings, change its color, and prey upon the unsuspecting.

In *The Financier*, Dreiser emphasizes the obsessive nature of Cowperwood, who early in life decides to be a moneymaker, and shows how the genius for this work is a matter of temperament, built into his nature. But like Zola and Norris, Dreiser saw that the economic process had its origin in nature; that, like a vast biological system, what happened in one realm rippled into another. When the Franco-Prussian War tied up European capital, Cooke's house failed – just as the Chicago fire of 1871 brought ruin to Cowperwood. In *The Titan*, Cowperwood's acquisitiveness engenders a swarm of wary but powerful enemies who finally overthrow him, just as the lead dog in a pack earns the respect and the enmity of those it displaces. All naturalistic fiction takes place in a quantifiable world of forces – with the exception of the life force – that eventually cancel each other out. Zola's and Dreiser's characters have moments – artistic moments like those of Claude Lantier and Eugene Witla and Cowperwood himself – when they intuit these biological secrets. Such understanding brings with it an awe of the mysterious workings of life, but those most sensitive to such meaning often fall victim to ideals or illusions, miscalculate the mechanistic meaning of reality, and perish in a disillusionment that often brings on physical decline. Such is the fate of Claude Lantier in *L'Oeuvre;* such also is Cowperwood's fate. In naturalistic fiction, once one dreams oneself out of tune with nature, the results are often fatal.

In *The Financier* and *The Titan,* Dreiser defined more clearly than ever before the biological and mechanistic nature of social reality: man is just once removed from the animals. A creative force talks through him in the form of "temperament." He lives by strength and cunning in a society of illusions, which upholds absolute justice and Christian restraint while the forces of greed, trickery, and self-interest work corruptingly, and in deadly combat, out of view. Like all men, weak or strong, Cowperwood demonstrated the nature of man in motion – a fury of activity, struggling, plotting, tricking – all heading nowhere but the grave. And yet – hungry for experience, power, love, beauty – he lived. Life is its own justification; the mad race goes in a strange circle; but to have lived is nothing and all. In the Cowperwood story, Dreiser was writing directly out of the naturalistic narrative mode: man's nature is fixed, the strong and the sly win for a time, all combat is eventually destructive, and life cancels itself out and then begins again – and this mysterious process is its own justification.

V

We can now return to some of the questions with which we began – such as, is there a literary naturalism? The answer, I have argued, is yes, if we mean by this a spectrum of ideas controlled by a literary method but used variously by a group of writers who brought the doctrine into being. But the answer is no, if we mean by this a coherent and self-sustained doctrine uniformly used by the same group of writers. Perhaps we can best avoid confusion by thinking of literary naturalism as involving a *synoptic* text – that is, a text similar to the three books of the New Testament that have elements in common at the same time as each text preserves its own uniqueness and difference. As a narrative mode, literary naturalism has a beginning and an end, a European origin and a multinational history. As we have seen, it depends upon a biological model, relying heavily on theories of evolution and devolution, seeing man as a product of his immediate environment. It is essentially mechanistic in its view of matter and deterministic in its attitude toward human will, moving toward theories of degeneration when viewing the individual, the family, the crowd, and finally the community itself, whether it be the city or the nation-state. As a narrative mode, literary naturalism involved a way of seeing. It rested upon the scientific assumption that history can be documented and the mind functions empirically. The naturalistic novel usually involved a double perspective: one point of view, delimited and incomprehensive, involved that of the characters who had little sense of the meaning of the world around them; the other was the more expansive view of the author or narrative commentator, which alerted the reader to the crises about to befall the characters. The two views resulted in the narrative irony that is the benchmark of naturalism – the constant play between what the characters anticipate and what the reader/narrator anticipate. As a literary way of presenting reality, naturalism dominated in Europe, especially in France, from 1870 to 1890, and in America from 1890 to the end of World War II.

Is this insistence that naturalism precedes as an idea its literary embodiments a question more academic than critically necessary? My answer is clearly no, because an understanding of the nature and ideology of naturalism can let us see the artistic limitations within which an author is working as well as save us from the many distortions that have crept into the discussion. Such distortions involve the claim that naturalism is transhistorical – that it is, for example, tragedy, a dubious claim if the assumption is based on the belief that there is common ground between (say) Sophocles and Dreiser: such a view avoids seeing the effects of the immediate environment upon the unfolding sequence of naturalistic events. An understanding of naturalism as an idea can also save us from the argument that it is economically grounded (see Michaels) or a form of neo-Marxism (see Howard) when these claims rest on the partial understanding that fails to see that such economics have a biological basis. And an understanding of naturalism as an idea can save us from the argument that naturalism is inseparable from language or language systems (see Mitchell), especially structuralist or self-referential language, when naturalism clearly refers us in an unmediated way back to the physical world of nature. But despite the compellingness of the naturalistic vision, such a view of life did place limitations on a sense of human complexity by reducing characters to the behavioristic and deterministic realms. The naturalistic hero is usually inarticulate, devoid of deep subjectivity and moral reflection, subject to poverty and suffering, the product of his biological makeup and immediate environment, and the victim of an inevitable sequence of events usually triggered by mechanistic forms of chance.

As a narrative method, naturalism eventually gave way to literary modernism (the movement, not the period of time). Modernism challenged the basic assumptions of naturalism, moving away from scientism toward a mythic/symbolic base, substituting cyclical for linear time, allowing a Bergsonian kind of subjective reality to replace scientific empiricism, and creating an elitist distinction between high and low culture. It is true that natural-ism relied heavily upon symbolism, but a symbolism that reinforced a given natural reality, whereas the literary symbolism of (say) Joyce in *Ulysses* became a prism through which reality was viewed: we see Leopold Bloom through the symbolic lens of the Homeric Ulysses, the contrast between the two marking the Viconian differences in the cyclical sweep from a heroic to a democratic era.

In the last generation there have been even more radical changes in the assumptions governing our sense of literary realism and naturalism. In the move away from modernism, postmodernism has attempted to bridge the distinction between elitist and popular culture. Individual conscious-ness, whether that of the author or his characters, is inseparable from the world of which it is a part: artistic consciousness cannot be divorced from an all-encompassing commercialism; the individual simply becomes another sign among signs, to be read by the critic just like any other cultural sign. The consciousness of modernism gives way to the semiotics of postmoder-nism. As a way of seeing, postmodernism undoes the naturalistic emphasis upon the biological while delimiting the notion of environment to a system of institutions held together by constructed forms of power.

Under the influence of structuralism and poststructuralism, the idea of the mimetic was seriously challenged. One could no longer refer narrative meaning to some reality in nature, governed by principles of revelation, symbolic unfolding, or evolutionary process. Roland Barthes has demon-strated that a realistic novella like Balzac's *Sarrasine* was just as convention-al as more self-conscious literary works and that a realistic text drew no more directly on "life" than any other kind of writing. Barthes maintained that narrative functions as part of a language system controlled by its own inner grammar. Instead of discussing Balzac in terms of theme, character, setting, plot, symbols, and point of view, Barthes divided the text into 561 meaning-units, or what he called "lexies," and then proceeded to read the text word by word, producing over two hundred pages of commentary on a thirty-page story.

Barthes's assumption is that we know the world only through language, which in turn encodes our understanding of reality. There are five such codes: the proairetic or code of action, the hermeneutic or code of puzzles, the cultural or code of fashions, the connotative or code of themes, and the symbolic or code of tropes. On first glance, this looks as if Barthes is simply bringing the old categories of theme, plot, and symbol in by the backdoor, but this is not the case. For while character, setting, and action look from the text outward to some aspect of reality, Barthes's codes look from the text inward to its language, which is an encoded barrier to reality. Whereas Zola told us the author of the experimental novel was comparable to the scientist in the laboratory, describing objectively the reality of the historical moment, Barthes insisted that all writers function within self-enclosed language systems. Under such a theory, the idea of reality gave way to the idea of relation, substance to a system of signs, and meaning to hermeneutics. Moreover, such encoding led to two kinds of texts: the writerly text, which a reader can rewrite by reading because the codes are still active and alive, and a readerly text, which cannot be rewritten in the process of reading because the codes are culturally exhausted. Barthes thus emptied literary realism of meaning by cutting it off from an essential reality that it supposedly embodied and by seeing it as encoding signs from a dead and empty past. If Roland Barthes did not kill literary realism/naturalism, he was conspicuous at the funeral.

Another European influence on the commentary affecting literary naturalism came as a by-product of the writings of Michel Foucault and has led to the practice of what has been called "the new historicism" – a term badly applied, as the method is neither a historicism (the belief that each era or period has a *geist,* principle of identity, or a definable sense of destiny) nor new. Rather, the new historicism sees culture through a series of tropes or metaphors, which are then historicized. The method depends upon textualizing history, seeing all aspects of culture – legal, artistic, behavioral – as forms of representation, as the product of discourse (hence the interest in tropes and other rhetorical forms) to be read like fiction. The most substantial application of this Foucauldian method to literary naturalism is Walter Benn Michaels's *The Gold Standard and the Logic of Naturalism.*

Michaels's literary naturalism is inseparable from a commodity culture. He believes consumerism and a money economy create the prism through which literary naturalism must be viewed, moving us radically away from the more traditional idea that biology is the discipline, and nature the norm, through which naturalism is best engaged. Michaels, in effect, argues that sex, art, and economics are all part of the same process, whereas a more conventional reading of naturalism sees them as distinct activities, as three different ways of relating to nature, existing in a hierarchy ranging from those activities closest to nature (sex), to those most abstractly removed (economics), to those which can give us an insight into their relationship (art). Michaels creates his own text: literary naturalism is subsumed to the motives of economics; commodity culture produces desires that reduce sex, art, and consumerism to the same order of reality.

One might ask what difference it makes if we substitute an economic for a biological reading. It makes a great difference, because naturalism is a mode of narrative reality that begins with nature and moves toward the culturally grotesque, whereas Michaels begins with the moneyed economy and never gets back to nature; he thus robs naturalism of its most basic meaning. The way a biological reading differs from an economic reading should help us to clarify this point. In Norris's *Vandover and the Brute,* Vandover's excessive gambling debts stem from brute motives that play into a degenerative process. But for Michaels such gambling losses are simply another form of expression in a commodity society: "a purchase that seems nonsensical only because it doesn't seem like a purchase at all" (Michaels, 143). Again, Michaels sees the miser and the spendthrift as simply two kinds of consumers in a money economy, whereas, one could argue, the novel depicts them as two distorted ways of relating to the needs of nature. Michaels reads Zerkow's obsession with gold in *McTeague* as an equation that links gold, language, and junk: "Junk, like language, can represent gold only because, for Norris, gold, like language, is already a representation. Loving language and loving gold, Zerkow also loves the junk that is the material condition of their representability and hence their identity" (Michaels, 159). But while Zerkow does substitute the story Maria tells for the reality of the gold dinner plates, Norris does not equate these elements as much as he shows how a greed that goes beyond natural necessity creates a pathological state of mind in which one is willing to murder for an illusion, a mirage. In a culture in which material goods become ends in themselves, the final reality will become junk. Thus Norris, like Zola and the other naturalists, shows how the farther we become removed from the rhythms of nature, the more grotesque our behavior can become. Rather than equating gold, junk, and language and seeing them as a kind of given in a commodity culture, Norris sees Zerkow's activity as a radical distortion of natural need, another grotesque displacement. And finally, in Zola and the other naturalists, the crowd is more than a collection of individuals; it has an animality that gives it a natural identity, an inseparability from nature. But in Michaels's discussion of the economy, the crowd, in the sense of an aggregate, equates with the legal status, and hence the constructed reality, of the corporation, rather than with any physical reality (Michaels, 179). In Michaels's readings of naturalistic texts, we not only lose the connection between man and nature, but the philosophical subject is collapsed into the money economy, which in turn becomes an extended form of textuality. Such critical maneuvering is a way of positioning oneself to both the culture and the text – a positioning that by necessity puts this kind of critic, despite Michaels's claim to the contrary, as much "outside" the culture he is examining as any other critic.

Michaels's method makes literary naturalism a by-product of postmodern theory; one would never know from his book that naturalism had a biological origin and a hierarchy of values based upon nature as the ultimate source of reference.

As an ideology and a mode of narration, literary naturalism rose and then fell. It was replaced by literary modernism and then by postmodernism. But even in this context its meaning was not entirely lost: new narrative modes transformed (or what can be called *re-presented*)[6] naturalism, rather than totally superseded it. The obsession with degeneration, for example, gave way to the modernist emphasis upon decadence, and in turn decadence gave way to the postmodern fascination with entropy – all different embodiments of the same idea. The difference between degeneration and decadence is the difference between physical decline and the cultural rot that sets in with overcivilization and the ways of the dandy, the difference between a biological and an aesthetic view of reality; just as the difference between degeneration and entropy is the difference between a decline built into the individual and a decline built into a system, the difference between a naturalistic and a structuralist biology.

All literary modes involve a prism through which to interpret "reality." Postmodernism has put more emphasis upon the prism than the reality – or, rather, the construct (the prism) has often become the reality itself. As a result, postmodernism has been a highly antirealistic movement, more idealized than any other narrative mode. When the biological basis for reality has not been destroyed, it has been challenged, as Stephen Jay Gould has challenged Edward O. Wilson's sociobiology: the assumption that there are physical connections between man and other species and that nature is a mirror for man. Once our contact with nature is mediated, as it is through the self-reflexive language of postmodernism, realism gives way to textuality, to the ludic, to mirrors reflecting other mirrors rather than to a window opening out onto nature. But it is unlikely that nature can be long suppressed: the rhythms of a day, of the seasons, the cycle of life (birth, sexuality, maturity, sickness, death) are all too strong to be distanced in our consciousness by forms of constructed reality. Life is too much with us, and realism as a literary perspective is too vital to our sense of being to be shut for long in the airless room of linguistic self-reflexivity.

NOTES

1   See Lars Ahnebrink, *The Beginning of Naturalism in American Fiction: A Study of the Works of Hamlin Garland, Stephen Crane, and Frank Norris with Special*

Reference to Some European Influences, 1891–1903 (Cambridge, Mass.: Harvard University Press, 1950). See also Marius Biencourt, *Une Influence du naturalisme français en Amérique* (Paris: Marcel Giard, 1933). Ahnebrink also has a study of Zola's influence on Frank Norris in *Essays and Studies on American Language and Literature* (Uppsala: A. B. Lundequistska Bokhandein, 1947). Another critic who sees a direct connection between French and other kinds of naturalism is George J. Becker; cf. his *Realism in Modern Literature* (New York: Frederick Ungar, 1980).

2　For other formalist readings of naturalistic authors, see William Dillingham's *Frank Norris: Instinct and Art* (Lincoln: University of Nebraska Press, 1969).

3　Other recent studies that delimit the connection between naturalism and nature are June Howard's *Form and History in American Literary Naturalism* (1985), primarily a neo-Marxist reading, and Lee Clark Mitchell's *Determined Fictions* (1989), a study of naturalism as a system of language.

4　Unless otherwise shown, all translations from the *Rougon-Macquart* series are from the E. Vizetelly edition (London, 1886). Since this edition is unreliable, all translated passages have been checked against the original French. There is a great need for a better translation of the lesser-known Zola novels.

5　The theme of decline, embodied in the impending death of the last degenerative offspring, is a theme that runs through literary modernism, as we see in Mann's Buddenbrooks and Faulkner's Compson families. Such degeneration and decline is also inseparable from the fate of characters like F. Scott Fitzgerald's Anthony Patch and Dick Diver, but by now the naturalistic explanation of such decline is omitted.

6　An excellent study involving *re-presenting* literary naturalism is Paul Civello's *"American Literary Naturalism and Its Modern and Postmodern Transformations"* (Ph.D. diss., UCLA, 1991). Civello shows how Frank Norris, Ernest Hemingway, and Don DeLillo created three narrative modes by making different uses of an overlapping literary ideology.

WORKS CITED OR CONSULTED

Baguley, David. *Naturalistic Fiction: An Entropic Vision.* Cambridge: Cambridge University Press, 1990.

Balzac, Honoré de. *Lost Illusions.* Translated by Herbert J. Hunt. New York: Penguin Books, 1971.

Splendor and Miseries of Courtesans. Paris: G. Barrie, 1895.

Becker, George J., ed. *Documents of Modern Literary Realism.* Princeton, N.J.: Princeton University Press, 1963.

Realism in Modern Literature. New York: Frederick Ungar, 1980.

Beer, Gillian. *Darwin's Plots: Evolutionary Narrative in Darwin, George Eliot, and Nineteenth Century Fiction.* London: Ark/Rouledge & Kegan Paul, 1983.

Bell, Michael Davitt. *The Problems of American Realism: Studies in the Cultural History of a Literary Idea.* Chicago: University of Chicago Press, 1993.

Bellos, David. *Balzac Criticism in France 1850–1900: The Making of a Reputation.* London: Oxford University Press, 1976.

Chamberlin, Edward J., and Gilman, Sander L., eds. *Degeneration: The Dark Side of Progress.* New York: Columbia University Press, 1985.

Chevrel, Yves. *Le Naturalisme.* Paris: Presses Universitaires de France, 1982.

Civello, Paul. "American Literary Naturalism and Its Modern and Postmodern Transformations." Ph.D. diss., UCLA, 1991.

Darwin, Charles. *Darwin: A Norton Critical Edition.* New York: W. W. Norton, 1979.

Dreiser, Theodore. *The Financier.* New York: Dell, 1961.

The Titan. New York: Dell, 1959.

Hemmings, F. W. J. *The Age of Realism.* New Jersey: Humanities Press, 1974.

Himmelfarb, Gertrude. *Darwin and the Darwinian Revolution.* New York: W. W. Norton, 1962.

Howard, June. *Form and History in American Literary Naturalism.* Chapel Hill: University of North Carolina Press, 1985.

Hugo, Victor. *Les Misérables.* Translated by Norman Denny. New York: Penguin Books, 1976.

Hunter, Allan. *Joseph Conrad and the Ethics of Darwinism: The Challenge of Science.* London: Croom Helm, 1983.

Kaplan, Amy. *The Social Construction of American Realism.* Chicago: University of Chicago Press, 1988.

Knapp, Bettina L. *Emile Zola.* New York: Frederick Ungar, 1980.

Lehan, Richard. "American Literary Naturalism: The French Connection." *Nineteenth-Century Fiction* (1984): 529–57.

Theodore Dreiser: His World and His Novels. Carbondale: Southern Illinois University Press, 1969.

Martin, Ronald E. *American Literature and the Universe of Force.* Durham, N.C.: Duke University Press, 1981.

Marx, Karl. *The Holy Family.* Moscow: Family Language Publication House, 1956.

Michaels, Walter Benn. *The Gold Standard and the Logic of Naturalism.* Berkeley and Los Angeles: University of California Press, 1987.

Mitchell, Lee Clark. *Determined Fictions: American Literary Naturalism.* New York: Columbia University Press, 1989.

Nelson, Brian, ed. *Naturalism in the European Novel: New Critical Perspectives.* New York: Berg European Studies/St. Martin's Press, 1992.

Norris, Frank. *McTeague.* New York: Rinehart, 1955.

The Octopus. New York: New American Library, 1964.

The Pit. New York: Grove Press, n.d.

Vandover and the Brute. New York: Doubleday, Doran, 1928.

Peck, Daniel. *Faces of Degeneration: A European Disorder, 1848–1919.* Cambridge: Cambridge University Press, 1989.

Pizer, Donald. *The Novels of Frank Norris.* Bloomington: Indiana University Press, 1966.

Realism and Naturalism in Nineteenth Century American Literature. Carbondale: Southern Illinois University Press, 1966; rev. ed., 1984.

The Theory and Practice of American Literary Naturalism: Selected Essays and Reviews. Carbondale: Southern Illinois University Press, 1993.

Twentieth-Century American Literary Naturalism: An Interpretation. Carbondale, Southern Illinois University Press, 1982.

Prendergast, Christopher. *Balzac: Fiction and Melodrama*. London: Edward Arnold, 1978.

Stromberg, Roland N., ed. *Realism, Naturalism and Symbolism: Modes of Thought and Expression in Europe 1848–1914*. New York: Harper & Row, 1968.

Sue, Eugene. *The Mysteries of Paris*. London: G. Routledge, n.d.

Walcutt, Charles Child. *American Literary Naturalism: A Divided Stream*. Minneapolis: University of Minnesota Press, 1956. Reprint. Westport, Conn.: Greenwood Press, 1973.

Zola, Emile. *L'Assommoire*. Translated by Leonard Tancock. New York: Penguin Books, 1970.

La Bête humaine. Translated by Louis Colman. New York: Julian Press, 1932.

La Débâcle. Translated by Leonard Tancock. New York: Penguin Books, 1972.

Germinal. Translated by Leonard Tancock. Baltimore: Penguin Classics, 1954.

Rougon-Macquart. London: Vizetelly, 1886.

La Terre. Translated by Douglass Parmee. New York: Penguin Books, 1980.

PART TWO

Contemporary critical issues

3

MICHAEL ANESKO

Recent Critical Approaches

The more things stay the same, the more they change. That paradox might well sum up a comparison of the new *Columbia Literary History of the United States* (1988) with its postwar predecessor, *Literary History of the United States* (1946).[1] As a measure of recent critical approaches to American realism and naturalism, the *Columbia History* offers a convenient frame of reference; indeed, many of the authors who contributed chapters relevant to this discussion (Brodhead, Fisher, Rowe, and Sundquist, for example) would also figure prominently in any bibliography of recent work in the field. One could hardly assert, however, that these critics (or the others gathered into part 3 of the *Columbia History*, which covers the years 1865–1910) bear a consistently oedipal relation to their counterparts in *Literary History of the United States*.

When one makes allowance for certain differences in topical arrangement – the fashionable segregation, for example, of "Women Writers and the New Woman" – the forty years separating the two books may not seem to have affected much. Separate chapters are still devoted to Henry James, Mark Twain, and Henry Adams, while Emily Dickinson has finally un-hitched herself from Sidney Lanier, meriting an overdue chapter to herself. Perhaps more surprisingly, Theodore Dreiser now loses that distinction, as he is merged with Stephen Crane, Frank Norris, and Jack London under the heading of "Naturalism and the Languages of Determinism." Previously, these last three writers had been grouped with Hamlin Garland under a similar heading, "Towards Naturalism in Fiction." Now Garland is classi-fied (and sensibly demoted) as a realist, his work associated with other local colorists. The more things change, the more they stay the same.

Such continuities can, of course, be deceiving, as is the comparatively abbreviated nature of the *Columbia* project. Whereas *LHUS* devoted nearly four hundred pages of closely printed text to roughly the same period (pre-cise calculation is impossible, because the earlier history did not insist upon neat chronological division – a distinction also worthy of remark), the

Columbia History affords its contributors only 250 pages for the corresponding task. This self-imposed restraint necessarily makes for economy and concision, but it also empowers a criticism of omission and/or replacement. If Lanier is sacrificed, so too are many other writers, especially in genres other than the novel. The poetry of Edwin Arlington Robinson, for example, commanded a separate chapter in *LHUS;* in the *Columbia* index, three separate page numbers follow his name, indicating sporadic reference rather than sustained comment, and none of his titles is listed at all. The *Columbia History* is also virtually silent with respect to American drama during these years; instead of the separate chapter offered by *LHUS,* "A New Nation's Drama," which takes the reader summarily from 1714 to 1900, it provides a three-page coda, recommending the work of James A. Herne, only one of several nineteenth-century playwrights endorsed previously. If nothing else, comparing these two volumes reminds one that the canon is very much a historical construct.

Such comparison also suggests that, at least in the past thirty years, the novel has become the normative focus of critical attention to realism and naturalism.[2] One might even say that genre and mode have become coterminous, not merely in practice but also in ideological conception. Wherever one looks in recent critical work, some variant of this rather smooth equation is bound to surface: "The subject of realism . . . leads directly to the larger problems concerning the novel: its nature as representation, its function within the culture, its life-cycle as an influential literary form, and its 'death' in our time" (Jenkins, 1). The sequence of these concerns concisely adumbrates the current critical agenda at the same time that it suggests both a narrowing and a concentration of interest.

If the *Columbia History* leaves certain things out, it also makes room for new additions, especially in chapters devoted to popular literature and the work of literary outsiders (recent immigrants and minorities). Deliberately revisionist, the *Columbia History,* like so much recent criticism, insists that traditional notions of what makes American literature either "American" or "literary" have suppressed or rendered marginal important voices and modes of expression (usually of protest). Despite the exclamatory rhetoric and aggressive contemporaneity with which such claims are frequently urged, one should remember that possibly the first person to make them was none other than William Dean Howells, the lonely realist so often ridiculed for his genteel temperament. His brilliantly hostile review of Barrett Wendell's *Literary History of America* (1901) anticipated almost everything since written on the subject, particularly as he exposed the Harvard professor's (woefully misplaced) New England fetishism. "No one can estimate the relative value of the New England episode of our literary growth more highly than I," Howells wrote, "but I cannot ignore the fact that our literary conscience, the wish for purity and the desire for excellence, which Professor Wendell recognizes as its distinguishing qualities, was not solely of Puritan origin."

For adopting such moralistic criteria (uncomfortably reminiscent of a Sunday-school vocabulary), Howells has usually been pilloried – even by his friend Henry James – as an outmoded Victorian, prudish and hopelessly bourgeois. But Howells also went on to remark, even more pointedly, that "Wherever Professor Wendell scents democracy or perceives the disposition to value human nature for itself and independently of the social accidents, he turns cold, and his intellectual tradition gets the better of his nature, which seems sunny and light and friendly. Something, then, like a patrician view of the subject results." What Howells read between the lines, others, including Vernon Louis Parrington, were exposed to in the classroom, where Wendell's smugness and condescension left indelible impressions. Twenty-five years after leaving Cambridge, and in the midst of preparing his monumental *Main Currents in American Thought* (1927–30), Parrington proudly announced that he was "up to [his] ears in the economic interpretation of American history and literature, getting the last lingering Harvard prejudices out of [his] system." He was becoming "more radical with every year," he told his college classmates, "and more impatient with the smug Tory culture which we were fed on as undergraduates."[3]

Parrington was graduated with the class of '93: a fateful year, as Alan Trachtenberg reminds us in *The Incorporation of America*. Harvard's commencement virtually coincided with the opening of the World's Columbian Exhibition in Chicago – the dazzling and deceptive White City – but the season was also marked by violent labor struggles and nascent agrarian unrest, social concerns that Parrington would emphasize in his chronicle of the nation's intellectual development. That the Exhibition opened its gates at the same time that banks and factories were closing theirs in the nation's worst financial panic was an irony lost neither on him nor on Trachtenberg (211). A remarkably convenient and pregnant site of contradiction, the fair has indeed become the *locus horribilis* of much cultural criticism, if only because to the many Americans who flocked there, it appeared to be a *locus amoenus*. That discontinuity itself suggests why, approached from almost any angle as a historical event, the Exhibition betrays all the "problematic" features that have achieved renewed prominence in critical discussions of realism and naturalism. As Trachtenberg concludes, "In retrospect, the Fair has seemed not only a culmination of the efforts of ruling groups since the

Civil War to win hegemony over the emerging national culture but a pro-
phetic symbol of the coming defeat of Populism and its alternative culture,
the alternative 'America' it proposed" (231). William Dean Howells made
the same point with alternative spelling. "Dere *iss* no more Ameriga any-
more!" the symbolically maimed character Lindau declares in *A Hazard of
New Fortunes* (1890); and it was Parrington's self-appointed task to explain
why.

A number of recent monographs have tried to rehabilitate Parrington's
social and economic framework for interpreting what he called "The Beginnings of Critical Realism" in America. Once consigned to the dustbin of
literary history (most famously by Lionel Trilling) because of its deliberate
rejection of narrowly "belletristic" criteria, Parrington's vision has almost
come full circle. Now his most relentless critics are (posthumously) on the
defensive. Significantly, an audible echo of Howells's attack on Wendell can
be heard in at least one repudiation of Trilling and the other so-called
consensus critics: "Such criticism, though it often purports to be about the
writer and his society, displays a patrician aloofness in regard to social fact,
resulting in a polished insensitivity to those sociological features of class and
ideological conflict which make their appearance in the literature and even,
from time to time, constitute its central concerns" (Spindler, 3). Renewed
examination of what has cleverly been referred to as American "dissensus"
has brought to the fore issues of race, class, and gender that previous criticism allegedly suppressed or ignored. As Amy Kaplan has forcefully suggested, Parrington's Cold War enemies (especially Trilling and Richard
Chase) "were recasting a literary tradition to echo their own generation's
disillusionment with oppositional politics and their disbelief in the efficacy
of human agency in what Trilling called the 'social field,' the province of the
novel itself" (*The Social Construction of American Realism*, 4).

Intentionally or not, this viewpoint gives a peculiarly American twist to
Lukác's famous indictment of subjective modernism (*Realism in Our Time*),
especially as it contends that postwar criticism "contributed to the broader
intellectual consensus which held that America was a classless society without internal ideological conflicts" (Kaplan, 4). Sanitized of the socially dis-
ruptive elements that brought realism into being in the first place, these
older assessments of realist or naturalist texts were obliged either to dispar-
age the books they examined or to elide the literature's political content by
way of patriotic platitudes. (Although heard much less frequently, these still
occasionally surface: "the realistic novel," one critic claimed in 1979, "was
the embodiment of the American dream, the expression of the democratic

hope, the articulation of the Protestant ethic" [Holman, 15]). Yet the damaging legacy of these critics, according to the newer school,

> extended beyond their own time to frame an American canon which equates the romance with the exceptional nature of American culture and which makes realism an anomaly in American fiction; as an inherently flawed imitation of a European convention, realism is, in effect, un-American. If the "thinness" of American culture cannot nurture social fiction, then those novelists who do confront contemporary social issues must be imaginatively handicapped, inorganically related to that culture.   (Kaplan, 4)

By turning the tables on this argument, more recent criticism insists that what makes American realism interesting is precisely its "flawed" nature, the slippage that occurs between the social perception of reality and its representation, whether in a work of "art" or in other manifestations of culture. "Those apparently unrealistic elements in realistic fiction," it has been suggested, "are not to be seen as aberrations in the writer's control over his own method but rather as crucial to the formative energy of the novel" (Levine, 253).

Recuperating realism (and, by extension, naturalism) has thus become a largely historical project, which helps to explain why so few comprehensive assessments of the subject have appeared in the past twenty-five years – or at least since Warner Berthoff's *The Ferment of Realism* (1965) and Jay Martin's *Harvests of Change* (1967). What once appeared to be an intellectual cul de sac is now an open-ended avenue of inquiry, intimidating (if not inimical) to categorical definition and evaluation. From a different, but reinforcing, point of view, modern developments in linguistics and philosophy have widened the "chasm" between subjects and objects "to the point where the referent itself is often now posited as a mere myth or mirage by post-structuralist theorists. This partly accounts, not only for the absence of any major development in the theory of Realism in our own time, but also for the fact that the nineteenth-century Realist movement itself has for the most part been described only in negative terms by modern critics unsympathetic to its general aims" (Lee, 28). Just one generation ago, realism "was less opposed than considered beyond the pale of discussion," because it "was taken as a servile, transparent copying of the world" (Arac, 161). Since then it has been casually appropriated by Roland Barthes and other postmodernists, used "more as a trampoline than as an altar, but one with well-tested springs, which allowed the critic to stay longer and longer in the air, returning to the text infrequently, and then only to gain bounce" (Hirsh,

235). Modern champions (and critics) of realism, rediscovering their roots – usually via Parrington or Howells (or both) – in the evolution of the phenomenon itself, have necessarily invoked the forces of history to justify their own critical projects.

To cite Parrington and Howells as necessary links to the past is, of course, to oversimplify; but in fact these figures can usefully represent the two more abstract epistemologies – Marxism and feminism – principally responsible for the retrieval and reconsideration of realist texts. Such a statement is not as outrageous as it might seem, given Parrington's explicitly materialist base and the astonishingly cogent reinvention of Howells as the nineteenth century's preeminent student – and victim – of gender distinctions (see, for example, Prioleau, Crowley, and Habegger). Indeed, on theoretical grounds, their obvious naïveté (Parrington is no Lukács – and certainly no Jameson – and no one would mistake Howells's geniality for the laugh of a Medusa) suggests why they have been so unusually provocative.

Even though Marxist and feminist writers are fond of trading accusations about each other's methods and assumptions, they both question and explore the relation between literature and social structure, especially as that relation centers on issues of representation. One particularly significant book displaying the productive confluence of these approaches is the 1982 collection of essays gathered by Sundquist, *American Realism*. Many of the pieces published here turned out to be seminal anticipations of important larger projects: Seltzer's *Henry James and the Art of Power* (1984); Brodhead's *The School of Hawthorne* (1986); Fisher's *Hard Facts* (1987); Michaels's *The Gold Standard and the Logic of Naturalism* (1987); and, indeed, the *Columbia Literary History* itself (1988). *American Realism* can rightly be viewed as a kind of watershed. The book earns this distinction, however, not by virtue of rigorous methodological consistency, but rather because it avoids any. Indeed, what the editor says of his subject might also be said of his fellow contributors: "American realism virtually has no school; its most dominating and influential advocate, William Dean Howells, often seems to ride along in a strange vacuum, nearly unheeded in his continual insistence on the proprieties of the everyday, stable characterization, and moral certainty, while almost every other important author of the period simply refused, in these terms, to become a realist" (4). (Howells himself, it should be noted, occasionally refused to become a realist "in these terms," but the point is still well taken.) This failure of coherence, then, is less a liability than a source of interest, because it reveals the peculiar instability of realism's aesthetic and social functions and the multiple ways in which that instability can be registered and analyzed.

Even though their methods differ, Sundquist's various contributors do share certain concerns. Prominent among them is a cultural paradox best articulated some years earlier by Leo Bersani. "The realistic novel," he observed, "gives us an image of social fragmentation contained within the order of significant form – and it thereby suggests that the chaotic fragments are somehow socially viable and morally redeemable." Indeed, as he extends the logic of this remark, Bersani anticipates the conclusions that Trachtenberg would reach about the cultural work achieved by Chicago's White City:

> A good part of the realistic novelist's imaginative energies – whatever his intentions may be – is devoted to sparing his society the pain of confronting the shallowness of its order and the destructiveness of its appetites. The ordered significances of realistic fiction are presented as immanent to society, whereas in fact they are the mythical denial of that society's fragmented nature. In a sense, then, the realistic novelist desperately tries to hold together what he recognizes quite well is falling apart. (60–1)

The desperation of that effort and the means of rendering immanent what is only mythical are, respectively, the sign and the work of ideology, a term that assumes great prominence in recent critical discourse.

To confirm this suggestion, one could turn (for the sake of convenience) to another collection of essays, *Ideology and Classic American Literature* (1986); but the student of realism and naturalism might initially be disappointed, for none of the contributors to this book focuses on late-nineteenth-century texts. Nevertheless, in the essays by Jehlen and Porter, the implications of ideological analysis become manifest, and in Porter's case are carried forward in other work.

Although she bases her argument mostly on antebellum fiction, Jehlen does not hesitate to offer a broader conclusion about the restricted social vision of the American novel, which has been crippled by our writers' addiction to an individualist ethos. By contrast, she claims, the European novel "more easily envisages alternative societies or at least their theoretical possibilities"; and the "source of the difference lies . . . in the different ways in which the middle class achieved its hegemony in Europe and in America" (126–7). Essentially repeating an older argument (Louis Hartz's) that America was born "liberal" and never had to become so (by struggling, often violently, against the feudal authority), Jehlen suggests that the triumph of bourgeois hegemony in the New World was comparatively effortless and, to all appearances, "natural": "America . . . was conceived not so much in liberty as in liberalism" (127). Starting from this premise, the very notion of

American "realism" (in Lukácsian terms) becomes absurd; for, even when it is most "critical," the American novel never discards a belief in "transcendent order or unifying purpose in . . . bourgeois culture" (128). Thus, even to so shrewd a reader as Henry James, *Madame Bovary* can be dismissed as "really too small an affair," while in France, as Jehlen observes, "she was either a national scandal or an international triumph"; at any rate, "no one seems to have doubted her significance" (134). The juxtaposition with *The Portrait of a Lady* is indeed telling, as, in his preface, James confesses how hard he worked to justify Isabel Archer as a proper subject, to make her predicament seem a very big affair, by casting her character in dimensions symbolically worthy of his International Theme. "For Flaubert," Jehlen notes, "it was a historical catastrophe that France had become bourgeois. For James the coming of America offered at last the possibility of transcending both class and history" (136).

For readers attentive to the ending of *The Portrait* (or, say, *The American Scene*), that gloss might seem rather queer. Indeed, in the first chapter of *Seeing and Being*, Porter accuses Jehlen of the same ahistoricism that she deplores as a national characteristic. What Jehlen ignores, according to Porter, is the inherently unstable nature of ideological hegemony, which, even in America, has been subject to the (frequently irrational) flux of historical circumstance. "What we need to understand," Porter urges, "is that if America is different, it is not only because of what it has lacked [i.e., overt ideological conflict], but also because of what that lack has fostered – a social reality constituted of the individual's atomistic freedom, a social reality breeding an extreme form of alienation" (20). If one abides by Marxian (or Lukácsian) priorities, a phenomenon most worthy of analysis is reification: the disabling process by which man not only becomes alienated from himself, but also projects his commodified consciousness into an illusory world of "things," hence leaving him twice removed from primary, or objective reality. Consequently, "bourgeois man does not deny history, but rather is incapable of apprehending it at all, except in reified forms. Yet at moments of crisis," Porter qualifies, "the contradictions inherent in bourgeois society surface, seem to break through the reified patina of the objectified world, revealing the incoherence of the rational systems by which [history] has been obscured, as well as the historically mediated nature of 'objectivity'" (30). At such moments of crisis the critic of realism finds his (or her) most salient opportunities.

James's bizarre novel *The Sacred Fount* (1901), with its helplessly anonymous narrator, gives Porter a nearly perfect (reified) textual environment in which to explore the implications of her project, the partial subtitle of which

("The Plight of the Participant/Observer") could easily be transferred to James's book. For the student of American realism and naturalism, Porter's chapters on James and Adams will probably be most compelling. In these she analyzes the textual strategies by which James and Adams attempt "to save the detached observer, to recontain the crisis to which his contemplative stance makes him vulnerable" (38). For James – outside of the autobiographical prefaces – this observer is usually a protagonist (Maggie Verver, for example), while Adams, of course, pretends to be detached from himself (or from history); but over time, Porter alleges, both writers become uncomfortably aware of their "impotence and complicity" as participants in the world beyond which they presume to stand (37). Their books, then, become veiled confessions of capitalist excess, the fitting emblem of which (in James's last unfinished novel, *The Ivory Tower*) is Abel Gaw, the businessman antihero, whose sharp beak, the narrative voice reveals, has pecked out so many hearts.

For all of its theoretical abstraction, Porter's speculations about capitalism's commodification of the world and of others might not come as a surprise to students who have read not only *The Sacred Fount* but also its close contemporary, Bradford Peck's *The World a Department Store* (1900). Indeed, one of the more curious aspects of the "historical" recovery of American literature and authorship is its tendency to overlook certain forms of evidence. Porter herself can be accused of this: her chapter on "Emerson's America," for example, would more accurately be titled "Leo Marx's Version of Emerson's America," since the primary sources on which her analysis of nineteenth-century political economy depends are, almost exclusively, cited as quotations from *The Machine in the Garden* (1964). It may be more than ironic that, in a book about the reification of consciousness, much of the evidence is reified, too.

Indeed, anyone who surveys much of the recent critical literature on realism and naturalism might well be afflicted (when he is not refreshed) by a certain claustrophobic awareness of overlap and reduplication – even when, as is frequently the case, it goes unrecognized in footnotes. Thus, one influential interpretation of Henry James's peculiarly commodified world (Agnew's) ignores another (Porter's), even though they both heavily depend upon the same primary text (*The Golden Bowl*) for justification. Likewise, the notes to Philip Fisher's essay on *Sister Carrie*, when first published in 1982 (in Sundquist's *American Realism*), referred mostly to a smattering of the same author's other essays. When republished in *Hard Facts* (1987), most of these references were cosmetically removed, nor were any added to acknowledge Rachel Bowlby's work, or June Howard's, even though these intervening books often speak to the very same issues: commodity fetishism and the naturalist plot of decline. Reading these interpretations in sequence, one might have to inquire which is which:

> Self-esteem is always material in Dreiser, and there is no more significant indication of the progress of Carrie's career than the details he gives of the gradual rise in her income while Hurstwood, out of a job, wastes away his limited capital[.]   (Bowlby, 59)

> Hurstwood's decline is measured . . . equally by the melting away of his savings, or rather his stolen savings: $1300 when he reaches New York, $500 by Chapter 33, $340 in Chapter 36, $100 and then $50 in Chapter 37, then finally he is a beggar for dimes and beds for a night.   (Fisher, 175)

If one has had the benefit of reading Fisher's essay on Twain (in the *Columbia History*), the answer is more obvious, since that too is preoccupied with dollar signs. The text he seizes upon, typically, is "The $30,000 Bequest."

The other numerals in this brief extract from *Hard Facts* point to another recurrent problem, however; for if one is reading the definitive Pennsylvania Edition of *Sister Carrie,* which restores many passages cut from Dreiser's manuscript, the balance-book evidence Fisher cites will not be found in chapters 33, 36, and 37, but rather in 36, 39, and 40, respectively. Fisher neither acknowledges this discrepancy nor feels obliged to explain (or defend) his choice of texts – a pregnant silence heard even amid the deafening roar of cultural criticism. The wholesale revaluation of American realism and naturalism that has occurred in the last twenty years has been accompanied by equally important advances in textual bibliography, even though (as so often happens) the left hand has failed adequately to appreciate what its partner has been up to. Dreiser criticism is a case in point. Even though some recent work addresses the newly available textual evidence (Bowlby and Howard, for example), no one has fully accepted the challenge posed by the Pennsylvania editors – that *Sister Carrie* "is in fact a new work of art, heretofore unknown, which must be approached freshly and interpreted anew" (Dreiser, 532). The "new" text of *The Red Badge of Courage* poses similar problems (Crane, 111–58). As one voice in the wilderness has ruefully noted, "the angels of hermeneutics have long feared to tread in the fields of textual/bibliographical studies, which are widely regarded, in fact, as a world well lost" (McGann, 181).

McGann's comments should not necessarily be construed as an endorsement of the editorial theory upon which either the Pennsylvania *Sister Carrie* or Norton *Red Badge of Courage* were based: indeed, he has specifically rejected the prevailing imperative (promulgated by the Center for Editions of American Authors) that would oblige an editor to choose an author's manuscript as copy text for an authoritative edition. His larger argument, however, is only more compelling because of this apparent contradiction.[4] Even though so much recent critical work bemoans the consequences of social and economic hierarchy in American life, that same work frequently reproduces and internalizes a stratified conception of criticism itself, which tends to devalue the labor of textual historians and bibliographers. Reintegrating the still too disparate fields of bibliography and the so-called higher criticism is one of the more profound challenges that awaits a new generation of scholars. For when we reevaluate realist or naturalist texts in a more comprehensive sociohistorical context – viewing them as "books, manuscripts, or otherwise materialized objects" – then we must approach the issues of criticism and interpretation "in a very different way, for the language in which texts speak to us is not located merely in the verbal sign system" (McGann, 191).

Much of the best recent scholarship on American realism and naturalism reflects this renewed awareness of literary sociology. Again, it is helpful to remember that certain chapters of the *Literary History of the United States* can be said to have anticipated the expanding interest in this field. The central concerns of "Literature as Business" and "Creating an Audience" – first published in 1946 – resurface with new vigor in a lengthening list of important monographs that explore the relationship between nineteenth-century writers and the marketplace. For a long time critics and theorists of literature have remarked upon the disappearance – or death – of the author, but any survey of recent contributions to the field of literary scholarship suggests that reports of this event have been greatly exaggerated. One might even say that he has been resurrected as an afflicted, but by no means terminal, exemplar of capitalist civilization. Not surprisingly, he returns a changed man: transubstantiated by newer modes of cultural analysis, he is now frequently a woman or, even more frequently, an aggregate – the idea of authorship itself. While a number of these newer studies have focused on a single author – such as Henry James (see Jacobson, Margolis, Anesko, and Freedman) – others have attempted comparative study of writers whose careers followed similar historical trajectories (Wilson, Coultrap-McQuin). The fact that one of the best of these, Henry Nash Smith's *Democracy and the Novel* (1978), has in most respects already been superseded suggests the rapid pace at which the newer historical scholarship has been advancing.

An instructive example of such work is Daniel H. Borus's *Writing Realism* (1989), which aligns the work of Howells, James, and (somewhat surprisingly) Frank Norris. Because "the contours of realism" are more important to this critic than "individual texts," differences among writers seem less important to him than shared interests, an attitude that may help to justify the unusual linkage of Norris to the seemingly more companionable Howells and James (9). All three had to come to terms with the commercial transformation of the literary marketplace in the late nineteenth century, and the emergence of literary realism can be understood, according to Borus, only in relation to this "central historical determinant" (24). The commodification of literature – its production, exchange, and circulation – serves to focus this wide-ranging inquiry, which draws freely and rewardingly upon an unusually broad base of sources: manuscript archives of both authors and publishers, runs of nineteenth-century periodicals, as well as the more conventional published materials. By recontextualizing American realism in terms of professional practice, this study posits more explicit and historically specific connections between writers and their social environments than literary criticism ordinarily admits.

The same motive asserts itself in the work of Kaplan and Michaels, who also emphasize the extent to which practitioners of realism and naturalism were complicitous with the very structures of power their work superficially seems to oppose. Borus tries to reconcile these competing claims by keeping the professional mechanism of authorship always to the fore. "Meeting the audience through the marketplace," Borus concludes, "writers of the late nineteenth century had before them the task of redefining just what it was that an author did. . . . In the course of writing, realists defined writing as 'work'; consumption of the resulting product depended upon the establishment of a common dialogue; and the writer's responsibility was to insure social cohesiveness" (188). Burdened by the cultural contradictions of capitalism, "realists tried to mold a position in which art was simultaneously in the world but not of it" (61). The inherent instability of that posture – resulting as much from questions of practice as from prevailing ideology – explains why so many realist texts arrive at inconsistent and aesthetically dissatisfying conclusions. As Kaplan puts it, "realistic novels have trouble ending because they pose problems they cannot solve, problems that stem from their attempt to imagine and contain social change" (160).

Such problems of containment, as Kaplan sees them, are a direct result of marketplace conditions, which placed the cultural work of writers like Howells, Wharton, and Dreiser in competition with other modes of representation: the emerging colossus of mass journalism, the domesticated remnants of the sentimental tradition, the vulgarized theatrics of the nineteenth-century stage. Unlike Borus, who deliberately understates the realists' individual differences, Kaplan exploits biography for the sake of illuminating the various challenges that realism had to confront. Edith Wharton, for example, proudly legitimated her commitment to realism as a form of productive labor (as did Howells, who began his career setting type in a frontier printshop); but her reasons for doing so stemmed even more from issues of gender than from those of class. As Kaplan reads it, the novelist's autobiography (*A Backward Glance*) shows how deliberately Wharton defined herself against the preceding generation of pious sentimentalists and wrote herself "out of the domestic sphere into an alternative realm of professional authorship" (72). Such a contest was made even more difficult because, in devoting herself to writing, Wharton also rejected the life of enforced idleness her upper-class status would have presupposed.

In her best work, then, Wharton achieves a new synthesis of culturally engendered spheres, fusing the interior (psychological) world of feminine ritual with the public (commercial) world of masculine enterprise. Negotiating the precarious interstices between these spheres is precisely the problem Wharton's most famous heroine, Lily Bart, is forced to confront in *The House of Mirth*. Although many other critics empowered by feminist theory have noted this before (Wolff, 109–33; Fetterley), Kaplan adds an interesting new twist to the argument by suggesting that the "novel maps a social terrain where these realms become increasingly interconnected not only through the relations of work and marriage but through the mediation of spectatorship" (89). The precious Four Hundred are threatened less by repeated assaults from parvenus among the Fortune Five Hundred than by a debilitating "need to turn the rest of society into an audience" (90). While voyeuristic crowds are kept apart from the numerous pageants, ceremonies, and rituals that make up the novel's social landscape, Wharton quietly – but insistently – records the presence of outsiders and registers the pressure they exert upon the vulnerable objects of their gaze. The most compelling but elusive goal in Lily Bart's world is to become an enviable center of attention, distinguished from and yet enhanced by the approving spectatorship of others. Lily and all the other elite figures in *The House of Mirth* are entrapped by their very need to be conspicuously consumed by the gaping mob. Ironically, then, their plight is not much different from that of Wharton as professional author in search of a popular market. Indeed, the phenomenal success of her novel would seem not merely to confirm but tangibly to exemplify the triumph of publicity in its representations of class power.

Henry James, too, had registered the implications of this sinister logic (tragically, in *The Bostonians* [1886]; comically, in *The Reverberator* [1887]; more ambiguously, in *The Ambassadors* [1903]); indeed, the reach of his career spanned the pivotal incorporating stage of the advertising industry. To be reminded of this can help one better appreciate just what is at stake in even so recondite a novel as *The Ambassadors*. "Strether's fictions deceive only himself, while Chad's are manipulated for the deception of others. If Chad and Strether are accordingly set up as rival authors of a sort, Chad, as the advertising writer, is invested in a kind of fiction-making that can penetrate back out into the world, one that can actively make things happen" (Wicke, 110). True to his form, then, Chad is the author of profoundest disappointment. Like any good advertisement, he both seduces Strether by embodying the ambassador's most powerfully repressed desires and reduces him to play the part of a voyeuristic consumer. He certainly makes Selah Tarrant (in *The Bostonians*) look like an amateur.

The examples of Lily Bart and Strether tend to confirm another critic's interesting suggestion that when American novels take money as their central concern, they "inevitably wind up chronicling the isolation of one character, his or her separation from the real world" (Vernon, 197). If it is true that the age of realism in America is "the age of the *romance of money*" (Sundquist, 19), then the triumph of realism (as a register of material life) implies its own collapse; for when class distinctions are determined solely by the power of money, "the novel of manners" cedes its authority to "the novel of single consciousness" (Vernon, 195). Manners are incompatible with a purely material world – as James lamented in *The Question of Our Speech* (1905) – and surely this is one aspect of what Michaels calls the "logic of naturalism" (one need only think of *McTeague!*).

Historical recontextualization is perhaps one way to escape from the prison-house of language (de)constructed by so much poststructuralist theory. It has almost become familiar in recent years for critics to offer their services to students as a scholarly kind of operation rescue. As one symptomatic book promises, "This narrative has as its end the 'socialization' of Henry James, of the concept of the 'single author,' not in terms of a particular Marxist utopianism but in terms of the sociopolitical forces of contemporary ideology at work in our most avowedly avant-garde and politically radical theories of literature, literary function, and humanistic study" (Rowe, 157). Such theories have indeed rejuvenated critical inquiry, as Rowe suggests, but they have not been explored without attendant risks. Warnings have been sounded, but perhaps not sufficiently heard. In "sophisticated flight" from the naïve epistemological assumptions associated with realism, much contemporary criticism promulgates "a conception of the novel as ideally and entirely self-reflexive" (Stowe, 172). Indeed, what one observer has said of twentieth-century literature's marked self-indulgence might well be even more applicable to criticism at the present time: "as the technical skills of writers of fiction have increased in disproportionate relation to the simple power of literature to hold an audience and move it with a new imaginative vision, technique *per se* has begun to seem more and more insistent. Too many works seem reducible to attempts to see how far an idea or a technical gimmick will go" (Stephens, 71).

This tendency (observable from even the briefest detour through the academic journals) inevitably betrays certain ironies, but it might also provoke useful self-reflection. As at least one critic has suggested, "It is surprising how, in the argument over realism, the relations between art and life, so little attention is paid to either art or life" (Stoehr, 165). And the same has been said about naturalism. "Theories that ignore the . . . oppositional character of naturalism have the attraction of all such reversals in that they astonish, but they have the disadvantage, if taken seriously, of detaching analysis from any anchor in experience. They may also cater to an unearned sense of moral and intellectual superiority to the writers to which they are applied because they claim access to a 'political unconscious'" (Seamon, 60, n. 4). The acutely self-conscious politics of much recent criticism tends to diminish the value of that unearned increment. Perhaps E. M. Forster had the best last word: "only connect." And the place to begin is with our writers themselves.

NOTES

1   Complete bibliographical information for all titles mentioned in the text can be found in Works Cited for this chapter.
2   It should come as no surprise that a companion volume, *The Columbia History of the American Novel,* has recently appeared.
3   Vernon Louis Parrington, "Class of 1893, Sixth Report, 1918," pp. 220–1 (Harvard University Archives). See also Richard Hofstadter, *The Progressive Historians* (New York: Knopf, 1969), for an excellent account of the historical factors that shaped Parrington's intellectual development.
4   For a competing view, see also G. Thomas Tenselie, "Textual Criticism and Literary Sociology," *Studies in Bibliography* 44 (1991): 83–143.

WORKS CITED

Agnew, Jean-Cristophe. "The Consuming Vision of Henry James." *The Culture of Consumption: Critical Essays in American History, 1880–1980,* pp. 65–99. Edited by Richard W. Fox and T. J. Jackson Lears. New York: Pantheon, 1983.

Anesko, Michael. *"Friction with the Market": Henry James and the Profession of Authorship.* New York: Oxford University Press, 1986.

Arac, Jonathan. "Rhetoric and Realism; or Marxism, Deconstruction, and the Novel." *Criticism Without Boundaries: Directions and Crosscurrents in Postmodern Critical Theory,* pp. 160–76. Edited by Joseph A. Buttigieg. Notre Dame: University of Notre Dame Press, 1987.

Barthes, Roland. "L'Effet de Réel." *Communications* 11 (1968): 84–9.

Bersani, Leo. *A Future for Astyanax: Character and Desire in Literature.* Boston: Little, Brown, 1976.

Berthoff, Warner. *The Ferment of Realism: American Literature, 1884–1919.* New York: Free Press, 1965.

Borus, Daniel H. *Writing Realism: Howells, James, and Norris in the Mass Market.* Chapel Hill: University of North Carolina Press, 1989.

Bowlby, Rachel. *Just Looking: Consumer Culture in Dreiser, Gissing, and Zola.* New York: Methuen, 1985.

Brodhead, Richard. *The School of Hawthorne.* New York: Oxford University Press, 1986.

Chase, Richard. *The American Novel and Its Tradition.* New York: Doubleday, 1957.

The Columbia History of the American Novel. Edited by Emory Elliott et al. New York: Columbia University Press, 1991.

Columbia Literary History of the United States. Edited by Emory Elliott et al. New York: Columbia University Press, 1988.

Coultrap-McQuin, Susan. *Doing Literary Business: American Women Writers in the Nineteenth Century.* Chapel Hill: University of North Carolina Press, 1990.

Crane, Stephen. *The Red Badge of Courage.* Edited by Henry Binder. New York: Norton, 1982.

Crowley, John W. *The Mask of Fiction: Essays on W. D. Howells.* Amherst: University of Massachusetts Press, 1989.

Dreiser, Theodore. *Sister Carrie.* The Pennsylvania Edition. Edited by Neda M. Westlake et al. Philadelphia: University of Pennsylvania Press, 1981.

Fetterley, Judith. "The Temptation to Be a Beautiful 'Object': Double Standard and Double Bind in *The House of Mirth.*" *Studies in American Fiction* 5 (1977): 199–211.

Fisher, Philip. *Hard Facts: Form and Setting in the American Novel.* New York: Oxford University Press, 1985.

Freedman, Jonathan L. *Professions of Taste: Henry James, British Aestheticism and Commodity Culture.* Stanford, Calif.: Stanford University Press, 1990.

Habegger, Alfred. *Gender, Fantasy and Realism in American Literature.* New York: Columbia University Press, 1982.

  Henry James and the "Woman Business." New York: Cambridge University Press, 1989.

Hartz, Louis. *The Liberal Tradition in America.* New York: Harcourt, Brace, 1955.

Hirsh, John C. "Realism Renewed." *Journal of American Studies* 25 (1991): 235–43.

Holman, C. Hugh. *Windows on the World: Essays on American Social Fiction.* Knoxville: University of Tennessee Press, 1979.

Howard, June. *Form and History in American Literary Naturalism.* Chapel Hill: University of North Carolina Press, 1985.

Howells, William Dean. "Professor Barrett Wendell's Notions of American Literature." *North American Review* 172 (1901): 623–40.

Ideology and Classic American Literature. Edited by Sacvan Bercovitch and Myra Jehlen. New York: Cambridge University Press, 1986.

Jacobson, Marcia. *Henry James and the Mass Market.* University: University of Alabama Press, 1983.

Jameson, Fredric. *The Political Unconscious: Narrative as a Socially Symbolic Act.* Ithaca, N.Y.: Cornell University Press, 1981.

"The Realist Floor-Plan." *On Signs.* pp. 373–83. Edited by Marshall Blonsky. Baltimore: Johns Hopkins University Press, 1985.

Jehlen, Myra. "New World Epics: The Middle Class Novel in America." *Salmagundi* 36 (1977): 49–68. Reprinted as "The Novel and the Middle Class in America," in *Ideology and Classic American Literature.*

Jenkins, Cecil. "Realism and the Novel Form." *The Monster in the Mirror: Studies in Nineteenth-Century Realism,* pp. 1–15. Edited by D. A. Williams. Oxford: University of Hull, by Oxford University Press, 1978.

Kaplan, Amy. *The Social Construction of American Realism.* Chicago: University of Chicago Press, 1988.

Lee, Brian. *American Fiction, 1865–1940.* New York: Longman, 1987.

Levine, George. "Realism Reconsidered." *The Theory of the Novel: New Essays,* pp. 233–56. Edited by John Halperin. New York: Oxford University Press, 1974.

Literary History of the United States. Edited by Robert E. Spiller et al. New York: Macmillan, 1946. 4th ed. rev. 1974.

Lukács, Georg. *Realism in Our Time: Literature and the Class Struggle* (1964) Translated by John and Necke Mander. Reprint. New York: Harper, 1971.

McGann, Jerome J., *Textual Criticism and Literary Interpretation.* Chicago: University of Chicago Press, 1985.

Margolis, Anne T. *Henry James and the Problem of Audience: An International Act.* Ann Arbor, Mich.: UMI Research Press, 1985.

Martin, Jay. *Harvests of Change: American Literature, 1865–1914.* Englewood Cliffs, N.J.: Prentice-Hall, 1967.

Marx, Leo. *The Machine in the Garden.* New York: Oxford University Press, 1964.

Michaels, Walter Benn. *The Gold Standard and the Logic of Naturalism: American Literature at the Turn of the Century.* Berkeley: University of California Press, 1987.

Mitchell, Lee Clark. *Determined Fictions: American Literary Naturalism.* New York: Columbia University Press, 1988.

Parrington, Vernon Louis. *Main Currents in American Thought.* 3 vols. New York: Harcourt, Brace, 1927–30.

Porter, Carolyn. *Seeing and Being: The Plight of the Participant Observer in Emerson, James, Adams, and Faulkner.* Middletown, Conn.: Wesleyan University Press, 1981. Chapter Two, "Reification and American Literature," reprinted in *Ideology and Classic American Literature.*

Prioleau, Elizabeth Stevens. *The Circle of Eros: Sexuality in the Work of William Dean Howells.* Durham, N.C.: Duke University Press, 1983.

Rowe, John Carlos. *The Theoretical Dimensions of Henry James.* Madison: University of Wisconsin Press, 1984.

Seamon, Roger. "Naturalist Narratives and Their Ideational Context: A Theory of American Naturalist Fiction." *Canadian Review of American Studies* 19 (1988): 47–64.

Seltzer, Mark. *Henry James and the Art of Power.* Ithaca, N.Y.: Cornell University Press, 1984.

Smith, Henry Nash. *Democracy and the Novel: Popular Resistance to Classic American Writers.* New York: Oxford University Press, 1978.

Spindler, Michael. *American Literature and Social Change: William Dean Howells to Arthur Miller.* Bloomington: Indiana University Press, 1983.

Stephens, Gary. "Haunted Americana: The Endurance of American Realism." *Partisan Review* 44 (1977): 71–84.

Sundquist, Eric J., ed. *American Realism: New Essays.* Baltimore: The Johns Hopkins University Press, 1982.

Trachtenberg, Alan. *The Incorporation of America: Culture and Society in the Gilded Age.* New York: Hill & Wang, 1982.

Trilling, Lionel. *The Liberal Imagination.* New York: Viking, 1950.

Vernon, John. *Money and Fiction: Literary Realism in the Nineteenth and Early Twentieth Centuries.* Ithaca, N.Y.: Cornell University Press, 1984.

Wendell, Barrett. *A Literary History of America.* New York: Scribner's, 1901.

Wicke, Jennifer A. *Advertising Fictions: Literature, Advertisement, and Social Reading.* New York: Columbia University Press, 1988.

Wilson, Christopher P. *The Labor of Words: Literary Professionalism in the Progressive Era.* Athens: University of Georgia Press, 1985.

White Collar Fictions: Class and Social Representation in American Literature, 1885–1925. Athens: University of Georgia Press, 1992.

Wolff, Cynthia Griffin. *A Feast of Words: The Triumph of Edith Wharton.* New York: Oxford University Press, 1977.

4

ELIZABETH AMMONS

Expanding the Canon
of American Realism

Iktomi surprised me, particularly as a part of this course, because the Sioux realism – a markedly *different* realism – is, first, not at all what I might define as "realism" and, second, it *must* be accepted as the reality of whoever subscribes to it.

Joseph Pelletier

These three books – *The Rise of Silas Lapham, Old Indian Legends, The Conjure Woman* – taught me to see that my idea of realism is not everyone's.

Emma Lockwood

Being able to write is a healing, an act that speaks to one's tangible existence and worth as one whose voice not only roars, but is given attention to.

Lucy Park

How does an artist of color express anger in a way that will not alienate a mainstream white audience predisposed to hostility?

Lisa Hom

When we say American realism, two immediate questions are: Whose reality? And: Whose America? To suggest those questions, I have opened with statements written by four of my students. Also, I begin with my students' words to anticipate two other core ideas. First, the whole issue of canonicity is at heart an issue of the classroom; what is at stake is which books get taught and which do not, which voices get heard. Second, I will be arguing in favor of a reconceptualization of American realism that holds at its center the principle of multiculturalism.

An excellent place to begin any discussion of canonicity and American realism is Amy Kaplan's overview of modern scholarship in *The Social Construction of American Realism* (1988). As Kaplan explains, post–Second World War opinion tended to go in two directions. Charles C. Walcutt's *American Literary Naturalism: A Divided Stream* (1956), Donald Pizer's *Realism and Naturalism in Nineteenth-Century American Literature* (1966), and Harold Kolb's *The Illusion of Life: American Realism as Liter-*

ary Form (1969) consider texts apart from their social contexts in order to offer close New Critical analyses. In contrast, Warner Berthoff's *The Ferment of Realism: American Literature, 1884–1919* (1965) and Jay Martin's *Harvests of Change: American Literature, 1865–1914* (1967) situate texts in their social contexts in order to see how they reflect those contexts. Challenging the premises that govern both of those approaches, more recent studies such as Eric Sundquist's *American Realism: New Essays* (1982), June Howard's *Form and History in American Literary Naturalism* (1985), and Kaplan's book respond to postmodern theoretical concerns. They raise questions about what is "real," what is knowable, and what is involved in the acts of creating, reading, interpreting, discussing, and writing about texts.

Kaplan cuts to the quick of postmodernism's impact on the concept of realism when she points to the "antimimetic assumption of poststructuralist theory which holds that reality is not reflected by language but that language in fact produces the reality we know."[1] This philosophical position leads to exciting new interpretive perspectives. But it can also, as Kaplan points out in her description of the Sundquist collection, deconstruct the whole idea of realism. If language does not reflect, but instead *creates,* reality, then what reality, or what knowable, communicable one, can realist texts logically be said to stand in relation to? Hence, as Kaplan says, postmodernist critics frequently "locate the power of realistic texts precisely in their ability to deconstruct their own claims to referentiality. Through the lenses of contemporary theories, those characteristics once considered realistic are revalued for exposing their own fictionality" (5). The outcome, too often but predictably, is pronouncement of realism's failure, extinction, or nonexistence and the concomitant reassertion of romance as America's best, only, and truest form.[2]

Scholars such as June Howard and Amy Kaplan deal with the challenge of poststructuralist theory by arguing, in Kaplan's words, that "Realists do more than passively record the world outside; they actively create and criticize the meanings, representations, and ideologies of their own changing culture" (7). Thus realism can be said simultaneously to reflect *and* to be part of, to be enmeshed in and produced by, its social context. What this accomplishes is a crucial complication of the idea that texts simply "reflect" their society. As Carl R. Kropf and R. Barton Palmer observe at the beginning of a special issue of *Studies in the Literary Imagination* devoted to narrative theory, when "issues relating to interpretation and the connection between texts and the 'real world' . . . figure prominently on the critical agenda" of contemporary scholarship, "such criticism today avoids both a naive reflectionism and the pseudo-Leavisite view that novels speak directly to readers, unmediated by the structural or technical aspects of storytelling."[3] Consequently, as Kaplan notes, recent critics have tended to reevaluate "realism's political stance, from a progressive force exposing social conditions to a conservative force complicit with capitalist relations" (7). (Dreiser is most frequently used to illustrate this argument.) Charting her own course, Kaplan builds on the historian T. J. Jackson Lears's contention that at the turn of the century "reality itself began to seem problematic, something to be sought rather than merely lived." Kaplan argues that realistic narratives enact this search – "not by fleeing into the imagination or into nostalgia for a lost past but by actively constructing the coherent social world they represent; they do this not in a vacuum of fictionality but in direct confrontation with the elusive process of social change" (9). Realists, in this view, "show a surprising lack of confidence in the capacity of fiction to reflect a solid world 'out there,' not because of the inherent slipperiness of signification but because of their distrust in the significance of the social" (9). Hence their art, which is "anxious and contradictory," simultaneously "articulates and combats the growing sense of unreality at the heart of middle-class life" (9).

The problem with this approach lies in the narrowness of the field of writers to which such a definition of realism applies. A Learsian, postmodernist perspective does illuminate works by Henry James, Theodore Dreiser, and Edith Wharton, the three authors Kaplan studies; and no doubt it can profitably be applied to work by other authors as well. Also, the way in which such a perspective engages important theoretical issues, particularly the question of how realism functions as social reflector even as it is social participant and product, is clear and useful. But how well does such a theory help us understand Zitkala-Ša, Pauline Hopkins, Charles Chesnutt, or Charlotte Perkins Gilman? Or Sui Sin Far, W. E. B. Du Bois, Alice Dunbar-Nelson, Anzia Yezierska, Simon Pokagon, María Cristina Mena, Frances Ellen Harper, Upton Sinclair, James Weldon Johnson? Can we really claim that floating feelings of personal disorientation – individualistic anxiety about the "elusive process of social change" and "a growing sense of unreality at the heart of middle-class life" – were the important issues facing writers who were people of color, feminist, working-class, or poor? Confronted with lynching, rape, Jim Crow laws, land dispossession, cultural erasure, domestic violence, deportation, anti-Semitism, economic oppression, racist immigration laws, and widespread disenfranchisement – to name only some obvious "realities" that, despite postmodernism's claims, were hardly linguistic fictions – many turn-of-the-century authors struggled with problems ignored (in some instances actively denied and suppressed – even caused) by privileged white writers such as James and Wharton. To reconceptualize the period so that a full range of authors can come into view, and to do so in a way that allows us not simply to introduce them as tokens but, rather, to place on an even footing Henry James and Sui Sin Far, Charles Chesnutt and Edith Wharton, I am proposing multiculturalism. It is a paradigm for canon-formation that is intellectually provocative, inclusive, historically sound, and pedagogically flexible.

I

In "Canonicity and Textuality," Robert Scholes explains that the curriculum – what students are told to read – stands at the center of all of our debates about literary canons, which is to say, the texts agreed upon as constituting the "best" or most important works one should read in order to be educated about a given period, author, genre, literary movement, or tradition. With the professionalization of literary studies in the United States early in the twentieth century, "the canon supported the literary curriculum and the curriculum supported the canon. The curriculum, in literary studies, represented the point of application, where canonical choices were tested in the crucible of student response. Works that proved highly teachable (like Shakespeare) remained central in the canon as well as in the curriculum." Professors added other writers they found especially "teachable," such as John Donne, whose poetry was particularly well suited to New Criticism's investment in complex, tight, textual explication by experts. At the same time, formerly admired but less "teachable," because more obvious, authors such as Oliver Goldsmith fell out of canonical favor.[4] Perhaps the most important thing about this process, Scholes observes, is how unconscious it was. Until the last twenty years or so, decisions about canonicity – who's in and who's out –

> were seen as "natural" – or even as not occurring at all. What has happened to literary studies in those decades is a part of larger cultural happenings that can be described (and deplored, if you like) as the politicization of American life. Once upon a time we believed that if the best men (yes) were appointed to the bench, we would get the best judicial decisions. Now, we know that one set of appointments to the Supreme Court will give us one set of laws and another set of appointments will give us others. What is happening is part of the evolution of a democratic society. With respect to the literary canon, [Northrop] Frye's statement about [Matthew] Arnold's touchstones was a political bombshell: "We begin to suspect that the literary judgments are projections of

social ones." Which is to say that the literary canon is a social, and therefore a political, object, the result of a political process, like so much else in our world. (147)

Canonicity is a human, not a divine or "natural," phenomenon. Professors decide what the "best" and most important books are on the basis of what they want to teach and write about. Those decisions, in turn, are grounded in social and political values that do not exist in a vacuum but in the context of faculty members' histories, training, and biases, which are, in their turn, inseparable from considerations of class, gender, race, ethnicity, sexual orientation, nationality, religion, and culture – among other things.

For the canon-making professoriat, then, the questions are not all that obscure. To which texts and authors is it important to expose the young and why? When I construct my syllabus for, say, American realism in the way that it was constructed for me by my professors ten, twenty, or thirty years ago, what social and political values am I perpetuating and endorsing? What version of America am I presenting? Even more specifically, if I make my reading list all white, or all white plus one lonely black as a token to "diversity," what story of "our" (whose?) national past am I creating? Likewise, if I say I have to make my list consist of 80 percent elite white writers because otherwise I will disserve my students, who will come away not having read the canonical authors they "need" to know, whose definitions of disservice, canonicity, and need am I employing?

The obvious point here is that syllabi and, behind them, canons, are all composed of choices. As Robert Hemenway observes, "Although it sounds immodest to say so, English professors largely define the literary canon by choosing to teach certain works. . . . No writer, no book, is likely to be accepted into the canon without the sanction of the university curriculum."[5] Even in English departments where freedom to design syllabi is denied, the design of syllabi is still recognized, at some level, as simply that: a design, a made-up construct. Departmental politics may make argument pointless, but that does not mean that argument about whether a book should or should not be on a syllabus actually *is* irrational – as opposed, for example, to arguing about whether to eat rocks. In short, every time we teach from a syllabus, whether we have designed it or it has been given to us, we participate in a canonical argument. We assert that this list of texts and authors, as opposed to all the lists we are not teaching, is the important one to engage at this time, in this place, and for these reasons, stated or unstated.

Given the constructed character of the canon, what construction shall we choose? My own position is that, if American realism means anything, it means attention to the multiple realities figured in the work of the broadest possible range of authors writing in the late nineteenth and early twentieth centuries. We are educating the young in a world where – to use my own city, Medford, Massachusetts, as an example – the high school was closed as I was writing this essay in 1992 because of a racial "brawl." Although 16 percent of the 1,250 students were black or Hispanic, there were only two black teachers. White teachers interviewed in the newspaper said they saw nothing offensive about white students dressing in Ku Klux Klan regalia for a Halloween party and having pictures of themselves in those costumes published in the yearbook. When the overwhelmingly white local and state police forces descended on the school, they arrested twelve black, two Hispanic, and one white male student. A story I have now heard several times repeats how an African American girl in a history course raised her hand to ask which black people the class would be studying, only to be told, none. In answer to her question, why, she was told because there were none.

None of us needs to look far to find this world. I could, instead of my town, refer to my university – Tufts – which, like any other, contains behind-the-scene rapes, swastikas scrawled on a dormitory door, suicides, racist complaints about the bad English of "foreign" teaching assistants, and on and on – all in a community that is committed to confronting and dealing with issues of discrimination, hatred, and fear. How shall I proceed in this world? It makes no sense to me. to teach American realism as a middle- to upper-class white, male, literary period preoccupied with ways of preserving privilege when, in fact, literary production in the period can be shown to have been more various and more contested by people traditionally denied access to publication than at any preceding time in United States history. My choice is to focus on the presence of diversity, conflict, and turbulence – as well as exuberance, idealism, and celebration – that a genuinely multicultural representation of authors and texts makes possible.[6] To illustrate, my most recent syllabus for American realism (1992) consisted of: Henry James, *Daisy Miller*; William Dean Howells, *The Rise of Silas Lapham*; W. E. B. Du Bois, *The Souls of Black Folk*; Charlotte Perkins Gilman, "The Yellow Wallpaper"; Zitkala-Ša, *Old Indian Legends*; Kate Chopin, *The Awakening*; Charles Chesnutt, *The Conjure Woman*; Pauline Hopkins, *Of One Blood*; Sui Sin Far, selections from *Mrs. Spring Fragrance*; Upton Sinclair, *The Jungle*; Edith Wharton, *Ethan Frome*; María Cristina Mena, "The Vine-Leaf"; Willa Cather, *O Pioneers!*; and selected stories from Anzia Yezierska, *Hungry Hearts*.

Typically, arguments in favor of multiculturalism as an organizing principle for curricula begin with the self-evident truth that the world is, and the

United States has always been, multicultural. Henry Louis Gates, Jr., states: "Whatever the outcome of the cultural wars in the academy, the world we live in is multicultural already. Mixing and hybridity are the rule, not the exception."[7] John Brenkman explains:

> As multiculturalism has begun to impinge on education and on contemporary cultural and literary criticism, neoconservative commentators like to blame an imaginary cabal of leftists who have surreptitiously (and unbeknownst to ourselves) taken over academia, hellbent on stirring racial and ethnic animosities. The neoconservatives, ever mindful of tradition and neglectful of history, will not own up to the real reasons multiculturalism has entered the scene so forcefully, namely, because the United States is rife with unsolved social and political problems whose history reaches all the way back to Columbus.[8]

For Gates, who provides thoughtful comments about weak arguments sometimes invoked in its defense, multiculturalism's imperative lies in its power to increase knowledge and tolerance. To those who worry about exacerbating divisions, he responds: "Ours is a world that already is fissured by nationality, ethnicity, race, and gender. And the only way to transcend those divisions – to forge, for once, a civic culture that respects both differences and commonalities – is through education that seeks to comprehend the diversity of human culture. Beyond the hype and the high-flown rhetoric is a pretty homely truth: there is no tolerance without respect – and no respect without knowledge."[9] For Brenkman, the goal is similar. "A democracy in the contemporary world cannot create a monocultural citizenry. . . . We must define and defend the equality, not the homogeneity, of citizens in the context of multiculturalism."[10]

Multiculturalism should not be confused, however, with simplistic white-oriented feel-good diversity. Paula Gunn Allen speaks with passion about the absence of real change in the academy. Native people, along with women, men, and gay people of color are "labeled as 'marginal,' the 'poor,' the 'victims,' or we are seen as exotica. Our 'allies' adamantly cast us in the role of helpless, hopeless, inadequate, incompetent, much in need of white champions and saviors, dependent upon an uncaring State for every shred of personal and community dignity we might hope to enjoy. Right, left, and center see us as their shadows, the part they disown, reject, repress, or romanticize."[11] White people's magnanimous decisions to "include" writers of color on undeconstructed white reading lists; descriptions of human beings as "marginal" or "Other"; arrogant projections of elite western theory onto cultural expressions of people writing outside western frameworks; patronizing assumptions that all art created by people of color is

obsessed with nothing but subverting dominant-culture forms, as if no referent could possibly exist except the master narrative[12] – all of these are just
the new colonialism. They are simply new ways of asserting the hegemony
of a western, Eurocentric perspective. They are not part of any genuinely
*multi*cultural perspective.

Allen especially attacks elite western academic assumptions that philosophical and literary theories invented by privileged white patriarchs can be
applied, willy-nilly, around the globe.[13] She rejects what many would argue
are the three basic propositions of fancy contemporary theory in the West.
To the notion that "gender (or sex) is a metaphor, a social construct," she
responds, "In other systems – systems not so bound in a self-referencing,
nearly psychotic death dance – meaning is derived and ascribed along different lines" (307). On the academy's obsession with language, she points out
that "western minds have supposed (wrongly) for some time that language
is culture and that without a separate language a culture is defunct" (308).
On the alleged politicalness of all human reality, she states: "In the world of
the patriarchs everything is about politics; for much of the rest of the world,
politics occupies little if any part of our preoccupations" (310).

As Paula Gunn Allen's challenges make clear, multiculturalism does not
consist of simply gathering various cultural expressions together under the
interpretive control of dominant-cultural paradigms. Multiculturalism, approached in the spirit of genuinely wishing to understand how different
people define, create, accept, and inhabit different cultural realities, is a
difficult and often threatening – even painful – undertaking that involves
opening ourselves intellectually and emotionally to various and frequently
conflicting cultural premises, practices, and values. How to do so in a way
that does not reproduce the existing power structure and yet deals with the
ways in which that power structure affects all of us is a basic question. The
task requires not only a new canon but also substantial new knowledge and
a significantly new pedagogy, both in theory and in practice.

When I apply these concerns to the question of how to expand the canon
of American realism, five models for the new construction of literary study
– suggested by Paula Gunn Allen, Henry Louis Gates, Jr., Paul Lauter,
Annette Kolodny, and Renato Rosaldo – strike me as particularly useful.

Allen advocates the obvious – starting over.

> Perhaps the best course is to begin anew, to examine the literary output of
> American writers of whatever stripe and derive critical principles based on
> what is actually being rendered by the true experts, the writers themselves.
> While we're at it, we might take a look at the real America that most of us
> inhabit – the one seldom approached by denizens of the hallowed (or is it

hollow?) groves of academe – so that we can discover what is being referenced beyond abstractions familiar to establishment types but foreign to those who live in real time. I am suggesting a critical system that is founded on the principle of inclusion rather than on that of exclusion, on actual human society and relationships rather than on textual relations alone, a system that is soundly based on aesthetics that pertain to the literatures we wish to examine. (309)

Allen's advice, for me, means building a definition of American realism not simply on William Dean Howells's famous prescriptions for realists, grounded as they are in white, middle-class ideas about what is ordinary, common, and representative of the lives of actual men and women in the United States, but also on Charles Chesnutt's articulations of what it means as an African American writer to try to render "reality"; Zitkala-Ša's definition of Sioux reality in *Old Indian Legends,* as well as her representation of mixed cultural realities in her autobiographical writing; and Sui Sin Far's fictional and autobiographical definitions of the "real" from her particular Chinese American point of view. In other words, to follow Allen's advice and start over with a truly heterogeneous set of writers, works, and life conditions is to arrive at a new conceptualization of American realism as a multiple rather than a unitary phenomenon, American realism as American realisms.

Allen's concept of foregrounding writers rather than preconceived inherited theories about American literature is echoed in Henry Louis Gates's recommendation that we think of American literature as a conversation among authors; Paul Lauter's suggestion that we construct American literary study on a comparativist model; and Annette Kolodny's proposal that we relocate American literary inquiry onto what she identifies as frontiers, borderland sites.[14] Gates, recognizing that debates about canonicity and American literature are really about "the twin problematic of canon formation and nation formation," says, "it is time for scholars to think of a comparative American culture as a conversation among different voices – even if it is a conversation that some of us were not able to join until very recently" (300). Lauter, referring to the metaphorical use of "mainstream" as "the Great River theory of American letters," argues that the model itself is the problem. It "presents variations from the mainstream as abnormal, deviant, lesser, perhaps ultimately unimportant. That kind of standard is no more helpful in the study of culture than is a model, in the study of gender differences, in which the male is considered the norm, or than paradigms, in the study of minority or ethnic social organization and behavior, based on Anglo-American society. What we need, rather, is to pose a comparative model for the study of American literature" (1). Kolodny, inviting us to think of the ways in which cultural differences meet, retain their separateness, and yet engage in exchange at those human boundaries we call frontiers, focuses on Hispanic and Anglo-American encounters but also invokes an imagined moment in turn-of-the-century United States history: "the crush of languages and cultures on a single day at Ellis Island in 1905." She says: "The texts that attempt to delineate these frontier moments – like the literary histories generated to accommodate them – will tell many different stories. . . . The singular identities and unswerving continuities that Americanists have regularly claimed for our literary history are no longer credible" (13).

Each of these models posits multiplicity of perspective as the premise – the governing idea – for the study of American literature. Also, all these scholars – Allen, Gates, Lauter, Kolodny – caution against reinscribing a patriarchal white model by talking in terms of centers, margins, others, subversions, and re-visions, as if, again, all cultural expression finally can do nothing but revolve around the great white western Center.

An undeniable difficulty in adopting such models is the threat that radical change poses to us as teachers. Who can possibly know everything that needs to be known if we have to become Americanist comparativists? One answer, Renato Rosaldo suggests, speaking of cultural studies in general, is that we *won't* know everything. Our authority as professors will change, and with it the character of our pedagogy and the dynamic of the classroom. As Rosaldo puts it, we already teach in a world classroom, which means that our authority as teachers is not what it was even a decade ago. Who among us can be Asian, African, lesbian, European, working-class, male, female, and of mixed blood, all on different days of the week or different parts of the hour? The question is how to teach when we cannot know, either through experience or training, everything – cannot be the complete authority.[15]

Obviously, multiculturalism means that faculty members have to commit themselves to lifelong continuing education in cultures other than their own – a situation different only in focus, not kind, from what is expected now. Also, it is already the case that graduate education is changing and that a younger generation, as has always been true, will be more skillful at performing what the emerging new project requires than their elders. But another part of the answer lies in a changed classroom, one where group exploration, team teaching, admission of the limits of one's own current knowledge, and encouragement of targeted serious research at the undergraduate level will represent the norm rather than the exception. Creating this kind of classroom without abrogating responsibility as the person paid and trusted to be knowledgeable and in charge *and* without exploiting students who happen to be members of culture groups to which the professor does not belong are key issues.

II

For a glimpse of the kind of canon that a multicultural construction of American realism opens up, let me juxtapose four of the texts on my syllabus: *Mrs. Spring Fragrance* (1912), "The Yellow Wallpaper" (1892), *The Conjure Woman* (1899), and *Old Indian Legends* (1901).[16] Others could be used, but these four work well in providing a broad range of cultural perspectives within a short time frame. (Although the book was published in 1912, many of the stories in Sui Sin Far's volume were written and published in the 1890s.) Since some of these texts and their authors may be unfamiliar, I will give brief biographies.

Sui Sin Far was the first Chinese American writer to publish serious fiction in the United States about Chinese American life. Born in 1865 and also known as Edith Eaton, she was one of fourteen children. Her father was English and her mother Chinese. She grew up in Canada and then, as an adult, supported herself as a single woman by working as a stenographer, reporter, and magazine-fiction writer, traveling and living in Canada, the Caribbean, and the United States, where she settled in Seattle for ten years. Because her appearance was not obviously Asian, she could have "passed" for white. She chose, however, to identify herself as Chinese American, despite the racist persecution consequent upon that choice, as she explains in her autobiographical essay, "Leaves from the Mental Portfolio of a Eurasian" (1909). Her only published book, *Mrs. Spring Fragrance,* appeared two years before her death in 1914; it is a collection of thirty-seven stories divided into two sections, the second of which is intended for children. The stories for adults take place in Chinese American communities and display a wide array of plots, issues, and characters, ranging from fictions that dramatize interactions between white Americans and Chinese Americans to fictions solely about relationships and issues within the Asian American community.[17]

Charlotte Perkins Gilman, born in 1860 and descended from the famous Beecher family, grew up in a repressive, white Protestant, middle-class household in New England. Her father abandoned his wife and children while Charlotte was young, leaving her mother bitter and impoverished; and, as an adult, Gilman found her own first marriage and experience of motherhood psychologically devastating. She suffered such severe, incapacitating mental breakdowns that she underwent treatment by the renowned rest-cure physician Dr. S. Weir Mitchell, which nearly drove her permanently insane. After divorcing and giving up her daughter to the child's father, she remarried, but had no more children and devoted her life to writing and speaking about women's rights. Best known for her short story "The Yellow Wallpaper," her book-length feminist analysis *Women and Economics* (1898), and her feminist utopia *Herland* (1915), Gilman, who died in 1935, dedicated her life to the cause of white middle-class feminism and became one of the leading theorists of the era. She published more than a thousand essays, in addition to writing poetry, novels, and short stories.[18]

Charles Waddell Chesnutt was born in 1858 in Cleveland, Ohio, to free black parents who had moved north from Fayetteville, North Carolina. Although the family returned to Fayetteville when Charles was eight, as an adult he moved his own family back to Cleveland in 1884. A member of the bar, Chesnutt's real ambition was to make his living as a writer, and with his short story "The Goophered Grapevine" in 1887 he became the first African American author to be published in the *Atlantic Monthly*. In 1899, by invitation of the publisher, he collected seven of his stories in *The Conjure Woman,* his first book. It was followed that same year by *The Wife of His Youth and Other Stories of the Color Line* and then three novels, *The House Behind the Cedars* (1900), *The Marrow of Tradition* (1901), and *The Colonel's Dream* (1905). Chesnutt's books sold poorly, which meant that, although he continued to publish occasionally, he could not make a living as a writer. In 1928, four years before his death, he was honored by the National Association for the Advancement of Colored People with the prestigious Springarn Medal.[19]

Zitkala-Ša, also known by her English name, Gertrude Bonnin, was born on the Pine Ridge Indian Reservation in 1876. Her mother was Yankton Sioux; her father, a white man, left the family. When she was eight, Zitkala-Ša persuaded her mother to let her go away to a missionary school for Indians in Wabash, Indiana, a traumatic experience that she chronicled in her autobiographical piece for the *Atlantic Monthly* in 1900, "Impressions of an Indian Childhood." Yet when she returned to the reservation from Indiana, Zitkala-Ša found herself so changed that she was unable to resume the life she had left; after a few years, she departed again, this time for Earlham College in Indiana, and then, because she was an accomplished violinist, the Boston Conservatory of Music. Zitkala-Ša published two books, *Old Indian Legends* (1901) and *American Indian Stories* (1921).

Her primary dedication was to Indian rights activism, however, and she devoted her life to public speaking, lobbying, and political advocacy. In 1926 she founded the National Council of American Indians; also, her labor contributed to the passage of the Indian Citizenship Bill. When she died in 1938, she was buried in Arlington National Cemetery in Washington, D.C.[20]

To group Sui Sin Far's *Mrs. Spring Fragrance,* Charlotte Perkins Gilman's "The Yellow Wallpaper," Charles Chesnutt's *The Conjure Woman,* and Zitkala-Ša's *Old Indian Legends* is to interrogate the very category "American realism." Although produced at about the same time and for much the same purpose – namely, to reach and affect the thinking of a hostile (or at the very least ignorant), conventional, white, educated readership, a readership such as that served by the *Atlantic Monthly* – each of these texts constitutes and employs realism in radically different ways from the others.

Mrs. Spring Fragrance, like many other texts at the turn of the century – W. E. B. Du Bois's *The Souls of Black Folk* (1903), Sarah Orne Jewett's *The Country of the Pointed Firs* (1896), Alice Dunbar-Nelson's *The Goodness of St. Rocque* (1899), Hamlin Garland's *Main-Travelled Roads* (1891) – is a communally focused, coherent, long narrative composed of collected stories. They can be read randomly as individual short stories, but the book can also be read straight through as a composite long fiction. Thus the effect of the work as a whole, even simply at this mechanical formal level, is to send a complex message about the relationship between individual and collective identity. Each individual's story is important; yet by the end no one individual's story can be said to be more important than another's. The emergent group focus, in addition to showing that the book's stories were written at different times for different magazines, implies an aesthetic and a definition of realism that privilege community and place the issue of culture itself at the center of narrative.

Filled with characters who embody distinctly diverse cultural perspectives – immigrant Chinese, native-born white American, many versions of Chinese American – *Mrs. Spring Fragrance* explores life in North America from a range of Asian American perspectives. The book is organized by no single protagonist's experience or point of view. We are asked to think about immigration, deportation, detention centers, feminism, marriage, art, love, language, clothing, social class, child-rearing, education, nationality, and internationality from multiple perspectives, seeing how an issue looks to a new immigrant in contrast to an "Americanized" inhabitant of Chinatown as opposed to a Caucasian American, all the time with age and gender entering the equation as well. Indeed, this is an ideal text to which to bring

Kolodny's concept of interpretive "frontiers," for it is composed of constantly shifting and frequently interfacing cultural perspectives, often in
conflict with each other. Multiplicity of viewpoint drives Mrs. *Spring Fragrance,* whose very subject is cultural relations. As Sui Sin Far has Mrs.
Spring Fragrance announce early in the book: "'Many American women
wrote books. Why should not a Chinese? She would write a book about
Americans for her Chinese women friends. The American people were so
interesting and mysterious.'" Lest we miss the flipped stereotype, Sui Sin
Far has Mrs. Spring Fragrance repeat, "'Ah, these Americans! These mysterious, inscrutable, incomprehensible Americans! Had I the divine right of
learning I would put them into an immortal book!'"[21] Attacking – and
sometimes reinforcing – stereotypes, Mrs. *Spring Fragrance* enacts cultural
clash in the United States. It is about the pain and struggle – and occasional
joy – of dealing with generational, racial, sexual, and cultural conflicts, all
within a dominant power structure set up to discriminate against people
who are not of European descent.

In contrast, "The Yellow Wallpaper," which Horace Scudder of the *Atlantic Monthly* rejected as too horrible and depressing to print, focuses narrowly on white upper-middle-class, feminine reality, which it locates – ap-
propriately – deep within one single, locked, hyperdomestic room. Gilman's
setting is the exaggeratedly privatized world of the genteel Victorian family. This environment is insular and male-dominated; literally cut off from
the public, commercial realm of open social exchange; scientifically ratio-
nalized (the authority figure is literally a physician); secretly and sadistically
violent (the paraphernalia of torture and imprisonment masquerade as nurs-
ery trappings); and organized by a bourgeois division of labor based on
formal servitude (there are two women in the story, one a privileged wife,
the other her servant). As with Mrs. *Spring Fragrance,* here too the narrative
form beautifully reflects and is the product of the cultural values it exam-
ines. Whereas Sui Sin Far's book is multiple and diverse both conceptually
and structurally, Gilman's story is very tightly aimed and unified. Its form
stages the private, secret, individual consciousness of its female narrator/
protagonist. As readers we enter this single mind, which is, at bottom, what
the story is about: experiencing the inside of one person's mind, the interior
life of one representative but highly individualistic, privileged, white woman
who is being forcibly held and reindoctrinated into a suffocating Victorian
ethic of decorous, dependent femininity. The aesthetic employed and en-
joyed, like the cultural reality the story reflects but is also produced by,
locates pleasure and meaning in the exercise of individual, isolated, autonomous intellect. That is, Gilman's story about cultural oppression – about

white patriarchal subjugation of women – attacks western patriarchal values at the same time that it endorses a modern, patriarchal, Eurocentric definition of mental health and creative genius which places a premium on the solitary, individualistic expression of human intelligence.

The Conjure Woman, in contrast, reflects and is generated by an emphatically *un*-unitary but instead complexly dual cultural consciousness, similar to that expressed by Chesnutt's famous compatriot W. E. B. Du Bois in his metaphor of the Veil in *The Souls of Black Folk* (1903). The seven tales comprising Chesnutt's book perform the clash between European American and African American cultures in the United States. Every tale begins with a frame story which, almost to the letter, reproduces the patriarchal white Anglo-Saxon Protestant culture pictured by Gilman, right down to centrally figuring a "sick" privileged wife, Annie, who is cared for by her ultrarational, successful, power-focused husband, John. Interacting with these two is Julius, an old rural Southern black man who bonds with and heals Annie and skillfully manipulates John, managing to keep for himself a healthy measure of economic and narrative control despite the white man's power. These envelope-narratives detailing the power struggle between Julius and John with Annie on the sidelines frame the book's seven conjure tales, which are inherited, oral, African American stories. Told by Julius, they constitute a significantly different realism from that contained in the frame stories.

In Julius's inner tales people change into animals and back again into people; a person can inhabit a tree, and then the wood sawn from it; a man can grow young and old with the seasons year after year. The power to make such things happen belongs to conjure women and men, powerful black people whose cultural heritage is African. For John, a successful white man, these tales are nonsense. For Annie, in contrast, they are compelling; she responds to the way Julius's stories define slavery from an African American perspective, and she is tempted to believe in their "magic." For us as readers able to hear all three characters, Julius, John, and Annie, there is yet a third rhetorical situation. The book's inner and outer tales set up a constant, complex, cultural dialogue – literally a conversation, to recall Gates's term – about the cultural construction of realism. The frame stories, we have no doubt, are "realism." After all, they mimic the economic, psychological, sociological, and historical "facts" of race relations, racism, and racial resistance in the United States as they are often represented. But what about the inner tales? *Is* conjure "realism"? Obviously, modern western wisdom – witness Chesnutt's white man, John – says no. But African and African American wisdom – the wisdom at work in the traditional tales – says otherwise. Conjure exists; it happens. Mysterious metaphysical powers that defy western reason inhabit the universe; and certain people have access to those powers, whether white people can accept it or not.[22] As Julius observes: " 'I don't know if you believes in conjure or not. Some of the white folks don't.' "[23] Camouflaged in downhome, nonthreatening, black dialect designed to make Chesnutt's tales appear no different from white Plantation School ditties, *The Conjure Woman* is a radical text. It asserts that an Afrocentric cultural reality not only exists in the United States but has actual power. In the final (Afrocentric) analysis, it is Julius's conjure, not modern science's medicine, that heals Annie.

Old Indian Legends makes an equally radical choice. It presents a single cultural reality, which is Sioux. Although the book exists in print and is written in English, it claims a place in Anglo-derived United States literature for a Native American, which is to say, a nonwestern, work of art. And Zitkala-Ša makes that claim in full awareness of her narratives' prior and prime identity on the North American continent. As she states in her preface: "I have tried to transplant the native spirit of these tales – root and all – into the English language, since America in the last few centuries has acquired a second tongue."[24]

Everything about *Old Indian Legends* challenges standard academic notions about American realism. Its announced, intended audience of children says that it cannot be "serious" literature (even though *Huckleberry Finn,* of course, is); and this announcement is reinforced by Zitkala-Ša's simplicity of language and presentation, her main characters' embodiment as animals, and the protagonist's identity as trickster – all of which distance and confuse the reader taught to expect and admire Henry James. Most disorienting, perhaps, is the complete, uncommented-upon absence of white people in *Old Indian Legends* – and with them the complete absence of any Judeo-Christian frame of reference. How do western-trained readers read this book? As Arnold Krupat, addressing the issue of academic critical methodology and Native American texts, points out, "Native American cultural production is based upon a profound wisdom that is most certainly different from a Western, rationalistic, scientist, secular perspective."[25] This leads me (despite Krupat's argument to the contrary) to try different ways of proceeding, ways that bring into the classroom oral and communal experiences of literature in addition to individual, analytic thinking.

Certainly, it is important to contextualize *Old Indian Legends* by providing conventional academic lectures and discussions that focus on Sioux culture and history, including, in particular, information about the Massacre at Wounded Knee, which occurred just eleven years before Zitkala-Ša's book and must have exerted a major influence on her decision to issue a

collection of traditional tales. Also, because the subject has been so neglected, in most United States classrooms some formal lecturing is necessary
to introduce students to the activity of thinking seriously about Native
American literary traditions, values, and aesthetic principles.[26] Still, a text
such as *Old Indian Legends* demands more than just intellectualizing. Without falling into sentimental, bogus attempts to "be" Indian, the approach to
this text needs, in some way, to stretch students' awareness. In representing
Sioux reality independent of European presence, *Old Indian Legends* asserts
a cultural integrity and strength – an indestructableness – which stands at
the very core of this book's realism. Iktomi the trickster constantly changes
shapes, plans, plots, roles, locations, faces, bodies, jokes, schemes, fates, and
futures. But all of this contradictoriness coheres in one created principle
within one complex universe that embraces – weblike – all worlds, visible
and invisible. Artistic principles of repetition, laughter, silence, orality, and
cyclicness reinforce Zitkala-Ša's realism of multivocal creational wholeness
and continuity, a realism both reflected in and productive of this book. To
try to open ourselves to some of this fullness, I have my class read a tale out
loud, and then I ask all the students to commit one story to memory, using
their own words but sticking close to Zitkala-Ša's telling. We then spend
time in class storytelling – *not* a high-status activity in the academy – which
leads us to reflect on which details got lost, why we are poor storytellers, the
relation between oral and printed forms, the structure of education in the
modern West, the reality embodied by Iktomi, and the realism of animals
and human beings exchanging form. Also, it might be worth mentioning,
before we start the book I give a quiz. The first question is: As you look at
the door in our room, what direction on the earth are you facing? The
second is: What time did the sun rise this morning?

To close by returning to Paul Lauter's recommendation that we use a comparativist approach to American literature: What is gained and what is lost
in adopting a multicultural definition of American realism? Lost is the high
degree of security and even comfort, not to mention tidiness, that a traditionally constructed Anglo-oriented canon offered many of us. I no longer
can present my students with a relatively uncomplicated, coherent, linear
story about United States prose fiction in the second half of the nineteenth
and the beginning of the twentieth centuries. The cultural line I once taught,
running unbroken from Henry James and Mark Twain through William
Dean Howells, Stephen Crane, Frank Norris, Charlotte Perkins Gilman,
Kate Chopin, Theodore Dreiser, Edith Wharton, Upton Sinclair, Willa Cather, and Sherwood Anderson (with, perhaps, James Weldon Johnson thrown

in for diversity), had the virtue of being very manageable and teachable. Except for trying to get students to think historically, the class could move smoothly through the semester, tracing variations on repeated themes.

Such a monocultural canon, however, does not begin to capture the multiplicity of cultural perspectives that literary production of the period – evincing what Warner Berthoff wisely called a ferment – brought into being. A multicultural canon yields no unified story about realism. Philosophically and artistically, the realism of *Old Indian Legends* clashes with the realism of "The Yellow Wallpaper" or *Mrs. Spring Fragrance,* two works that, in turn, contrast strongly (though not entirely) with each other. At the same time, *Old Indian Legends* shares some strong affinities with *The Conjure Woman,* both of which, for example, insist on the reality of conjure and interspecies transformations. In short, a multicultural construction of American realism does reveal sharp, fundamental disjunctions: Henry James and Anzia Yezierska, Edith Wharton and Sui Sin Far, Pauline Hopkins and Frank Norris. But it also generates provocative new links and connections: *Daisy Miller, Of One Blood,* and *The Autobiography of an Ex-Colored Man,* on the "international theme"; *Mrs. Spring Fragrance, O Pioneers!* and *Hungry Hearts,* on immigrant experience; *Old Indian Legends, The Conjure Woman,* and *The Custom of the Country,* on tricksters; *Iola Leroy, The Awakening,* and "The Vine-Leaf," on women's liberation. Most important, as Martha Banta eloquently argues in "Melting the Snows of Yesteryear; or, All Those Years of a White Girl Trying to Get it Right," an expanded canon looks, little by little, more like America.[27] A multicultural canon contains the cultural range, complexity, conflict, and contradictions of the nation itself. As Jules Chametzky has pointed out, the melting-pot theory of the United States was contested from its very beginning late in the nineteenth century. There has never been "an" American culture. "There *is* only . . . now as 'then' only *contention,* struggle, unmaking and making, discovery and invention, loss and gain."[28] Expanding the canon of American realism creates a canon that represents that contention.

NOTES

1 Amy Kaplan, *The Social Construction of American Realism* (Chicago: University of Chicago Press, 1988), p. 5.
2 Ibid., p. 6.
3 "Editors' Comment," 25 (1992): 1.
4 Robert Scholes, "Canonicity and Textuality," *Introduction to Scholarship in Modern Languages and Literatures,* ed. Joseph Gibaldi (New York: Modern Language Association of America, 1992), p. 147.

5 Robert Hemenway, "In the American Canon," *Redefining American Literary History,* ed. A. LaVonne Brown Ruoff and Jerry W. Ward, Jr. (New York: Modern Language Association of America, 1990), p. 63.

6 For a similar argument, see Hemenway, who advocates incorporation of African American literature into all literature classes (pp. 63–72).

7 Henry Louis Gates, Jr., "Pluralism and Its Discontents," *Profession 92,* ed. Phyllis Franklin (New York: Modern Language Association of America, 1992), p. 38.

8 John Brenkman, "Multiculturalism and Criticism," *English Inside and Out: The Place of Literary Criticism; Essays from the 50th Anniversary of the English Institute,* ed. Susan Gubar and Jonathan Kamholtz (New York: Routledge, 1993), p. 88.

9 Gates, *Profession 92,* p. 37.

10 Brenkman, pp. 94, 96.

11 Paula Gunn Allen, " 'Border' Studies: The Intersection of Gender and Color," *Introduction to Scholarship,* p. 304.

12 I take the concept "master narrative," of course, from Frederic Jameson, *The Political Unconscious: Narrative as a Socially Symbolic Act* (Ithaca, N.Y.: Cornell University Press, 1981).

13 The Latin Americanist Francine Masiello similarly argues against the global application of western high theory, with its presumption that abstract, translatable constructs exist that can validly be employed anywhere. In Masiello's view, the academy must attend to and learn from the theory of local people (in her case, people living in Latin America), which is in her opinion embedded irretrievably in particular histories, languages, and local contexts. Untitled paper, Modern Language Association Convention, New York, 1992.

14 Henry Louis Gates, Jr., " 'Ethnic and Minority' Studies," *Introduction to Scholarship,* pp. 288–302; Paul Lauter, "The Literatures of America: A Comparative Discipline," *Redefining American Literary History,* pp. 9–34 (also see Lauter, *Canons and Contexts* [New York: Oxford University Press, 1991]); Annette Kolodny, "Letting Go Our Grand Obsessions: Notes Toward a New Literary History of the American Frontiers," *American Literature.* 64 (1992): 1–18.

15 Renato Rosaldo, untitled paper, Modern Language Association Convention, New York, 1992.

16 For other discussions that proceed similarly, see Lauter's comparativist treatment of Henry James and Charles Chesnutt in "The Literatures of America"; or, broadening the field of vision dramatically, Marilyn Sanders Mobley's excellent study, *Folk Roots and Mythic Wings in Sarah Orne Jewett and Toni Morrison: The Cultural Function of Narrative* (Baton Rouge: Louisiana State University Press, 1991); or my book, *Conflicting Stories: American Women Writers at the Turn into the Twentieth Century* (New York: Oxford University Press, 1991).

17 For extended discussion, see Amy Ling, *Between Worlds: Women Writers of Chinese Ancestry* (New York: Pergamon, 1990); also, I discuss Sui Sin Far in *Conflicting Stories* and in "The New Woman as Cultural Symbol and Social Reality: Six Women Writers' Perspectives," *1915, The Cultural Moment,* ed. Adele Heller and Lois Rudnick (New Brunswick, N.J.: Rutgers University Press, 1991), pp. 82–97. Although *Mrs. Spring Fragrance* does not exist in paperback,

the University of Illinois Press is issuing one, along with a book-length critical biography of Sui Sin Far by Annette White-Parks. Until then, individual stories and the autobiographical essay, "Leaves," can be found in two accessible paperback anthologies: *The Heath Anthology of American Literature*, vol. 2, ed. Paul Lauter et al. (Lexington, Mass.: D. C. Heath, 1990), and *American Women Regionalists, 1850–1910*, ed. Judith Fetterley and Marjorie Pryse (New York: W. W. Norton, 1992).

18 For representative discussions of Gilman, see Ann Lane, *To Herland and Beyond: The Life and Work of Charlotte Perkins Gilman* (New York: Pantheon Books, 1990); Susan S. Lanser, "Feminist Criticism, 'The Yellow Wallpaper,' and the Politics of Color in America," *Feminist Studies* 15 (1989): 415–41; and my chapter on Gilman in *Conflicting Stories*.

19 Excellent discussions of Chesnutt can be found in William L. Andrews, *The Literary Career of Charles W. Chesnutt* (Baton Rouge: Louisiana State University Press, 1980); and Houston A. Baker, Jr., *Modernism and the Harlem Renaissance* (Chicago: University of Chicago Press, 1987). Also, the biography written by Chesnutt's daughter, Helen M. Chesnutt, remains an important source: *Charles Waddell Chesnutt: Pioneer of the Color Line* (Chapel Hill: University of North Carolina Press, 1952).

20 Little scholarship on Zitkala-Ša exists. See Dexter Fisher, "Zitkala-Ša: The Evolution of a Writer," *American Indian Quarterly* 5 (1979): 229–38.

21 Sui Sin Far, *Mrs. Spring Fragrance* (Chicago: A. C. McClurg & Co., 1912), pp. 22, 31.

22 For two excellent relevant studies, see Henry Louis Gates, Jr., *The Signifying Monkey: A Theory of Afro-American Literary Criticism* (New York: Oxford University Press, 1988), and Lawrence W. Levine, *Black Culture and Black Consciousness: Afro-American Folk Thought from Slavery to Freedom* (New York: Oxford University Press, 1977).

23 Charles Chesnutt, *The Conjure Woman* (1899; rpt. Ann Arbor: University of Michigan Press, 1969), p. 11.

24 Zitkala-Ša, *Old Indian Legends* (1901; rpt. Lincoln: University of Nebraska Press, 1985), p. vi.

25 Arnold Krupat, *The Voice in the Margin: Native American Literature and the Canon* (Berkeley and Los Angeles: University of California Press, 1989), p. 14.

26 Among the many useful books on the subject designed for teachers are Houston A. Baker, Jr., ed., *Three American Literatures: Essays in Chicano, Native American, and Asian-American Literature for Teachers of American Literature* (New York: Modern Language Association of America, 1982); Paula Gunn Allen, ed., *Studies in American Indian Literature: Critical Essays and Course Designs* (New York: Modern Language Association of America, 1983); and A. LaVonne Brown Ruoff, *American Indian Literatures: An Introduction, Bibliographic Review, and Selected Bibliography* (New York: Modern Language Association of America, 1990).

27 Martha Banta, unpublished paper, Modern Language Association Convention, New York, 1992.

28 Jules Chametzky, "Beyond Melting Pots, Cultural Pluralism, Ethnicity – or, Deja Vu All Over Again," *MELUS* 16 (1989–90): 13.

PART THREE

Case studies

5

JOHN W. CROWLEY

The Portrait of a Lady and *The Rise of Silas Lapham:* The Company They Kept

The company they kept, very often, was each other. Henry James and William Dean Howells first met in 1866, at Cambridge, Massachusetts. Howells was the newly hired assistant editor of the *Atlantic Monthly,* the organ of New England's literary dominance. James was a promising young writer, six years Howells's junior, whose stories had begun to appear in the magazine, thanks in large part to the advocacy of the assistant editor. From 1866 until James departed for Europe in 1869, the two men were nearly inseparable companions. In a public letter on the occasion of Howells's seventy-fifth birthday, James paid tribute to the "frankness and sweetness" of Howells's hospitality and the inspiration of his sympathy during their Cambridge years. "You showed me the way and opened me the door," he recalled; "you wrote to me, and confessed yourself struck with me – I have never forgotten the beautiful thrill of *that.*"[1] As Howells remembered, in an essay left unfinished at his death in 1920, "We seem to have been presently always together, and always talking of methods of fiction, whether we walked the streets by day or night, or we sat together reading our stuff to each other."[2]

In one of their long talks, according to Howells, he and James "settled the true principles of literary art."[3] It is tempting to imagine that this particular dialogue culminated in a pact between these ambitious young men, eager to beard their literary elders and to assert their own originality in a mutually supportive fashion. It might have gone something like this:

> "Well, my dear Howells, the Civil War, to which a horrid even if an obscure hurt made me a bystander – and you too, for that matter – is gloriously over; and the time is ripe for a new literary movement, since future literary historians will seize, inevitably, upon the convenience of using our wars to discriminate our literary periods."
>
> "We both know, so much better than our untraveled contemporaries, that 'realism' is the next thing."
>
> "It's the rage in France, of course."

"What's needed, my dear James, is an *American* realism; that's the way to go!"

"So let us beautifully have an understanding, just between us. We can divide the territory so that we don't trammel each other. I'll take Americans in Europe – let's call it –"

"What about 'the international novel'?"

"Yes, that's fetching. And you can take Americans at home."

"We'll boost one another in reviews."

"Realism will supplant romance –"

"And both of us – or you, at least – will be famous forever!"

Even if it didn't happen quite this way, Howells and James have often been regarded as cofounders of the movement for "realism" that is seen to have dominated American literature after the Civil War.

The term *realism* is sometimes used these days – in the wake of literary theory and its transformation of the literary-academic complex – with a certain trepidation. Realism, after all, has been charged by some advocates of poststructuralism with various crimes against humanity, not least of which is allegedly brainwashing captive readers with the very idea that humanity (as opposed to "humanity") exists! Interrogated, as they say, under the thousand-watt glare of a (supposedly) liberating critique, realism has been exposed as an insidious agent of the capitalist–imperialist– bourgeois hegemony. Through such timely intervention, a program of reeducation has now been installed, and realism has been duly resituated; shown, that is, to be relative to the ideological formations of particular Western cultures in different periods.

Within the context of "American literature" (which itself may be unmasked as a discursive artifact), the kind of writing with which Howells and James were affiliated has borne several different labels. As Donald Pease suggests, what was known as "realism" in the late nineteenth century and as "critical realism" early in this century was refashioned during the 1950s into "American literary realism," a "subfield within American studies that developed out of collective interest in the ways in which literary conventions produced 'realistic' effects." Howellsian "realism," in particular, has been variously re(de)constructed (but invariably denigrated) by successive critical movements: "Progressivists found it reactionary, modernists believed it banal, formalists criticized it as unliterary, deconstructivists exposed its mystifications, feminists censured its masculinism, and new historicists have demystified Howells's realism as a romance."[4]

One speaks of realism at all, then, at some peril. For purposes of this essay, however, let us understand that the term has limited reference to the kind of fiction both written and critically championed by Howells during the quarter-century from *Their Wedding Journey* (1872) to *The Landlord at Lion's Head* (1897), respectively his first realistic novel and his last major realistic novel. Although Howells continued to produce realism during the last two decades of his career, his best work moved closer to romance as it became more and more psychological and nonrepresentational. As for James, it should be recognized that he neither began nor ended his career as a realist. Rather, as Alfred Habegger points out, "James was a realist for a time – roughly 1876 (*Roderick Hudson*) to 1890 (*The Tragic Muse*)."[5] *The Portrait of a Lady* (1881) and *The Rise of Silas Lapham* (1885) represent, then, the highest degree of James's and Howells's commitment to the idea that realism embodies "the true principles of literary art."

The principles of realism, which each writer would articulate somewhat differently, derived from their common experience as Americans abroad. Throughout his peripatetic education, James had been steeped in European literature, especially French fiction. Howells, an autodidact in several languages, served four years as American consul to Venice during the Civil War; and the success of his Italian travel writing paved the way for his triumphal rise from rural Ohio to the seat of American letters.

James's fiction, in Howells's view, expressed an "alien quality and circumstance" reflective of its author's European immersion ("The American James," 398). This formative experience, Howells argued in his review of *A Passionate Pilgrim* (1875), meant "the loss of that tranquil indifference to Europe" characteristic of their "untraveled" compatriots. "The American who has known Europe much can never again see his country with the single eye of his old ante-European days. For good or for evil, the light of the Old World is always on her face; and his fellow-countrymen have their shadows cast by it." Such awareness, Howells believed, took the form of either "refinement" or "anxiety." He detected both in James's work, adding that "he is able to confront his people with situations impossible here, and you fancy in him a mistrust of such mechanism as the cis-Atlantic world can offer the romancer."[6]

Was James a "romancer" or a "realist"? These terms entered early into James's and Howells's mutual criticism as each tried to pull the other in a slightly different direction, even as both agreed they were fellow travelers at heart. Before discussing *The Portrait of a Lady* and *The Rise of Silas Lapham*, produced when Howells and James had reached their full maturity as writers, it is worth examining their earlier readings of one another for signs of a formative rhetoric of realism.

In a review of *A Foregone Conclusion* (1875), James marveled at Howells's ability to score a popular success without appeasing "that great majority of people who prefer to swallow their literature without tasting." Howells's earlier novel, *A Chance Acquaintance* (1872), had been "very maliciously contrived," James thought, to "hit the happy medium." Howells had managed "at once to give his book a loose enough texture to let the more simply-judging kind fancy they were looking at a vivid fragment of social history itself, and yet to infuse it with a lurking artfulness which should endear it to the initiated." Now, in *A Foregone Conclusion*, Howells displayed the artfulness of the "cabinet-picture" or the painted "miniature": every stroke "plays its definite part, though sometimes the eye needs to linger a moment to perceive it." In particular, he had achieved a mastery of characterization, of bringing recognizable Americans fully to life despite the Venetian setting. More remarkable still was his portrait of Don Ippolito, a disaffected priest. Although "Italians have been, from Mrs. Radcliffe down, among the stock-properties of romance," Don Ippolito transcended the stereotypes of the "romancer's art."[7]

Present in this early review are all the rudiments of realism as James and Howells would define it. Realism eschews the devices of romance, especially reliance on melodrama and exotic backgrounds. Realism seeks subtly to raise the taste of an unrefined audience while appealing to "initiated" readers capable of detecting artfulness, however "lurking." Realism depends on character rather than story for its effects. Realism values the particularity of ordinary life. Realism is ultimately a matter of *seeing* the world accurately. Writing of Howells in 1882, Thomas Sergeant Perry linked realism to the empirical method: "Just as the scientific spirit digs the ground from beneath superstition, so does its fellow-worker, realism, tend to prick the bubble of abstract types." Realism, declared Perry, is nothing less than "the tool of the democratic spirit, the modern spirit by means of which the truth is elicited."[8]

Although Howells identified many of the same literary qualities in James that James had ascribed to him, Howells also found his friend's work wanting in the democratic spirit. In his review of *A Passionate Pilgrim*, Howells noted that the artfulness of James was apparent in the construction of his stories, the drawing of his characters, and "the precision with which he fits the word to the thought." He attributed an "old-time stateliness" to James, a "certain weight of manner" that affiliated him with "the writers of an age when literature was a far politer thing than it is now." James's "reverent ideal of work" set him above contemporary writers of popular fiction, with their "latter-day sins of flippancy, slovenliness, and insincerity." But his rarefied literary ideals rubbed against the democratic grain of realism. Howells confessed a "whimsical doubt" whether James's sheer intelligence had not produced an unfortunate superiority of tone – an appeal "less to men and women in their mere humanity, than to a certain kind of cultivated people, who, well as they are in some ways, and indispensable as their appreciation is, are often a little narrow in their sympathies and poverty-stricken in the simple emotions" (*Discovery of a Genius,* 63–4, 74).

From the start of their careers, Howells and James recognized some important differences in each other's approach to the true art of fiction. Howells, for instance, differentiated the "more strictly romantic" or "purely romantic" tales in *A Passionate Pilgrim* ("The Romance of Certain Old Clothes," "The Last of the Valerii") from those with an admixture of realism; and he appreciated the romancer in James as much as he esteemed the realist. The result was such seemingly paradoxical formulations as: "The Madonna of the Future is almost as perfect a piece of work, in its way, as A Passionate Pilgrim. It is a more romantic conception than Madame de Mauves, and yet more real"; or, "Eugene Pickering is, like Madame de Mauves, one of those realistic subjects which we find less real than the author's romantic inspirations" (*Discovery of a Genius,* 64, 70–2).

What finally mattered to Howells was less the genre of James's fiction than its psychological acuity. James's realism consisted precisely in the verisimilitude of his characters, whose depth and roundedness were achieved by his rejecting the traditional primacy of story. As Howells wrote in 1879, in defense of *Daisy Miller,* "It is certainly evident that the author of Roderick Hudson and The American has not the genuine story-telling gift, the power of inventing a story interesting for its own sake. His talent lies in another field, that of keen observation and fine discrimination of character, which he portrays with a subtle and delicate touch."[9]

Howells reiterated this point in an 1882 essay on James that unexpectedly triggered the so-called Battle of the *Century* – a protracted exchange of polemical thrusts and parries between Howells, as champion of American realism, and British defenders of those revered English novelists at whose expense Howells had advanced his claim for James's artistic superiority.[10] Noting James's refusal to wrap up his novels neatly, Howells insisted that in this "new kind in fiction" the "pursuit and not the end . . . should give us pleasure." James left his portrait of Isabel Archer unfinished, for instance, because "it is the character, not the fate, of his people which occupies him; when he has fully developed their character he leaves them to what destiny the reader pleases." Analysis of character, which in *The Portrait of a Lady* might seem a "superabundance if it were not all such good literature," was for Howells the hallmark of the truly modern novel: "The novelist's main business is to possess his reader with a due conception of his characters and the situations in which they find themselves. If he does more or less than this he equally fails." James the "annalist, or analyst" represented the wave of the future insofar as he inspired younger American writers to imitate his methods; but whether the audience would "accept a novel which is an analytic study rather than a story" remained to be seen (*Discovery of a Genius*, 115–16, 121–2).

In this important essay, Howells never pinned the label of "realism" on James's work, for which he offered no name other than "his own way of storytelling – or call it character-painting if you prefer." On the contrary, he asserted that James was fundamentally a romancer: "Looking back to those early stories, where Mr. James stood at the dividing ways of the novel and the romance, I am sometimes sorry that he declared even superficially for the former. His best efforts seem to me those of romance; his best types have an ideal development. . . . But, doubtless, he has chosen wisely; perhaps the romance is an outworn form, and would not lend itself to the reproduction of even the ideality of modern life" (*Discovery of a Genius*, 122, 117–18). As Sarah B. Daugherty has suggested, "Henry James, Jr.," despite the way it was read by indignant British reviewers, was "no radical defense of realism but a thoughtful appraisal of a writer who had adapted Hawthorne's aesthetic to his own more skeptical point of view."[11]

Was James, then, *not* a realist? The key distinction for Howells was not between realism and romance, but rather between the novel and the romance. In Howells's view, James had no choice but to adopt the novel – since the romance had become "an outworn form" – but the Jamesian method inclined the novel toward the romance.[12] James's work was sui generis, after all. In a review of *The Tragic Muse* (1890), Howells asserted that "Henry James is not recognizable as anything else, and must be called a novelist because there is yet no name for the literary kind he has invented, and so none for the inventor."[13] Firing another fusillade in the Battle of the *Century,* Howells sardonically distinguished James the modern American from his reactionary British contemporaries:

> To spin a yarn for the yarn's sake, that is an ideal worthy of a nineteenth-century Englishman, doting in forgetfulness of the English masters and grovelling in ignorance of the Continental masters; but wholly impossible to an American of Mr. Henry James's modernity. To him it must seem like the lies swapped between men after the ladies have left the table and they are sinking deeper and deeper into their cups and growing dimmer and dimmer behind their cigars. To such a mind as his the story could never have value except as a means; it could not exist for him as an end; it could be used only

illustratively; it could be the frame, not possibly the picture.   (*Discovery of a Genius*, 165)

Although he agreed that character had rightly supplanted story in the modern novel, James thought that Howells showed far too little care in framing the picture. In an 1886 essay, written in reaction to "Henry James, Jr." and the controversy it had incited, James praised Howells's "work of observation, of patient and definite notation." There was no other novelist in English, he thought, whose work was "so exclusively a matter of painting what he sees, and who is so sure of what he sees." And the object of the novelist's eye, as Howells insisted in his own criticism, was "the common, the immediate, the familiar and vulgar elements of life." Howells, said James, "adores the real, the natural, the colloquial, the moderate, the optimistic, the domestic, and the democratic; looking askance at exceptions and perversities and superiorities, at surprising and incongruous phenomena in general."[14]

For James, Howellsian realism had two major limitations, however. First, although it grasped "a large part of the truth" – the optimistic truth of the American average – it blinked the darker elements: "If American life is on the whole . . . more innocent than that of any other country, nowhere is the fact more patent than in Mr. Howells's novels, which exhibit so constant a study of the actual and so small a perception of evil." Second, Howells's conviction that "style" mattered little in the novel led him to hold "composition too cheap" and to allow his work to become artistically unruly. Howells's fondness for the dramatic method was, moreover, all too keen: "a critical reader sometimes wishes, not that the dialogue might be suppressed (it is too good for that), but that it might be distributed, interspaced with narrative and pictorial matter. The author forgets sometimes to paint, to evoke the conditions and appearances, to build in the subject" ("William Dean Howells," 152–3, 155).

If the problem with James for Howells was an undemocratic detachment from "men and women in their mere humanity," then the problem with Howells for James was his obsession with surface details. It may be useful to think of Howellsian realism as resembling Madame Merle's theory of personal identity. As she tells Isabel Archer:

"When you have lived as long as I, you will see that every human being has his shell, and that you must take the shell into account. By the shell I mean the whole envelope of circumstances. There is no such thing as an isolated man or woman; we are each of us made up of a cluster of appurtenances. What do you call one's self? Where does it begin? Where does it end? It overflows into everything that belongs to us – and then it flows back again. I know that a large part of myself is in the dresses I choose to wear. I have a great respect for *things!* One's self – for other people – is one's expression of one's self; and one's house, one's clothes, the books one reads, the company one keeps – these things are all expressive."[15]

Jamesian realism, by contrast, has much in common with what Isabel opposes to Madame Merle's "metaphysical" analysis. Isabel advances instead a theory of personal identity that is redolent, as critics have often noted, of American transcendentalism:

"I don't agree with you. . . . I think just the other way. I don't know whether I succeed in expressing myself, but I know that nothing else expresses me. Nothing that belongs to me is any measure of me; on the contrary, it's a limit, a barrier, and a perfectly arbitrary one. Certainly, the clothes which, as you say, I choose to wear, don't express me; and heaven forbid they should!" (186–7)

The contrast between Howellsian realism and Jamesian realism is not absolute, however. In practice, both writers worked within and across the dialectic defined by the positions of Madame Merle and Isabel Archer; and although Howells gravitated toward the former's pole and James (at least in his earlier work) toward the latter's, neither novelist can be identified solely with either extreme.

Although their realism always centered on character, Howells and James differed in the extent of their reliance on external signs – the "cluster of appurtenances" – to represent character. In both *The Rise of Silas Lapham* and *The Portrait of a Lady*, the central figure first appears in a fully dramatized scene. But whereas the further development of Silas Lapham's character depends almost entirely on his speech and actions in other such scenes, the portrait of Isabel Archer emerges not only through the dramatic method, but also through direct commentary on her inner life and indirect narrative access to her consciousness.

As an example of Howells's technique, consider a passage from the opening chapter. Silas Lapham, in an interview with the newspaper reporter Bartley Hubbard, is defending his use of outdoor advertising – an increasingly common and controversial method of promoting consumer products:

"In less'n six months there wa'n't a board-fence, nor a bridge-girder, nor a dead wall, nor a barn, nor a face of rock in that whole region that didn't have 'Lapham's Mineral Paint – Specimen' on it in the three colors we begun by making." Bartley had taken his seat on the window-sill, and Lapham, standing before him, now put up his huge foot close to Bartley's thigh; neither of them minded that.

"I've heard a good deal of talk about . . . the stove-blacking man, and the kidney-cure man, because they advertised in that way . . . but I don't see where the joke comes in, exactly. So long as the people that own the barns and fences don't object, I don't see what the public has got to do with it. And I never saw anything so very sacred about a big rock, along a river or in a pasture that it wouldn't do to put mineral paint on it in three colors. I wish some of the people that talk about the landscape, and *write* about it, had to bu'st one of them rocks *out* of the landscape with powder, or dig a hole to bury it in, as we used to have to do up on the farm; I guess they'd sing a little different tune about the profanation of scenery. There aint any man enjoys a sightly bit of nature – a smooth piece of interval, with half a dozen good-sized wine-glass elms in it – more than *I* do. But I aint a-going to stand up for every big ugly rock I come across, as if we were all a set of dumn Druids. I say the landscape was made for man, and not man for the landscape."

"Yes," said Bartley, carelessly; "it was made for the stove-polish man and the kidney-cure man."

"It was made for any man that knows how to use it," Lapham returned, insensible to Bartley's irony. "Let 'em go and live with nature in the *winter*, up there along the Canada line, and I guess they'll get enough of her for one while."[16]

Bartley Hubbard's cynicism, already familiar to readers of Howells's *A Modern Instance* (1882), must quickly become apparent to the uninitiated reader as well. For although Lapham misses the reporter's irony, it is more significant that Bartley, preoccupied with scoring witticisms at Lapham's expense, remains "insensible" to the depths of his character. Despite Hubbard's success in drawing out the braggadocio in the mineral-paint king and thus in exposing his vanity and vulgarity, Lapham does not come across simply as a ridiculous braggart. We are shown, on the contrary, a complex man in whose character exists a mixture of tactlessness and shrewdness, rigidity and resilience, ignorance and knowledge (Lapham's familiarity with Druids is quite unexpected!). In contrast to Bartley's egoism, Silas's fundamental dignity, sincerity, and decency stand out even when he is expressing his most dubious opinions.

The characterization of Lapham depends in this first chapter, and throughout the novel, on such telling details as his "huge foot" and hamlike hands, which signify an immense animal vitality but also mark his social distance from the manicured elegance of the aristocrat Bromfield Corey. But Howells's main emphasis falls on the vernacular (and slightly ungrammatical) vigor of Lapham's own speech. With more intelligence and skill than Hubbard would likely credit to him, Lapham aggressively confronts his imagined critics: lovers of Nature with a capital *N*, who deplore any "pro-

fanation" of the "sacred" scenery and affirm a public interest in the conser-
vation of the "natural" state.[17] Silas argues, in part from the bitterness of
his own experience, that the "natural" bears little resemblance to what is
conjured up by the sentimental attitudinizing of those who have never endured nature's hardships. Unlike the "dumn" Druids, whose animistic beliefs discovered gods within even the ugliest of rocks, Lapham places his
faith in the more modern divinity of the Protestant Work Ethic. Like the
New England settlers in Emerson's poem "Hamatreya," Lapham arrogantly
claims possession of the land and its treasures as his own property.[18] Although he attributes a conventionally picturesque beauty to the elms (at
least when they assume the classical wine-glass shape), he believes that
nature, like the family paint mine, exists primarily to turn a profit through
human ingenuity and hard work.

There is a defensive edge to Lapham's talk, however, that suggests something unspoken. The idea of his outer toughness compensating for a tenderness within reappears at the beginning of the fourth chapter, when Howells
provides a page or two of narrative summary about Lapham's past. Most
notably, we learn here that his conscience still rankles over his dealings with
Rogers, a former business partner. But very little characterization of
Lapham is accomplished through this kind of narrative intervention. The
reader instead must constantly read between the lines, drawing inferences
from the dialogue.

Such indirection is entirely typical of realism, and similar strategies are
employed by James in drawing Isabel Archer's portrait. After her arrival
upon the scene of Gardencourt in the novel's second chapter – an entrance
so unobtrusive that the dog senses her presence before her cousin Ralph
Touchett does – Isabel's initial conversation with Ralph shows her to be the
independent American Girl that her aunt's cryptic telegram has led the
Touchett men to expect. While their banter may seem inconsequential, it
brings out in Isabel what qualifies her as Ralph's ideal of an "interesting"
woman. In one passage, for example, James uses extended play on the word
settle to raise a major issue in the novel: the question of Isabel's own role in
her European resettlement. Ralph has just expressed his hope that his American cousin will stay for a long time at Gardencourt:

> "You are very kind. I hardly know. My aunt must settle that."
> "I will settle it with her – at a quarter to seven." And Ralph looked at his
> watch again.
> "I am glad to be here at all," said the girl.
> "I don't believe you allow things to be settled for you."
> "Oh yes; if they are settled as I like them."

"I shall settle this as I like it," said Ralph. "It's most unaccountable that we should never have known you."

A few lines later, Ralph inadvertently unsettles Isabel's sense of control over her own affairs. She has spoken of the kindness of her aunt (Ralph's mother) in bringing her from Albany to England:

> "I see," said Ralph. "She has adopted you."
>
> "Adopted me?" the girl stared, and her blush came back to her, together with a momentary look of pain, which gave her interlocutor some alarm. . . .
> "Oh, no; she has not adopted me," she said. "I am not a candidate for adoption."
>
> "I beg a thousand pardons," Ralph murmured. "I meant – I meant –" He hardly knew what he meant.
>
> "You meant she has taken me up. Yes; she likes to take people up. She has been very kind to me; but," she added, with a certain visible eagerness of desire to be explicit, "I am very fond of my liberty." (19–20)

James here suggests the centrality to Isabel's character not only of her fondness for liberty per se, but also of her eagerness in asserting that fondness. Her desire covers an underlying insecurity about which Isabel does *not* wish to be explicit, even to herself.[19] The intensity of her declarations of independence betrays the emotional pain, which is reflected in her sensitive cousin's alarm and embarrassment, of her uncertain future, her potential *dependence* on her English connections. Liberty may be a matter of the highest philosophical principle to Isabel, but her enjoyment of personal freedom will ultimately depend as much on her impulses as on her beliefs.

Like Howells, James was capable of using dialogue very effectively as a means of characterization. He did not, however, depend as heavily as did Howells on the dramatic method to create a dense and expansive interiority for his characters. As he explained to the actor-producer Lawrence Barrett in 1884, *The Portrait of a Lady* could not easily lend itself to stage adaptation: "The book is before all things a study of character – descriptive, analytic, psychological, concerned with fine shades, emotions, etc. . . . I don't think the *action* of the 'Portrait' vivid enough to keep a play on its legs, even if bolstered up by numerous changes."[20] James must certainly have had in mind his celebrated chapter forty-two, in which Isabel meditates before her parlor fire on the disastrous failure of her marriage to Gilbert Osmond, the scent of whose treacherous intimacy with Madame Merle is becoming faintly detectable. But he must also have meant such passages as the two-and-a-half-page paragraph that opens chapter six, in which the narrator, acting self-consciously as Isabel's "biographer," offers a descriptive, analytic, and psychological exposition that is almost invariably quoted whenever critics describe Isabel's character.

We are told, for instance, that Isabel's aunt is quite in error to think that Isabel has any literary ambitions:

> She had no talent for expression, and had none of the consciousness of genius; she only had a general idea that people were right when they treated her as if she were rather superior. Whether or no she were superior, people were right in admiring her if they thought her so; for it seemed to her often that her mind moved more quickly than theirs, and this encouraged an impatience that might easily be confounded with superiority. It may be affirmed without delay that Isabel was probably very liable to the sin of self-esteem; she often surveyed with complacency the field of her own nature; she was in the habit of taking for granted, on scanty evidence, that she was right; impulsively, she often admired herself. Meanwhile her errors and delusions were frequently such as a biographer interested in preserving the dignity of his heroine must shrink from specifying. (47)

There is decisiveness in the urbane irony of this passage and authority in its use of psychological generalization. Such a passage inspires the reader's confidence; it promises to reveal the very essence of Isabel's character.

By positing such an essence, James's narrator implicitly affirms Isabel's theory of identity. *She* may not succeed in expressing herself, as she admits to Madame Merle, but nothing else expresses her because there *is* something to Isabel beyond or beneath or besides the company she keeps. As *The Portrait of a Lady* develops, it becomes clear that a materialist reading of identity, of the sort advocated by Madame Merle with her "great respect for *things,*" imposes a limit to understanding. But this limit is not, as Isabel imagines, a "perfectly arbitrary" barrier. The novel clearly shows her to be mistaken in supposing that *nothing* that belongs to her can be any measure of her.

With some philosophical inconsistency around the issue of free will versus determinism, James believed that although the "the whole envelope of circumstances" may be constitutive of identity, the "shell" is not finally coextensive with the "self." Even in Madame Merle's formulation, one's house, books, clothes, and the "company one keeps" are "all expressive" of a self "*for other people*" (my emphasis). She implies that whatever self is thus being expressed must exist apart from the "cluster of appurtenances": a self for one's self, as it were, within an interior room of one's own. This notion of self underlies Henrietta Stackpole's warning to Isabel about her dangerous illusions: " 'You think that you can lead a romantic life, that you can live by pleasing yourself and pleasing others. You will find you are mistaken. Whatever life you lead, you must put your soul into it – to make any sort of success of it; and from the moment you do that it ceases to be a romance, I assure you; it becomes reality!' " (201). Paradoxically, then, the presence of the immaterial soul gives reality its substance.[21]

Like James, Howells was deeply influenced by his father's adherence to the mystical doctrines of Emanuel Swedenborg. Both men were familiar, if not entirely comfortable, with the idea of the "soul" as the irreducible core of human identity. The term they preferred, however, was "character"; and they understood character in much the same way as did James's brother William, whose *Principles of Psychology* (1890) attempted to reconcile "soul" with "self" by translating the supernatural concepts of Swedenborg into the discourse of modern science. In his review of this landmark book, Howells endorsed the idea that good character results from the discipline of good habits:

> It would be hard for us, at least, to find a more important piece of writing in its way than the chapter on Habit; it is something for the young to read with fear and hope, the old with self-pity or self-gratulation, and every one with recognition of the fact that in most things that tell for good or ill, and much or little in life, we are creatures of our own making. It would be well for the reader to review this chapter in the light of that on the Will, where the notion of free-will is more fully dealt with. In fact the will of the weak man is *not* free; but the will of the strong man, the man who has *got the habit* of preferring sense to nonsense and "virtue" to "vice," is a *freed* will, which one might very well spend all one's energies in achieving. It is this preference which at last becomes the man, and remains permanent throughout those astounding changes which everyone finds in himself from time to time.[22]

Character, according to William James, is formed by an accretion of innumerable moral choices; character is a construction that becomes "permanent" through sheer force of habit. If "we are creatures of our own making," then anyone lacking good character has consistently failed to prefer sense to nonsense and virtue to vice.

In the late nineteenth century, *character* referred interchangeably to literature and to life, and it marked the interpenetration of the fictional and the real that realism posited in its claims to verisimilitude. *Character* for James and Howells implied, as Amy Kaplan says, "more than a neutral descriptive term for a structural element in a novel; it carried the moral connotations of personal integrity – 'to have character.' "[23] This conception of character is basic not only to the American realism of James and Howells during the

1880s, but to realism in general. As Catherine Belsey remarks, "Classic realism tends to offer as the 'obvious' basis of its intelligibility the assumption that character, unified and coherent, is the source of action." Typically, realism "presents individuals whose traits of character, understood as essential and predominantly given, constrain the choices they make, and whose potential for development depends on what is given."[24]

To a point, this statement accurately describes *The Portrait of a Lady* and *The Rise of Silas Lapham,* both of which are founded on the intelligibility of character and concerned with how the "given" traits of their central characters constrain choices and influence moral development. Beneath the "obvious" level of these novels, however, character is neither unified nor entirely coherent. As in *The Principles of Psychology,* character is understood to be constituted by choice before it constrains choice.

Both *The Portrait of a Lady* and *The Rise of Silas Lapham* focus on the development and exercise of "freed will" in their title characters. Despite obvious differences in age, gender, and social background, the bookish young orphan from Albany and the rough-hewn entrepreneur from rural New England are much alike in their abounding energy, overweening pride, and fierce independence. Both Isabel and Silas are ambitious and provincial American innocents for whom a rise in wealth and social standing leads to a falling away from the traditional middle-class values impressed upon their puritan consciences.

The resemblance of Isabel Archer to Silas Lapham has been obscured to some extent by James's revision of *The Portrait of a Lady* for the New York Edition of 1908. Isabel, who would have reached her fifties by then, was made over stylistically; the result was less a face lift than an elevation of consciousness, such that she became more like Milly Theale in *The Wings of the Dove* (1902) than her contemporary fictional counterparts, Daisy Miller and Catherine Sloper in *Washington Square* (1880). As Anthony J. Mazzella argues, the revised Isabel "embraces multiple levels of existence"; her motives and actions spring from "a compelling level of mind." Those of the original Isabel, however, are "perhaps best ascribed to the folly of her youth and the esthetics of her incompleteness."[25]

Nina Baym has arrived independently at similar conclusions. James's revisions, she argues, transformed *The Portrait of a Lady* into "a drama of consciousness" in which Isabel was endowed with "the acute, subtle consciousness required for a late James work." "Intellectual agility" displaced "emotional responsiveness" as Isabel's primary trait, and James's concern with such topical issues of the 1880s as the New Woman and the question of female independence was painted over:

The matrix of values which radiates out from "independence" in 1881 centers in "awareness" in 1908, with attendant dislocations of emphasis. Awareness in 1881 is a means toward the end of an independent life; in 1908 the independent life is attained only in awareness – the two things are almost identical. The only possible independence is the independence of perfect enlightenment. Consequently, Isabel is no longer perceived as having failed, and, not having failed, she has no limitations or shortcomings of thematic consequence.[26]

Because failure for the Isabel of 1881 was not so unequivocally transcended, as it was to be in 1908, by a triumph of late-Jamesian consciousness, the original *Portrait of a Lady* seems more clearly related to *The Rise of Silas Lapham*. The theme of failure versus success – and the overlapping of material and moral measures of each – is central to both novels.

What Isabel and Silas have most in common, in fact, is the dilemma of being nouveau riche. In distinguishing Isabel Archer from Maggie Verver and other late Jamesian heroines, Philip Rahv suggests that the latter represent a more ethereal version of "the heiress of all the ages" whose life "may be designated, from the standpoint of the purely social analyst, as a romance of bourgeois materialism, the American romance of newly got wealth divesting itself of its plebian origins in an ecstasy of refinement!"[27] Because of her *un*refinement, in contrast either to Maggie Verver or to herself in the retouched *Portrait,* the original Isabel Archer experiences no "ecstasy." On the contrary, she painfully learns, as Lapham does, the falsity of such romance.

Realism for James and Howells debunks the romance of dematerialization, where leaden riches seem transmutable not merely to gold but also to a beauty beyond all exchange. What Wai-Chee Dimock says of *The Rise of Silas Lapham* is also true of *The Portrait of a Lady*: "by dramatizing the permeable relation between the moral and the economic, and by focusing on liability as a problem in moral conduct, Howells not only makes morality a vital issue in business dealings, he also makes economics a vital instrument in moral arbitration."[28]

In a scene at the center of *The Rise of Silas Lapham,* Howells considers the corrupting influence of romantic fiction. The guests at Bromfield Corey's dinner party are discussing *Tears, Idle Tears,* a "'perfectly heartbreaking'" popular novel whose "'dear old-fashioned'" hero and heroine "'keep dying for each other all the way through and making the most wildly satisfactory and unnecessary sacrifices'" for one another. "'You feel as if you'd done them yourself,'" adds Miss Kingsbury, whose credibility on this matter is undercut – within the ironic climate of the novel – by the extravagant cleverness of her expression (197). Miss Kingsbury's opposite, the

Reverend Mr. Sewell, denounces the noxious effect on public morals of such sentimental claptrap: " 'And the self-sacrifice painted in most novels . . . is nothing but psychical suicide, and is as wholly immoral as the spectacle of a man falling upon his sword' " (198).

Although Sewell has, according to many critics, the weight of authorial approval behind him, his views are not, in fact, completely privileged. Sewell's allusion to the "immoral" spectacle of ritual suicide reveals a cultural bias in his own moral standards. He is incapable of entertaining the claims of a code of honor – one foreign to his American Victorian sensibilities – that might render such an act not only intelligible but even admirable. As an advocate of what he later calls the "economy of pain," in which moral rightness is determined by the rational and pragmatic minimizing of human suffering, Sewell detests "unnecessary sacrifice" so vehemently that he cannot admit the idea of *necessary* sacrifice – and thus of its possible moral legitimacy and emotional appeal. " 'One suffer instead of three, if none is to blame?' " Sewell insists. " 'That's sense, and that's justice' " (241). Yet as another of Corey's guests points out, the popularity of such novels as *Tears, Idle Tears* cannot be accidental: " 'We do like to see people suffering sublimely' " (197).

The novel, in fact, places Lapham in the morally contested field that lies between the sublimity and the psychical suicide of self-sacrifice. In terms of Dimock's analysis, these poles may be said to define the self-limiting cognitive structure of late-nineteenth-century American life by which moral entanglements were simultaneously produced and released: "on the one hand, there is a movement toward expanded connectedness, which implicates everyone, and makes everyone responsible for everyone else. Complementing it, however, is a movement in the opposite direction, a movement that restores limits, that tries to minimize not only suffering but also the obligations that suffering entails" (*New Essays on The Rise of Silas Lapham*, 70–1). That is, although a humanitarian ideal of mutual human responsibility – what Howells called "complicity" in *The Minister's Charge* (1886) – may have been sublime, it was also potentially exhaustive of emotional and financial resources, and thus ultimately suicidal as well.

This counterpoise of limitation and excess creates a certain ambiguity in *Silas Lapham* that has led, in turn, to contradictory readings of the interrelationship of its love plot to its business plot.[29] Whereas the romantic fortunes of Irene Lapham, Penelope Lapham, and Tom Corey seem to be apportioned by a strict and parsimonious "economy of pain," the moral rise of Silas Lapham seems to depend on the awesome totality of his financial ruin.

In the love plot, one suffers instead of three, when none is really to blame for the confusion that surrounds Tom Corey's romantic intentions. From the perspective of the one who endures the pain – in this case, Irene – such a distribution might seem unfair; but within a larger moral context it becomes reasonable and humane. For Donald Pizer, the utilitarian principle of attaining the greatest good for the greatest number by placing common interest before individual need also governs Lapham's actions in the business plot, thereby assuring the "ethical unity" of the novel by reconciling within a "single moral system . . . the apparent conflict between the attack on self-sacrifice in the subplot and Lapham's self-sacrifice in the main plot."[30]

In some recent criticism, this "apparent conflict" has been read as a transparent contradiction. In the business plot, Lapham's moral culpability always remains somewhat in doubt, and his scrupulousness with Rogers and the English investors exceeds what were normal business ethics in the 1880s. Yet he must lose everything before he can regain his moral integrity. Silas's bankruptcy seems to be the kind of unnecessary sacrifice proscribed by the "economy of pain" (a satanically parodic version of which, ironically, underlies Rogers's proposal to spread around the loss on Lapham's worthless land). As John Seelye remarks: "Where Howells was willing to argue that self-sacrifice is wrong in affairs of the heart, being equated with sentimentality, he convinces us that in matters of social and business arrangements it seems to be still a fictive necessity." Or, as Daniel T. O'Hara puts it, Howells uses the language of capitalism "to support a morality the novel both entirely disapproves as unrealistic in principle even as it clearly approves such extravagant moral sacrifice in practice by enacting it in the fate of the hero."[31]

" 'One suffer instead of three, *if none is to blame?*' " (my emphasis). *The Rise of Silas Lapham* implies that if blame *can* be ascertained, then the "economy of pain" does not apply so easily, because responsibility for evil should justly weigh upon the evildoer. The assessment of such responsibility depends implicitly on the existence of individual character as a formation of "freed will." An individual's capacity for morally meaningful self-sacrifice is directly proportional to his or her strength of character; at the limit of moral perfection, such sacrifice would become sublimely redemptive. Lapham's rise gains sublimity, therefore, from the nearly annihilating degree of his suffering.

For Isabel Archer, likewise, deep failure becomes an opportunity for moral triumph. Whereas Howells's double plot allocates the ethical problems of romance and business along gender lines, dividing moral responsibility between Silas Lapham and his daughter Penelope, James combines the issues of love and of money in Isabel Archer. Her inheritance leads directly to her disastrous marriage – in part because, as Isabel admits in her meditation, she has sought relief from the burden of her unaccustomed wealth. But once she has inherited so much more of the Touchett fortune than she could ever have expected, Isabel's financial security is never thereafter in doubt. At the moral climax of the novel, when she is weighing whether or not to return to Osmond, Isabel need not concern herself with any economic factor; for even if she were to succumb to the passionate entreaties of the wealthy Caspar Goodwood, there would be no diminution of her material comforts.

For Isabel, then, the economy of pain bears only on her emotional life. If, like Lapham, she is ultimately to blame for her errors, then she may deserve to suffer accordingly, especially since an innocent party, Pansy, will otherwise bear the emotional brunt. A common reading of *The Portrait of a Lady*, especially in its revised version, stresses the morally redemptive effect of Isabel's personal sacrifice. The encounter of Isabel's American innocence with European experience is seen to result in a moral chastening through which her innocence is recovered at a higher level. As Joel Porte summarizes this "humanistic" view of the novel, "Europe will provide not only the trap for her innocence but also the opportunity for her to repossess her dignity and sense of freedom by identifying with those who have been compromised before her."[32] By "affronting her destiny," as James said in his preface, by repulsing Caspar Goodwood in the final chapter and willfully embracing the fate she has helped to create for herself out of pride, ignorance, and self-deception, Isabel's terrible future becomes morally sublime.

Some readers, however, have always found this ending to be unsatisfying. As Donatella Izzo observes, the nature of Isabel's final act "remains utterly ambiguous: does going back to Osmond mark her decision to accept consciously the role in which she found herself to be trapped – thereby transforming deception into free choice (or, to be consistent, paying for her own mistake)? Or is it a flight from the responsibilities of the autonomous life she could still lead away from Osmond?"[33] Is Isabel motivated by moral choice or merely driven by neurotic fear? – by an unconscious dread of sexuality that holds her in the grip of a puritanical and masochistic severity?

The Portrait of a Lady, like *The Rise of Silas Lapham*, offers contradictory answers to such questions. Through its ironic treatment of the "romance of bourgeois materialism," the realism of these novels reassesses the cost of living in terms that speak both to the materialist economics of Karl Marx and to the transcendental economics of his American contemporary Henry David Thoreau. The cost of a thing is calculated in *Walden* as "the amount of . . . life which is required to be exchanged for it, immediately or in the long run."[34] In James and Howells, where "life" is equivalent to "character," a double-edged moral economy inevitably involves the exchange of material as well as spiritual substance.

NOTES

1 "Letter to William Dean Howells," in Leon Edel, ed., *The American Essays of Henry James* (New York: Vintage, 1956), p. 157.

2 "The American James," in Mildred Howells, ed., *Life in Letters of William Dean Howells* (Garden City, N.Y.: Doubleday, Doran, 1928), 2:397.

3 Howells to E. C. Stedman, 5 December 1866, in George Arms et al., eds., *Selected Letters of W. D. Howells; Volume 1: 1852–1872* (Boston: Twayne, 1979), p. 271. Howells praised his friend to Stedman as "a very earnest fellow, and I think extremely gifted – gifted enough to do better than any one has yet done toward making us a real American novel."

4 Introduction to Donald E. Pease, ed., *New Essays on The Rise of Silas Lapham* (Cambridge: Cambridge University Press, 1991), pp. 2, 3. Pease's own commentary is written, evidently, from a metahistoricist position.

5 *Gender, Fantasy, and Realism in American Literature* (New York: Columbia University Press, 1982), p. 105.

6 Albert Mordell, ed., *Discovery of a Genius: William Dean Howells and Henry James* (New York: Twayne, 1961), pp. 64–5. Other quotations from this handy collection of Howells's writings on James will be identified in the text.

7 Edwin H. Cady and Norma Cady, eds., *Critical Essays on W. D. Howells, 1866–1920* (Boston: G. K. Hall, 1983), pp. 7–9.

8 "William Dean Howells," in ibid., p. 23.

9 "The Contributor's Club," *Atlantic Monthly* 43 (February 1879); repr. in *Discovery of a Genius*, p. 86. By design, "The Contributor's Club" contained only anonymous material. The comments on James have been attributed to Howells by Albert Mordell, but there is no definitive proof of his authorship.

10 See William L. Stull, "The Battle of the *Century*: W. D. Howells, 'Henry James, Jr.,' and the English," *American Literary Realism* 11 (1978): 249–64. The British took offense chiefly at the following passage: "The art of fiction has, in fact, become a finer art in our day than it was with Dickens and Thackeray. We could not suffer the confidential attitude of the latter now, nor the mannerism of the former, any more than we could endure the prolixity of Richardson or the coarseness of Fielding. These great men are of the past – they and their methods and interests; even Trollope and Reade are not of the present" (*Discovery of a Genius*, p. 120).

11 "Howells Reviews James: The Transcendence of Realism," *American Literary Realism* 18 (1985): 155.

12 This view was echoed by Richard Chase in his widely influential chapter on *The Portrait of a Lady*: "It is an important fact about James's art that he gave up what he considered the claptrap of romance without giving up its mystery and beauty. . . . [A] part of James's great program for improving the novel consisted of the reconstitution, on new grounds, of romance." *The American Novel and Its Tradition* (New York: Anchor, 1957), pp. 118–19.

13 In a review of *The Portrait of a Lady*, William Crary Brownell proposed a suggestive term, "romantic sociology," to characterize the novel's combination of "a scientific value with romantic interest and artistic merit." Lyall H. Powers, ed., *The Merrill Studies in The Portrait of a Lady* (Columbus, Ohio: Charles E. Merrill, 1970), pp. 15, 18.

14 "William Dean Howells," in Edel, *The American Essays of Henry James*, pp. 150–2.

15 Oscar Cargill, ed., *The Portrait of a Lady* (New York: New American Library, 1963), p. 186. All other quotations are taken from this Signet Classic, which reprints the text of the first English edition of 1881. The novel was substantially revised by James for the New York Edition of 1908. (The interpretive implications are considered below.) For my purposes, it is more appropriate to use the version that Howells and all other nineteenth-century readers actually read.

16 Walter J. Meserve and David J. Nordloh, eds., *The Rise of Silas Lapham* (Bloomington: Indiana University Press, 1971), pp. 14–15. All other quotations are taken from this standard edition.

17 One of Lapham's critics turns out to be his daughter Penelope's future father-in-law, Bromfield Corey, who jokes to his wife that " 'We don't really care what business a man is in, so it is large enough, and he doesn't advertise offensively; but we think it fine to affect reluctance' " (p. 102). As it turns out, Lapham's views surpass even Bartley Hubbard's sense of the "limitations of decency"; much to his regret, the reporter believes that readers must be spared from knowing " 'just what Colonel Lapham thought of landscape advertising in Colonel Lapham's own words' " (p. 21).

18 See the famous opening lines of "Hamatreya":

> Bulkeley, Hunt, Willard, Hosmer, Meriam, Flint,
> Possessed the land which rendered to their toil
> Hay, corn, roots, hemp, flax, apples, wool and wood.
> Each of these landlords walked amidst his farm,
> Saying, " 'Tis mine, my children's and my name's.'

Like these men, Lapham remains deaf to the humbling and chilling words of the Earth-song:

> 'They called me theirs,
> Who so controlled me;
> Yet every one
> Wished to stay, and is gone,
> How am I theirs,
> If they cannot hold me,
> But I hold them?'

Edward Waldo Emerson, ed., *The Complete Works of Ralph Waldo Emerson*, Autograph Centenary Edition (Cambridge: Houghton Mifflin 1904), 9:35–7.

19 The same psychological dynamic is apparent later in the novel, when Isabel haughtily, but nervously, dismisses Caspar Goodwood: " 'If you were in the same place as I, I should feel as if you were watching me, and I don't like that. I like my liberty too much. If there is a thing in the world that I am fond of,' Isabel went on, with a slight recurrence of the grandeur that had shown itself a moment before, 'it is my personal independence' " (p. 149).

20 Leon Edel, ed., *Henry James Letters; Volume III, 1883–1895* (Cambridge, Mass.: Harvard University Press, 1980), p. 46.

21 Late in the novel, in trying to explain the nature of Osmond's evil, Madame Merle accuses him of drying up her soul. " 'Don't you know the soul is an immortal principle?' " he mocks her. " 'How can it suffer alteration?' " In accordance with her materialist beliefs, Madame Merle retorts: " 'I don't believe at all that it's an immortal principle. I believe it can perfectly be destroyed. That's what has happened to mine, which was a very good one to start with; and it's you I have to thank for it. You are very bad' " (p. 482).

22 "Editor's Study," *Harper's Monthly* 83 (July 1891); repr. in James W. Simpson, ed., *Editor's Study by William Dean Howells* (Troy, N.Y.: Whitston, 1983), p. 324.

23 *The Social Construction of American Realism* (Chicago: University of Chicago Press, 1988), p. 24.

24 *Critical Practice* (London: Methuen, 1980), pp. 73, 74.

25 "The New Isabel," in Robert D. Bamberg, ed., *The Portrait of a Lady* (New York: Norton, 1975), p. 619. Mazzella's analysis of the revisions demonstrates convincingly that "there are two *Portraits*, not one, and that each is a different literary experience." The transformation of Isabel and several other characters in the 1908 version is so palpable that "we are responding in a new way to new characters in a new work" (pp. 597–8).

26 "Revision and Thematic Change in *The Portrait of a Lady*," *Modern Fiction Studies* 22 (1976); repr. in Harold Bloom, ed., *Henry James's The Portrait of a Lady* (New York: Chelsea House, 1987), pp. 72, 86.

27 *Image and Idea: Twenty Essays on Literary Themes*, rev. ed. (Norfolk, Conn.: New Directions, 1957), p. 67.

28 "The Economy of Pain: Capitalism, Humanitarianism, and the Realistic Novel," in Pease, *New Essays on The Rise of Silas Lapham*, p. 79.

29 The double plot of this novel has long been an interpretive crux. For a summary of the criticism on this point and for a formalist defense of Howells's artistic design, see G. Thomas Tanselle, "The Architecture of *The Rise of Silas Lapham*," *American Literature* 37 (1966): 430–57.

30 *Realism and Naturalism in Nineteenth-Century American Literature*, rev. ed. (Carbondale and Edwardsville: Southern Illinois University Press, 1984), pp. 123, 125.

31 Seelye, "The Hole in Howells/The Lapse in *Silas Lapham*" and O'Hara, "Smiling Through Pain: The Practice of Self in *The Rise of Silas Lapham*," both in Pease, *New Essays on The Rise of Silas Lapham*, pp. 56, 96.

32 Introduction to Joel Porte, ed., *New Essays on The Portrait of a Lady* (Cambridge: Cambridge University Press, 1990), p. 3.

33 "*The Portrait of a Lady* and Modern Narrative," in ibid., p. 37.

34 Michael Meyer, ed., *Walden and Civil Disobedience* (New York: Penguin, 1983), p. 73.

6

TOM QUIRK

The Realism of *Adventures of Huckleberry Finn*

"Hast seen the White Whale?" gritted Ahab in reply.

"No; only heard of him; but don't believe in him at all," said the other good-humoredly. "Come aboard!"

"Thou are too damned jolly. Sail on. Hast lost any men?"

"Not enough to speak of – two islanders, that's all; – but come aboard."

Herman Melville, *Moby-Dick,* chap. 115

"It warn't the grounding – that didn't keep us back but a little. We We blowed out a cylinder-head."

"Good gracious! anybody hurt?"

"No'm. Killed a nigger."

"Well, it's lucky; because sometimes people do get hurt."

Mark Twain, *Adventures of Huckleberry Finn,* chap. 32

The second of these passages, too familiar to require much commentary, is frequently instanced as a dramatic rendering of much that is noteworthy about *Huckleberry Finn:*[1] The centrality to the novel's purpose of questions of racial prejudice; the transparent irony disclosed in Aunt Sally's anxious question and her genuine relief that no "people" were injured; the canniness of Huck himself, who, though perplexed by this sudden relative who calls him "Tom," knows enough about human nature to invent yet another fictional experience and adopt yet another persona on the instant, but is totally unaware of the satire, irony, or humor of his own remark. Huck knows his audience *inside* the novel; time and again he sizes up his situation in an antagonistic adult world and plays to the several desires, fears, and biases of those who confront or question him. However (despite his amiable introduction to us in the opening paragraph, his final summary complaint about the "trouble" he has had telling his story, and his closing adieu – "YOURS TRULY, HUCK FINN") Huck is often indifferent to or ignorant of his effects upon an audience *outside* the book, which is to say, us as readers.

Reprinted from *Coming to Grips with Huckleberry Finn: Essays on a Book, a Boy, and a Man* by Tom Quirk, by permission of the University of Missouri Press. Copyright© 1993 by the Curators of the University of Missouri.

If realism depends upon a certain consensual understanding of the world, an understanding of what Henry James said we cannot, one way or another, "not know," then the realism of *Huckleberry Finn* stands in peculiar relation to other realist works. As Michael Davitt Bell has shown, Twain's attachment to the proclaimed principles of literary realism is tenuous at best,[2] and what is true for Twain is even more true for his young narrator. For Huck not only does not knowingly participate in this consensual understanding, he is supremely unqualified to render it in his narrative. Time and again, Huck proves that he can readily adapt to the moves of the game; but no one has taught him the logic of it. The origins of feuds, the behavior of pirates and robbers, the decor of the Grangerford house, the prerogatives of royalty, all these remain obscure and mysterious to him, but he quickly sizes up the situation and plays his part as best he can.

The first epigraph comes from as famous a book. Yet so far as I know this exchange, and its coincidentally parallel expression in *Huck Finn*, have gone virtually unnoticed. There may be several explanations for this. Among them, and one perhaps worth exploring, involves the difference between the romanticism of *Moby-Dick* and the realism of *Huckleberry Finn*. That difference may be as simple as the distinction between motive and action, the difference, that is, between quest and escape – between the pursuit (all defiant of necessity and contingency, fixed upon some insane object and driven by some overruling passion) and the "scrape" (the unanticipated event somehow managed, eluded, or negotiated). Ahab bends the will of his crew to his purpose and dispenses with genial observances and courtesies; Huck caters to whim and courts favor, always with an eye to the nearest exit. The unmarried captain of the *Bachelor*, like most of Melville's bachelors, is an emblem of moral complacency and lavish good humor, in command of a full cargo and homeward bound. Aunt Sally is a type, an equal mixture of Christian goodwill, blind bigotry, and doting affection, glad to receive the boy whom she takes to be her nephew. *Moby-Dick* is characterized by its symbolic trappings, its metaphysical inquiries, its lyrical spontaneity, its Shakespearean "quick probings at the very axis of reality," as Melville said in "Hawthorne and His Mosses."

But *Huckleberry Finn* works by other means: it subverts the same high drama that promotes its episodes. (Boggs's drunken swagger, for example, results in his murder, but the dramatic emphasis is upon the town's perverse fascination with his dying; a distempered gang calls for the lynching of Colonel Sherburn, but what they get is an upbraiding lecture on mob cowardice.) Through the benign auspices of folklore, superstition, and enviable credulity, Huck and Jim are on the happiest terms with reflection and meditation. Ishmael's crow's-nest reverie is blasted by the anxious recognition that he hovers over "Descartesian vortices," but Huck and Jim argue the origins of stars – the moon must have laid them after all – and no one gets hurt. *Huckleberry Finn* displays much less of the Melvillean interest in an "Anacharsis Clootz deputation" of humanity than in the solidarity of two, a "community of misfortune," as Twain would later describe the partnership of Huck and Jim. In the above cited passages, Melville's is a throwaway line, Twain's an epitome of vernacular realism.

Huckleberry Finn, like *Moby-Dick,* is a storyteller's story. In both books the teller and the tale vie for our attention. Ishmael, the yarn-spinner, is intent on chasing to their dens the significances of his experiences, though it is seldom the case that we as readers feel these adventures are existentially *his* at all. Huck, too, is a receptacle of impressions, but they are filtered through a distinctively adolescent consciousness – quick to perceive, slow to comprehend. The realism of *Huckleberry Finn* is disclosed alternately by the thread of Huck's consciousness, not yet come to full awareness of how fully implicated in events it is, and by the palpable events that seem randomly strung upon it, namely, by the narrative itself. These are inevitably blended, and often tangled, but it is well to take up the teller and the tale separately.

<h2 style="text-align:center">I</h2>

One of the things to be observed about the realism of *Huckleberry Finn* is that Huck's voice functions much like Whitman's multivalent "I" in "Song of Myself": he is the narrator of his chronicle and the author of his book; he is the chief witness of events and, emotionally at least, the principal victim of them; he is ruled and to a degree protected by the laws of the republic and the customs of place, but only accidentally a citizen of, and never a voice in, the dominant culture that so mystifies him.

Both as "author" and as narrator, Huck typically foregoes representational depiction. He himself has seen the Aunt Sallys of the world before, and he is far less interested in disclosing her character than in dealing with the situation. Huck's own considerable experience in the world (the result of having fended for himself most times, not of playing the detached observer of life), as remarkable as it is regrettable in a fourteen-year-old child, outfits him for his adventures. In this sense, the realism of the quoted passage above, and dozens of others like it, is presupposed in the telling itself.[3] Unlike Ahab, Huck takes the world on its terms, not his own, and experience has taught him how best to navigate its treacheries and delight in its beauties.

Huck's wary canniness is frequently a source of the sort of narrative detachment so often associated with realist writing; it is also the source of its special pathos. When Huck sees the king and duke tarred and feathered, men who "didn't look like nothing in the world that was human," he is incapable of hardening his heart to their plight. Huck finally concludes, "Human beings *can* be awful cruel to one another" (290). This familiar scene is moving not because it effectively dramatizes Twain's attitudes toward the damned human race, nor for that matter because it serves as moral pronouncement (these two con-men are scalawags through and through and deserve the sort of treatment they at long last receive). Nor, I believe, does it signal Huck's moral development or, as Leo Marx would have it, "a mature blending of his instinctive suspicion of human motives with his capacity for pity."[4] Rather, it is the unlooked-for and disquieting revelation, somewhat surprising in a boy as familiar with the world as Huck is, that gives the moment force.

For Huck has earlier witnessed far greater and more disturbing cruelty than this: the murderous treatment of Jim Turner on the *Walter Scott;* the killing of Buck Grangerford that still troubles his sleep; Boggs's gasping out his last breath under the weight of a family Bible; not to mention the thievery and calculated deceptions of the king and duke themselves. What he hasn't before recognized, indeed does not fully recognize even as he speaks his sad conclusion, is the universal human condition of cruelty. Nor has he yet developed the righteous, which is to say "civilized," indignation that would serve as defense against his own spontaneous impulses.

Huck and Tom have no opportunity to help these con-men, and they go on home. But Huck is feeling "kind of ornery and humble," not so brash as before, even though he knows he hasn't done anything to cause the event he has just witnessed. Only two chapters earlier, in his famous decision to tear up the letter to Miss Watson and "go to hell" and help Jim, Huck's sympathies had prevailed against his training. Twain once observed, in reference to this internal struggle, that this is a chapter "where a sound heart and a deformed conscience come into collision and conscience suffers defeat."[5] Its triumph is temporary, however; as Harold H. Kolb, Jr., remarked, "Huck never defeats his deformed conscience – it is we [as readers] who do that – he simply ignores it in relation to Jim."[6] Nonetheless, when he sees the punished king and duke, Huck finds that a conscience, deformed or otherwise, has little to do with whether you do right or wrong or nothing at all. And precisely at that moment conscience moves in on him: "If I had a yaller dog that didn't know no more than a person's conscience, I would pison him. It takes up more room than all the rest of a person's insides, and yet ain't no good, nohow" (290).

Perhaps Huck is never so vulnerable as at this moment. His unwanted recognition, followed hard and fast by voracious conscience, has its inverted equivalent in *Moby-Dick* when Ahab realizes that his quest is self-destructive but he must press on nevertheless, and he drops his tear into the sea. For in Huck's response to the frenzied throng of townspeople exacting their revenge on these rapscallions and the image of the pair who do not look human, he concludes upon the human condition. Ahab is driven by interior impulses that extinguish all "natural" longings and lovings; but Huck, just as relentlessly, and simply by virtue of being alive and growing up, is being drawn into this inhuman, human world.

Robinson Jeffers, in "Shine, Perishing Republic," would have his children keep their distance from the "thickening center" of corruption:

> And boys, be in nothing so moderate as in love of man, a
>   clever servant, insufferable master.
> There is the trap that catches noblest spirits, that caught –
>   they say – God, when he walked the earth.

This is a belated wisdom, reduced to fatherly advice, that, boys being boys, will likely go all unheeded. But Twain (or Huck, rather) dramatizes his troubled understanding at the moment of its birth; his conclusion is the unstudied remark, not yet a conviction, no longer a perception. For Huck, corruption has no center but spreads out evenly before him, just as he has left it behind in the wake of his flight; it presents no scrape to be mastered or outlived, but the general human condition. And Huck is not yet wise; his insight yields instantly to vague, unaccountable feelings of guilt. And this, too, is a dimension of the realism of the book, for he is a boy ruled more by feeling than by sober reflection.

Huckleberry Finn has sometimes been described as a picaresque novel without the picaro. This may be a meaningful statement if our understanding of the genre is qualified by the variations of it Cervantes accomplished in *Don Quixote,* a novel Twain read several times, Tom Sawyer at least once, and Huck not at all. Still, Huck is not quite an idealist, not yet a rogue. His mischievousness is typical of a boy his age, and it is combined with a special, sometimes ridiculous tenderness.

Huck is often capable of pseudomoralizing, citing his Pap as authority for lifting a chicken or borrowing a melon. This is also true when, in chapter 22, he dodges the watchman and dives under the circus tent: "I had my twenty-dollar gold piece and some other money, but I reckoned I better save it. . . . I ain't opposed to spending money on circuses, when there ain't no other way, but there ain't no use in *wasting* it on them" (191). Once inside, though the audience is hilarious, Huck is "all of a tremble" to see the danger of the drunken horseback rider. When, at length, he recognizes that he has been taken in by this performer, he is so admiring of him and the bully circus itself that he claims if he ever runs across it again, "it can have all of *my* custom, every time" (194).

In this relatively slight episode are compactly blended the multiple functions of Huck as author, character, narrator, and comic device. As author, he tries to make the circus scene vivid to us, but is not equal to the task. His rendering of the performance is notable for its descriptive flatness. The passages are sprinkled with a few vernacular metaphors, but unlike his disturbing description of his Pap in chapter 5, Huck's language here is indefinite and vague. The men are dressed in their "drawers and undershirts," he says, and the ladies have lovely complexions and are "perfectly beautiful." What *is* vivid, however, is his faltering speech, his slightly breathless excitement. As narrator, he gropes for adjectives and falls into abstractions and platitudes. Huck is mastered by the spectacle, which is simultaneously his experience and his subject matter. But as boy, he is true to childlike enthusiasm and typically replaces descriptive detail with hyperbolic affidavits of his rapt attention: It was "the splendidest sight that ever was"; the women looked like "real sure-enough queens"; it was a "powerful fine sight"; "I never see anything *so* lovely"; "they done the most astonishing things" (191–2). At length, he becomes the straight man to his own joke. So pleased is he with the sight that he promises they can have his business any time, evidently unaware of the humor of the remark, that his "custom" has in no way damaged his purse.

Huck is worldly wise but never jaded, as this episode dramatizes, but the significance of his pranks are defined less by youthful motive than by the terms of the adventure. The charm of what Neil Schmitz calls his "Huck-speech" (speech "written as spoken, talked into prose")[7] can be, and is, radically redefined by narrative context. There is prankishness involved, for example, when Huck plays his joke on Jim after they have been separated in the fog, but he receives a tongue-lashing that so cuts him that he "humbles himself to a nigger." Huck's manufacture of his own murder in order to escape the potentially lethal abuse of his Pap is grotesque, to be sure, but it is highly dramatic too, and Huck regrets that Tom is not handy to throw in "the fancy touches" (41). He laments Tom's absence as well in an episode that is a mixture of romantic escapade and existential urgency when, in chapter 12, he and Jim undertake to save Jim Turner from certain death. The same may be said for his efforts to preserve the Wilks girls' fortune from the hands of the king and duke.

As humorist Huck is humorless, as hero he is only accidentally heroic, and as narrator he seems never to quite know where to place the accent. He is constitutionally incapable of distilling from his supposed experience either the ultimate conditions or the deeper significance of his adventures. He never doubts the existence of the "bad place" and the "good place," in fact believes them to be all that Miss Watson has told him. However, while he can imagine the fires of hell and the monotony of playing harps and singing forever, he scarcely comprehends eternity and has little interest in it. His famous declaration "All right, then, I'll *go* to hell" (271) is not accompanied with an exclamation point. The statement is matter of fact and to be taken literally, for Huck is a literal-minded boy. He is temperamentally suited to the bad place (wickedness is in his line, he says), and he will give up trying to achieve the other place. But his decision is also the resignation of self-acceptance, a declaration, that is, of the acceptance of the world's judgment upon him, not the resolution to abide by some higher moral authority, as is sometimes claimed. It is just this quality that gives the scene its special pathos. Huck is not built right, and the fact that he is social and moral refuse is hardly arguable.

Huck is caught between stern rebuke ("Don't scrunch up like that, Huckleberry"; "Don't gap and stretch like that") and enforced social acceptance ("Pray every day, Huckleberry"; "Chew your food, Huckleberry"). But he remains the same boy the town allowed to sleep in a hogshead, stay away from school, and make do for himself. Caught on the horns of this dilemma, there is nevertheless a strong undercurrent of self-affirmation; Huck is filled with self-recrimination and self-condemnation, but never self-loathing. When Jim is bitten by the rattlesnake, he curses himself as a "fool" for not remembering that the mate was apt to join the dead one he had placed in Jim's blanket; he is sorry for the outcome and his stupidity, but not the impulse. Huck devoutly tries to admire Emmeline's poetic "tributes" and drawings because he accepts the Grangerford family faith that she was a saint; he even steals up into her room and browses through her scrapbook when he begins to "sour" on her. He often regrets that Tom Sawyer is not around to throw some style into his plans, but Huck never fully accepts the world's corrections or refusals of him. And this same realistic disclosure of a young boy's self-consciousness, in the hands of Mark Twain, becomes a satirical vehicle as well.

Twain often employs a satirical strategy in Huck that he seems to have observed in himself and to have dramatized in *A Tramp Abroad*. The narrator of that book does not condemn violent alien customs (most particularly the revolting German student duels) but instead curses himself for failing to comprehend the wisdom of received tradition. The same is true of countless occasions in *Huckleberry Finn* where Twain's intent, as opposed to Huck's, is to expose sham, pretense, and outright silliness: Huck is perplexed that the widow makes him "grumble over the victuals" even though there is nothing wrong with them; he takes it on faith that Emmeline Grangerford's pictures are "nice," but they always give him the "fan-tods"; he goes to church with the Grangerfords and hears a sermon about brotherly love and "preforeordestination," and every one agrees it was good sermon, and it must be so because, for Huck, it proved to be "one of the roughest Sundays" he had ever run across.

Tom Sawyer variously describes Huck as a lunkhead, an idiot, or a saphead for failing to comprehend the observances required of pirates, robbers, or royalty. Huck never disputes Tom's basic superiority or his own cultural and moral ignorance; after all, Tom is "full of principle" (307). In fact, Huck is flabbergasted that Tom is willing and eager to help him free Jim, and he regrets his own betrayal of his friend for not insisting that he not sink so low: "Here was a boy that was respectable, and well brung up; and had a character to lose; and folks at home that had characters; and he was bright and not leather-headed; and knowing and not ignorant; and not mean, but kind; and yet here he was without any more pride, or rightness, or feeling, than to stoop to this business, and make himself a shame, and his family a shame, before everybody. I *couldn't* understand it, no way at all" (292–3). As a realistic portrayal of one boy's concern for another, the statement is touching; as satire, it is deadly – all the more so when we learn that Miss Watson has already freed Jim in her will and that Tom knows it.

Twain once astutely remarked that, unlike *Tom Sawyer, Huckleberry Finn* is not a book for boys but for those who used to be boys. It is not altogether clear that Twain recognized this distinction at the time of writing the novel, so strong was his identification with his created character, but the instinctive decision to have an unwashed fourteen-year-old outcast tell a story ultimately meant for readers whose own innocence was behind them proved to be an enabling one. As a character or narrative consciousness, Huck is pure possibility – his future casually spreads out before him, luxuriant in meandering adventures and antics, freedom and easiness. But he is doomed as well – for every adult reader knows (though because we are adults we are often reluctant to admit it) that his delightful caginess and high jinks depend less on moral purpose than on youthful energy; his escapes and accommodations are destined to become evasions and compromises in the end.[8] Huck does not know this, he hasn't even considered the issue; but we his grown-up readers do, and every vile specimen of humanity surveyed in this rich cross-section of America confirms it. Huckleberry Finn set out to tell a story and did the best he could. By degrees, it became apparent to Mark Twain that the boy was writing a novel.

II

Perhaps *novel* is too narrow a word. In his "Notice," and apparently after some deliberation, Twain chose to describe his book as a "narrative." In any event, the tale Huck tells is all slapdash and oh, by the way, as mixed up in its way as the king's recitation of Hamlet's soliloquy; the book Twain wrote is another matter.

Huckleberry Finn is a highly episodic book, and the arrangement of episodes observes no incontestable narrative logic. The feud chapters precede rather than follow the Boggs shooting, not for self-evident artistic reasons, but because we are to suppose that is the order in which Huck lived them. The episodic density of the book thins considerably as the narrative progresses, the last half being dominated by the lost heirs episode and the Evasion chapters. But this is not because these events are more important than earlier ones, but because in the long gestation of the book Twain himself had acquired the capacity to make more of less. That capacity, it is true, sometimes degenerates into artifice and burlesque, as in the strategy to acquire one of Aunt Sally's spoons, but it likewise betrays an author's professionally calculated attitude toward his material. Moreover, Twain had commercial as well as artistic motives impelling him to finish his book; undoubtedly, in the final burst of composition in 1883, he approached his narrative, in part, as a commodity that was too long in production. Besides, he had his own newly formed publishing company ready to print and promote it.

The *reason* why some episodes follow others might be more confidently pursued by examining how the novel grew and took shape during the seven years of its intermittent composing. That is a story too complicated to tell here.[9] It is enough to say, perhaps, that Huck Finn, as character and voice, was a metaphor for Twain's mind: through his identification with the boy, he might indulge nostalgically in vagrant thoughts and happy recollections, and particularly in the early stages of composition, he might satisfy his own desire to escape the cares of a world that was too much with him. And when he was in more aggressive moods, through the satirical latitude Huck's perspective on events permitted him, Twain could deal scathingly with his several hatreds and annoyances – racial bigotry, mob violence, self-righteousness, aristocratic pretense, venality, and duplicity, along with several lesser evils. His complaints about these and other matters found their way into Huck's narrative.

William Dean Howells once affectionately complained that he wished Mark Twain might rule his fancy better, and for his part, Twain contributed to the public image of him as a jackleg novelist. However, not since the work of such critics as Sydney Krause, William Gibson, Walter Blair, Victor Doyno, or Henry Nash Smith, to name only a few, has anyone been able to celebrate Twain's maverick genius at the expense of his literary art. Still, we cannot dismiss out of hand Mark Twain's claim that he merely served as the "amanuensis" to his creative imagination, and in fact on the first page of the manuscript of the novel he gave his book the working title "Huckleberry Finn/Reported by Mark Twain." By the end of the first paragraph, however, even that modest claim seems too much.

From the manuscript we know that Twain had at first begun his tale with "You will not know about me . . ." before he fully accepted Huck's ungrammatical authenticity and, with it, all the multiplying implications of the decision. "You don't know about me," Huck begins, "without you have read a book by the name of 'The Adventures of Tom Sawyer.'" Clearly, Mark Twain cannot serve even as the reporter of Huck's narrative, and, besides, he is not to be trusted, for we have it on Huck's authority that he told some "stretchers" in recounting Tom's story. Within the first three sentences, Huck has politely dispensed with "Mr. Mark Twain" and introduced himself as an orphan in more ways than one.

Except perhaps for the opening lines of "Song of Myself," there may be no more audacious beginning to an extended work of the imagination. Mysteriously, we are forced, or rather agree, to assume what Huck assumes, not because we are in the seductive presence of someone afoot with his vision, but because Huck amuses us. He makes us laugh and, later, cry; we want to be with him and to hear him speak. Just as mysteriously, we assume, or rather never ask, how such a book written by a boy could come to be, nor do we require of it even the most fundamental elements of fictional probability.

Even without Kemble's illustration of Huck writing a letter to Mary Jane Wilks in chapter 28, we can easily imagine him in the act of writing itself – squinting one eye, holding his tongue between his teeth, tightly clenching his pencil as he begins to record his adventures. It is somewhat more difficult, however, to imagine when or why Huck tells his story. We know that he has finished it before he lights out for the Territory, and presumably has spent about as much time writing as it took for Tom's bullet wound to heal. But the only apparent motive he has in the writing is to correct the forgivably exaggerated account of Tom and himself Mark Twain had published as "The Adventures of Tom Sawyer." (It would be out of character for Huck to assume that anyone might actually be interested in his thoughts or exploits.) More perplexing is the fact that *Tom Sawyer* was published in 1876, but the novel takes place in the 1830s or 1840s, and it never occurs to Huck that he ought to explain this curious discrepancy. It is equally unimaginable that Huck should have lit out for New York instead of the Indian Territory to seek a publisher for the completed manuscript. The very conditions of the fiction that is his book are perhaps the biggest stretcher of all.

It is not for nothing that Twain added the elaborate introductory apparatus to his novel: the heliotype image of him as a frontispiece, sternly presiding over his book; his parenthetical identification of Huck as "Tom Sawyer's Comrade"; his setting of the scene and the time of the novel; his "Notice" and his "Explanatory." These were no doubt, in part, attempts to reassert his own authorial presence in the narrative to follow, but Twain also rather generously and succinctly made up for some of Huck's literary failings. Huck, after all, never tells us the when or where of this narrative, but Twain does – the Mississippi Valley forty to fifty years ago. Perhaps Huck did not know, after all, that his story ought to display some interest in motive, plot, or moral, and Twain in his "Notice" somewhat protectively, and very authoritatively, warns us away from even noting their absence in the narrative. At the same time, in his "Explanatory," Twain calls attention to one of the book's chief virtues, the careful attention to and realistic rendering of dialect. We can imagine Huck straining to parse out a sentence, but we hardly expect him to have taken the same pains Twain did in fashioning the speech of his characters.

Huck's story as novel is impossibility followed by implausibility and linked together by unlikelihood. To give a merely incidental example, when in chapter 17 Huck wakes up after his first night at the Grangerford house, he has forgotten that he is now George Jackson. That much is realistic; the reader, too, is apt to get lost in the dizzying array of Huck's aliases. But Huck tricks Buck into giving the name away:

> "Can you spell, Buck?"
> "Yes," he says.
> "I bet you can't spell my name," says I.
> "I bet you what you dare I can," says he.
> "All right," says I, "go ahead."
> "G-o-r-g-e J-a-x-o-n – there now," he says. (136)

Then Huck privately writes the name down because "somebody might want *me* to spell it, next." One need not be a metafictionist to see the difficulty here. Huck, as narrator, has spelled George Jackson correctly from the beginning, along with any number of other more difficult names – Harney Shepherdson, Emmeline Grangerford, Lafe Buckner, Silas Phelps, "Henry the Eight," Colonel Sherburn (how Huck was able to sound out *Colonel* is a permanent puzzle). Are we to suppose that in the few months since this exchange with Buck occurred that Huck has undergone some orthographically redemptive experience? My point here is not to indulge in fastidious fault-finding but rather to note that in the course of reading these sorts of questions simply don't come up. The enchantment, the atmosphere of mind, conveyed by Huck's narrative presence is too pleasing, too hypnotic, to permit skepticism. There is considerable magic in the realism of *Huckleberry Finn*.

However improvised and shapeless the boy's narrative is, it nonetheless miraculously coheres almost in spite of itself. More often than not, the plot thickens only to dissolve into another overlapping adventure. We expect Colonel Sherburn to get lynched; he does not. What really happened to Buck Grangerford?; Huck won't tell us. We become interested in the romance of Miss Sophia and Harney Shepherdson, but all we know of their star-crossed love affair is that they got across the river safely. We pity Boggs's sixteen-year-old daughter and ask for revenge; what we get in her potential hero, Buck Harkness, is a coward and someone looking "tolerable cheap" at that. We hope that the king and duke get their just desserts and then are made to feel sorry for them when they do. We wish to see the Wilks girls reunited with their money and their nearest kin, but in the climactic scene of this episode the crowd rushes forward to the coffin and Huck takes the opportunity amid the confusion to get away, and we, his readers, however much a part of us might want to linger, are willingly drawn after him. The Wilks girls' adventure is abruptly over; Huck's has acquired new life.

And the two principal plot devices, it turns out, are false leads, Hitchcockean Maguffins: Huck is fleeing from Pap, but Pap, we learn at last, was the dead man in the floating house thirty-four chapters and several hundred miles ago. Jim is escaping from the dreadful edict of Miss Watson to sell him down the river, but, again, we eventually discover that he had been freed in her will two months earlier. Time and again, the action that enlists our interest is discarded, diverted, or thwarted. In "Chapter the Last" Twain, through several disclosures made by several characters, goes about tying up the loose ends of the story as quickly and efficiently as a calf roper with the rope clenched between his teeth: Jim owns himself, and his early prophecy that he will be a rich man is fulfilled; Pap is dead, and thus Huck has free use of his $6,000 to finance a trip West; Tom is recovered from his bullet wound, and we now know why he had consented to free Jim.

If there is no plot to speak of, there remain nevertheless discernible mythic, structural, and satirical patterns throughout the novel – patterns of flight and absorption, prophecy and fulfillment, retreat and return, death and rebirth, initiation and emergence, repetition and variation. And there are multiple themes and issues as well – the comic and devastating effects of Christian piety and absurd sentimentality, obnoxious aristocratic privilege and backwater vulgarity, marginalization and cooptation, intuitive sympathy and utilitarian conduct, inflexible racist bigotry and the dignifying enlargements of open friendship. Then there is the clear advance over and inestimable contribution to the tradition of American humor that is accomplished in the example of the book itself. These patterns, themes, and achievements are certainly "there" within the novel to the extent that criticism and interpretation can make them so, but they would be invisible to Huck and likely hazy to Twain himself. All of them may be comprehended, perhaps, in the insightful remark of Henry Nash Smith: Twain's "technical accomplishment was of course inseparable from the process of discovering new meanings in his material. His development as a writer was a dialectic interplay in which the reach of his imagination imposed a constant strain on his technical resources, and innovations of method in turn opened up new vistas before his imagination."[10]

The four groups of "Working Notes" for the novel Twain jotted down between 1879 and 1883 nevertheless reveal that Twain's imaginative reach was at times blind groping. Among other things, Twain considered including in his narrative: a Negro sermon, the legend of a Missouri earthquake, a house-raising, a village fire, a hazing, elocution lessons, an encounter with alligators, a quilting bee, a candy-pulling, a temperance lecture, a duel, a lynching, an accidental killing with an "unloaded" gun, an auction, a dog messenger, and (most improbably of all) an elephant given to Huck and Tom so that they might ride around the country and "make no end of trouble."[11] Twain was always tempted by burlesque, of course, and the fact that he resisted the several temptations suggested by this list of creative brainstorms testifies to more than a bit of artistic restraint. However, many have felt he so yielded to his fondness for burlesque in the final Evasion episode that he irreparably damaged Huck's integrity and credibility, subjected Jim to a series of unnecessary degradations, subverted the terms of Huck and Jim's friendship he had so patiently developed, and ultimately betrayed his readers' confidence.

That is an issue individual readers will decide, but the "Working Notes" indicate at least the range of possibilities Huck's adventures suggested to the author, a range so vast as to become arbitrary. The only requirements of his then developing narrative, it seems, were that Huck should have been witness to the events, or to a recitation of them by another, and that he narrate them. This is merely to say that Twain banked on the realism of a literary manner over and above the realism of subject matter. Any and all of the events recorded in his working notes conceivably could have happened along the Mississippi, of course, but they indicate no definite narrative direction. And many episodes he did dramatize are no less adventitious than those he contemplated. After all, he did choose to include witch pies and rope ladders, hidden treasure and secret tattoos, sideshows and soliloquys, feuds and romances, ghost stories and fistfights. And as palpable as the River is in the book, it is absolutely incredible that a runaway slave should be trying to get to Canada on its current.

If Twain did not in every instance manage to rule his fancy, he does seem to have tried to coordinate the several products of it. The most obvious example of this sort of artistic management is in the telling juxtaposition of the Boggs shooting with the drunken bareback rider at the circus. In the first episode are mixed the actual physical suffering of Boggs and the emotional grief of his daughter with the sham of pious sentiment and the predictably perverse fascination of the townspeople, who shove each other aside to get a good look at a dying man. At the circus, Huck's worry over the supposed drunk is sincere, but the man's peril is merely show business. There are other paired episodes or details as well: the actual deafness of Jim's daughter and the deaf-and-dumb hoax of the duke; the real rattlesnake that bites Jim on Jackson's Island and the garter snakes with buttons tied to their tails in the shed at the Phelps farm; Huck's captivity in his Pap's cabin and the gruesomely imagined evidence of his invented murder and Jim's captivity in the shed on the Phelps farm and the ridiculous traces of Tom's romantic prescriptions that convince the townsfolk that Jim is a raving lunatic; Huck's efficient attempts to save Jim Turner aboard the *Walter Scott* and Tom's embroidered and leisurely efforts to rescue Jim in the Evasion episode. Each of these correspondences, and others as well, mark with deadly satirical effect the difference between realistic urgency and contrived hoax. They mark as well how artfully Twain blended the two.

Many of the characters and episodes in *Huckleberry Finn* can be explained as inspired narrative twists that keep the plot moving along, broaden the range of Huck and Jim's adventures, and permit the author to indulge in such imaginative improvisation as might occur to him. The most important of these are the introduction of the king and duke in chapter 19 and the reemergence of Tom Sawyer in chapter 33. When Twain allowed the king and duke to commandeer the raft, he violated the sanctity of the craft and the River itself. But it was also an enabling move, for now his characters could travel in daylight and the author could survey in freer fashion the manners and language of life along the River. The maneuver also helped explain away the difficulty of moving an escaped slave into the deep South, since Huck and Jim now have considerably less say in events. The fantastic reintroduction of Tom Sawyer, who suddenly becomes the superintendent of affairs and relaxes the deadly serious consequences of Huck's decision to help Jim in chapter 31, turned Huck's experiences and commitment into disappointingly fanciful pranks. But at least it provided a strategy, however improbable, for concluding a book that might have drifted along forever.

Huckleberry Finn was published in England in 1884; coincidentally, Henry James published his famous essay "The Art of Fiction" the same year. Twain's novel passes most of the tests for the art of the novel that James proposes there – that it be interesting, that it represent life and give the very "atmosphere of mind" in contact with experience, that it "catch the color, the relief, the expression, the surface, the substance of the human spectacle." It also happens to fulfill the requirements of some critics and the expectations of many readers that James holds up to skeptical scrutiny – that it have a "happy ending," that it be full of incident and movement, that it have an obvious moral purpose. Coincidentally, too, James compares in the same essay two novels he had been reading at the time: Robert Louis Stevenson's *Treasure Island* and Edmond de Goncourt's *Chérie*. The first, he notes, "treats of murders, mysteries, islands of dreadful renown, hairbreadth escapes, miraculous coincidences, and buried doubloons"; the second seeks to trace "the development of the moral consciousness of a child." James approves of Stevenson's novel because it achieves what it attempts, whereas the second, in his estimation, does not. James probably did not imagine, even as he struck the comparison, that any writer, much less an American writer, might effectively fuse both attempts in a single project, but he certainly would have approved the attempt.

Not that Twain would have given a fig for James's approval. In such matters, Howells was Twain's admired comrade, as Hawthorne was Melville's. Even so, after Twain had finished his novel and was making revisions, he wrote Howells with a certain petulant self-confidence that he, at least, was happy with the result: "And *I* shall like it, whether anybody else does or not." Melville's summary remark to Hawthorne upon the achievement of *Moby-Dick,* to risk one final comparison, is similarly defiant: "I have written a wicked book, and feel spotless as a lamb." The wickedness of *Huckleberry Finn* is not the wickedness of *Moby-Dick*, of course, but it was the sort one might expect of Huck Finn, and perhaps Mark Twain. For Huck had been brought up to it, and the rendering of it was right in Twain's line.

NOTES

1 *Adventures of Huckleberry Finn*, ed. Walter Blair and Victor Fischer, vol. 8, *The Works of Mark Twain* (Berkeley and Los Angeles: University of California Press, 1988), p. 279. Subsequent references will be to this edition and will be indicated parenthetically in the text.

2 See "Mark Twain, 'Realism,' and *Huckleberry Finn*" in *New Essays on Huckleberry Finn*, Louis J. Budd, ed. (Cambridge: Cambridge University Press, 1985), pp. 35–59.

3 Shaped as he is by experience, however, Huck remains innocent in an important way. Unlike Colonel Sherburn, say, who has traveled in the North and lived in the South and is therefore able to proclaim on the cowardice of the "average" man (p. 190), Huck's perspective has not frozen into an attitude. Not only is the narrative point of view of this novel presexual, as has so often been observed, but it is also prepolitical, even preideological. Huck, in his efforts to help Jim, may worry that he may become a "low-down Abolitionist," but the quality of that anxiety is rather more like a thousand childhood myths – e.g., the worry children have that, having made an ugly face, it will "stick."

4 Leo Marx, "Mr. Eliot, Mr. Trilling, and *Huckleberry Finn*," *The American Scholar* 22 (1953): 423–40.

5 Quoted in Walter Blair, *Mark Twain and Huck Finn* (Berkeley and Los Angeles: University of California Press, 1960), p. 143.

6 "Mark Twain, Huck Finn, and Jacob Blivens: Gilt-Edged, Tree-Calf Morality in *The Adventures of Huckleberry Finn*," *Virginia Quarterly Review* 55 (1979): 658.

7 *of Huck and Alice: Humorous Writing in American Literature* (Minneapolis: University of Minnesota Press, 1983), p. 96.

8 Twain knew this, too; in a cranky moment, he predicted that Huck would grow up to be just as low-down and mean as his Pap.

9 Walter Blair and, more recently, Victor A. Doyno have provided us with full and perceptive book-length studies of the evolution of the novel. See *Mark Twain and Huck Finn* and *Writing Huck Finn: Mark Twain's Creative Process* (Philadelphia: University of Pennsylvania Press, 1960, 1991), respectively.

10 *Mark Twain: The Development of a Writer* (Cambridge, Mass.: Harvard University Press, 1962), p. 113.

11 The "Working Notes" for *Huckleberry Finn* are reproduced in the California/Iowa edition of the novel, pp. 711–61.

7

J. C. LEVENSON

The Red Badge of Courage and *McTeague*: Passage to Modernity

Convenience of remembering is often at odds with historical accuracy. For convenience we divide a past into epochs, and then we fall into thinking of epochs as if they were uniform and simple and followed each other in a regular march of events; then we begin thinking of actual people as if they had modeled themselves on the historians' models. For example, take Stephen Crane (1871–1900) and Frank Norris (1870–1902), who are frequently paired as the first wave of an American naturalist movement. They would hardly have said so. Crane was content with the name of realist, and Norris wanted no part of realism. Norris called himself a naturalist, to be sure, but, then, he unblushingly called himself a romantic, too. And as for their being part of an identifiable movement, the two men met only once, and they did not take to each other at all. In an exemplary way, they illustrate the constant need for renewing historical inquiry.

Their meeting took place in 1898, when they were both sea-going war correspondents trying to cover Caribbean and Cuban operations in the Spanish-American War. Whatever they had in common was not enough to spark instant recognition of shared literary goals. Crane, who had once tasted college and fraternity life, had by then overlaid the style of clean-cut gregarious youth with the worldly-wise journalist and the free-spirit bohemian; given the tropical heat and the pitching tugboat, he sat around in loose pajamas, neglected to shave, and drank beer while he worked. Norris, who had lived among bohemians in Paris when still in his teens and who wrote regularly for the press, was neither bohemian nor stage-typed news-paperman; on board *The Three Friends,* he seemed conspicuously "college-bred" – too good for the rest of the company. To Norris's eyes, Crane appeared grimy and unkempt, the sort of person who drank beer – from the bottle. Norris also had reservations about Crane as a writer, thinking him too far above his characters in ironic detachment and, at the very next moment, too close to them in the rendering of "microscopic" impressions. Crane for his part did not know the work of Norris, whose first published novel was still in the works, and he felt no personal rapport of the sort that leads to friendship.

Despite the look of a missed chance for history, however, that first and only meeting is worth taking seriously. Although they did not bother to find out, the two young men had a good deal in common, not only in birth and background, but also in present circumstance. By their own choice, they were far from home, and farther from any supposedly tranquil literary life. They were reporters for the new press syndicates, the latest technological instruments for the making and marketing of collective responses. They were covering the violence and boredom of war, hoping to combine eye-witness accuracy with sensational appeal. The popular audiences for whom they wrote and the literary institutions through which they tried to reach them were closely connected to what and how they wrote. And to the way they lived: tropical disease, which killed so many soldiers, struck them too. The malaria they contracted did not kill them – Crane died of tuber-culosis, Norris of peritonitis – but the hazards of the unsheltered life had a cumulative effect. Their being young and adventurous, and their being engaged with new media and new audiences, may tell more about what they had in common than such conventional topics as narrative technique (such as thickly detailed representation) or subject matter (such as the mod-ern city or the consumer society) or ideology (such as relentless scientistic explanation of all behavior and events), which apply to them only sporad-ically.

Even the non-take of literary friendship may be taken as an example of the deception of appearances: what these ambitious, active, engaged young writers had most in common simply did not meet the eye. Each in his own way explored an inner space of psychic experience that an older generation was mostly not prepared to enter. William James might have responded to Crane's ventures into the stream of consciousness, and Freud to Norris's ventures into the depths of the unconscious, but most people, whether professional critics or ordinary readers, simply had no terms by which to grasp the new kind of narrative. Crane and Norris were at the very edge of what was possible in the 1890s. They were, to be sure, explorers rather than colonizers of territory that other, later writers would develop on a grand scale. But they were more than accidental precursors. They helped jolt American fiction out of its nineteenth-century conventions, and those who came after them were in their debt, knowingly or not. Their work leads very uncertainly to that of twentieth-century naturalists like Farrell and Dos Passos, but it decidedly points the way to the fiction of Stein and Heming-way, Anderson and Faulkner. The pairing of the two can still be suggestive in new contexts because the novels they wrote are still disclosing new facets to an ever-changing audience.

William Dean Howells, in an essay written shortly after their shocking early deaths, first talked of Norris and Crane together. Howells – older by more than three decades – was acutely aware that memorializing his juniors turned the order of generations upside down; by writing about them, he poignantly affirmed the continuity of literary history. In claiming the younger writers as second-generation realists, he was establishing connections both with them and between them. He thought his common ground with Crane and Norris lay in their having explored radically fresh literary material, the newly populous, newly gigantic cities that by the 1890s dominated the American scene. He himself, after moving from secure, familiar Boston to massive, unfamiliar New York, had written about his own actual exploration of a new city; still in the flush of first discovery, he set *A Hazard of New Fortunes* (1890) in a broader, fuller social scene than any other of his novels. By the same token, he praised Crane and Norris for their venturing into the "tragically squalid," the "grotesquely shabby" streets of the modern city and rendering the "half-savage" life that they observed there.[1] Although his own practice had done much to identify American realism with the restricted scene of the comedy of manners, Howells had all along believed in the classic mission of realism as placing private lives in the context of current history. Although a middle-class domestic temperament made his own fiction acceptable in the drawing-rooms of *Atlantic* subscribers, open-mindedness and insatiable literary curiosity made him well aware of worlds beyond. A devoted reader of French, Russian, Italian, and Spanish realists, he never thought that realistic American fiction had to be just like his.

So Howells's critical approval of Crane and Norris, reaffirmed after their deaths, had been there back when it could make a practical difference. Upon reading the privately printed version of Crane's *Maggie, A Girl of the Streets* (1893; revised and published 1896) and, later, after reading Norris's *McTeague* in manuscript (written 1895–7, read by Howells in 1898, published in 1899), Howells had gone out of his way to praise and help the younger writers. He saw them as practicing, like himself, a realism that could extend social awareness and "widen the bounds of sympathy."[2] He generously publicized their work, and besides his authoritative literary judgment, he offered his personal friendship. They for their part responded warmly to the older writer. Nevertheless, understanding between the generations was only partial.

For both younger writers, the city was one subject among many, not the dominant historical actuality in which the moral life must now be worked out. Crane's link to Howells was more – or less – basic than a choice of urban subject matter. In his mind, the word *honesty* was the point of connection – he was utterly committed to honest reporting of the world as he saw it. As a nineteen-year-old newspaper reporter, he first became acquainted with Howells, not through reading his novels, but through hearing about his ideas. As he later put it, he felt indebted to the older man "for a certain re-adjustment of his point of view victoriously concluded some time in 1892."[3] He thought his own creed to be "identical" with Howells's, namely, to come as near as possible to "nature and truth."[4] (In his youthful enthusiasm, he felt no need to define "nature" or "truth.") Crane never recanted this allegiance or the filial gratitude that went with it. When, at the age of twenty-five, he thought of making a will – he was in Florida en route to cover the Cuban revolution from inside insurgent territory – he hoped that the novelist-critic would serve as his literary executor. Assuming an intimacy on the basis of Howells's expressed good will, he obviously wanted the approval and counted on the judgment of a literary father.

The good will on Howells's side had at first been unstinted. He believed that the middle-class discovery of the urban poor was a natural extension of bourgeois decency and clear-sightedness, a widening of sympathies that went with the advance of civilization. So he admired *Maggie* for living up to the claim of its subtitle, "A Story of New York." To see into Rum Alley, Devil's Row, and other mean streets that the casual tourist never saw demanded, for Howells, no special readjustment of point of view. The method of simple transcription would do, not just for sight but for hearing. To Howells's ear, the tough dialogue and even the swearing in *Maggie* sounded like authentic transcription, and he warmly approved.

When it came to *The Red Badge of Courage*, however, Howells found the vernacular dialogue to be such as he had never heard and the "close-at-hand impression of battle" less convincing than he found in other books. He appreciated, as others have then and since, the "subjective" narrative, the "sense of deaf and blind turmoil" in which the "tawdry-minded youth" was sunk. He even commended "the skill shown in evolving from the youth's crude expectations and ambitions a quiet honesty and self-possession manlier and nobler than any heroism he had imagined."[5] As time passed, though, Howells felt more and more discomfort with the subjective aspects of the novel, and when he looked back after Crane's death, he regretfully decided that the young man had "lost himself in a whirl of wild guesses at the fact from a ground of insufficient witness."[6] Subjectivity had turned into an anarchic violation of the realist's code. The difference between "a whirl of wild guesses" and learning "the rage of conflict on the football field"[7] – Crane's version of how he came to write about battle as he did – was a difference over literal representation, a difference that turned out to center on a definition of reality.

Aided by hindsight, one can locate the fault line between Howells's realism and Crane's very early on. Crane had his introduction to literary theory in the summer of 1891 when, covering the New Jersey resorts for his brother's press agency, he attended a lecture by Hamlin Garland. Garland, who had a strong interest in the newly popular impressionists in painting, gave a twist of his own to Howells's critical doctrine: "He does not insist on any special material, but only that the artist be true to himself and to things as he sees them."[8] In the young reporter's account, a shift from the verifiable observed to the eye of the observer had unobtrusively taken place.

The shift to the eye of the beholder, the new concentration on the contents of consciousness, implied a philosophical revolution whereby the nineteenth-century split between objective and subjective knowledge was called into question.[9] Crane's critical view of so-called objectivity developed in the years after he reported Garland's seaside lecture. In 1894, when he had graduated to reporting for a national syndicate, Howells, as a kindness to a protégé, granted him a press interview. What took place seems to have been a genuine dialogue rather than a neutral question-and-answer session, with odd results. The ideas are Howells's and the quotation marks are presumably legitimate, but the phrasing bears the marks of his interlocutor:

> "It is the business of the novel to picture the daily life in the most exact terms possible with an absolute and clear sense of proportion. That is the important matter – the proportion. As a usual thing, I think, people have absolutely no sense of proportion. Their noses are tight against life, you see. They perceive mountains where there are no mountains, but frequently a great peak appears no larger than a rat-trap. An artist sees a dog down the street – well, his eye instantly relates the dog to its surroundings. The dog is proportioned to the buildings and the trees. Whereas many people can conceive of that dog's tail resting upon a hill-top."[10]

Howells argued that art – the realist's art – brushing aside the immediate phenomena of consciousness and seeing through to a higher, deeper, or, as we should say, conventionalized "reality," transcribed an objective, rational, Newtonian world. What the reporter's words suggested, however, was that shaping by internal attitude was going on, and that Newton's optics was the convention that determined the shaping. The reader is invited to imagine people who look at life so closely as to lose perspective or, better, to exercise an accordionlike expansion and contraction of field as illusions become mountainous and mountains shrink to the size of rat-traps. The wordplay – Crane's wordplay – makes it clear that while many people can, few people do conceive of a "dog's tail resting upon a hill-top"; only heavy-handed analysis – or an artist's lightness of touch – gets us to abandon Newtonian convention and imagine the unmediated sensation that makes a joke of our everyday rationality. Art in this latter sense offers a comic liberation and a psychological insight; but if the reader resists a change of premises, it can seem to make the world unstable, it can threaten anarchy.

Crane's unorthodox play of perspective has a comic aspect that goes well with the story of growing up, which affirms life-enhancing powers that are associated with comedy. On the other hand, the ordeal of fear that is under-gone is a matter of life and death. The narrative, as Crane presents it, is generated in the inner flux of consciousness as well as in quasi-documentable events such as realists allegedly transcribed. Reading about the "reality" of warfare, like the battle of Chancellorsville which was to provide the objective ground of his narrative, he had found that the existing accounts left him dissatisfied. The more he dug out facts from the monu-mental series of articles in *Century* magazine known as *Battles and Leaders of the Civil War*,[11] the more impatient he became with the inadequacy of direct witness: "I wonder that *some* of these fellows don't tell how they *felt* in those scraps! They spout eternally of what they *did,* but they are as emotionless as rocks."[12] The articles supplied details of topography or the order of events, but they offered scant help to someone who wanted, as he put it, to "see war from within."[13]

In his own way, Crane was doing something radically new. In contrast to the "realist" witnesses of *Battles and Leaders,* Crane so deeply suffused his story with subjectivity that even the "objective" narrative conveys it. At the very beginning of the novel, the third-person narrator personifies the land-scape in the act of seeing it. At dawn "the cold *passed reluctantly* from the earth," and at night, across a stream of "*sorrowful* blackness," impersonal simile turns into felt metaphoric actuality: "one could see across it the red, *eyelike* gleam of hostile camp-fires *set in the low brows of distant hills.*"[14] A chapter later the metaphor of the narrator is displaced upon the young recruit whose worries about courage are turning into self-induced fear: "From across the river the red eyes were still peering. . . . Staring once at the red eyes across the river, he conceived them to be growing larger, as the orbs of dragons advancing" (92, 93). The modulation from narrator to protago-nist, from objective, to subjective, and back again, is characteristic. It leads to the seemingly contrary literary classifications of Crane's style as impression-istic – that is, giving the verifiable look of things detail by detail – and as expressionistic – bodying forth the feel of things in images that are private to someone's personal experience. The extremes of inner and outer view, and the instability that arises from the jumps back and forth and in between, would be found objectionable by Norris and others, but Crane's method has a function in the text. It establishes the young soldier in a recognizably modern world where both external and internal experience are in flux and where the two flow into one another so that the boundary between them is hard to determine.

The psychological revolution that operates at the heart of *The Red Badge of Courage* has some of the commonsense pragmatic quality of Howells's psychology. Henry Fleming evolves, as Howells put it, from crude ambition to manly self-possession. He stands up well enough in his first skirmish; he panics in his second and runs with other fleeing soldiers, though perhaps a little faster; having had the luck to return to his unit, he joins battle in his third skirmish like a "madman," possessed by the "red rage of battle"; in his fourth skirmish, even though he knows how bad the odds are for his unit, he fights courageously, carried away perhaps in his eagerness to take over as color-bearer, but by no means overcome with a mad excess of zeal. By contrast, his friend Wilson undergoes a fairly pat, conventionally literary initiation: at the outset he is the "loud soldier," boastful and yet full of terrible fears; once he has undergone the ordeal of battle, he comes through as modest, brave, individualized; from then on, he is "Wilson," modest, brave, comradely, and endowed with an identity. Nothing so sure can be said about the protagonist, who, at the end of his *series* of trials, is not exempt from future trial and error. Although in one context the would-be *hero* has become a *man,* he is also still "the youth." When the "sultry nightmare" of fear is over, his mind turns to the next phase of life as if he could expect "an existence of soft and eternal peace." It looks very much as if the learning process must start all over again, just as in common experi-ence. We know enough of him to think that the case is not hopeless, but Crane has trained us to recognize that experience does not entirely wipe out the capacity for foolish dreams and the need for corrective experience.

Crane's variant on the usual story of initiation had an everyday proba-bility that Howells would have seen as an improvement on literary conven-tion. (What Howells might have seen as replacing convention with reality, we tend to see as using convention parodically to suggest a more complex version of experience.) In other respects, Crane departed more radically from Howells. The shift of subject helps define the difference; in the modern city, the violence and unpredictability of the world were to be thought of as deplorable and correctible, and the novel that represented them realistically served the cause of progress; in the world of battle, violence and unpredictability were built into the way things happen, and the war novel that represented them was presumably an adventure story, a melodramatic entertainment. To Howells, the world of chance was one that decent people had to reduce to order, and violence was an evil for which somebody must bear the blame. To Crane, chance was part of the order of things and violence could erupt into experience without a moral explanation. In "The Open Boat" (1897), the distilled narrative of his being shipwrecked off the coast of Florida and of the thirty-hour ordeal in a dinghy that followed, he summed up both these principles: "Shipwrecks are *apropos* of nothing."[15] Crane was prepared to see the world as flux rather than order. Or, more precisely, flux containing elements of order, everyday order within a larger context that exceeds known rules. Once the old rules of perspective or conduct are no longer taken as absolute and universal, it is by no means certain that trial and error will come out as we have previously believed and hoped. Henry Fleming happens to come out all right, but for Newtonians bothered by the element of uncertainty, such coming out all right is not good enough. Instability of perception seemed to go all too easily with instability of conduct and might lead to moral anarchy.

The point where Crane's psychology parted from Howells's marks the rift between them. A slight difference in literary theory opened up into a difference between men and between epochs. Howells believed, in effect, that on the other side of convention was a reality as orderly as any rational man could wish; he believed that accurate observation and literal representation would necessarily confirm that his truths were axioms of the universe, statements about the way things "really" are. Given this belief, failure to come up with the right, reassuring conclusions resulted from technical error, from a failure to observe accurately and transcribe literally. So, in 1895, he thought that Henry Fleming's growth from "frenzy" to "quiet honesty and self-possession" was psychologically striking, though not perfectly clear in all respects.[16] With time, his uneasiness grew stronger. By 1902, he was ready to come out with his strictures about "wild guesses" and "insufficient witness."[17]

Crane, for his part, had all along worried about the question of literal witness. Indeed, one of his most famous statements about *The Red Badge of Courage* takes up exactly this question: "I know what the psychologists say, that a fellow can't comprehend a condition that he has never experienced, and I argued that many times with the Professor. Of course, I have never been in a battle, but I believe I got my sense of the rage of conflict on the football field, or else fighting is a hereditary instinct, and I wrote intuitively. . . ."[18] The alternatives to eyewitness observation were metonymic inference, widely viewed as the staple of all realistic narrative, or dubious instinct, a popular form of nonexplanation then as now. Metonymy, "the power to guess the unseen from the seen, to trace the implication of things," had been put forth as the basis of experience and of writing realistic novels, and when Henry James formulated that principle thus in "The Art of Fiction" (1885), Howells had been glad to support the cause.[19] When Howells eventually found Crane's inferences "a whirl of wild guesses," he was refusing to believe in Henry Fleming's inner world and putting the blame on faulty observation. The difference between "a whirl of wild guesses" and learning "the rage of conflict on the football field" is a difference over literal representation that finally gets down to a definition of reality.

Violence and unpredictability in the outer world were more obvious and so perhaps less disturbing than the psychological revolution of Crane's inner narrative. Howells had begun with a sense that, despite the violence and unpredictability of the emotions being presented, Henry Fleming illustrated an orderly evolution of character. Crane, too, thought that through experience we may learn to control our wilder impulses. But he would not have agreed with Howells that moral prudence, like Newtonian perspective, derives from an "absolute and clear sense of proportion." Howells's notion of prudence was based on an outdated conception of the mind. He reasoned from a kind of Aristotelian-Scholastic faculty psychology in Victorian dress. In his commonsense conventional analysis, Reason sits in judgment on Desire and after deliberation issues rational orders to Will. Crane worked from a dynamic psychology whereby desire and will are no longer categorically set apart from each other and are no longer vassals of the judging reason. The rational "self" that Lee Clark Mitchell imputes to the realistic novelists generally[20] simply disappears. Radically dissenting from that commonsense version of faculty psychology with its multiplied abstractions, William James was teaching a younger generation to think of mind and body as one. Starting from the laboratory instead of from accumulated moral theory, James argued that "bodily changes follow directly the perception of the exciting fact, and that our feeling of the same changes as they occur is the emotion." Common sense might say that "we meet a bear, are frightened and run," but James replied that

> this order of sequence is incorrect, that the one mental state is not immediately induced by the other, that the bodily manifestations must first be interposed

between, and that the more rational statement is that we feel sorry because we cry, angry because we strike, afraid because we tremble, and not that we cry, strike, or tremble because we are sorry, angry, or fearful, as the case may be. Without the bodily states following on the perception, the latter would be purely cognitive in form, pale, colorless, destitute of emotional warmth. We might then see the bear and judge it best to run, receive the insult and deem it right to strike, but we should not actually *feel* afraid or angry.[21]

James thus revolutionized psychology, returning us not only to our emotions, but also to our bodies: "A disembodied human emotion is a sheer nonentity. . . . emotion dissociated from all bodily feeling is inconceivable."[22] In an age when psychic states like Desire have often been hypostatized as surely as Reason was a century ago, James's view is restorative. In any age, his immediate value to the novelist is to establish the principle that "Action is character."[23]

James gives us an interpretative key to Henry Fleming's more and more pressing curiosity about fear and courage. The answer to the youth's self-questioning cannot be deduced, for he knows that his conventional literary ideas about heroism are useless and that he himself is an unknown quantity. In his bafflement, he is "obliged to experiment" (88) – "the only way to prove himself was to go into the blaze, and then figuratively watch his legs to discover their merits or faults" (91).

This experimental psychology excludes several possibilities. One is the constitutional monarchy of Reason, to which the alternative – in the eyes of many – was the iron rule of (supposedly scientific) necessitarianism. The necessitarian view is ruled out too. The shibboleths of popular Darwinism come into Crane's text only when Henry Fleming is rationalizing his flight. The panic-stricken youth, having noted that squirrels and rabbits run when frightened, classes human reflexes with those of other animal species. Clearly, a character trying to palliate his bad behavior cannot be taken as speaking for the author. In his revision of the manuscript, Crane cut some of the youth's self-serving interior speech-making, content that a little such characterization could go a long way. Yet another interpretative scheme, that of depth psychology, comes into view when the youth's flight deeper and deeper into the forest leads him through a gothic arch of trees to the clearing where he encounters a ghastly corpse: retreat to the peace of the womb is a regression that leads to an end in death, and be it said for the youth, at that ultimate point, he recoils and starts toward a reengagement with life. But reengagement, like initiation, is for him a matter of multiple trials, interventions of chance, eruptions of spontaneity. The flux of inner experience, like that of outer event, seems to balk simple systematic interpretation.

Meaning and moral content do nevertheless emerge. The youth's hardest battles are with himself. His panic is largely self-induced, brought on by his dwelling on fear and the question of whether he might run. His focus of attention, the control of consciousness, defines the exercise of will. He may not choose to run, but the relation of consciousness and event is statistically probable: given the youth's frame of mind, if he hadn't run in the first or the second skirmish, he'd have run the third time around. At times, consciousness seems to induce event, almost as in a fairy tale. The youth wishes for a wound such as could justify his having been separated from his outfit – and he gets such a wound. He wishes the army would break into panic, such as could justify his having run himself – and he is almost overwhelmed by fleeing troops; that is how he gets his wound. But Crane goes deeper. The youth in his misery becomes almost despondent: ". . . he thought that he wished he was dead. He believed that he envied a corpse" (146). As the indirect discourse suggests, the wish is not a wish of the first order. Just as his early ambition to be a hero was out of scale with the actualities of combat and fear, so his ideas about dying are incommensurate with his actual will to live. The crucial problem of narrative is to persuade readers that "he *thought* he wished" does not induce the way he acts, and that watching his legs is the best means of discovering his merits or faults.

One incident foreshadows this climactic reversal of intent and disclosure of character: when the youth had panicked under fire and run, he had regressed into the very womb of the forest and there confronted death itself in the ghastly corpse – and he had recoiled. The incident does not foreshadow in the sense that we might have predicted the sequel all along; rather, it confirms Crane's practice of showing that the major tests of character, for those who survive them, tend to come up again. So, at the climax, he has reason to hate himself. Ashamed at being mistaken for one of the wounded, he reacts in anger to the tattered man's solicitude and wrenches himself away. But he and the tattered man have just witnessed the horror of Jim Conklin's dying alone and unprotected, and he knows that desertion of the tattered man, beyond help though he may be, is the betrayal of a fellow creature to whom he owes the same solicitude that has been expressed for himself:

> The youth went on. Turning at a distance he saw the tattered man wandering about helplessly in the field.
> He now thought that he wished he was dead. (141)

In the event he has other impulses. When the fleeing column bears down on him, his old wish for heroics reasserts itself; in the critical moment he has "the impulse to make a rallying speech." It only comes out as "incoherent questions" put to "heedless" soldiers (148). His stammered and stuttered "Why – why –" is ineffective, and when he actually clutches one of the running soldiers, the man strikes him on the head with his rifle in order to break free. "Suddenly his legs seemed to die" (149), and writhing on the grass, he finds himself engaged in a "sinister struggle," which Crane has led the reader to recognize as ultimate:

> He fought an intense battle with his body. His dulled senses wished him to swoon and he opposed them stubbornly, his mind portraying unknown dangers and mutilations if he should fall upon the field. He went tall soldier fashion. He imagined secluded spots where he could fall and be unmolested. To search for one he strove against the tide of his pain.   (149–50)

However despondent he thought himself, in the test he did not make the easy, passive choice, to yield to pain and die. This was courage, the characteristic Crane so much admired. It was not premeditated. It was not deliberated. It was not, in the conventional sense, decided. But in the battle with his body, Henry Fleming summoned what in our time has been called the Courage to Be. More clinically, he focused attention on a spot of safety, and by the control of consciousness exercised what William James called free will. Or simply "will":

> The ethical energy *par excellence* has to . . . choose which *interest* out of several, equally coercive, shall become supreme. . . . What he shall *become* if fixed by the conduct of this moment. Schopenhauer, who enforces his determinism by the argument that with a given fixed character only one reaction is possible under given circumstances, forgets that, in these critical ethical moments, what consciously *seems* to be in question is the complexion of the character itself. The problem with the man is less what act he shall now resolve to do than what being he shall now choose to become.   (174)

The courage which, ironically, is really there underneath the other ironies of *The Red Badge of Courage* is worth taking at face value. It gives the story a moral center even though there are plenty of indeterminacies around the edges. On the one hand, shame at his panic is more easily overcome than guilt at deserting the tattered soldier. Even so, "gradually he mustered force to put the sin at a distance" (212). In Crane's pragmatic moral economy, to err is human, and to forgive oneself is also human. On the other hand, given that the raw recruit turns into a toughened soldier who can behave well under fire, does it *make a difference* at the end when the episode of war seems to be ending? When Henry Fleming turns his thoughts to "an existence of soft and eternal peace," isn't he fabricating another delusion such as that of Greeklike heroism with which he began? The moral center, ironic and qualified as it may be, reminds us that Crane held tight to the old-fashioned virtues – courage, loyalty, grace under pressure – in a world of flux so inhospitable that his commitment could seem absurd. Howells was right in his first praise for the book "on the psychological side." He was wrong, as the coming century would prove, in thinking that a whirling chaos of events and behavior was beyond the probabilities of common life.

Norris, too, ventured into new kinds of psychological narrative that took him beyond the then recognized probabilities of common life. But a complicated web of widely held ideas clothed and half-concealed his newness. His relation to Howells, in effect his relation to accepted ideas and established institutions, differed from Crane's. For one thing, he was much more of a reader than Crane. He admired Howells the consummate storyteller at the same time that he tried to disentangle himself from Howells the critic. Where Crane departed from Howells on the question of the observer's point of view, Norris separated on the question of subject matter. Telling the truth was essential, but young Norris insisted that truth could not be contained, could only meagerly be found, in the circumscribed world of Howells's fiction. That world, urban though it might be, was all too parochial: "Howells's characters live across the street from us, they are 'on our block.' We know all about them, about their affairs, and the story of their lives. One can go even further. We ourselves are Mr. Howells's characters, so long as we are well-behaved and ordinary and *bourgeois,* so long as we are not adventurous or not rich or not unconventional."[24] If realism was to be defined by the probable, the ordinary, and the familiar – as Howells said it was – Norris would sooner be known as a romantic or, to use his preferred term, a "naturalist." For him, a difference of milieu – getting away from "our block" to the other, larger city – meant a difference of kind: the change of subject matter meant a change of narrative genre.

In rejecting Howells's principle of probability to average experience as banal, Norris made it clear that his hero was Emile Zola. He thought that Zola's naturalism combined the realist's accuracy with the romantic's truth – truth, that is, to the strong emotions felt by men and women in their encounter with extreme situations and large-scale events. The desire for stirring events and strong feelings in no way compromised his belief in accuracy. In his commitment to direct observation, Norris argued at least as strongly as Howells that the serious artist transcribed reality and added nothing of his own: "Imagination! There is no such thing; you can't imagine anything that you have not already seen and observed" (1117).[25]

The idea of literal transcription, though it seemed secondary to choice of subject matter, was far from being a mere technical point of literary theory. The claim of witness is a claim of detachment, of "objectivity," and a disclaimer of personal involvement: other people have done the deeds; the novelist has "seen and observed" the kind of events he writes about, not imagined them or projected them from his own experience. Yet personal involvement was there. As Joseph McElrath has pointed out, Norris had impulses, spontaneous inner reactions, that rarely met the eye: in a couple of early sketches, he left traces of how he reacted to evils that he could not bear to witness – a deaf blind child, a shameless drunken derelict – with irrational, destructive rage.[26] Also, in *Vandover and the Brute,* the first novel he wrote,[27] he evinced an almost obsessive concern with the cultural contradictions he grew up with in a late-Howellsian middle-class environment – work ethic versus self-cultivation, unflagging acquisitiveness versus high-minded indifference to wealth, and (what even Howells occasionally hinted at) courteous regard for women versus demonstrated aggressive machismo. The motives for introspection and imaginative projection were there. On the other hand, in *McTeague,* as he invented and explored bizarre feelings and lurid events, Norris claimed not to be guessing the unseen from the seen, but to be reporting what he had observed. In a curious way, otherness became a means to candor. Confident that an author's rage of conflict on the football field or elsewhere bore no relation to his novel, Norris freed his imagination to go where serious American writers had not gone before.

Norris started from the relatively familiar and the literarily probable. In the opening chapter of *McTeague,* he practiced the conventions of representation so well as to convince himself, and Howells, and generations of readers, that he was giving a literal report on life a few blocks down from the upper-middle-class fastnesses of San Francisco's hilltops. In contrast to *The Red Badge of Courage,* which juxtaposes the unpredictable, unstable world of war with the mythic pastoral security of farm and village from which Henry Fleming comes, *McTeague* presents at first no clear-cut boundary between the secure world we are familiar with and a world where anything can happen. Norris's Polk Street, with its sights, sounds, movement, and daily round of working, shopping, living, has some of that wonder of the great city that readers know from Whitman or Dreiser or Saul Bellow, and that readers of the 1890s knew from Balzac, Dickens, or Zola. Easy literary reference is matched by familiar literary technique: the life of the street is seen from McTeague's window. The fixed perspective and the rounded cycle of day and night conventionally assure the reader of stability. The contiguity of neighborhoods becomes clear because shoppers from up the hill frequent Polk Street during business hours. Aside from commercial intercourse, however, the sense of a shared world is quickly called into question.

An out-of-the-ordinary world, not familiar to the civic experience of most novel readers, is also there from the beginning of the novel, though at first glance it seems safe enough. McTeague is a dentist enjoying a lazy, restful Sunday afternoon. Like the little shopkeepers who live where they work, McTeague sleeps on a daybed in his "dental parlors" (263)[28] ("parlors" is plural, but the place is really just one room), and on Sunday he can conveniently nap in his lean-back operating chair. His nap is assisted by the pail of steam beer he picked up when coming home from lunch. The beer is a signal of class that differentiates Polk Street from such levels of society as may be characterized by either temperance or a palate for wines. At any rate, the poor, the middling poor, even the not rich, relatively genteel lower-middle class, differ from people who dwell in a higher cultural neighborhood. If one recalls Frank Norris's disapproval of Stephen Crane, the rumpled war correspondent who drank beer on the job, one may detect a hint of disapproving superiority that crosses with his local pride in San Francisco's special brew.

Other differences presently appear. First of all, McTeague is not quite professional. He has apprenticed with an itinerant dentist who once came through the mining hamlet where he grew up, he has worked through the standard dental textbooks of his time, and he has acquired considerable skill through experience; but he is unlicensed all the same. In an age of widening professionalism, he is a relic of frontier conditions, a social anachronism – the sort of dentist that poor people can afford and that fashion-conscious shop girls do not choose. The difference from the well-ordered world of middle-class stability becomes more apparent when a friend whom he has treated for free brings in a pretty cousin as a patient: the sexual and psychological complications that follow are not the sort that Norris knew how to portray in characters from his own neighborhood.

Although Norris the would-be naturalist intended candidly to present his characters as sexual beings, he had a hard time finding a vocabulary for such narrative material. Getting started was simple enough, as he postulated a presexual phase of life: McTeague at the opening of the story is an "overgrown boy," suspicious "of all things feminine," and Trina, the pretty patient who is to become his wife, is virtually "without sex," "almost like a boy" in her manner (279). Prepubescent sexual amorphousness was a mark of innocence.[29] Such innocence is lost once the dentist feels attracted to the pretty young woman who is anesthetized and helpless in the dental chair. To describe the event, there is a confusion of biological and moral terms: "Sud-

denly the animal in the man stirred and woke; the evil instincts that in him
were so close to the surface leaped to life, shouting and clamoring" (283).
Once the impulsive kiss wakes the brute within, there is no going back.
Suddenly released is a "perverse, vicious thing that lived within him, knitted
to his flesh" or, in another figure, a foul, subsurface "stream of hereditary
evil, like a sewer" (285). "Evil," "perverse," "vicious," and "foul" convey
moral condemnation, and moral condemnation evidently makes it all right
to talk about what is conventionally forbidden. But the mixed vocabulary
has a nearly opposite effect as well. The theological language that makes
McTeague's yielding to temptation into a curious reenactment of the Fall
saves Norris from the limitations of his popular science. Influenced by the
progress-preaching evolutionism of Joseph Le Conte and the pessimistic
sociology of Max Nordau, Norris sometimes suggests that McTeague's brutality is a case of genetic development gone wrong, a matter of bad blood
and consequent degeneration.[30] The brutal inheritance is perhaps from
McTeague's unique family line, perhaps from his "race": "The vices and sins
of his father and his father's father, to the third and fourth and five hun-
dredth generation, tainted him. The evil of an entire race flowed in his
veins" (285). Almost despite himself, however, the novelist words his discourse so that "the evil of an entire race" can refer to the human race as a
whole and the problem that faces McTeague "sooner or later . . . faces every
child of man" (285). By his archaic phrasing, Norris allows himself (and his
reader) to feel a modicum of human kinship with a protagonist whom he
otherwise treats as someone radically other than himself or his neighbors.
Although his implied sympathy for McTeague is tenuous, obscure, and
confused, for one moment at least he can imagine this non-neighbor like
himself.

Such instability of moral premise, though it violates the canons of clear
writing, has an effect much like Crane's vivid changefulness of point of
view; it creates an unstable world in which anything can happen, the improbable, indecent, and rash as well as the probable, decent, and prudent.
The improbable does happen: Trina wins five thousand dollars in a lottery.
Her reaction – "Why should I win?" – makes it clear that the simple
rational universe does not work, that events occur which bear no relation to
"effort or merit" (340). The prize sets off her proclivity for miserliness; and
it prompts in her cousin Marcus Schouler, who had easily yielded his priori-
ty as a suitor to McTeague's manifest passion, an emotional transformation
– from a high sense of his own generosity to a fierce, jealous hatred of the
lucky bridegroom. The unpredictable leads to the indecent and the shocking. When Marcus secretly informs the authorities, McTeague is barred

from practicing dentistry for lack of a proper diploma. The ruin of the McTeagues is sped by Trina's compulsive avarice – her money cannot be touched no matter how rainy the day – and by McTeague's turning to alcohol and wife abuse. *Hereditary* alcoholism and *hereditary* brutality help to explain the plot, but even granting that the advanced ideas of the 1890s look like a crude and mixed-up explanation a century later, the bare events retain a plausibility.[31] The robbery-murder in which the marriage ends now seems less a matter of genetic criminology than a case of a sado-masochistic relationship gone to its terrible conclusion. Neat scientific explanation seems less convincing than the glimpse into the unpredictable possibilities of the human heart.

How can an author present a world more complex than his scientific or moral theories can cover? How could the equipoise of otherness and like-ness release Norris's imagination to explore mysteries of human behavior that had been generally taboo and were only beginning to be the focus of modern psychological investigation? Given a narrative imagination, it can be said that, although he made no psychological discoveries to compete with James or Freud, Norris did figure out a way to write about the unconscious mind. And an important clue to his method lies with a rhetorical oddity of the novel. As Alfred Kazin has observed, no other novelist ever so belabored his protagonist with the epithet "stupid" as Norris did.[32] (The word or its cognates occurs more than twenty-five times in the text of the novel.) By making McTeague stupid, Norris expressed a contempt that seemed to place this low specimen at a safe distance. At the same time, he was enacting a psychological revolution in narrative curiously like that of Stephen Crane: functionally, McTeague's being stupid got rid of the whole apparatus where-by reason judges desire and orders behavior. Instead of engaging in self-debate, as Vandover does, over gentlemanly courtesy versus sexual aggression, McTeague and the characters in this novel react directly to situation, event, and chance, and the resulting dramatic immediacy creates narrative interest.

One need not be stupid or genetically defective to take part in Norris's pageant of psychopathology – one need only be "other." McTeague's room-ing house is a warren of odd cases. Least obvious are the dear old couple, Grannis and Miss Baker, who for years before they speak to each other sit on opposite sides of the partition between their rooms, the doors left ajar, going their separate ways together. They are not called stupid, but they are past sixty, in their "second childhood" (273), and their shared erotic thrill at *virtually* "occupying the same room" (275) is clearly meant as an instance of reciprocal pathology. Genteel reviewers might find them the great sentimental attraction in an otherwise repulsive book, but Norris the anti-highbrow was working out a grotesque travesty of Emily Dickinson, that new poet of the 1890s whom Howells had supposedly read aloud to Crane:[33]

> Elysium is as far as to
> The very nearest room,
> If in that room a friend await
> Felicity or doom.
>
> What fortitude the soul contains,
> That it can so endure
> The accent of a coming foot,
> The opening of a door![34]

Norris relents after a time and lets the old couple enter "a little Elysium of their own creating" (384; repeated verbatim, 493), but he makes it clear that theirs is an autumnal garden of second childhood where the heyday of the blood runs thin.

At a further remove from the average and probable are those whose otherness is attested by racist stereotypes; the Latino maid of the rooming house, Maria Macapa, and the Jewish junkman with "claw-like, prehensile fingers" (293), Zerkow, who lives down the alley behind. They, too, enjoy a pathological codependency: Zerkow feeds alcohol to Maria to induce her yarn-spinning about a glorious coffee-plantation past and her family's enormous service of gold plate, and the stories of gold plate in turn feed the fantasies of the junkman's avarice. After they marry, the trauma of childbirth and then of watching her puny infant die puts an end to Maria's storytelling. Norris pointedly leaves the question open: is she cured of her delusion or repressing her past? Either way, Zerkow's unsatisfied appetite for Maria's story turns into an unsatisfiable search for her gold plate. The maddened junkman ends by horribly killing the woman who quit her side of the fantasy game.

With McTeague and Trina, a slightly subtler racism comes in. Their red-blooded Americanness is qualified: Norris's ethnic chauvinism put "Anglo-Saxons" at the forefront of progress, whereas their Celtic and Germanic cousins, not quite so far advanced, retained a higher proportion of primitive genetic stuff and could more easily slip into regression. McTeague's brutishness comes from his father's side, not stage-Irish comical but much closer to the apelike caricatures of *Harper's Weekly* cartoons. Trina inherits thrift (and a talent for carving) from her Swiss-German peasant ancestors, though the same genetic pool produces Cousin Marcus, stereotyped as a German

socialist agitator, and her father, a stage-German paterfamilias who organizes picnics like military campaigns. When things go well for the couple,
the ruling ideology seems to resolve all problems: marriage to a good woman civilizes the brutish male and sets him on the high road of evolutionary
progress; women like "being conquered and subdued" (390), and in marital
submission they satisfy their passional needs. In marriage, McTeague gives
up steam beer and learns to enjoy consumer recreations like window-
shopping. He starts wearing a silk hat and commences to "have opinions"
(398). Since, patently, opinions are socially constructed, McTeague's stupidity seems not very different from Marcus Schouler's smartness. When it
comes to thinking rather than opinion, McTeague perceives anomalies that
others miss. One, at least. Among his most loved possessions is the great
gilded tooth that Trina had given him as an engagement present and that
hangs as a sign outside his dental parlors window; psychologically, it au-
thenticates him as no diploma ever could. After marriage, on an evening
stroll down Kearney Street, he looks up at a similar golden tooth, the sign of
a really prosperous dentist who has a really top location. But this golden
tooth has *four* roots, such as never existed in a human jaw: McTeague can
only stare (401). (Norris, whether tickled by the surrealist invention of a
four-pronged molar or contemptuous of the fools born every minute, also
tactfully holds his tongue. Silence is clearly the mark of intelligence as much
as it is of stupidity.) Such is McTeague's evolutionary progress up until his
reversal of fortune. Then, when he loses his identity as a dentist, he loses his
place in civilized society, and degeneration quickly sets in.

Degeneration, like progress, is a social process best seen in the reciprocal
relations of interlocked lives. The marriage is based on an imperfect equilibrium. McTeague's erotic interest subsides with time, while Trina's grows
stronger; McTeague's economic ambitions, beyond wanting the golden
tooth as his badge of identity, are never more than vague, while Trina's thrift
turns into avarice. In both respects, life seems to go contrary to the supposedly natural order of male conquest and female submission.[35] If marriage brings into existence an autonomous sexual being, and if the lottery
prize brings into existence an autonomous economic being (Trina asserts
without serious dispute that the money is hers, not "ours"), so much the
worse for the natural order. Once McTeague is deprived of his identity as a
dentist, a more or less normal disequilibrium begins to come apart at the
fault line, and unnaturalness becomes the prevailing characteristic of the
relationship. So, after Trina has refused even to let him keep back carfare
out of his own earnings and sends him job hunting on foot, McTeague is
heading home rain-soaked and chilled when a friend stands him to a first

fateful drink of hard liquor. Anger at Trina, made vicious by drink, comes out in stages – first verbal abuse, then striking, then pinching, then weirdly biting her fingers – and eventually ends in murder.

The changes in Trina are more complex. During the prosperous early years of their marriage, her "brusque outbursts of affection" (395) or her compulsive, and for McTeague compulsory, thrift are apparently subsumed in the more feminine assertiveness of establishing a neat and pretty household or training her husband to his station in the matter of silk hats. When the downward turn toward ruin occurs, a pattern of conquest and submission is restored in grotesque fashion: McTeague's conquerings become sadistic, and she takes masochistic pleasure in the brutal treatment. At the same time, her saving money for saving's sake becomes obsessive "I-can't-help-it" miserliness. While suffering (and inflicting on her husband) the hardships of poverty, she keeps adding to her five thousand dollars. Also, she gradually displaces the saving of money in the abstract (a caricature of capital accumulation) by the hoarding of gold. For her, gold coins have more than economic value. She buries her head in them. She mouths them. Eventually, she spreads them on her bed, strips herself naked, and lies down on them in sensual rapture. Danaë raped by Zeus as a shower of gold is transformed into modern psychopathology. In this world of taboo imaginings, there is a kind of common sense: Trina comes to see that her private pleasure with the gold is preferable to the human reciprocal pleasure in being abused. There is also the uncommon sense of a writer who scorned the ordinary, average, probable truths of so-called realistic fiction. In the remote, other, vital world of Polk Street, the prevailing sexual code of mastery and subservience might be imagined as a form of sado-masochism, and the prevailing economic virtue of acquisitiveness might be imagined as a weirdly sensual narcissism.

Even the melodramatic ending of the novel, which Howells deplored, conveys rich suggestions of more than realistic truths. McTeague loses his dental practice and the gilded tooth, poor symbol that proved weaker than a slip of official paper stating that he was no dentist, but he hangs on to shreds of identity that antedate his Polk Street existence. The concertina on which he can play six mournful little tunes and the canary in its gilded cage are signs that he never was pure brute and, as long as he has them, never will be. If he reasoned, he would know that a fugitive carrying a birdcage is ludicrously easy to track. The caged bird – friend to miners, symbol of spirit, or simply last worldly possession – goes with him even into Death Valley. Unlike ourselves as we may think McTeague to be, he thus retains a last modicum of human dignity that allows for pity and fear.

Marcus Schouler, his fierce pursuer, also goes with McTeague into the dread alkaline desert, and, handcuffed to his quarry, does not release him even in death. In a novel rife with examples of codependency, this is a linkage that persists long after the Polk Street scene has been left behind. It is not simply a matter of handcuffs. Marcus is bound to McTeague by passionate hatred, and McTeague is bound to him in a way that leads Norris to speak of "that strange sixth sense, that obscure brutish instinct" (550) which makes the quarry aware of the hunter. As a mode of perception, the "sixth sense" is unconvincing, but the term alerts readers to the uncanny relation between McTeague and a kind of double, a figure he evokes just when all other human ties have been broken. In most respects, Marcus is a kind of anti-self, articulate, clever, greedy, and aggressive, a mirror-image of McTeague. But the connection is not just in their complementarity. Early on, when McTeague first fell in love with Trina, "the jealousy of Marcus Schouler harassed him," and, his racking desire crossed with frustration and bewilderment, he lay in bed "gnawing at his fingers in an excess of silent fury" (291). During the long degenerative process, he shifts the object of his finger-biting to Trina, and eventually her infected fingers have to be amputated. When Marcus Schouler shows up in pursuit of McTeague the wanted murderer, he is not the same as he was on Polk Street. His story is a curious mixture of popular fantasy and narrative appropriateness. Having fulfilled his ambition to become a cowboy, he has blustered his way into a gunfight and had two fingers shot off. The coincidence is striking with Henry James's "The Jolly Corner" (1908), in which Spencer Brydon eerily confronts his double, a coarse, aggressive, acquisitive alter ego who has similarly lost two fingers. Aggressiveness does not preclude vulnerability any more than brutishness precludes humanity. The luridly unrealistic death scene leaves readers with more to think about than just a clinical history of regression and criminality.

While other reviewers found *McTeague* just such a case study and an offense against ideality in literature, Howells came through with a perspicacious review. He praised Norris for catching in his own way Zola's epic scope and romantic color; and he singled out, as he had with *The Red Badge of Courage,* the psychological acuteness of the narrative. He recognized the boldness with which Norris had transgressed "the provincial proprieties" and brought into American fiction "the passions and the motives of the savage world which underlies as well as environs civilization."[36] With all due respect for Howells's readiness to support an expanding universe for the American novel, it must be pointed out that he used the term *civilization* with a specific social geography in mind. He seems not to have believed that chaotic forces from outside the sheltered world of middle-class security could make incursions into ordinary, well-regulated lives; war or shipwreck must be a distortion of rational perspective. And he seems to have thought that "semi-savage" natures of the sort that *McTeague* portrayed were to be found "along the low social levels which the story kept, and almost never rose or fell from."[37] After a century in which the fragile social order and the discontents of civilization have demonstrably kept to no social or geographic limits, Howells's own provincialism seems as striking as his generosity and good intentions. Crane and Norris, though they came "from the same block," left it and headed for the fluid, unpredictable, and often dangerous world that has become familiar since their time – a matter not of social and physical surroundings only, but of the mind.

NOTES

1 "Frank Norris," *North American Review*, 175 (1902): 769–78; the quoted phrases are from pp. 770, 773.

2 *Criticism and Fiction* (New York, Harper, 1891), p. 15; the quoted phrase, from section 2, appeared in *Harper's Magazine* in 1886.

3 *The Correspondence of Stephen Crane*, ed. Stanley Wertheim and Paul Sorrentino, 2 vols. (New York: Columbia University Press, 1988), 1:247.

4 Ibid., 1:63.

5 *Harper's Weekly*, 39 (1895): 1013.

6 *North American Review*, 175:770.

7 To John Northern Hilliard, [1897?], *Correspondence*, 1:322.

8 Stephen Crane, "Howells Discussed at Avon-by-the-Sea," *New York Tribune*, August 18, 1891; rpt. in *Stephen Crane: Prose and Poetry*, ed. J. C. Levenson (New York: The Library of America, 1984), p. 457.

9 The split between objective and subjective can, of course, be traced back to Descartes, as numerous historians have done, and the philosophic terms were in widespread use in the eighteenth century; but it was Coleridge who made them current in literary discourse and prepared the way for their becoming commonplace.

10 "Howells Fears the Realists Must Wait," McClure Syndicate: *New York Times*, October 28, 1894; *Stephen Crane: Prose and Poetry*, p. 616.

11 *Battles and Leaders of the Civil War: Being for the most part contributions by Union and Confederate officers, condensed and arranged for popular reading*, 4 vols. (New York: Century, 1887) reprinted the series of articles that had appeared in *Century* magazine from 1884 to 1887.

12 Quoted by Crane's close friend at the time of writing and the lender of the old copies of *Century* that Crane was devouring, Corwin K. Linson, in *My Stephen Crane*, ed. Edwin H. Cady (Syracuse, N.Y.: Syracuse University Press, 1958), p. 37.

13 Crane quoted by his editor at D. Appleton and Company, Ripley Hitchcock, in the preface to the 1900 edition of *The Red Badge of Courage,* (New York: D. Appleton, 1900), p. vii.

14 *Stephen Crane: Prose and Poetry,* p. 81; emphasis added. The first edition (1895) of *The Red Badge of Courage,* as reprinted in the Library of America edition, is hereafter cited parenthetically in the text.

15 *Stephen Crane: Prose and Poetry,* p. 891.

16 *Harper's Weekly,* 39:1013.

17 *North American Review,* 175:770.

18 *Correspondence,* 1:322.

19 "The Art of Fiction," originally published in *Longman's Magazine* in 1884 and then collected in *Partial Portraits* (1888); rpt. in *Henry James: Literary Criticism,* ed. Leon Edel (New York: Library of America, 1984), p. 53.

20 Lee Clark Mitchell, *Determined Fictions: American Literary Naturalism* (New York: Columbia University Press, 1989), chap. 1.

21 William James, *Psychology: Shorter Course* (the widely used, one-volume textbook edition of his 1890 *Principles of Psychology;* New York: Holt, 1892), p. 376.

22 Ibid., p. 380.

23 The thrice underscored (capitalized) final entry of "Notes for The Last Tycoon," in F. Scott Fitzgerald, *The Last Tycoon: An Unfinished Novel* (New York: Scribner's, 1941), p. 163.

24 "Zola as a Romantic Writer" (1896), in *Frank Norris, Novels and Essays,* ed. Donald Pizer (New York: Library of America, 1986), p. 1106. Parenthetical page citations in the text refer to this volume.

25 From "Fiction Is Selection" (1897).

26 Joseph R. McElrath, Jr., *Frank Norris Revisited* (New York: Twayne, 1992), p. 14, notes the "hysterical" responses disclosed in "Little Dramas of the Curbstone" (1897) and suggests that a more discreet editor would have kept Norris from going public with his private impulses.

27 Norris began and nearly completed the novel during his year at Harvard (1894–5). He submitted it to publishers at least twice: once it was rejected; once he withdrew it before getting a decision. It was finally published posthumously in 1914.

28 *McTeague: A Story of San Francisco* (New York: Doubleday and McClure, 1899). Parenthetical page citations in text refer to the Library of America edition cited above (n. 24).

29 The implications of the language here are supported by Norris's use of cross-naming in *Vandover and the Brute,* where *Turner* Ravis is the pure young woman and *Dolly* Haight is the pure young man. The title character of *Moran of the Lady Letty* (1898) is a much more vigorous instance of androgyny, a female ship's captain; yet even she, though androgynous, is sexless, and once conquered by the male protagonist in physical combat (adolescent polymorphous play turned into an almost deadly "battle of the sexes"), she is transformed into a conventionally submissive woman.

30 An indispensable guide to Norris's debts to current ideas is Donald Pizer, *The Novels of Frank Norris* (Bloomington and London: Indiana University Press, 1966), esp. pp. 3–18, 55–63.

31 Just as Crane, in the fictional time of a few days, shows that incidents are not necessarily final, and that second chances do come in life, so Norris, telling a story that continues over fictive years, conveys the sense that some events are irreversible and that long chains of consequences, affected by both genetic *and* social circumstances, may follow from them. What both novelists show is something far different from either a deterministic or a man-controlled universe; their novels take place in a disorderly world in which both second chances and irreversibilities exist.

32 Alfred Kazin, introduction to *McTeague* (New York: Vintage Books, 1990), p. xii.

33 Unfortunately, we need independent confirmation for any events in Crane's life for which our knowledge derives from Thomas Beer's 1923 volume, *Stephen Crane: A Study in American Letters.* Beer did not distinguish between historical novel and biography.

34 Emily Dickinson, *Poems,* ed. Mabel Loomis Todd and T. W. Higginson (Boston: Roberts Brothers, 1890), p. 46. Todd and Higginson gave the poem the title "Suspense." Although they changed Dickinson's capitalization and punctuation, they left her words as written.

35 The supposition was not merely that of Norris or of genteel America. Freud, in *Fragment of an Analysis of a Case of Hysteria [Dora's Case]* (1905), names "surrender" as the proper female response to love, and either abandonment to or repudiation of sexuality as a sick ("neurotic") response (New York: Collier, 1963; p. 107).

36 "A Case in Point," *Literature* 4 (March 24, 1899): 370–1.

37 "Frank Norris," *North American Review,* 175:774.

8

BLANCHE H. GELFANT

What More Can Carrie Want?
Naturalistic Ways of Consuming Women

"Know'st me not by my clothes?"

Cymbeline

A recent magazine article evokes the perennial mystery of human desire by asking why a movie star who "has it all" – "a perfect body, happy marriage, wealth," and "success" – is "not yet satisfied."[1] Beginning with a play of words, "Why Demi Moore Wants More," the article ends by finding the word *more* "elusive." This elusive *more* is the subject of my essay, which links a desire for *more* to determinism as a doctrine of causation common to literary naturalism, behavioral psychology, modern advertising, and consumerism. Once consumption figures in a discussion of literary naturalism, at issue in this essay, the lines of argument move centrifugally in various directions to include such seemingly far-flung and unrelated matters as the Vietnam War, kleptomania, the "packaging" of American politics, women's fashion, material culture studies, fitness diets, images of burning bodies, the commodification of books, Jane Fonda's self-transformations, and indecent proposals to Demi Moore.[2] All these matters converge at a single point of origin where a woman character, an American literary heroine, stands and looks. The consequences of this simple, ordinary act – which leads the woman to consume and be consumed – seem to me laden with literary and cultural meanings I must necessarily condense. To do so, my first tactical move will be to leap over an entire century in order to compare Theodore Dreiser's famous novel *Sister Carrie*, published in 1900, with a contemporary story that leaves one shaken by its brilliance and horror. I ask the reader to imagine the gap between the two texts as an ellipsis – a *dot, dot, dot* – filled in by decades of turbulent historical change that have redefined what an American heroine wants but not why she wants more.

A century ago, when little Oliver Twist said, "Please, sir, I want some more," he was, in Dickens's words, "desperate with hunger." The child said "want" but meant "need" – a basic, biological need for food. As we know, Dreiser's *Sister Carrie* begins with a poignantly needy heroine, a poor working-girl without a job, skill, or money. The novel ends with Carrie

Meeber, now a Broadway star, sitting in her luxurious hotel suite with a hundred and fifty dollars "in hand" and contemplating the meaning – or rather the meaninglessness, the "impotence," to use Dreiser's word – of money: "Her hotel bill did not require its use. Her clothes had for some time been wholly satisfactory. Another day and she would receive another hundred and fifty."[3] Dreiser's little actress now has everything she wanted: money, clothes, comfort, recognition, rich men proposing marriage. And still she thinks, and cannot help thinking, "she must have more – a great deal more."

What more, I wonder, can Carrie want? What is the meaning of desire that so exceeds the demands of need it seems insatiable? In the 1950s, the psychologist Abraham Maslow popularized the term *self-actualization* as a synonym for the human "desire to become more and more what . . . one is capable of becoming."[4] Self-actualization depended upon an incessant satisfaction of needs that, Maslow believed, were hierarchical, ranging from the physiological need for food to a need for safety, love, self-esteem, and self-fulfillment. Each satisfied need released a new and higher need, making desire insatiable. Maslow was to complain that women who have it all soon begin "asking for *more*. . . . After a period of happiness, excitement, and fulfillment comes the inevitable taking it all for granted, and becoming restless and discontented again for *More!*"[5] The complaint was gratuitous, since Maslow, like Dreiser, considered desire genetic, a biologically determined component of a self driven to seek satisfaction.

As a naturalistic novel, *Sister Carrie* dramatized biological determinism through a plot that made every action consequential. No matter how casual a character's gesture, look, or comment seemed, it became the cause of an effect, the stimulus to a response that could produce a significant but unforeseen, and perhaps tragic, outcome. Determinism evoked Dreiser's famous comparisons of human beings to insects and animals, all subject to ineluctable drives that characters experience as desire. Desire is a natural force in the novel, but the objects of desire are socially constructed artifacts imbued with impossible dreams of happiness. Insatiability is thus ontologic and cultural, an innate human condition and the sign of social conditioning. Poor Carrie. Her desire is illimitable, but her imagination is limited to the world of goods. Carrie is always looking to see what else in the world she could want, and as Dreiser shows, she is conditioned biologically and culturally to want and buy – or buy into – what she sees. I would argue that this simple sequence of seeing, wanting, and buying constitutes a deterministic structure of desire underlying naturalistic novels, like *Sister Carrie,* and advertisements psychologically programmed to motivate the modern consumer. In the 1920s, when creating consumer desire became a serious profession, the well-known behavioral psychologist John B. Watson left his academic chair at The Johns Hopkins University for a position with the J. Walter Thompson Company, at the time a leading advertising agency. Watson's departure from Baltimore uncannily reproduced the circumstances in *Sister Carrie* that surrounded Hurstwood's flight from Chicago. Both men headed for New York in disgrace, an illicit attraction to a young woman having cost them their marriage, their money, and their respectable positions.[6] Unlike Hurstwood, however, the penniless Watson had marketable psychological techniques that would earn him and the advertising firm a fortune – techniques of Pavlovian conditioning said to produce determinable responses to stimuli associated with elemental emotions – fear, pleasure, desire.[7] Desiring a beautiful woman, one desires the Coca-Cola associated with her billboard image.[8] Desiring beautiful clothes, Carrie yearns for something more she associates with money and material goods.

If we had a literary text devoid of the goods and advertisements associated with consumerism, a text that creates a world without department stores – the site and *sight* of consumption[9] – without restaurants, theaters, hotels, and the parade of fashion, an emptied world antithetical to Dreiser's Chicago and New York, would it be devoid of *Sister Carrie*'s pattern of desire? What, if anything, could a young woman see and want if she were suddenly transposed to a stark, empty landscape where there is no shop, no need for money, nothing to buy? This is the situation in my second text, a hauntingly resonant story that tests the possibility of escaping American consumerism and undermining the ways of consuming women.

First to Carrie.

As soon as she arrives in Chicago, poor desirous Carrie Meeber begins to dream and despair. Other women have what she, a poor working-girl, can never possess. Wandering through the city, she is a perennial outsider looking in at glamorous interiors through plate-glass windows that, Dreiser tells us, were becoming common in the city – office-building windows and the display windows of Chicago's new department stores. These glass windows revolutionized the relationship between insider and outsider by reflecting an image of the outsider upon goods arrayed within. Just looking thus drew the shopper inside the store as she saw her image superimposed upon and enhanced by dazzling things she was learning to desire. In effect, plate glass changed the concept of shopping from satisfying to creating desire, and turned shopkeepers into "amateur psychologists" delving into the secrets of human behavior. The Parisian shopkeepers who conceived the grand design of The Bon Marché, usually considered the first department store, foresaw that glass windows and cases would bring goods close to a woman who is just looking and evoke in her desires *"she did not know she had until she entered the premises."* By linking consumption with women and evocative desire, with eroticism, department stores supplanted a longstanding "commercial principle of *supply* [with] . . . that of *consumer seduction."*10

Carrie discovers Chicago's great department stores on her weary quest for "a likely door" – a strange and wonderfully elliptical phrase that suggests possibilities. When the door of a shoe factory opens, Carrie enters hopefully only to discover, all too soon, that she should have been looking for an *unlikely* door, a magical door to which the key was money. Years later, as she anticipates her first hundred and fifty dollars, she imagines this door finally opening: "What a door to an Aladdin's cave it [the money] seemed to be. Each day . . . her fancies of what her fortune might be, with ample money, grew and multiplied. She conceived of delights which were not – saw lights of joy that never were on land or sea" (334).

Carrie sees what is not there except in imagination, illusion, or desire, and she projects "the perfect joy" she cannot see upon material things readily visible to the eye.11 In this respect, she is not unlike the writer of a literary text, who has imbued its material objects with symbolic meanings, or the reader of the text, who learns to interpret its symbolic codes. Carrie learns by studying the semiotics of clothes, for she understands that "clothing constitutes a generally understood language of society."12 To learn this language, she becomes a willing student of her lover Drouet, a salesman alert to distinctions in dress, and of women friends like "the dashing Mrs. Vance," a fashion plate who arouses Carrie's desire and envy (230–1).13 These characters fulfill the function of modern advertisements by associating commodities with satisfaction and social class and creating, in their well-fashioned selves, enviable images for a shopper's avid eye to see. The city itself is, preeminently, a place to see, as Drouet tells Carrie when they first meet on the train to Chicago: "So much to see – theaters, crowds, fine houses" (5); "Chicago is a wonder. You'll find lots to see here" (7). Even Carrie's meager sister Minnie tells her, "You'll want to see the city first," and Carrie responds, "I think I'll look around tomorrow" (9).

Carrie starts out looking for a job and ends up – rather endearingly, I think – looking around in a department store. Just looking transforms Carrie from a shop-girl, the term applied to her, into a shopper who sees an array of commodities she is learning to want. Commodities speak to Carrie in tender voices with erotic overtones sounded by the salesmen of consumerism and condemned by its critics. " 'My dear,' said the lace collar she secured from Partridge's, 'I fit you perfectly; don't give me up.' 'Ah, such little feet,' said the leather of the soft new shoes; 'how effectively I cover them'" (75). Through a typical Dreiserian inversion, Carrie is inarticulate, while little jackets, silk cravats, shiny buttons, and soft shoes speak in a seductive language structured by a grammar of difference, envy, and desire. Carrie succumbs to this language as she makes what Thorstein Veblen famously called "invidious distinctions" and "invidious comparisons."[14] In Chicago, she compares her shabby, shop-girl clothes to the elegant fashion of lady shoppers who "elbowed" their way past her to buy the "dainty," "delicate," "dazzling" goods displayed in department store showcases. Invidious comparison lights a "flame of envy" in Carrie's heart, and envy arouses mediated desires. Carrie begins to want what she sees other women have – their clothes, and something more incorporated in contemporary definitions of consumerism: the self that is delineated by acquisition.[15] In Carrie's mind, clothes make the woman, and in Dreiser's representation, clothes make the man, as the text immediately asserts in its description of Drouet: "Good clothes, of course, were the first essential, the things without which he was nothing" (3).[16]

The possibility of being or becoming nothing – a fear of anomie – haunts Dreiser's characters. Like Carrie in Chicago and Hurstwood in New York, they know themselves to be dispossessed faceless figures in an urban crowd, and they seek to fashion a distinctive self in the only way they can conceive – by wearing the latest fashion. In the theaters of Broadway, where Carrie will again look for a likely door, clothes obviously create the person: a gray suit transforms Carrie into a "little Quakeress," and a scanty dress, into an oriental harem beauty. On stage where all can see, fashion fulfills its promise to confer identity, though the self it creates is factitious and unstable, subject to fashion's notorious vagaries. Fashion used properly – that is, used up and discarded – makes consumption visible, especially in the theater, where consumption becomes inseparable from acts of seeing and being seen.[17] Intuitively, Dreiser's little actress links seeing with fashion, consumption, and social value. As soon as she sees Hurstwood, she evaluates his worth – his wealth, position, and sexuality – by his "rich" plaid vest, mother-of-pearl buttons, and soft black shoes "polished only to a dull shine." Dull is sometimes better than shiny in a text gleaming with "a thousand lights" (1). Seeing Drouet's shiny patent leather shoes, "Carrie *could not help* feeling that there was a distinction in favor of soft leather" (73; emphasis added).

Somehow naïve little Carrie Meeber has learned to make distinctions, the basis of personal tastes which, we are being told, reflect social class and cultural encoding.[18] Long before the term *distinctions* was to be given its current prominence in cultural criticism, Dreiser had translated it into dramatic action by having Carrie reject one man for another with superior taste, and into authorial judgment by finding Carrie's taste inferior to that of "the greatest minds" (like, presumably, the writer's). In reflective passages, the text comments upon the many minute but momentous social distinctions made by its characters – characters Dreiser views critically, but with a much-noted compassion. They are, after all, helpless creatures, driven by innate desire and "the lure of the material." In Dreiser's famous, and infamously clichéd, image, they are moths drawn to the flame – and Hurstwood is finally consumed.

The etymological root of the words *consume, consumer,* and *consumerism* is the Latin *consumere:* "To take up completely, make away with, eat up, devour, waste, destroy, spend" (*OED*). While economists define *consumption* as use in satisfaction of wants, the *Oxford English Dictionary* gives as its primary meaning "to use up destructively. Said chiefly of fire: To burn up." These contrary meanings suggest why acts of consumption elicit ambivalent feelings, attracting and repelling as *using* melds into *using up* or wasting, turning something into nothing. The end of *Sister Carrie* shows Dreiser's Hurstwood, once a man to be envied, reduced to nothing: he has no money, no clothes, no one, and, dangerously in a market economy, no exchange value. Ironically, the discovery of a likely door marked the beginning of Hurstwood's decline. By coincidence, it seems, Hurstwood finds the door of his employer's safe open on the night he feels most persecuted by his wife, most driven by desire for Carrie, and most befuddled by whiskey. Like Carrie later on, Hurstwood has stumbled upon a magical door and entered Aladdin's cave only to find its golden treasures illusory. The little actress came to see the impotence of money, and the manager saw its evanescence. Hurstwood's estranged wife takes the now ex-manager's small fortune, and detectives take the stolen money. Having lost his money, reputation, and natty clothes, the essence of his self, Hurstwood loses all desire, and his last suicidal words stand as Dreiser's last words in the Pennsylvania edition of *Sister Carrie* – "What's the use?"

Hurstwood ends up "a nameless body" drifting to a pauper's grave in Potter's Field, and Carrie becomes a name used to advertise the pleasures of illusion: "At Broadway and Thirty-ninth Street was blazing, in incandescent fire, Carrie's name. 'Carrie Madenda,' it read, 'and the Casino Company.' All the wet, snowy sidewalk was bright with this radiated fire." The source of the radiation is "a large, gilt-framed posterboard, on which was a fine lithography of Carrie, life-size" (362). Poor Carrie. She wanted a real self and ends up a fiery figure of consumption. Her blazing billboard image holds her in arrest, as though she were "under the spell of one activity . . . to be sold" – which is how cultural theorists picture goods in a department store window.[19] As an image that promises pleasures only illusion can fulfill, Dreiser's little actress is as much a victim of deception as she is a deceptive representation among all the misrepresentations sadly catalogued in the novel's much-quoted conclusion: "In fine raiment and elegant surroundings, men seemed [to Carrie] to be contented. Hence, she drew near these things. Chicago, New York; Drouet, Hurstwood; the world of fashion and the world of stage – these were but incidents. Not them, but what they represented, she longed for. Time proved the representation false" (368). Today, influential cultural critics contend that representation itself has become an act of falsification as it "substitut[es] signs of the real for the real itself."[20] I quote Jean Baudrillard, who argues, along with Guy Debord and others, that the evocative images circulating in consumer societies have no referents and that the representations these images bring to the eye are devoid of reality, as is the name Carrie Madenda. For Carrie Madenda, like Carrie Drouet, Carrie Murdock, and Carrie Wheeler, is a false name for Carrie Meeber which is, after all, a fiction.

I turn now to 1990 and a story called "Sweetheart of the Song Tra Bong" in Tim O'Brien's highly acclaimed collection of Vietnam War stories, *The Things They Carried*.[21] The "Sweetheart" is an actual sweetheart of a young American soldier, Mark Fossie, a medic assigned to an aid station deep in the Vietnam bush, near the village of Tra Bong, an ideally remote place, Mark believes – and we are asked to believe – for his childhood sweetheart to visit. Mary Anne Bell duly arrives in Tra Bong, a seventeen-year-old blond with "blue eyes and a complexion like strawberry ice cream" dressed in "white culottes and this sexy pink sweater" and carrying a plastic cosmetic kit (105, 102). Thus begins a highly compressed story of initiation that describes a young woman's passage from innocence to experience as she assimilates the values of a new world and becomes a new person. To Mary Anne, Vietnam is as immanent with possibilities for self-actualization as Chicago was to Carrie, and as evocative of desire even though it offers nothing to buy. Mary Anne has been transported to a world without department stores, without hotels, restaurants, and theaters, a world beyond "the lure of the material," to recall Dreiser's phrase, and beyond the need for money. Mary Anne never expresses a desire for money and never appears, as Carrie does, with money in hand. Nevertheless, she begins to act like a shopper as she wanders about, just looking. Guarded by three soldiers,

Mary Anne browses through the village, a dangerous place run by the Vietcong, looking with such burning intensity at "the wonderful simplicity of village life" – so different from the city's complexities – that "her pretty blue eyes begin to glow."[22] If the glow is that of a tourist appreciating the sights of an unknown land, it burns with the acquisitive desire of a consumer. For tourism, like consumerism, begins with seeing and often ends with shopping, getting something. "She couldn't get enough of it," Rat says of Mary Anne (107), and then adds cryptically: "She wanted more" (124).

What more, I wonder, can O'Brien's Mary Anne want in the dematerialized terrain of Vietnam? As with Carrie, clothes offer a significant clue. Mary Anne exchanges her pink sweater for "filthy green fatigues" which, like Carrie's little tan jacket, mark her initiation into a rite of passage. Short stories require a rapid transit, and Mary Anne falls almost precipitously "into the habits of the bush. No cosmetics, no fingernail filing. She stopped wearing jewelry, cut her hair short and wrapped it in a dark green bandana. Hygiene became a matter of small consequence" (109). Giving up deodorant, creams, maybe even soap, this "half-equipped little knight," to borrow Dreiser's phrase, equips herself with "a standard M-16 automatic assault rifle" (113). She learns how to disassemble the weapon, care for its parts, and shoot. She discovers "she had a knack for it" (109). Like the re-fashioned Carrie who sees a new and prettier, plumper self in the mirror, Mary Anne becomes a new and "different person." She develops "a new confidence in her voice, a new authority in the way she carried herself" (109), and new visions of her future with Mark, less definite and less conventional. When Mark, troubled by the changes he sees, mentions home, she tells him to forget it: "Everything I want, she said, is right here. . . . To tell the truth, I've never been happier in my whole life. Never" (109–10). Hedonistic desire keeps Mary Anne in Vietnam, Carrie in Chicago, and consumers in the marketplace where, economists claim, they expect to purchase pleasure, the implicit promise of goods waiting to be possessed. In a single statement, Carrie wonderfully compresses the intention, desire, and future of the consuming woman: "She would be happy."[23]

For Mary Anne, as for Carrie, happiness centers upon the self – or more precisely, upon self-actualization, a dream of *more* fostered by individualistic societies.[24] Mary Anne wants to actualize "possibilities" deep within her self that draw her to the "dark green mountains to the west." "The wilderness seemed to draw her in," Rat says, describing a helplessness before determining forces that links America's sweetheart to Carrie as a naturalistic character. Driven by innate desire, neither can help being drawn to what she sees as symbolically charged means to happiness: clothes, comfort, and fame; or secrecy, violence, and death. Through different means, each becomes a different person, different from her uninitiated self, outwardly different from each other, and inwardly different from the real self each desired. Even the color of Mary Anne's eyes changes, turning from cheerleader blue to jungle green. "I saw those eyes of hers," Rat says, "I saw she wasn't even the same person no more" (117).

Mary Anne is changed by the Green Berets, who evoke her desire for killing, just as sporty men and fashionable women had evoked Carrie's desire for clothes and jewelry. *Made in Vietnam* could be the label on Mary Anne's new jewelry, a necklace strung with human tongues: "Elegant and narrow, like pieces of blackened leather, the tongues were threaded along a length of copper wire, one overlapping the next, the tips curled upward as if caught in a final shrill syllable" (120).[25] Silent and yet eloquent, the eviscerated tongues speak persuasively, telling of seductions that leave a woman solitary after drawing her from one dream to another, one man to another. Carrie leaves Drouet for Hurstwood, and Mary Anne leaves Mark for the Green Berets. The mutual attraction between America's sweetheart and these lethally secretive men is inexplicable but irrevocable: Mary Anne follows the Greenies into the night to become a killer.[26] Like Carrie, transformed into an incandescent fiery image of consumption, Mary Anne turns into a nocturnal silhouette, the residue of a consuming fire ignited by desire. She is consumed – and her killer self consummated – through a desire to devour what she sees: "Vietnam, I want to swallow the whole country – the dirt, the death – I just want to eat it and have it there inside me. That's how I feel. It's like . . . this appetite . . . but it's not *bad* . . . it's like I'm full of electricity and I'm glowing in the dark – I'm on fire almost – I'm burning away into nothing – but it doesn't matter because I know exactly who I am. You can't feel that anywhere else" (121; original emphasis). O'Brien's narrator describes Mary Anne as "lost inside herself," but she believes she has found her self by incorporating into her own body Vietnam, the war, death. Like Carrie, she ends up the embodiment of the values of her world and, like Carrie, strangely disembodied. Carrie becomes a fiery image, and Mary Anne, burned out by fire, becomes an ominous shadow slipping through the jungle where she is now "part of the land." Wearing her necklace of human tongues, she spreads silence over this land, though she has given a voice to the narrator Rat Kiley and the writer Tim O'Brien, who ends by saying, "She was dangerous. She was ready for the kill" (125).[27]

Mary Anne Bell belongs to a new breed of woman personified in recent movies and novels by the "hard body," so called in a 1991 article in *New York Magazine* entitled "Killer Women."[28] In such movies as "Terminator

II," these new women emerge as "combat-trained outlaws" who establish a "new standard of beauty" by appearing, like Mary Anne, without makeup, jewelry, or fancy clothes. For her role as terminating woman, the actress Linda Hamilton trained for months to transform her image – and her body – from that of the good, winsome, fashionably dressed Beauty she played in the television series "Beauty and the Beast." To become a Killer Woman, the Beauty who saved man from his bestiality had to release the violent impulses of the Beast suppressed within her breast.[29] Drawn to the site of men's violence, she will transform herself through an act of consumption – a suicidal gesture of discarding or destroying her own self. In the movies, Thelma and Louise consume their socially formed selves by dying; in O'Brien's story, Mary Anne burns away into nothing. The Killer Woman has survived, however, to become a popular pinup in Desert Storm. Appearing originally in a jeans advertisement, she reappeared in the desert war zone: a "slim, lanky" figure, "tough, fit, cool, and lethal," she leans against a police car and casually dangles a carbine – a dream woman ready for combat.[30]

The famous exponent of hard bodies, Jane Fonda, has said that *Playboy* images from Vietnam made her look at her body with "new eyes."[31] The softness of her Barbarella-self, she saw, had become complicit in the sexual consumption of Vietnamese women who were having themselves "Americanized" – eyes rounded, breasts enlarged – to enhance their value to American soldiers. Fonda's famous slogan to "go for the burn" thus traces back, through sordid images of consumption, to Vietnam, where O'Brien's Mary Anne Bell would carry out its mandate by "burning away into nothing." A simple but insatiable desire for profit ties this savagely exhilarating and anorexic vision of the burning body to a multibillion-dollar diet industry, as well as to books and movies.[32] Fonda turns the story of her self-transformation into a personal testimony that will help sell her aerobics *Workout Book,* just as countless products – face creams, perfumes, cigarettes – are sold through a movie star's endorsement. The *New York Magazine* attributes the emergence of "Killer Women" movies to the film industry's notorious pursuit of profit: "To appeal to women repulsed or bored by male action movies, they ["movie-moguls"] have created these woman warriors" (29). Killer Women sell. They have, indeed, become stylish artifacts used to sell designer killer clothes: black leather bike jackets, gold hip-hop chains, Chanel ammo bands – violence fashioned into chic.[33]

This trajectory of an American woman consumer, traced with elliptical starkness by two male writers, raises aesthetic, moral, and cultural questions. Does the recurrence of the same deterministic structure of desire in stories set in different times and places point to static elements in human behavior, in the literary forms that represent them, and in the shaping forces of consumerism? Is O'Brien's Mary Anne, a woman wandering in a global village, continuing an itinerary laid out for Dreiser's Carrie? Chicago, New York, and, eventually, Tra Bong – might this have been Carrie's progression if ninety years after *Sister Carrie,* Dreiser were to describe a young desirous woman following her man to Vietnam? There she would encounter a land seemingly beyond the consumer capitalism emerging in Chicago and New York, and yet a land that had become the ultimate *site* of consumption – and the *sight* of an ultimate consumption – as it was destroyed and wasted, consumed by the fires of war. Indeed, Baudrillard sees the Vietnam War as an insidiously involuted expression of modern consumer capitalism that functions as a society of the spectacle – to use Debord's phrase.[34] In this society, as in Carrie's world, "it's all theatre."[35]

When O'Brien's narrator accused his fellow soldiers of having "blinders on about women . . . [about how] gentle and peaceful they are" (117), he apparently meant to clear himself of sexism. Nevertheless, I believe, his story redacts a stereotypical male fear of females who step out of their prescribed social roles. Drawn into the heart of darkness that is war, Mary Anne rejects these roles to become, she believes, her real self, the killer woman who devours, wastes, and wastes away into a fiery image. Moralizing about a woman's fall, the narrator fitfully forgets that men created Vietnam, men transported Mary Anne to Tra Bong, and insidiously secretive men mediated her desires. As she enters a man's world and begins to want what she sees, Mary Anne seems sadly, if savagely, "a Waif amid Forces," to use Dreiser's words, a "wisp in the wind," a moth drawn to the flame.

Mary Anne's helpless submission to her surroundings dramatizes Dreiser's dictum that to see is to succumb. Defining the human mind as "a mere reflection of sensory impressions," and tracing impressions to the "flood of things" (203), Dreiser made an equation between seeing and succumbing irrefragable. Carrie's mind is flooded by sensory impressions of the city's material things, and it succumbs; Mary Anne's mind is flooded by impressions of darkness, mystery, and violence. As in *Sister Carrie,* the most striking impressions in *The Things They Carried* are visual, and they are all of war. Another story in the collection states explicitly that war "fills the eye. It commands you" (85), a view shared by an *Esquire* article entitled "Why Men Love War." Written by a Vietnam veteran, the article traces men's intense feeling for war, a feeling fit to be called love, to a "fundamental [human] passion . . . to see things, what the Bible calls the lust of the eye and the Marines in Vietnam called eye fucking."[36] "Sweetheart of the Song Tra Bong" describes its heroine's blue eyes constantly looking, staring, narrowing, squinting, focusing, and reflecting the world they see by turning jungle-green. This physiological response makes visible the force of stimuli so driving and deterministic that they transform desire into a craving need, and the self into a helpless and atavistically craving creature.

Thus O'Brien's story displaces the biological determinism it reinscribes to the trope of addiction, a reality to countless American soldiers: "Vietnam had the effect of a powerful drug: that mix of unnamed terror and unnamed pleasure that comes as the needle slips in." Seduced and pleasured, Mary Anne "wanted more . . . and after a time the wanting became needing, which then turned to craving" (123–4). *Sister Carrie* had described the city as a powerful drug, producing upon the newcomer's "untried mind" the same "craving" that "opium" produced upon the body (214). In both texts, the trope of addiction coalesces with that of male seduction as a powerful man overcomes a helpless woman whose passivity requires a passive grammatical voice: Carrie is seduced by Drouet and that "inhuman" or "superhuman" tempter, the city; and Mary Anne is "seduced by the Greenies." Social historians who describe "customer seduction" or commodities "wrapped in an aesthetic of seduction" – common and recurrent descriptions – place modern consumerism within the same paradigm of male power over a fatally submissive female.[37]

This submission raises complicated moral issues in both texts. In Vietnam, O'Brien's narrator says, everyone comes in clean and goes out dirty; how dirty is "a question of degree" and of moral integrity. In Dreiser's city, we are told, a young woman "becomes better, or . . . becomes worse" (1), though the difference seems equivocal in *Sister Carrie*.[38] Would a poor working-girl have become a better person if she had remained in a shoe factory punching holes for four dollars a week? Did she become worse by accepting "two soft, green, handsome, ten-dollar bills" – perhaps the most sensuously seductive dollar bills in American literature? Should the blue-eyed sweetheart of Sigma Chi have remained untouched by the violence she saw in Vietnam and blithely returned home to await marriage and motherhood in a "gingerbread house" with "yellow-haired children"? Or should she have stayed to bear witness in her own being to the atavistic savagery of war by retreating farther and farther into its darkness to become its terrible realization?

Moral questions became legal problems when succumbing to the "drag of desire," as Dreiser phrased it, led to criminal behavior. Oliver Twist's innocent request for *more* evoked an awful, if comic, prophecy: "That boy will be hung . . . I know that boy will be hung" (37). In Victorian England, respectable middle-class ladies were lured into crime in glamorous new department stores where they suffered sudden attacks of kleptomania, a hitherto unknown disease of women overcome by an irresistible urge to steal. Women apprehended for department-store thefts had a common plea: "I couldn't help myself."[39] Like moths drawn to the flame, they responded to glass showcases designed "to force people to possession." Victorian doctors explained that women "forced to steal" had been seduced by material things and victimized by their "sexual organs."[40] Treatment of their "pelvic diseases" might entail surgery, to which kleptomaniacs swooning in Victorian courtrooms tearfully assented in hope of being freed from the blight of "biological determinism."

Critics of American consumerism, tracing back to Veblen and beyond, have described the deliberate evocation of acquisitive desire as conspiratorial, if not criminal, a secret attack by "hidden persuaders" – to use Vance Packard's famous phrase – upon an unsuspecting public. Discerning a businesslike "application of the wisdom of advertising, public relations, and behavioral science to . . . modern elections," historians have argued that the political "packaging and sale of candidates to voter-consumers" has resulted in an impersonalized mediated relationship of "packages to packages . . . shaped by managers who are themselves for sale."[41] In this view, everyone in modern politics is a salesman, like Dreiser's perennial Drouet, or like Hurstwood, a manager, or like Carrie, an actor – no one less so, perhaps, than our country's telegenic presidents. The vocabulary of politics has become synonymous with that of an advertising industry concentrated upon image-making, perception (as opposed to a putative reality), and selling.[42] Public policies, like brand-name products, have to be sold, and politicians, like traveling salesmen, energetically take to the road or to the shopping mall to buy a pair of socks.

Historians have claimed that the commodification of books, begun with the invention of the printing press, created an autonomous space for verbal advertisements. Books destined for a competitive marketplace carried the printer's own unabashed testimonials to their excellence. In time, these commendatory inserts were printed separately and distributed as publicity flyers, the precursors, historians believe, of modern advertisements and the endorsements still printed in today's paperbacks.[43] *The Things They Carried* contains six introductory pages of single-spaced excerpts from glowing reviews not unconscious of their incitements to buy. "If I can't get you to go out and buy this book," one reviewer writes, "then I've failed you." The profuse advertising of *The Things They Carried* contrasts with the lack of advertising that initially repressed the sales of *Sister Carrie*. The story of the novel's virtual censorship is famous in literary history both for its apocryphal versions, generated mainly by Dreiser, and its elusive truth.[44] In 1907, *Sister Carrie* was reissued by a publisher apparently impressed by a comment on the novel's appearance and quick disappearance: "In this country, the popularity of a book depends upon 'judicious advertising.' "[45] The publisher's ten-page advertisement recapitulating *Sister Carrie*'s infamous lack of advertising suggested that the novel had been considered too daring, too raw, for the American public. What better way to sell the book?

Today, the serious consideration being given to *Sister Carrie* attests to its sheer inexhaustibility.[46] Absorbing all the attention it has received, the text, like its insatiable heroine, cries out for more, the promise of a future that seems assured by its past. The future of *The Things They Carried* remains to be seen. It may be bought and used and then used up. Or it may withstand the fickleness of fashion, critical and literary, and resist consumption through the strength of its highly praised style. Although clumsiness of style or lack of style has been considered Dreiser's weakness, *Sister Carrie* is a book that critics, in their insatiability, cannot consume. And yet unless it is consumed – bought, read, used, and used again – it ceases to exist. It needs for its self-actualization, its fulfillment as a work of art, the consumerist society that had depleted its characters, even the woman it enhanced, a rich and famous actress. Like Carrie Meeber, the novel must always have more: more readers, more appreciation, more sales – ultimately, an elusive *more* that represents the mystery of human desire.

"The ultimate meaning of desire," we have been told, "is death,"[47] but the death of desire in characters who seem beyond consumerism – because like homeless Hurstwood they cannot buy, or like Mary Anne they see nothing material worth buying – turns out, in the two texts I compare, to be deadly. When Hurstwood comes to the end of desire, when he does not want anything more, he dies. When Mary Anne has everything she wants, she becomes an agent of death. Wanting more, Carrie goes on living, dreaming of a happiness that, fortunately perhaps, she will never know. Thus she remains, forever, the producer's ideally insatiable consumer.

I began by asking what more Carrie could want and ended with an unlikely sister to Carrie – a young woman who had found "everything" she wanted, so she said, in the violence of Vietnam. This kinship might have been anticipated if one believes, as various critics do, that Vietnam was as much the site of late capitalism as the modern American city, and that capitalism and a culture of consumption are inextricably intertwined.[48] In *Sister Carrie,* the mediation of consumerism through a woman's desire produced a sequence of seeing, wanting, consuming, and being consumed that I find reproduced in the distinctly different postmodern text of the "Sweetheart of the Song Tra Bong." Strangely enough, time has not altered the sequential pattern of desire inscribed in Dreiser's *Sister Carrie*. Nor has a drastic change of setting disrupted its design. Indeed, the ways of consuming women in naturalistic fiction appear to be static, impervious to the historical changes effected by a seemingly radical change of setting, of time and place. In a Vietnam bush as in burgeoning Chicago, a fixed relationship between stimulus and response determines female behavior and transforms an innocent young American woman, a small-town girl from the Midwest, into a consumer. Her desire, her insatiability, seems synonymous with a sense of lack she finds irradicable.[49] Seeing what others have and she lacks, this unconsummated and consuming woman believes that she must have *more,* and that having *more* will allow her to become (as Maslow put it) more and more the person she sees herself capable of becoming. This desire for self-actualization, a culturally inscribed individualistic desire, turns Carrie and Mary Anne into consuming women whose generic similarities should not remain hidden by differences in appearance. A fashionably dressed Broadway star and a camouflaged killer waiting to strike – in either guise, naturalism's consuming woman glows with a devouring fire. In *Sister Carrie,* the fiery image of a body that had been consumed with desire appears in an advertisement designed to ignite desire in others. In O'Brien's story, a burning body becomes the site of consumption as a woman is consumed by what she sees in a land wasted by war. There, as in America's cities, her fate, like her desire, is determined; in both settings, the place where determinism and desire intersect is the body of a gazing woman. The woman herself is a static figure, arrested in a pattern of desire, but she generates a vortex of forces that flow inexorably toward consumption and death. Men should fear this woman, for a man who gazes upon her may be doomed, as may be those upon whom she gazes. In *Sister Carrie,* Hurstwood becomes a nameless pauper who must die because his eyes once glowed at the sight of Carrie Meeber. In "Sweetheart of the Song Tra Bong," nameless others die because Mary Anne Bell's eyes glow with the green of Vietnam's jungle.

As for Demi Moore the actress – like Carrie, she ended up with money. In the movie *Indecent Proposal,* the actress portrays a woman who sells her body for a million dollars. One thing has changed in the last hundred years: a consuming woman's price and reward. In Dreiser's novel, poor Carrie Meeber accepted two soft, green, handsome ten-dollar bills for her desirous self, and when she had "in hand" a hundred and fifty dollars, Carrie Madenda the actress found herself rich beyond belief and, for a moment, happy.

NOTES

1   Peter Wilkinson, "Why Demi Moore Wants More," *Redbook*, January 1993, pp. 48–51 and 91–92. The blurb for the article reads: "Don't envy her perfect body, happy marriage, wealth, or success. Though this actress has it all, she's not yet satisfied" (48). Perhaps one clue to Demi Moore's desire for more lies in her eyes: "delicate, slightly startled ovals that *take in* every detail" (48, emphasis added). As this essay will argue, what the eyes "take in" determines what the person wants literally to take in or consume.

2   Needless to say, each of these subjects is surrounded by a mass of critical theory and controversy, most of which I must relegate to the ellipsis in which I have placed historical time. However, I would like to mention some of the works that have helped me see the links between literary naturalism and desire, consumption, and determinism. From a collection of essays on free will, I have taken as a working definition of determinism the succinctly stated necessitarian view that "every event and state of affair is 'causally necessitated' by preceding events and states of affairs" (*Free Will*, ed. Gary Watson [New York: Oxford University Press, 1982], p. 2). Critics usually equate literary naturalism with determinism, particularly Dreiser's critics who see the writer linking cause and effect into a binding chain. In an early essay (1943), Philip Rahv distinguished naturalism from realism by "its treatment of the relation of character to background." In naturalistic fiction, he said, the individual is not merely "subordinate to" his background; he is "wholly determined by it." Rahv pointed to Dreiser as an example of an American writer who plotted "the careers of his characters strictly within a determinative process" ("Notes on the Decline of Naturalism," *Documents of Modern Literary Realism*, ed. George J. Becker [Princeton, N.J.: Princeton University Press, 1963], p. 584). Donald Pizer has slightly modulated the equation of naturalism with determinism by substituting *circumscribed* for *determined*. At the "ideological core of American naturalism," he writes, is "a sense of man more circumscribed than conventionally acknowledged" (*Twentieth-Century American Literary Naturalism: An Interpretation* [Carbondale: Southern Illinois University Press, 1982], p. 6). Lee Clark Mitchell has linked naturalism to a "scientific concept of determinism" according to which the individual's actions are subject to "insidious" constraints, and the writer's attention directed "to innate traits and socialized habits . . . [and] scenes of coercions" ("Naturalism and the Languages of Determinism," *The Columbia Literary History*, ed. Emory Elliott et al. [New York: Columbia University Press, 1988], pp. 534–49). Contributing to the rise of literary naturalism, Mitchell says, was the growth of industrialism, urbanization, and "a new consumer society" (527). In his recent study of American naturalism, Mitchell has shifted his critical attention from "scientific to linguistic forms of determinism," for reasons he explains in a preface entitled "Taking Determinism Seriously" (*Determined Fictions: American Literary Naturalism* [New York: Columbia University Press, 1989], pp. vii–xvii. Mitchell's reading of *An American Tragedy* focuses upon "the psychopoetics of desire"; desire is an inevitable subject in writing about Dreiser who, as we know, entitled his Cowperwood novels *A Trilogy of Desire*.
    Among the many subjects drawn into debates over determinism is women's

dress – a subject of consequence to Dreiser's Carrie and hence to this essay. Women's dress, we are told, still raises the "ever-controversial question" of determinism by asking whether biological differences between women and men determine differences in their dress (Mary Ellen Roach, "The Social Symbolism of Women's Dress," *The Fabrics of Culture: The Anthropology of Clothing and Adornment*, ed. Justine M. Cordwell and Ronald A. Schwarz [New York: Mouton, 1979], pp. 415–22). Like fashion, material culture has been linked to determinism. See, for example, Jules David Prown's claim that "[t]he fundamental attitude underlying the study of material culture is, as with most contemporary scholarship, a pervasive *determinism*" ("Mind in Matter: An Introduction to Material Culture Theory and Method," *Winterthur Portfolio: A Journal of American Material Culture* 17 [1982]: 6; original emphasis).

As we know, the influence of deterministic thinking upon the conduct of human affairs has been continuous, profound, and highly consequential; and as we shall see, it has figured in the development of American advertising, architecture, and politics, at least as they are represented in much theoretical and critical writing and in American literature. This is not to say that the deterministic views inscribed in various disciplines and cultural theories remain unchallenged. See, for example, the challenge to classical views on the determination of human needs made by Edmond Pretteceille and Jean-Pierre Terrail in *Capitalism, Consumption and Needs,* trans. Sarah Matthews (New York: Basil Blackwell, 1985).

3 *Sister Carrie,* ed. Donald Pizer (New York: Norton, 1970; 1900), p. 335. Another *Sister Carrie,* published in 1993, transports Dreiser's waif to a surrealistically hip contemporary American scene where she finds adventure in the advertising world, prostitution, and murder. See Lauren Fairbanks, *Sister Carrie, a Novel* (Normal, Ill.: Dalkey Archive Press, 1993). Among this novel's bizarre and zany scenes is one in which Carrie responds to a Narrator's synopsis of a "masterpiece" that describes a "sweet little girl" who has "all her needs met." "The poor little fuck – will she ever be this happy again?," the Narrator asks. "Is she enjoying it at all? Probably not enough, we all tend to think there is MUCH MORE" (61; original emphasis). Carrie's incongruous comment, "How strange," fits into all the incongruities of this strange and irreverent book. I read Fairbanks's book after I had written this essay, and though it interests me as an attempt to imagine a contemporary Carrie, it does not serve as the test case I am seeking, which is a text that imagines a contemporary woman transported to a place where there is nothing to buy.

4 Abraham H. Maslow, "A Theory of Human Motivation (1943)," *Motivation and Personality* (New York: Harper & Row, 1970; 1954), p. 46. Maslow finds self-actualizing people *"flexible,"* capable of adapting themselves realistically to any people, any environment" (xxi; original emphasis). Such flexibility allows the consuming women of this essay to adapt to the disparate and difficult settings described in the texts I discuss. Maslow contextualizes a desire for more within a psychological theory that seeks benignly to show people the way to happiness. Others contextualize the desire within an economic system that seeks to maximize profit. To sell products, advertisers, for example, need to understand that "[w]e all want more," we all measure our own improvement, as well as social

change, "by getting more" (Ronald Berman, *Advertising and Social Change* [Beverly Hills, Calif.: Sage, 1981], pp. 68–9).

5 Maslow, *Motivation and Personality,* pp. 98 and xvi–xvii.

6 See David Cohn, *J. B. Watson, The Founder of Behaviorism: A Biography* (London and Boston: Routledge & Kegan Paul, 1979). "When Watson got off the train in New York," Cohn writes, "he had no money, no job and no prospects" (159). If the name were switched from Watson to Hurstwood, the sentence could have appeared in *Sister Carrie* – and, with another switch, in Dreiser's biography. In 1903, when *Sister Carrie* seemed a dismal failure, Dreiser arrived in New York depressed and impoverished, lamenting the failure of his novel and his life. Cohn's description of the "indiscreet affair" that led to Watson's terrible troubles also applies to Dreiser and to his character, each of whom had been drawn irresistibly and ruinously to a young woman who "stirred something very deep in him" (*Watson,* 148). Cohn is misleading, however, when he says that Watson arrived in New York with "no prospects," for the behaviorist had long thought of applying his psychological theories to business, particularly the business of advertising. The rupture in his academic career became an opportunity for Watson to begin another career which he saw as a logical extension of his experimental work: he would apply the techniques of behavioral conditioning he had studied in the laboratory to the marketplace. On Watson's belief that psychology should be used as an instrument of "social control" and, specifically, used in advertising to create "a society of consumers," see Kerry W. Buckley, "The Selling of a Psychologist: John Broadus Watson and the Application of Behavioral Techniques to Advertising," *Journal of the History of the Behavioral Sciences* 18 (1982): 207–21. Buckley quotes Watson as saying that "the consumer is to the manufacturer, the department stores and the advertising agencies, what the green frog is to the physiologist" (212).

7 Cohn attributes Watson's phenomenal success in advertising to the "great god, the consumer [who] had made Watson so rich that he lived at one of the best addresses in Manhattan." Like Dreiser, Watson "began to dress in a very dandified fashion" that may have made him look "more attractive," though it gave him, Watson's biographer says, "a slightly ridiculous air in retrospect" (192). Obviously, men re-fashion themselves through their clothes as hopefully as women (or women characters), at once seeking and advertising a new self through a change of costume. Like Watson the psychologist, Dreiser the writer became a supersalesman. For after he had fallen into bad times in New York, he went on to earn the considerable salary of $10,000 as director of the Butterwick publications, *The Designer, The New Idea Woman's Magazine,* and *The Delineator,* magazines advertising Butterwick dress patterns and featuring articles on women's fashion. I should add that eventually Dreiser lost this position because of "amorous misconduct."

That the psychologist could teach the businessman how to "coerce" the consumer into buying was the belief of William Dill Scott, Ph. D., with whom Watson and others were affiliated in organizing the Scott Company, a consulting firm that showed businessmen how to use psychology to their profit. The author of influential books on the art of advertising, Scott held various prestigious positions, including that of Director of the Psychological Laboratory of North-western University and Director of the Bureau of Salesman Research, Carnegie Institute of Technology. In one of his books, Scott "assumed the pleasant task" of "systematizing" and "presenting" the "subject of the psychology of advertising" in a form that would "be of distinct practical value to all who are interested in business promotion" (*The Psychology of Advertising: A Simple Exposition of the Principles of Psychology in Their Relation to Successful Advertising* [Boston: Small, Maynard & Company, 1917], pp. 5–6). He dedicated another book to the "YOUNG BUSINESS MAN . . . who is studying to make his arguments more convincing and his suggestions more *coercive*" (*Influencing Men in Business: The Psychology of Argument and Suggestion,* rev. Delton T. Howard, Ph. D. [New York: The Ronald Press, 1928; 1911]; emphasis added). Scott believed that modern psychology showed man to be "a creature who rarely reasons" (35), and women to be particularly impetuous buyers whose "deliberation is interrupted by a sudden extreme feeling of value" that attaches itself to a commodity (62).

The irrational choices women make, especially in the marketplace, usually seem to psychologists more marked and censorious than those made by men. A putatively objective "mathematical examination" of the forces that determine choice ends up pointing to the particular irrationality of women: "Women in a supermarket are susceptible to the tricks of the advertiser and packer; they do not make rational choices" (Ludwig von Bertalanffy, *General System Theory: Foundations, Development, Applications* [New York: George Braziller, 1968]). Even irrational choices can be conditioned and manipulated, Bertalanffy asserts, illustrating once again how human behavior can be deliberately determined: "In our society, it is the job of an influential specialty – advertisers, motivation researchers, etc. – to *make* choices irrational which essentially is done by coupling biological factors – conditioned reflex, unconscious drives – with symbolic values" (115–16; original emphasis).

Among the many studies explicating the ways that symbolic values are imputed to material things – aside from Marx's quintessential study of the fetishization of commodities in *Capital* and of consumption in *Grundrisse* – I list here only a few highly selected works pertinent to this essay (and these are aside, also, from the Frankfurt school of critical theory to which many on this abbreviated list are indebted): Stuart Ewen, *Captains of Consciousness: Advertising and the Roots of the Consumer Culture* (New York: McGraw-Hill, 1976); Mary Douglas and Baron Isherwood, *The World of Goods* (New York: Basil Blackwell, 1979); W. F. Haug, *Critique of Commodity Aesthetics* (Cambridge, Mass.: Polity Press, 1986; 1971); Colin Campbell, *The Romantic Ethic and the Spirit of Modern Consumerism* (New York: Basil Blackwell, 1987); Patricia Springborg, *The Problem of Human Needs and the Critique of Civilisation* (London: George Allen & Unwin, 1981); Richard Lichtman, *The Production of Desire: The Integration of Psychoanalysis into Marxist Theory* (New York: Macmillan, The Free Press, 1982); Valerie Steele, *Fashion and Eroticism: Ideals of Feminine Beauty from the Victorian Era to the Jazz Age* (New York: Oxford University Press, 1985); *The Psychology of Fashion,* ed. Michael R. Solomon (Lexington, Mass.: Lexington Books, 1985); Thomas Richards, *The Commodity Culture of Victorian England: Advertising and Spectacle, 1851–1914* (Stanford, Calif.: Stanford University Press, 1990). Though this last book begins in London with the spectacle of the Crystal Palace, it goes on to refer to American fiction and, perhaps fittingly, bestows upon Dreiser's character yet another false name, erroneously calling the little actress Carrie Meacham (207).

8 Writing at the time of the Cold War, E. J. Kahn, Jr., wondered why the Communists "picked" on Coca-Cola as an emblematically invidious American product. "It's because Coca-Cola is a champion of the profit motive, and wherever it goes, it spreads profits," a Coca-Cola man explained: "Everyone who has anything to do with the drink makes money and becomes a member of the bourgeoisie" (*The Big Drink: The Story of Coca-Cola* [New York: Random House, 1960], p. 32).

9 According to Stuart Ewen and Elizabeth Ewen, "The department store was more than a site for consumption; it was the *sight* of consumption. . . . Shopping was a perceptual adventure" (*Channels of Desire: Mass Images and the Shaping of American Consciousness* [New York: McGraw-Hill, 1982], p. 68; original emphasis). Or in the words of Marx, "The need which consumption feels for the object is created by the perception of it" (*Grundrisse: Foundations of the Critique of Political Economy*, trans. Martin Nicolaus [New York: Vintage, 1973; written in the winter of 1857–8 and published in German in 1939 and 1953], p. 92). For an analysis of how the considered use of space in department stores reflects a managerial purpose to "indoctrinate the customer in the culture of consumption," see Susan Porter Benson, "Palace of Consumption and Machine for Selling: The American Department Store, 1880–1940," *Radical History Review* 21 (1979): 199–221. Benson argues that department store managers consciously manipulated space in order "to convey a lofty impression of consumption as the key to status, happiness, and personal fulfillment while at the same time attending to the crasser mechanics of buying and selling" (202). Benson's phrase "Palace of Consumption" calls to mind Daniel J. Boorstin's earlier discussion of the first department stores as "Consumer Palaces" (*The Americans: The Democratic Experience* [New York: Random House, 1973], pp. 101–9). Boorstin traces a historical relationship between the rise of department stores with their plate-glass windows and the growth of city crowds and public transportation systems, in particular, streetcar lines (which figure significantly in *Sister Carrie*). William R. Leach has described "a transformative moment in history" that occurred when women first entered newly designed and conceptualized department stores ("Transformation in a Culture of Consumption: Women and Department Stores, 1890–1925," *Journal of American History* 71 [1984]: 319–42). These grand settings evoked an "upsurge of longing, a diffuse desire for something better . . . [that] was a hallmark of the consumer culture" (337). Leach has expanded his study of American consumer culture in his recently published book *Land of Desire: Merchants, Power, and the Rise of a New American Culture* (New York: Pantheon, 1993). *Land of Desire* appeared after I had written this essay, for which it provides (if belatedly) a detailed historical context. In *The Bourgeois and the Bibelot* (New Brunswick: Rutgers University Press, 1984), Rémy G. Saisselin describes the general impact of early American consumer habits upon shoppers, noting in passing characters in Dreiser's *Sister Carrie* and Zola's *The Ladies' Paradise* who encounter the department store as a "cultural space" (33–49). For an analysis of how the "sensual appeal of stores and the central modern experience of shopping" have "affected the novelistic

sensibility" of William Dean Howells, Sinclair Lewis, F. Scott Fitzgerald, as well as of Dreiser, see Neil Harris's interesting essay, "The Drama of Consumer Desire," *Yankee Enterprise: The Rise of the American System of Manufactures,* ed. Otto Myr and Robert C. Post (Washington, D. C.: Smithsonian Institution Press, 1981), pp. 189–216.

10 *The Golden Age of Shop Design: European Shop Interiors 1880–1939,* ed. Alexandra Artley (New York: Whitney Library of Design, 1976), pp. 6–7. For a history of The Bon Marché, see Michael B. Miller, *The Bon Marché: Bourgeois Culture and the Department Store, 1869–1920* (Princeton, N.J.: Princeton University Press, 1981). Drawing upon the Bon Marché for the setting and plot of his novel *The Ladies' Paradise (Au bonheur des dames),* Emile Zola dramatized the myriad ways that a department store sought to seduce women into buying. See *The Ladies' Paradise* (Berkeley and Los Angeles: University of California Press, 1992, published in English by Henry Vizetelly in 1886). In a study of English department stores, Alison Adburgham claims that Bainbridge's of Newcastle and Kendal Milne & Faulkner of Manchester, rather than The Bon Marché, should be "nominated as the first department stores" (*Shops and Shopping 1800–1914: Where, and in What Manner the Well-dressed Englishwoman Bought Her Clothes* [London: George Allen and Unwin, 1964], p. 137).

11 Drawing upon Marx and his understanding of the commodity as fetish, William Leiss describes "a dynamic interaction between the material and symbolic correlates of human needing" (*The Limits of Satisfaction: An essay on the problem of needs and commodities* [Toronto and Buffalo: University of Toronto Press, 1976], p. 67). Leiss states the widely shared view that through a complex "network of symbolic mediations" modern market economies "orient [human] needs entirely toward commodities" (67). In his study of the symbolic value of goods, Grant McCracken relates the need for self-refashioning to consumption as it is expressed through purchases. Acts of buying can initiate the creation of a new self as they initiate a new rite of passage. See *Culture and Consumption: New Approaches to the Symbolic Character of Consumer Goods and Activities* (Bloomington: Indiana University Press, 1988). Even the chair on which both Carrie and Hurstwood famously rocked owed its popularity, at least in good part, to advertisements that imbued it with symbolic values. As Richard L. Bushman explains, rocking-chairs melded the values of "comfort and gentility," a combination touted in early-nineteenth-century advertisements: "The refined rocker stood for the changes going on . . . as the American middle classes . . . tried to assimilate parlor culture into the modest domestic economies of ordinary people" (*The Refinement of America: Persons, Houses, Cities* [New York: Alfred A. Knopf, 1992], p. 272). In seeking out general "clues" to the "historical roots of consumer culture" in *Sister Carrie,* Michael Schudson notes that for a woman "the road to success" is paved not "by work and career alone but by lifestyle and consumption" (*Advertising, The Uneasy Persuasion: Its Dubious Impact on American Society* [New York: Basic Books, 1984], p. 148). We should note, however, that Carrie achieves success by working and that her style of life as a conspicuous consumer follows upon, rather than paves the way to, her success as an actress. This is not to minimize the importance of sex, sexu-

ality, and gender in Dreiser's novel, but to point out that Carrie is, significantly, a working woman. (I might note parenthetically that Schudson's discussion of *Sister Carrie* contains some minor misreadings: Carrie does not actually "seek a job at several department stores" [149] – she feels too inferior and intimidated; the good-natured and affable Drouet is hardly "sinister" [149]; and Carrie's "world" is not really of the "1880s" [159], as the novel begins in August 1889, and events of the 1890s – like the streetcar strike – significantly affect the plot).

12 *Channels of Desire* (1982), p. 126.

13 On the importance of clothes to the so-called fashionables of Carrie's time, see Lois W. Banner, *American Beauty* (New York: Knopf, 1983), pp. 17–27. As a subject for study, fashion has interested a vast range of theorists and cultural critics, figuring peripherally in works of diverse interests, and centrally in articles and books that have approached the subject from diverse directions. Approaching fashion as a system of signs, Roland Barthes presented a semiological interpretation that he himself declared out-moded – old-fashioned – in his Foreword to *The Fashion System*, trans. Matthew Ward and Richard Howard (New York: Hill and Wang, 1983; 1967). Alison Lurie also approached clothes as a sign system in her much more easy-going, popular history of fashion, *The Language of Clothes* (New York: Random House, 1981). Both semiotic studies confirm the view expressed in Ewen and Ewen's polemical work, *Channels of Desire* (1982), that "clothing constitutes a generally understood language of society" (126). This is a language that Banner's "fashionables" knew and Carrie was acquiring. For a considered discussion of the differences between "the codes of clothing and language" and the significance of these differences to the study of material culture, see McCracken, "Clothing as Language," *Culture and Consumption*, pp. 57–70.

Through an ingeniously punning use of language, Jacques Lacan has turned the "profound bivalence of . . . analytical theory on the subject of the symbolism of clothes" into a means of evaluating "the impasse reached with the notion of the symbol . . . in psychoanalysis (*The Seminar of Jacques Lacan: Book VII, The Ethics of Psychoanalysis 1959–1960*, ed. Jacques-Alain Miller, trans. Dennis Porter [New York: Norton, 1992, published originally in 1986 as *Le Seminaire*], p. 226). Lacan creates "a fable" concerning "the power of cloth" as it reveals the relationship between hiding (by clothing) and the hidden (the phallus, of course), between need and desire, privation or lack and the frustration, rather than gratification, of desire – among other matters ("The function of the good," pp. 218–30).

14 The idle fashionable rich whom Carrie longed to emulate were mercilessly dissected by Thorstein Veblen in *The Theory of the Leisure Class* (New York: Viking Penguin, 1976; 1899). In his essay "The Economic Theory of Woman's Dress" (1894), Veblen distinguished between clothing as articles of "comfort," and dress as "display of wasteful expenditure" (Veblen, *Essays In Our Changing Order*, ed. Leon Ardzrooni [New York: Viking], p. 68 and passim). When Carrie is a poor shop-girl, her threadbare jacket cannot give her the comfort of warmth. She needs comfort; she wants display. When she becomes an actress; the clothing she wears on the stage is pure display or "dress."

15 I draw upon a succinct but assured equation of terms: "Consumption – better

put, the delineation of a self by acquisition . . ." (Berman, *Advertising and Social Change,* 107).

16 Dreiser's dictum that clothes make the man undergoes a significant refinement in a modern study of fashion and its relation to the images of art. In *Seeing Through Clothes* (New York: Viking, 1978), Ann Hollander writes, "Clothes make not the man, but the image of man" (xv). Whereas Dreiser's Carrie wants to look like the well-dressed women she sees, in actuality, Hollander argues, people want to look like the representations of the human figure they see in the art of their times. Hollander describes the eye as mediating for the self as it presents images of images rather than, as writers as diverse as Dreiser and O'Brien show, images of "real" others. I would describe the eye as etiolating the self when it offers a person representations to emulate – which is not to deny that many real people fashion themselves upon artifactual images.

Clothes literally make the man in H. G. Wells's novel *The Invisible Man: A Grotesque Romance* (1897). Well's famous character loses his social identity when he loses his "appearance" by becoming invisible. In an attempt to become "a human being again" he goes to a department store (aptly named the Omnium) to look for clothes. Like Dreiser, Wells lists everything the store displays: stockings, gloves, lambswool pants, lambswool vests, trousers, lounge jacket, overcoat, slouch hat; and like Carrie, the Invisible Man wants everything he sees. The more clothes he puts on, the more "acceptable" he becomes as a "figure" in the city; without proper clothes he was, as Dreiser put it, "nothing" (chap. 22, "In the Emporium). While the Omnium allows the Invisible Man to find clothes he desperately needs, a department store stirs another strange character, a modern Robinson Crusoe, with desire for superfluity. Inexplicably stranded in an inexplicably depopulated but fully stocked department store, the protagonist of James Gould Cozzens's novella *Castaway* looks around to find things he might want; the sight of abundance "liberates" him from necessity. "There was no reason why he should not have all the clothes he wanted," he thinks; "More, if he chose, than he could ever use (*S.S. San Pedro and Castaway* [New York: Random House], pp. 150-2 and 158). Like consuming women, male characters see possibilities for self-actualization in department stores which, as apparently planned, generate a desire for more.

17 For a discussion of theater as "metaphor for perpetual spectatorship," see Deborah M. Garfield, "Taking a Part: Actor and Audience in Theodore Dreiser's *Sister Carrie,*" *American Literary Realism* 16 (1983): 223-39. For a pertinent psychoanalytic critique of the "relation between viewing and devouring," see Anne Friedberg, "A Denial of Difference: Theories of Cinematic Identification," *Psychoanalysis and Cinema,* ed. E. Ann Kaplan (New York: Routledge, 1990), pp. 36-45. As I have indicated, an etymological meaning of *consume* is *to devour,* and an equation of devouring with seeing implies that seeing is, or can be, an act of consumption. In 1935, Otto Fenichel had published a paper on a "symbolic equation" he considered familiar to psychoanalysts, the equation between seeing and devouring. As he put it: "to look at = to devour. When someone gazes intently at an object, we say that he 'devours it with his eyes'" ("The Scoptophilic Instinct and Identification" in *The Collected Papers of Otto Fenichel,* 1st ser. [New York: Norton, 1953], pp. 373-97). Drawing upon

Freud, Fenichel traced the scoptophilic instinct to libidinal drives that may express themselves in sadomasochistic actions, in art, in empathetic feelings, or in displacements such as that from the "phallic eye" to the camera. Thus, the unconscious drive behind seeing can become objectified in an image that the camera creates as it imitates the eye in its power to turn a person into a sight. Indeed, in a much quoted work, *Ways of Seeing,* John Berger has described woman as an "object of vision" or a "sight" to be seen, in effect, as a commodity available for consumption (New York Penguin Books, 1979; p. 47). Berger's dicta on sexual difference in ways of seeing have influenced feminist film theory and, more generally, studies of women as objects, rather than the subjects, of desire. "Men look at women," Berger wrote; "Women watch themselves being looked at" (47). As a man obsessed with looking at women, Dreiser understood the personal and cultural implications of sexually differentiated ways of seeing and dramatized them in *Sister Carrie.* Drouet and Hurstwood see Carrie; and Carrie sees clothes. Dreiser's male characters are, however, unusually attentive to, and even obsessed by, clothes, but they generally see clothes as a means of possessing a woman. In *An American Tragedy,* Clyde Griffiths thinks that a coat displayed in a department store window will win him the young woman he desires; and in *Sister Carrie,* Drouet woos Carrie in the department store by buying her a fashionable outfit.

In an interesting discursive essay on actresses, Jane Blair points out the implications to be deduced from watching a woman occupy the public space of a theater ("Private Parts in Public Places: The Case of Actresses," *Women and Space: Ground Rules and Social Maps,* ed. Shirley Ardener [New York: St. Martin's Press, 1981], pp. 205–28). Blair believes that in the theater an actress "could be her own woman, and speak her own mind" (p. 212) – a view that I have argued elsewhere does not apply to Dreiser's Carrie as an actress permitted, indeed commanded, to speak the words assigned to her by others. See "Speaking Her Own Piece: Emma Goldman and the Discursive Skeins of Autobiography," *American Autobiography: Retrospect and Prospect,* ed. Paul John Eakin (Madison: University of Wisconsin Press, 1991), pp. 235–66.

18 By defining taste as "the product of upbringing and education," Pierre Bourdieu has linked it to a learning process"; the "eye," he says, "is the product of history reproduced by education" (*Distinction: A Social Critique of the Judgement of Taste,* trans. Richard Nice [Cambridge, Mass.: Harvard University Press, 1984; published originally as *La Distinction: Critique social du jugement,* 1979], p. 3). Bourdieu links taste also to a "social hierarchy of . . . consumers" created, he believes, by a differential education, and he argues that the social construction of this hierarchy "predisposes taste to function as markers of 'class'" (1–2). According to him, "the capacity to see (*voir*)" is a "function of the knowledge (*savoir*), or [the] concepts . . . [and] words . . . available to name visible things." The history of the construction of seeing and taste is usually forgotten, Bourdieu asserts, but by remembering he believes he can discern "limits" to the "autonomy" that individuals, especially "intellectuals," have in making classifactory distinctions (483–4). Bourdieu proleptically answers the critic who might argue that his views on conditioning are culturally conditioned by asserting that they are based upon "scientific observation" (1). Literary

naturalism has also appealed to "scientific observation" as a basis for its representation of human behavior. The basis itself can be questioned, since scientific observation may be a social construction (as various critics and historians now believe).

19 "[I]n shop windows, things stand still . . . under the spell of one activity only; to change owners. They stand there waiting to be sold" (Alfred Sohn-Rethel, *Intellectual and Manual Labour: A Critique of Epistemology* [Atlantic Highlands, N. J.: Humanities Press, 1978], p. 25). Walter Benjamin supported his claim that advertisement is "superior" to criticism by evoking an image of burning incandescence that, I believe, comments obliquely upon Dreiser's billboard Carrie, for this looming life-sized figure, which appeals to "the mercantile gaze," may strike onlookers as more real than Carrie's actual presence. According to Benjamin, "Today the most real, the mercantile gaze into the heart of things is the advertisement," particularly "the huge images" characteristic of an "American style" of display seen in cities. "What, in the end, makes advertisements so superior to criticism?," Benjamin asks and then points to a burning image: "Not what the moving red neon sign says – but the fiery pool reflecting it in the asphalt." See "This Space for Rent" in *One-Way Street* (1955), reprinted in Walter Benjamin, *Reflections: Essays, Aphorisms, Autobiographical Writings,* trans. Edmund Jephcott, ed. Peter Demetz (New York: Harcourt Brace Jovanovich, 1978).

20 Jean Baudrillard, "The Precession of Simulacra," *Simulations,* trans. Paul Foss, Paul Patton, and Philip Beitchman (New York: Semiotext(e), Inc., 1983), p. 4. By a simple and deadly transposition, Baudrillard undermines referentiality: "Whereas representation tries to absorb simulation by interpreting it as false representation, simulation envelops the whole edifice of representation as itself a simulacrum" (11).

21 Tim O'Brien, "Sweetheart of the Song Tra Bong," *The Things They Carried* (New York: Penguin, 1990), pp. 98–125.

22 O'Brien economically condenses the conventions of a character's first encounter with a new ambient world by focusing upon seeing as the stimulus of desire and the sign of appropriation – a "mutual appropriation" in which Mary Anne will be consumed by the landscape she consumes with her eyes. In a study of early travel writings, Mary Louise Pratt has described this "mutual appropriation" (her phrase) as a way of structuring an "arrival scene": the eye mediates the appropriation as it scans a landscape in which curious others look and "gratify *themselves*" (*Imperial Eyes: Travel Writing and Transculturation* [New York: Routledge, 1992], p. 80 and passim; original emphasis). In O'Brien's story, as in much of the travel writing Pratt discusses, the others remain invisible; they are the repressed element in a discourse of conquest. Mary Anne's encounters with others, with Vietnamese, take place at night and are occluded from the story as told; and her "transculturation," to use Pratt's term, assimilates her to the ways of fellow Americans, the deadly night-ravaging Green Berets. In the end, Mary Anne may have joined the Montagnards in the far-distant mountains scanned by her desireful appropriative eyes.

23 In an essay that focuses mainly on *Sister Carrie,* Philip Fisher describes an "anticipatory self [that] has as its emotional substance hope, desire, yearning,

and a state of prospective being for which the notion of acting is merely a convenient cultural symbol" ("The Life History of Objects: The Naturalist Novel and the City," *Hard Facts: Setting and Form in the American Novel* [New York: Oxford University Press, 1985], p. 159). Fisher's essay deals with such details as plate-glass windows, discussed here and, also discussed here, with such themes as the self and its commodification, "the importance of clothes," and "the plot of decline." Fisher sees the city as the essential milieu for the emergence of the details and themes he discusses. To me, the city has also seemed a determining force in Dreiser's writing. In an early study, I had called *Sister Carrie* "the generic novel" of twentieth-century American city fiction and Dreiser its "generic novelist" (*The American City Novel* [Norman: University of Oklahoma Press, 1970; 1953], p. 64); and in an essay on women in city fiction, I alluded to *Sister Carrie* as a realization of a subgenre of urban literature I described in "Sister to Faust: The City's 'Hungry Woman' as Heroine," *Novel: A Forum on Fiction*, 15 (1981): 23–38. Here, however, I am setting the novel within a pattern of determinism that I believe may pertain to women characters as consuming figures who appear in different guises in different times and places – places other than the American city – and yet remain, in their desires and their acts of consumption, essentially the same. By taking a synoptic view of literary developments, rather than concentrating upon a single text and time, I am asking whether certain patterns persist in naturalism, consumption, and the representation of women.

24 Although obviously men are individualistic and consuming, women often become the personification of cultural traits and effects that writers dramatize as destructive. The soldiers in "Sweetheart of the Song Tra Bong" are medics – men who nurse the needy (who have assumed traditional feminine roles), while the most visible and committed killer is a young woman. In another story, the narrator Rat Kiley disintegrates under the pressures of war, and ends up with a self-inflicted wound that will get him discharged from the army. Like Hurstwood, he turns his destructive powers against himself, while Mary Anne, like Carrie, lives on to pursue her self-fulfillment. For a Marxist study of American individualism that discusses the generation of needs and desires in ways pertinent to this essay, see James O'Connor, *Accumulation Crisis* (New York: Basil Blackwell, 1984).

25 Mary Anne's necklace serves the function Richard Slotkin has ascribed to trophies: "to provide visual and concrete proofs of the self-justifying acts of violent self-transcendence and regeneration that produced them" (*Regeneration Through Violence: The Mythology of the American Frontier 1600–1860* [Middletown, Conn.: Wesleyan University Press, 1972], p. 564). The Green Berets' hootch where Mary Anne finds her place as a Killer Woman is full of trophies that "stink of the kill" – the decayed head of a black leopard. . . . And bones. Stacks of bones – all kinds" (119). Slotkin believes that the myth of regeneration through violence, which he traces back to Indian captivity tales, has been used throughout American history to sanctify imperialistic ventures. Most recently, he says, it helped President Johnson escalate the war in Vietnam. In O'Brien's story, regeneration does not entail rescue of others but transformation of the self: Mary Anne becomes a new woman through acts of violence inseparable from the violation of a land.

Like Slotkin, T. J. Jackson Lears has linked American militarism to "social and personal regeneration," arguing that "war has offered men the chance to escape the demands of bourgeois domesticity" and find the "intensity of experience" they sought (*No Place of Grace: Antimodernism and the Transformation of American Culture 1880–1920* [New York: Pantheon, 1981], p. 98). The argument Lears develops about men – an argument that links "the quest for intense experience" to militarism, and both to "a secular culture of consumerism" (138) – applies to O'Brien's Mary Anne as she pursues her self-transformation in Vietnam. Lears's argument applies also to Dreiser's Carrie, a character in quest of a "self-fulfillment" she will never attain. The "vision of a self in endless development," Lears writes, "is perfectly attuned to an economy based on pointless growth and ceaseless destruction." Within this economy, advertisers early recognized "the cash value" of manipulating individual needs and underwriting "a notion of self-fulfillment through voracious acquisitions" (304). Both Carrie and Mary Anne succumb to this notion.

26 That a Special Forces unit, made up of meticulously and thoroughly trained individuals, would allow a raw young civilian woman to join its nocturnal guerrilla raids is unbelievable, no more so than that such a woman would be able to visit a lover stationed in Vietnam's In Country – even though O'Brien's narrator insists upon the truth of his account of her arrival, accommodation, and acceptance. O'Brien has acknowledged that "Sweetheart of the Song Tra Bong" is "so far from one's ordinary expectations as to be a fable," but he claims "that of all the stories in the book [it] . . . comes the closest to an actual event." As O'Brien had not "witnessed" the event but "been told about it," he was creating a story out of a story he had heard in order, he said, "to make credible what to me was incredible." (See Michael Coffey's interview, "Tim O'Brien" in *Publishers Weekly* 237 [February 16, 1990]: 60–1.) What O'Brien finds credible, apparently, is that a woman can be transformed into a killer more lethal and savage than all the male figures in his book, and that any American woman who appears in Vietnam, even if only in a photograph that a soldier carries, brings death (as in the story "In the Field," 192). Robin Moore has also insisted upon the truth of his fictionalized account of the Green Berets, an invented story that brought the then little known United States Army Special Forces to popular attention (*The Green Berets* [New York: Crown, 1965]). Moore's hyperventilated fiction became the basis of the John Wayne movie that further popularized the Green Berets. Colonel Charles M. Simpson, a group commander, has given a tempered, basically laudatory account of Special Forces missions in his book *Inside the Green Berets, The First Thirty Years: A History of the U. S. Army Special Forces* (Novata, Calif.: Presidio, 1985). As for Vietnam, Colonel Simpson asks, "Can the full story of Special Forces in Vietnam be told?" (96). This is a recurrent question raised in *The Things They Carried*.

27 In Bobbie Ann Mason's novel *In Country, a novel* (New York: Harper & Row, 1985), the young woman protagonist tries to imagine herself into the Vietnam War, in which the father she never knew had died. Horrified to discover that her father had actually killed Vietnamese, she draws a distinction between men and women that O'Brien's story subverts. "Women didn't kill," young Samantha or "Sam" thinks; "Men wanted to kill. . . . It was their basic profession" (209–

10). Even though she wants to disavow the war she had sought to know, Mason's heroine is gratified, rather than repelled, to find her own name – and "all the names of America" – on the Vietnam Veterans Memorial wall. As "SAM A HUGHES," she shares in the killing and cleansing symbolized by the Memorial.

28 Julie Baumgold, "Killer Women: Here Come the Hardbodies," *New York Magazine,* 24 (1991): 23–9. For an account of real killer women, see Eileen Mac-Donald's report of her interviews with women who have committed acts of terrorism in *Shoot the Women First* (New York: Random House, 1991). Mac-Donald concludes that women terrorists – that is, women who kill to further a political cause – "have proved that a woman is just as capable as a man of learning how to make bombs, plant them, and detonate them, and is just as likely to be a good shot with a gun" (233). Reputedly, the injunction to shoot the women first was given to antiterrorist squads because women terrorists were considered more dangerous than men (xiv).

29 For a psychoanalytic critique of the relationship between Beauty and the Beast in horror movies, see Linda Williams's insightful essay "When the Woman Looks," *Re-Vision: Essays in Feminist Film Criticism,* ed. Mary Ann Doane, Patricia Mellencamp, and Linda Williams (Los Angeles: University Publications of America, 1984), pp. 83–99. Focusing upon the woman as subject rather than object of the gaze, Williams says that in narrative cinema "to see is to desire" (83) – a point I am making about women characters in American naturalistic fiction. The monster that the woman sees in horror films, Williams argues, often is a double of herself, which may explain the "strange sympathy" that creates a sentimental bond between Beauty and the Beast (or America's Sweetheart and the Green Berets).

30 *Channels of Desire,* rev. ed. (1992), p. 209.

31 Jane Fonda, *Jane Fonda's Workout Book* (New York: Simon and Schuster, 1981), p. 20. For a discussion of Jane Fonda's changing personae and their relationship to her reactions to the Vietnam War, see Richard Dyer, *Stars* (London: British Film Institute, 1979), pp. 72–98. Dyer reproduces a still of Fonda as Barbarella dressed in metal and armed with a gun – the sex goddess as killer woman. In *The Things They Carried,* "Sweet Janie" appeals to O'Brien's most unappealing character, Azar, who makes an obscene joke about the way Janie "boosts a man's morale" ("The Ghost Soldiers," 232). As Tim the narrator notes, the movie *Barbarella* had been playing for eight nights in a row – a "lousy movie," he says (232). Dyer says that Fonda expressed her views on war and women through documentary and commercial films (*Vietnam Journey,* 1972, and *Coming Home,* 1978). As a movie star, however, Fonda was, like any actor, a "phenomenon of consumption" (19 and 39–48). The relation Dyer traces between the star and salient patterns of consumption, particularly conspicuous consumption, extends the arguments of this essay from fictional characters to actual women who enact in contemporary times the cultural roles that Dreiser's little actress had assumed a hundred years ago.

32 For a highly polemical argument that links a "culture of slimming" to late capitalism, and both to political practice, consumption, and the "manipulation" and "constant frustration of desire," see Hillel Schwartz, *Never Satisfied: A Cultural History of Diets, Fantasies and Fat* (New York: The Free Press,

1986), pp. 327–36 and passim. "An expanding Late Capitalist world requires that no one ever be satisfied" (329), Schwartz writes, describing the state of women characters who incessantly want more. Quoting passages in Fonda's *Workout Book* to which I have referred, as well as passages from Fonda's critic, Charles Krauthammer, Schwartz connects capitalism and the culture of slimming to Vietnam. As Krauthammer had noted, Fonda's prescribed diet was that of "the pre-war Vietnam peasant" (335); and as Schwartz notes, Fonda's exhortation to go for the burn "was compatible with the practices of the Thin Society and the profits of Hollywood capitalism" (336) – as, one might add, befits the current Mrs. Ted Turner.

33 Baumgold, "Killer Women," 23–9.

34 Baudrillard sees the Vietnam War as "a crucial episode in a peaceful coexistence" of Communist China with capitalistic America. By its nonintervention, China allowed a "passing from a strategy of world revolution to one of a [presumably capitalistic] sharing of forces and empires" (*Simulations,* 67). Inside Vietnam, Baudrillard argues, the adversaries seemingly in "a struggle to the death," shared a single objective: to liquidate " 'primitive' precapitalistic and antiquated structures." Once this end was accomplished, a "scenario" for ending the war could be enacted. Though the deaths were real and "heinous," the war was "a mere simulacrum" (69–70). For an elaborate discussion on the staging of reality through representations that are mere simulacra or appearances, see Guy Debord, *Comments on the Society of the Spectacle,* trans. Malcolm Imrie (London: Verso, 1990; published originally in 1988 as *Commentaires sur la société du spectacle*).

35 I quote from a monumental novel of our times, Thomas Pynchon's *Gravity's Rainbow* (New York: Viking, 1973), p. 3. The novel's highly involuted plot grows out of a psychological experiment in Pavlovian conditioning that is comic, bizarre, and ominous; the themes meld determinism with science and sheer spectacle, and both with war and myriad other matters. If I had world enough and time, I might have extended this essay to include *Gravity's Rainbow* as (in a Faulknerian phrase) the apotheosis and *reductum ad absurdum* of the essay's arguments.

36 William Broyles, Jr., "Why Men Love War," *Esquire* 102 (1984): 56. David Wyatt discusses the connection among looking, desire, and shame that Michael Herr drew in *Dispatches,* a book based on Herr's experiences as a journalist – essentially an onlooker or witness – in Vietnam. As Wyatt put it, "The endlessness of looking, its uncanny resemblance to the rhythms of desire – this is what Herr discovers in Vietnam, and it finally has less to do with the quantity and texture of the information coming in than with the sheer and permanent logic of the act of looking itself" (*Out of the Sixties: Storytelling and the Vietnam Generation* [New York: Cambridge University Press], pp. 182–3). Wanting more seems an inevitable consequence of separating "the permanent logic of the act of looking" from what one sees, whether the dead bodies Herr looks at or the clothes in a department store window a woman sees. In either instance, the act of looking impresses its logic of insatiability upon the onlooker, who must continue to look and want and, in this endless process, always want more: "Looking, like desire, is an act that is never ended" (182).

37 See *The Golden Age of Shop Design*, p. 7; *Channels of Desire* (1982), p. 74; and Rachel Bowlby, *Just Looking: Consumer Culture in Dreiser, Gissing, and Zola* (New York: Methuen, 1985), p. 20. See also Antoine Hennion and Cécile Méadel, "The Artisans of Desire: The Mediation of Advertising between Product and Consumer," trans. Geoffrey Bowker, *Sociological Theory* 7 (1989): 191–209, which describes "the discourse of advertising wandering between marketing and seduction" (197). These examples can only suggest, and they can hardly suggest, a countless number of references to the seductiveness of commodities and the seduction of the consumer.

38 As Charles Child Walcutt has pointed out in his important early study of naturalism, "Dreiser believes in a determinism which destroys or modifies the moral view of conduct" (*American Naturalism: A Divided Stream* [Minneapolis: University of Minnesota Press, 1956], p. 193).

39 Elaine S. Abelson, *When Ladies Go A-Thieving: Middle-Class Shoplifters in the Victorian Department Store* (New York: Oxford University Press, 1989), p. 74. Abelson quotes trade journals of the times that advocated the use of department-store window displays to "force" onlookers to want what they see: " 'Goods should be so displayed,' the DGR [*Dry Goods Reporter*] advised, 'as to force people to feel that they really wish to possess them' " (quoted on 73). The "respectable shoplifter" or kleptomaniac presumably felt the full power of the display, and her legal defense, which had "a softening effect in the courts," was that she "literally" had been " 'forced to steal' " (185). Lower-class women who stole were simply thieves. Thus *the constitution* of kleptomania *as a mental illness* takes place as social class converges with consumerism in the Victorian department stores where women of means can be captivated by display. To suggest *the zero point* of kleptomania – the historical moment before the disease was differentiated – I have appropriated and emphasized here and in the sentence above terms from Michel Foucault's well-known work, *Madness & Civilization: A History of Insanity in the Age of Reason* (New York: Vintage, 1965; published originally in 1961 as *Histoire de la Folie*), p. x.

That the "kleptomaniac is not a free agent, in respect of his stealing" became a philosophical matter to Sir Alfred J. Ayer, who believed that the kleptomaniac did not, could not, "go through any process of deciding whether or not to steal. Or rather, if he [*sic*] does go through such a process, it is irrelevant to his behavior. Whatever he resolved to do, he would steal all the same" – his, or her, action was determined ("Freedom and Necessity," in Watson, ed., *Free Will* [n. 2 above], 20). Ironically, department store thefts, whether by kleptomaniacs or ordinary thieves, opened new job opportunities to women, hired as in-house detectives to apprehend the women shoplifters who were increasing in number and decreasing business profits. On the early employment of women detectives in American department stores, see "Women Thief Catchers," Pittsburgh *Labor National Tribune*, no. 18 (April 23, 1896).

40 See Abelson, *When Ladies Go A-Thieving*, pp. 173–96, on the medical, legal, and cultural aspects of kleptomania as a newly defined disease associated with women, department stores, and window displays calculated to created irresistible desire. In his "social" (rather than "business") history of The Bon Marché, Miller makes the same associations about kleptomania (*The Bon Marché*, n. 10

above, 197–206). That Miller reiterates such terms as *seduction, irresistible desire, overpowering urges,* incitement and stimulation of *desire* – words connoting force and sexuality – may help explain why he turns briefly but ultimately to medical, legal, and cultural questions about women and kleptomania.

41 Robert B. Westbrook, "Politics as Consumption: Managing the Modern American Election," *The Culture of Consumption: Critical Essays in American History, 1880–1980,* ed. Richard Wightman Fox and T. J. Jackson Lears (New York: Pantheon Books, 1983), p. 145.

42 For an indicting account of the complicity of fashion, selling, and modern American politics, a conscious and invidious complicity, see Debora Silverman, *Selling Culture: Bloomingdale's, Diana Vreeland, and the New Aristocracy of Taste in Reagan's America* (New York: Pantheon Books, 1986). For a clear-sighted analysis of the deliberate muddling of spectacle with secrecy during the Reagan and Bush presidencies, see Michael Rogin, "'Make My Day!': Spectacle as Amnesia in Imperial Politics," *Representations* 29 (1990): 99–123. Rogin points out that "spectacles, in the Marxist modernist view, shift attention from workers as producers to spectators as consumers of mass culture"; and that "in the postmodern view," as described by Debord and Baudrillard, spectacles produce, among other effects, a skilled diversion of the public's attention from an "object" or "the real" to "its hyperreal, reproducible representation," to mere "display" (106).

43 Elizabeth L. Eisenstadt, *The Printing Press as an Agent of Change: Communications and cultural transformations in early-modern Europe,* 2 vols. (Cambridge: Cambridge University Press, 1979). Eisenstadt describes medieval publishers as "*both* business men *and* literary dispensers of glory. They served men of letters not only by providing traditional forms of patronage but also by acting as press agents and as cultural impresarios of a new kind. . . . The printer could take satisfaction in serving humanity at large even while enhancing the reputation of authors and making money for himself" (1:23; original emphasis). For interesting literary criticism that begins with the prehistory of advertising as contained within the history of printing and proceeds to fictions that contain – and are contained by – advertisements as "one vast textual system," see Jennifer Wicke, *Advertising Fictions: Literature, Advertisement, & Social Reading* (New York: Columbia University Press, 1988).

44 For two of the many accounts and revisionary tellings of the novel's publishing history, see Jack Salzman, "The Publication of *Sister Carrie*: Fact and Fiction," *Library Chronicle of the University of Pennsylvania* 33 (1967): 119–33; and Stephen C. Brennan, "The Publication of *Sister Carrie*: Old and New Fictions," *American Literary Realism* 18 (1985): 55–68. For letters and documents involved in the publishing controversy and its "legend," see the Norton Critical Edition of *Sister Carrie* (n. 3 above), 433–70. Like advertisements, literary criticism can revitalize desire for a text; critics make certain texts fashionable, as we know, and increase their consumption, though critics have also displaced desire from literary texts to literary theory.

45 Quoted from John H. Raferty, "By Bread Alone," *Reedy's Mirror* (Dec. 5, 1901), in Richard Lingeman, *Theodore Dreiser: At the Gates of the City, 1871–1907* (New York: G. P. Putnam's Sons, 1986), p. 298; see also 415.

46 Even a selective list of indispensable recent studies of *Sister Carrie* (aside from those already noted) requires more space than this essay allows. The studies I note here suggest the fecund diversity of critical approaches the novel has inspired. See, for example, *New Essays on Sister Carrie*, ed. Donald Pizer (New York: Cambridge University Press, 1991); Walter Benn Michaels, "*Sister Carrie's* Popular Economy," *The Gold Standard and the Logic of Naturalism: American Literature at the Turn of the Century* (Berkeley and Los Angeles: University of California Press, 1987); Amy Kaplan, "The Sentimental Revolt of *Sister Carrie,*" *The Social Construction of American Realism* (Chicago: University of Chicago Press, 1988), pp. 140–60; June Howard, *Form and History in America Literary Naturalism* (Chapel Hill: University of North Carolina Press, 1985). Among earlier studies of the novel, I note only two germinal critiques: F. O. Matthiessen, *Theodore Dreiser* (New York: William Sloane Associates, 1951), pp. 55–92; and Ellen Moers, *Two Dreisers* (New York: Viking, 1969), pp. 73–152.

47 René Girard, *Desire, Deceit, and the Novel: Self and Other in Literary Structure,* trans. Yvonne Frecerro (Baltimore: The Johns Hopkins University Press, 1965), p. 290.

48 Or this conclusion might have been anticipated if one pursued Fredric Jameson's conjecture that historical periods should be defined as a "restructuration" of the "elements" of a previous period's dominant style, rather than a rejection of the period's "content" ("Postmodernism and Consumer Society," *The Antiaesthetic: Essays on postmodern culture,* ed. Hal Foster [Seattle: Bay Press, 1983], pp. 111–25). I am suggesting that restructuration leaves intact an underlying pattern of desire ascribed to consuming women in texts produced in different historical times. The effect is to minimize the literary or cultural effects of restructuration. For though the destructive power of a woman who embodies, and is consumed by, capitalistic values may seem central to O'Brien's story and only marginal to Dreiser's novel, the difference between center and margin, I would argue contrary to Jameson, is more illusive than real, and the similarity is more culturally significant than the difference. At the center of both texts there is a woman who wants more; at the margins are the available objects of her desire. If we look closely at these objects, we see they are all products of the same culture of capitalism and they are all produced for consumption. Dreiser may be more ambivalent than O'Brien about the consuming woman he describes, and he is clearly closer to her and more sympathetic, but in other respects he seems to me O'Brien's contemporary rather than his "genealogical precursor" (the term is from Jameson's essay, "Postmodernism, or The Cultural Logic of Late Capitalism," *New Left Review* 146 [1984]: 56).

49 Theories on the etiology of desire are too numerous and well known to recapitulate here. Philosophical theories trace back at least to Hegel, if not further, indeed to the Bible; and psychological theories, to Freud. It would be supererogatory to cite here such contemporaries as Lacan, who formalized the concept of *lack,* the relation between conscious and unconscious desire, and of both to the acquisition of language (*Ecrits*); and of French feminists, like Irigaray, Cixous, and Kristeva, who sought to define woman's desire. Another approach to an understanding of desire is through Marxist materialism. Cather-

ine Belsey has merged Althusser's revisionary views of Marxist materialism with Lacan's revisionary views of Freud to produce a critique of literary practices that reveals the role of ideology in the criticism and consumption of books. "[B]ooks are literary commodities," she writes, but "conventional literary criticism" suppresses "the process of production" crucial to the making of books, mystifying or eliminating the writer's "work" in the same ways that a laborer's work is eliminated in the presentation of a commodity (*Critical Practice* [London and New York: Methuen, 1980], pp. 126–9). Belsey sees advertisements as comparable to literary realism insofar as each "constructs its signified out of juxtapositions of signifiers which are intelligible not as direct reflections of an unmediated reality but because we are familiar with the signifying systems from which they are drawn, linguistic, literary, semiotic" – systems which, like individuals, are "interpellated," she believes, with ideology (48).

9

BARBARA HOCHMAN

The Awakening and The House of Mirth: Plotting Experience and Experiencing Plot

> . . . the trouble was with plot. . . .
> Kate Chopin, "Elizabeth Stark's One Story"

Many women novelists tell a story of female defeat. Nineteenth-century fiction is particularly full of women characters who cannot make peace with the options available to them in their society, characters who cannot fulfill their needs or resolve their conflicts. Rarely if ever do these protagonists find a form through which to tell others their story as (at least to some extent) their novel-writing creators did.

Like their protagonists, Kate Chopin and Edith Wharton are often said to have failed in creating a "new plot" for "women's lives."[1] Yet the identification of writer and character should be entertained with caution. For Chopin and Wharton themselves, professional authorship meant redefining their position as women within turn-of-century American society. The novelistic enterprise also meant reaching an audience with their version of a woman's life – only partially a version of their own. Many aspects of the fiction-writing experience itself, inscribed in The Awakening and The House of Mirth, suggest the complexity of the relationship between these authors and the characters they create. In both texts a tension emerges between the figure of a defeated female protagonist and, obliquely yet insistently, that of a writer forging grounds of articulation and thereby a place in the world.[2]

Certain parallels between these authors and their characters are inescapable, of course. Edna and Lily stem from the same class and background as their creators. For the young Chopin and Wharton themselves, as for many a "frail vessel" in nineteenth-century fiction, life options were severely limited by convention: marriage was the prime locus of adult female choice. The presumed "career" for a woman of Chopin and Wharton's class and background was social and domestic. Professional authorship was socially dubious – particularly "indelicate in a female," as Wharton put it.[3] Her autobiography repeatedly notes the disapproval that her literary ambitions encountered within her family and throughout her social world.

The notion of art as a socially precarious borderland is clearly expressed in both *The Awakening* and *The House of Mirth*. When Edna Pontellier sketches and thinks of becoming an artist, the misanthropic musician, Mlle Reisz, warns her that art is only for "the brave soul . . . that dares and defies."[4] As for Lily, though aesthetic taste is one of her defining qualities, her own closest approach to *making* art is the notorious scene of *tableaux vivants*. There, in one of her finest (or most devastating) moments, Lily temporarily makes a work of art out of herself, appearing on stage as a figure in a painting.[5]

I suggest that despite certain self-evident grounds of analogy between Chopin or Wharton and their characters, the question of art becomes a watershed, a clear sign of the writer's separation from the protagonist who enacts her conflict rather than either resolving or articulating it. Unlike the writer who achieves pleasure, control, and distance in the act of writing, Lily and Edna are at best partial or failed artists. However, to reflect upon Lily and Edna as failing in the search for voice and form is not only to underscore their distance from women writers who have found both; it is also to clarify the two novels' recurrent focus on the nature and function of aesthetic experience, including the experience of narrative.

Up to a point, both *The Awakening* and *The House of Mirth* neatly exemplify the "naturalist" plot of individual decline, with its concern for the pressures of environment and circumstance, and its focus on forces (both inner and outer) beyond the control of the characters.[6] Like many "naturalist" writers, Chopin and Wharton reject a plot in which marriage becomes the ground of closure (as it does in the work of Dickens, George Eliot, William Dean Howells and sentimental/domestic American fiction). Instead, raising questions about marriage at the outset, both *The Awakening* and *The House of Mirth* follow their protagonists through progressive isolation to death (as in such naturalist works as *L'Assommoir,* the Hetty plot of *Adam Bede, Maggie: A Girl of the Streets, McTeague, Sister Carrie*).

Chopin and Wharton's use of the naturalist mode has several interesting implications. A woman's decision to write fiction for the late-nineteenth-century literary marketplace immediately signaled a bid for position in a male-dominated professional world. By employing a "naturalist" structure, Wharton and Chopin also sought authorial status beyond the confines of "women's" writing.[7] It would be difficult to find a late-nineteenth-century fictional model more clearly associated with male authorship and "virile" fiction[8] than the naturalist plot of decline. However, in adapting the naturalist plot to their purposes, Chopin and Wharton made some original changes. Through their handling of narrative time, in particular, they complicated the sense of downward slide typical of most naturalist texts – that relentless descent with its "few landings or level places."[9]

Throughout *The Awakening*, the forward movement of narration is modified by lyric passages and recurrent leitmotivs that foster a sense of stasis or free play without hampering the progress of the story.[10] As we shall see, *The House of Mirth*, too, intermittently undercuts the reader's sense of straightforward progression through narrative time – while maximizing other rewards of temporary immersion in a fictional world. Thus, for Chopin and Wharton, "naturalism" becomes both a vehicle for conceptualizing a woman's vulnerability and a way of redefining certain pleasures of the fiction-reading experience.

Compared to such naturalist heroines as Trina McTeague, Carrie Meeber, or Maggie Johnson, Edna and Lily are well educated and very sophisticated. Their greater access to "culture," however, does not give them either a sense of autonomy or a sense of community. *The Awakening* was originally entitled *A Solitary Soul*. Both that phrase and the following early description of Edna are equally applicable to Lily: "She had all her life long been accustomed to harbor thoughts and emotions which never voiced themselves. . . . They belonged to her and were her own, and she entertained the conviction that she had a right to them and that they concerned no one but herself" (48). When Edna tells Mme Ratignolle that she would give up "life," but not her "self," for her children, Edna's friend cannot grasp the distinction. The two women "did not appear to understand each other or to be talking the same language" (48). Despite increasing self-awareness as the novel unfolds, Edna's attempts at expression are never understood by others. Lily's efforts to articulate the life-issues that concern her are similarly fitful and unsatisfactory.

A failure of voice separates Edna and Lily from the writers who created them. Yet an illuminating analogue emerges between the challenge of the novelist *as* novelist and the protagonists' groping attempts at articulation. In a sense, Edna and Lily fail precisely where their authors succeed, defeated in "life" by their lack of several elements indispensable to fiction writing: not just a sense of plot, of how to structure and articulate one's story, but a sense of the relationship between fiction and reality, artists and audience, teller and tale. If we pursue the contrasts and parallels between the writers and protagonists with care, we shall clarify certain aspects of the characters' defeat while elucidating the meaning and function of fiction writing for Chopin and Wharton themselves.

At a critical juncture in the plot of *House of Mirth,* Gerty asks Lily to explain the events that result in Lily's disinheritance and ostracism from society. "[W]hat *is* your story," Gerty asks, "I don't believe anyone knows it yet."[11] "My story?" Lily replies: "I don't believe I know it myself. You see, I never thought of preparing a version in advance as Bertha did – and if I had, I don't think I should take the trouble to use it now" (236). Lily never takes that "trouble"; after her death, Selden struggles pointlessly to "unravel . . . the story" from Lily's "mute lips" (347).

Unlike Selden, Gerty tries valiantly to elicit that story while Lily is alive. "I don't want a version prepared in advance," Gerty insists,

> "but I want you to tell me exactly what happened from the beginning."
> "From the beginning?" Miss Bart gently mimicked her. "Dear Gerty, how little imagination you good people have!"   (236)

Lily claims that there is no way to establish the "beginning" of her story; it was in her cradle, she speculates – in her upbringing, or perhaps in her blood, via some "wicked pleasure-loving ancestress" (236). Moreover, Lily argues that the believability of a story is in any case relative, dependent on the power and influence of the teller. Thus, unlike Gerty, Lily sees no point in telling her friends "the whole truth" (235).

> "The whole truth?" Miss Bart laughed. "What is truth? Where a woman is concerned, it's the story that's easiest to believe. In this case it's a great deal easier to believe Bertha Dorset's story than mine, because she has a big house and an opera box, and it's convenient to be on good terms with her."   (236)

As Lily sees it, stories need to be planned, preconceived, carefully plotted, in order to persuade. But this is precisely what Lily cannot or will not do – either after her retreat from Monte Carlo or later, when Rosedale proposes his own well-made, if melodramatic, "plot" to neutralize incriminating rumors about her. "I don't believe [those] stories," Rosedale says (268), offering to marry Lily if she will silence Bertha by threatening to reveal her old love-letters. "But [the stories] are there," Rosedale continues, "and my not believing them ain't going to alter the situation" (268). Now it is Lily's turn to be naïve:

> "If they are not true," she said, "doesn't *that* alter the situation?"
> He met this with a steady gaze. . . . "I believe it does in novels, but I'm certain it don't in real life."   (268)

Although Lily sees Rosedale's point, she refuses his offer. Throughout the novel, Lily herself is repeatedly accused of "art," of achieving only "premeditated effects" in her social relations (3, 69, 70, 75); but she is singularly incapable of the kind of sustained and painstaking plotting that ensures Bertha's or Rosedale's success in society.

By refusing to tell anyone her story and rejecting all plots, Lily renounces the project of being believed or even heard, progressively isolating herself until, alone in her boardinghouse room, she seeks oblivion in drug-induced sleep. Cradling an imaginary baby in her arms, she finds the greater oblivion of death. Rosedale's distinction between "novels" and "real life" is cogent here, for whereas Lily renounces plot and is destroyed, it was precisely by articulating and controlling Lily's story that Wharton became a best-selling novelist.[12]

It is particularly illuminating to juxtapose Lily's storytelling failure with Edith Wharton's storytelling success. In Wharton's own account, "storytelling" was not merely her "job" or "vocation" (BG 119). In A Backward Glance storytelling is also given the credit for creating Wharton's "personality," being her "first-born," her own "real self," her very soul (112, 115, 119, 124). Such metaphors reflect a sense of deep identification, even merger, between Wharton and her stories. Yet, at another level, Wharton maintained a considerable distance from what she wrote for publication. For one thing, House of Mirth tells the story of a fictional character -- not her own. For another, Wharton exerts impressive control over the very elements of Lily's story that Lily fails to conceptualize. Lily may not know what her story "is," or even where it began; but Wharton cannot possibly tell Lily's story (indeed no one can tell any story) without, at the very least, a firm idea of beginnings and endings. Moreover, as we shall see, Lily lacks not only the novelist's gift for narration, but also the writer's perspective on the difference between what Rosedale calls "novels" and "real life."

Like Lily, Edna Pontellier fails to tell her story. Unlike Lily, however, Edna repeatedly tries her hand at art. She not only sketches, she is (again, unlike Lily) both a reader and a responsive music-lover. Thus the figure of Edna, making "art" and responding to it, reflects many aspects of aesthetic experience. From this point of view, one of the most resonant scenes in The Awakening is the one where Edna does tell a story – a story that (perhaps like Chopin's own) both is and is not about herself.

The occasion for Edna's storytelling is the dinner to which her husband invites his friend and family physician Dr. Mandelet. Disturbed by the sense that his wife is "not herself" (57), Mr. Pontellier hopes that the doctor will observe Edna at dinner and perhaps offer some insight. With the help of warm claret and cold champagne, Mr. Pontellier is impelled to share his "amusing plantation experiences [and] recollections." Edna's father, in turn, tells a more "somber" story that seems to prompt an equally dubious tale on the doctor's part: "the old, ever new and curious story of the waning of a woman's love . . . [and its return] to its legitimate source after days of fierce unrest" (70). Implicitly, this story gives rise to Edna's own:

> [The doctor's] story did not seem especially to impress Edna. She had one of her own to tell, of a woman who paddled away with her lover one night in a pirogue and never came back. They were lost amid the Baratarian Islands, and no one ever heard of them or found trace of them from that day to this. It was a pure invention. She said that Madame Antoine had related it to her. That, also, was an invention. Perhaps it was a dream she had had. But every glowing word seemed real to those who listened. They could feel the hot breath of the Southern night; they could hear the long sweep of the pirogue through the glistening moonlit water, . . . they could see the faces of the lovers, . . . drifting into the unknown. (70)

Edna's storytelling is a brief but crucial moment in *The Awakening,* one that dramatizes many issues in both Edna's life and Chopin's art. The passage, to begin with, repeatedly stresses the indistinct boundaries between reality and fiction. Despite Edna's attribution of a source for the tale, the narrative voice twice repeats that Edna's story is her own "invention," – "[p]erhaps . . . a dream." Nonetheless, "every glowing word seemed real to those who listened" (70). Few readers fail to perceive the resemblance between Edna's situation and that of the "imaginary" woman she describes. Her own recent boat ride with Robert is the high point of her summer's experience, the touchstone to fairy-tale pleasures she can never recapture. Moreover, the image of the woman lost in the sea without a trace points forward to Edna's own end. The doctor, for his part, directly identifies Edna with the woman in her story:

> He was sorry he had accepted Pontellier's invitation. . . . He did not want the secrets of other lives thrust upon him.
> "I hope it isn't Arobin," he muttered to himself as he walked. "I hope to heaven it isn't . . . Arobin." (71)

The doctor's response to Edna's story sharpens the focus on Edna's inner state and raises questions about her future. From the doctor's point of view, those "glowing word[s]" that seemed so "real to those who listened" simply reveal Edna's own wishes, thinly disguised. Yet by presenting Edna's story both as "invention" and as personal revelation, the passage invites speculation not only about the relationship between Edna's narrative and the feelings or events in her own life. It also raises questions about *Chopin's* "invention": what does Chopin herself mean by telling the story of an imaginary woman in *The Awakening?*

Some of the differences between Edna's act of narration and Chopin's become clearer when we juxtapose Edna's storytelling with other moments of representation dramatized in the novel. Edna repeatedly makes sketches in the course of *The Awakening,* gaining "satisfaction from the work in itself" (73) and even earning money in the process. Yet her sketching has neither the impact nor the intensity of her single storytelling moment. One reason for the difference, I suggest, is the clear separation between artist and object that informs Edna's every attempt to draw. She works, at her best, with "sureness and ease" (73) – never with passion or abandon. In this sense, Edna's relation to sketching is not unlike Mme Ratignolle's relation to music. Mme Ratignolle plays the piano partly for her children's benefit, partly to fulfill a social function. Her musical evenings occur regularly, "once a fortnight." They were "widely known, and it was considered a privilege to be invited to them" (55).

Mme Ratignolle's music (like Edna's sketching) provides pleasure and diversion for both artist and audience. It constitutes neither disruption nor danger to anyone. By contrast – and more like Edna's storytelling experience – the piano playing of Mlle Reisz has the power to disrupt Edna's equilibrium, eliciting passionate responses. Edna's relationship to Mlle Reisz's music thus raises questions about the nature of aesthetic response, the accompanying sensation of freedom, and even the dynamics of narrative. The questions raised by Edna's recurrent abandon and "exaltation" when listening to music are similar to those raised by her storytelling interlude: questions about loss of self and the threat of inner dissolution; questions about the boundary between the self and surrounding reality.

Hearing the strange, ugly Mlle Reisz play the piano, Edna feels as if her entire being is absorbed into the intensity of aesthetic response. Edna herself associates such experience with freedom: by way of "her divine art," Mlle Reisz "set [Edna's] spirit free" (78). Yet the "joy and exaltation" (80) that Edna experiences when listening to Mlle Reisz is full of contradictions. Edna's responses to this music are more problematic than her own view of them. Directly arousing Edna's "passions" (27) in one instance, Mlle Reisz's piano leaves her "sobbing" in another – "just as she had wept one midnight at Grand Isle when strange new voices awoke in her" (64). Despite the awakening of new voices in Edna, she only sobs. In fact, the scene at Grand Isle presents Edna's state as more conducive to incoherence and dissolution than to any articulation (such as "new voices" might imply). Far from

moving toward articulation in the course of her experience, Edna progressively refuses the orderly sequences and constraining forms not only of
social reality but of language itself.[13]

Thus, in the scene just alluded to, after a quarrel between Edna and her
husband, Edna refuses to speak. She withdraws to the porch alone, rocking
and crying: "There was no sound abroad except the hooting of an old owl
. . . and the everlasting voice of the sea that broke like a mournful lullaby
upon the night" (8). Edna is figured here as both mother and child. Inarticulate and overwrought, she cries, simultaneously rocking and soothing herself. Like many other elements in *The Awakening*, this early image of Edna
points to a state of emotional or developmental nondifferentiation – confusion, or fusion – for which the most resonant recurrent image is the sea.

The sea, repeatedly evoked in the course of *The Awakening*, is seductive
to Edna throughout. The epitome of a fluid, unbounded, "everlasting"
space and "unceasing" sound, the sea is figured here and elsewhere as a
voice. Yet the sea-voice, singing its "mournful lullaby," also provides a
sharp contrast both to the voice of any actual singing mother and to any
human voice that uses language: "The voice of the sea is seductive, never
ceasing, whispering, clamoring, murmuring, inviting the soul to wander for
a spell in abysses of solitude, to lose itself in mazes of inward contempla-
tion" (15). Maze and abyss, "clamoring, murmuring," "never ceasing," the
undifferentiated voice of the sea, unlike a speaking voice – certainly unlike a
narrative voice – is everything but linear and sequential. Inviting the soul to
"lose itself," suggesting a physical enclosure in which to "wander for a
spell," the sea-voice is neither articulate as language nor conducive to differ-
entiation or autonomy. On the contrary, like Mlle Reisz's music, it invites
loss of self, merger, immersion. It also refuses the traditional requisites of
every story: not only no language, but ("never-ceasing") no beginning and
no end.

All of Edna's most intense, responsive moments are explicitly marked by a
blurred sense of beginnings and endings. Not only is the boundless, fluid,
"unceasing" aspect of the sea often underscored; Edna herself repeatedly
associates the sea with her one extended and recurrent childhood memory:
"[walking through] a meadow that seemed as big as the ocean . . . [the little
girl] threw out her arms as if swimming when she walked, beating the tall
grass as one strikes out in the water. . . . I felt as if I must walk on forever
without coming to the end of it" (17–18). The experience of endless, non-
purposive movement through an unbounded area is directly linked for Edna
not only with field and sea but, still more inclusively, with her emotional
state during her experience at Grand Isle ("Sometimes I feel this summer as

if I were walking through the green meadow again, idly, aimlessly . . ."
Edna says [18]). In addition, the very qualities associated with the endless
field walk, the "never ceasing" voice of the sea, and the summer that Edna
hopes will never end, also characterize Edna's most intensely vital aesthetic experience: when Mlle Reisz plays Chopin in the city, Edna is so absorbed and exalted, that she "did not know when the Impromptu began or
ended" (64).

I have said that Edna's obliviousness to beginnings and endings is an
indispensible component of her "joy and exaltation" (80). She is repeatedly
drawn to a space or a state characterized by its lack of apparent beginning
or end. Still, *The Awakening* shows with brutal clarity that exaltation itself
always comes to an end. And when it does, the result is neither freedom nor
articulation – only increased vulnerability: "the exuberance which had sustained and exalted [Edna's] spirit left her helpless and yielding to the conditions which crowded her in" (32).

Thus, throughout *The Awakening* there is destructive as well as liberating
potential in Edna's experience of the "sensuous," "seductive," "never ceasing" sea (as in the sense of "endlessness" associated with her field walk).
The well-known passage about the "whispering, clamoring" sea – invoked
again during Edna's final swim – is preceded by a less frequently noted
comment: ". . . the beginning of things, of a world especially, is necessarily
vague, tangled, chaotic and exceedingly disturbing. How few of us ever
emerge from such beginning! How many souls perish in its tumult!" (15).

Although the language of Genesis here heightens the sense of potential
creation implicit in Edna's "beginnings," this passage simultaneously under-
scores the danger Edna faces, the difficulty of emergence. From Edna's
earliest childhood memories, through her rocking/crying/self-soothing experience and her engagement with the sea, her chances of "emerging" are in
doubt. Thus the text is pervaded by a concern with the complex relation
between beginnings and endings; yet Edna herself seems to live only in the
present moment. Unlike the novelist (who uncharacteristically identifies
herself with Edna's dilemma here: "How few of *us* ever emerge from such
beginning"; my emphasis),[14] Edna never conceptualizes or articulates for
herself the clash between her wish for merger and her need for emergence.
Indeed, like Lily, who repeatedly "crave[s] . . . the darkness [and silence]
made by enfolding arms" (157), Edna seeks not to articulate her plight, but
rather to escape from the inexorable forward march of chronological or
historical time, from all plots and stories with beginnings and endings.[15]
Even more than Lily, who cannot say where her own story begins and
yearns to "drop out of the race" (40), Edna actively courts immersion in

experiences that reproduce the "exaltation" of timelessness, the feeling of walking on forever with no sense of an ending.[16]

We have noted that Lily's experience, like Edna's, is characterized by the wish to disregard beginnings, refuse prearranged versions, renounce all plots. In addition, the figure of Lily, like the figure of Edna, raises questions about the status of exalted moments, whether triggered by life or by art. Lily's experience, like Edna's, repeatedly involves moments of intensity that seem to liberate the self, but that may instead merely hasten its destruction. Nowhere in *The House of Mirth* are the rewards and dangers of such moments more apparent than in Lily's stage appearance as Reynolds's Mrs. Lloyd. Moreover, this episode as a whole, and Lily's self-representation on stage in particular, are directly informed by the writer's concept of narration itself.

Among the "vision-making influences" (140) singled out for particular emphasis in Wharton's evocation of the tableaux is one element in the "the producing of . . . illusions" (141) that draws attention to the very question raised by Edna's doctor/dinner story – the relation between the storyteller (or, in this case, actress) and the character represented:

> the participators [in the tableaux] had been cleverly fitted with characters suited to their types. . . .
> Indeed so skillfully had the personality of the actors been subdued to the scenes they figured in that even the least imaginative of the audience must have felt a thrill of contrast when the curtain suddenly parted on a picture which was simply and undisguisedly the portrait of Miss Bart.   (141)

Until the moment Lily herself appears on stage, the "personalit[ies] of the actors" are "skillfully . . . subdued to the scenes" represented. If we now substitute the idea of an *author's* personality for "the personality of the actors," we have here a formulation that might have been written by any of Wharton's novelist contemporaries, describing late-nineteenth-century American fiction. Indeed, the norm of representation as expressed with regard to the actresses at the Welly Brys's sounds very like the typical realist or naturalist aesthetic.

In critical essays and reviews, Frank Norris, Theodore Dreiser, Henry James, and Wharton herself repeatedly emphasized the importance of effacing authorial presence and letting "situations speak for themselves," in James's words.[17] Norris explicitly advocated "the suppression of the author's personality" in fiction.[18] Wharton herself rejected the notion of the author's "intrusion . . . among his puppets."[19] But to underscore the connection between this cornerstone of realist narration and the artistic strategy in the Brys's tableaux is further to highlight the problematic exemplified by Lily: "when the curtain suddenly parted on a picture which was simply and undisguisedly the portrait of Miss Bart . . . there could be no mistaking the predominance of personality. . . . Lily Bart . . . had shown her artistic intelligence in selecting a type so like her own that she could embody the person represented without ceasing to be herself" (141–2).

In this passage Lily's aims are seen to be quite different from those of the other actresses. Far from subduing her personality to the represented scene, Lily's "artistic intelligence" is said to consist in her capacity to represent another woman – a figure not herself – while remaining, even representing, herself at the very same time. This description thus raises a number of questions. Like Edna's storytelling it points beyond the character's momentary performance to her daily life in society. At the same time, it points beyond Lily altogether to Wharton's position in relation to her own projected fictional "illusion."

The difficulty of representing one personality while remaining another can be easily applied to Lily's problem in "reality," her life-problem. When the novel begins, Lily thinks she can become Mrs. Percy Gryce without ceasing to be "herself." But in the course of her experience she encounters the difficulty (even impossibility) of this particular balancing act. Perhaps, the novel suggests, there *is* no way to represent otherness and yet remain oneself – except in art.

Even within the confines of stage illusion, however, Lily's approach creates difficulties. After the performance Lily delights in her sense of success. She "had not an instant's doubt as to the meaning of the murmur greeting her appearance. . . . it had obviously been called forth by herself and not by the picture she impersonated" (143). Yet Lily's certainty about the "meaning of the murmur greeting her appearance" is misplaced. As the text demonstrates in some detail, the "unanimous 'Oh!' of the audience" is comprised of multiple and contradictory responses to Lily's "flesh-and-blood loveliness" (141). Those responses range from Van Alstyne's lascivious sense of "what an outline Lily has" (146) or Stepney's disapproval of Lily "standing there as if she was up at auction (166) to Gerty and Selden's conviction that the stage has revealed nothing less than "the real Lily . . . , divested of the trivialities of her little world and catching for a moment a note of that eternal harmony of which her beauty was a part" (142).

Paradoxically, Selden's sense of contact with transcendent harmonies through Lily is quite as dependent upon the visible presence of Lily's body as the responses of Stepney or Van Alstyne. For Selden, Lily's "poetry" is inseparable from her physical being. Selden is entranced by "the suggestion of soaring grace . . . the touch of poetry in her beauty that Selden always felt in her presence yet lost the sense of when he was not with her" (142). If Lily's "poetry" is embodied in her body, however, the fact returns us once more to our point of departure: the difference between author and protagonist. Unlike a novelist, Lily uses her own body to project images. Moreover, for her – as for Edna telling her dinner story – total immersion in (and immediate feedback from) the act of representation is an indispensable element of aesthetic performance. For susceptible members of the audience, Lily's effectiveness on stage, like the impact of Edna's storytelling (or like Edna's response to Mlle Reisz's piano) depends upon the blurring of boundaries between art and life, fiction and reality, being oneself and being another. Lily's impact on her audience, the intensity of her delight in performance – like Edna's – joins teller/actress and listeners/spectators by temporarily transposing all concerned to an unaccustomed mode of being.

Such epiphanies – the sense of participation in a magic realm – may be seen as a major component of all aesthetic experience, including reading. (Indeed, nineteenth-century educators and librarians often argued against reading fiction on related grounds. Wharton herself was forbidden to read novels as a child.) As we have seen, neither Lily nor Edna accepts the limitations of aesthetic experience: they deny both their own separation from the objects represented and the short-lived nature of aesthetic response. On the contrary, they wish to prolong or reproduce such moments in "reality." That desire becomes a source of considerable danger to Edna and Lily alike.

Both *The Awakening* and *House of Mirth* invoke fairy-tale motifs to serve a double function: to underscore not only the delight of make-believe but also its time-bound tenuousness. Both books insistently thematize the question of time, setting Edna and Lily's escapist and transcendent impulses against multiple signs of time running out. Thematically, the protagonists' wish to escape or deny time is presented as a hopeless struggle. Yet, as we shall see, the desire for access to another world also provides an analogue to specific rewards of the reading experience.

The high point of Edna's dawning intimacy with Robert in the early chapters of *The Awakening* is their visit to the *Chenière Caminada*. This journey is punctuated by gamesome talk of the whispering "Gulf Spirit" and the pirogue they would sail in by moonlight someday. During the church service on the island, Edna is overcome by "a feeling of oppression and drowsiness" that causes her to flee – just as she fled in childhood from the Presbyterian service presided over by her father, finding refuge in the open field for her never-to-be-forgotten walk. When Edna leaves the island church, Robert takes her to a cottage "at the far end of the village":

> The whole place was immaculately clean, and the big, four-posted bed, snow-white, invited one to repose. . . . She took off her shoes and stockings and stretched herself in the very center of the high, white bed. . . .
>
> Edna awoke . . . with the conviction that she had slept long and sound-ly. . . .
>
> "How many years have I slept?" she inquired. "The whole island seems changed. A new race of beings must have sprung up, leaving only you and me as past relics. . . ."
>
> "You have slept precisely one hundred years. I was left here to guard your slumbers; and for one hundred years I have been out under the shed reading a book." (37–8)

Suggestions of Snow-White, Sleeping-Beauty, and Rip Van Winkle reinforce Edna and Robert's sense of shared magic. But after her return from the island, Edna is abruptly confronted by signs of passing time and change. The very next chapter opens with the news that Robert is going to Mexico. If he has realized that idylls do not last, Edna herself is startled: she does not understand how Robert can leave Grand Isle.

Several early encounters between Selden and Lily in *House of Mirth* reproduce the clash between transcendent impulses and time-bound realities. Lily and Selden's first meeting, setting the tone, is figured ironically as the "rescue" of a damsel in distress (4). Later, Lily and Selden's hilltop afternoon at Bellomont exhibits both the sense of delight and the sense of fleeting magic that characterize Edna's island experience.

> [Lily] had risen, and he stood facing her with his eyes on hers. The soft isolation of the falling day enveloped them; they seemed lifted into a finer air. . . .
>
> They stood silent for a while after this, smiling at each other like adventurous children who have climbed to a forbidden height from which they discover a new world. The actual world at their feet was veiling itself in dimness, and across the valley a clear moon rose in the denser blue. (76)

Then, all at once, the mood is broken, with the abruptness of midnight striking:

> Suddenly they heard a remote sound, like the hum of a giant insect, and following the high-road, which wound whiter through the surrounding twilight, a black object rushed across their vision.
>
> Lily started from her attitude of absorption; her smile faded and she began to move toward the lane. (76)

Intruding upon the "finer air" of Lily's "new world," the motorcar puts an end to all magic. The sound of the motor returns Lily to social reality and passing time, to the story she had told the others (of having a headache that would keep her inside all afternoon), and to her own master plan of marrying the rich and stolid Percy Gryce – the very plot she has taken a break from by spending the afternoon with Selden.

Both Lily and Edna are approaching thirty when their stories begin. Both feel increasingly trapped by their sense of coercive "reality" shaping their lives. From the outset, both texts underscore the clash between the pleasures of impulse, idleness, and aimlessness on the one hand and the inexorable realities of social convention and time itself on the other. As we have seen, the experiences most relished by Edna and Lily are incompatible with their everyday lives, attainable only by denying social reality, or through dream, fantasy, "invention" – and art. Nonetheless, as we have also seen, both characters associate certain elements of art (particularly narrative art) with the very aspects of "reality" they most strongly resist. For them, magic moments are destroyed, not created, by those indispensible attributes of fiction which bring the imaginary worlds of *The Awakening* and *The House of Mirth* themselves into being: beginnings and endings, story or plot.

All fiction requires strategies for structuring plot and representing time. Naturalism, with its thematic emphasis on the conflict between the relentless movement of time and the characters' impotent resistance to that movement, generally presents its sequence of events in straightforward chronological order, with little of that flare for subverting the surface coherence of plot that we associate with the fiction of modernism or postmodernism. Both *The Awakening* and *The House of Mirth* have the extremely clean, streamlined, linear plots typical of naturalist texts. One extended flashback early in *House of Mirth* (chap. 3) and another in *The Awakening* (chap. 7) give a selection of details about Edna and Lily's childhoods, contextualizing their relation to their parents and providing perspective on the present situation of each heroine. Beyond that point, both stories seem to move ahead quite directly, with little perceptible circling. Yet despite the general sense of unimpeded progression characteristic of both plots, sophisticated maneuvers are at work in the manipulation of narrative time. Chopin, for example, would seem to conceive of *The Awakening* not primarily as a sequence of events, but rather as a seductive enclosure into which she would invite the reader. ("The voice of the sea is seductive, never ceasing, whispering, clamoring, murmuring . . .".) We have emphasized the contrast between the "unceasing," undifferentiated voice of the sea on the one hand and the articulation of a narrating voice on the other. Paradoxically, however, narration in *The Awakening* seems designed to evoke for the reader, through the reading process, an experience analogous to Edna's immersion in the boundless realm of field and sea.

The link between Chopin's sense of her own text and Edna's sense of the sea is not merely fanciful. After Robert's return from Mexico, when Edna runs into him in a garden restaurant, he notices that she is reading a book he himself has already read. He tells her how the book ends, "to save her the trouble of wading through it," as he says (105). Robert's image of "wading" for reading is worth some attention in a book so pervaded by the image of the sea. To "wad[e] . . . through" a book merely to find out what happens at the end is a chore, something Robert would like to save Edna "the trouble of." I suggest that it is also antithetical to the reading experience that Chopin promotes in *The Awakening* itself. To wade in the sea is to keep one's feet on the bottom, to forestall the immersion that could make for a feeling of free forward movement (swimming) on the one hand, a danger of submergence (even the risk of drowning) on the other.[20]

All novel reading (at least until modernism) implicates a reader in a plot that creates suspense or curiosity, stimulating the reader to wonder "what will happen next," and especially "how will it end?" But a novel must keep the reader's wish to answer that question within bounds – must regulate the reader's involvement with the text, keeping him or her implicated in, and gratified by, the *process* of anticipation and delay itself. Otherwise, what is to prevent a reader from skipping ahead to the final scene?

Every writer must harness the forward movement that is indispensible to writing and reading fiction. Reading always involves such movement and encourages the projection of possible (anticipated) endings. In *The Awakening*, where the traditional momentum of the naturalist plot is modified by lyric passages and recurrent leitmotivs, Chopin generates a reading experience informed by a sense, not of rapid descent, but of timelessness or containment in a space that seems "free" even as it is always moving forward.

One measure of Chopin's control over narrative time is precisely her subversion of the forward thrust that characterizes most realist and naturalist plots.[21] The recurrent images and lyric passages in *The Awakening* complicate, even abrogate, a reader's concern with what will *happen* next. Unlike some of Chopin's own stories – and unlike *The House of Mirth* – *The Awakening* resists melodramatic encounters,[22] refusing climax altogether, creating instead a virtual sense of fusion between beginnings and endings.[23] That sense of fusion is reemphasized in the final passage by the repetition of previous motifs, the evocation of Edna's childhood memories, and the birth imagery that accompanies her disappearance in the sea.

Insofar as the act of reading fiction always separates one from habitual concerns and immerses one in a world of make-believe, the reading process may be seen as an undifferentiated state which one enters and from which one emerges.[24] As we have seen, the problem of emergence itself is underscored at an early point in *The Awakening,* with particular emphasis on the difficulty of emerging from the chaos that accompanies the beginning of "a world, especially." In the narrator's uncharacteristically explicit identification with Edna here ("how few of *us* ever emerge from such beginning . . . ") that "us" can of course be taken to include the reader as well as Edna and the narrator. However, while the aesthetic experience provided by *The Awakening* may approximate Edna's sense of immersion in a timeless realm (field, sea, or music), the act of reading allows fusion or merger only within safe boundaries. By engaging imaginatively with the fluid medium of narrative time, Chopin (like Wharton) makes the creation of an "in-between state" for readers a source of strength and satisfaction, even while demonstrating the inexorable power of time in "reality" and explicitly underscoring its role in destroying the protagonist.

Recent discussions of women's literature often concern themselves with the question of woman's "space." The issue is not merely one of physical space – a room of own's own – nor is it simply a question of woman's "place" in relation to either society or the literary canon. Many feminist critics speak of women's writing itself as "another 'medium'" (Jacobus), a "wild zone" (Showalter), a border or margin between established modes (Jehlen).[25] Far from constituting a purposive hurtle toward an end, the process of reading itself is a kind of "in-between state" that shares many qualities with the kinds of unbounded, or timeless, "magic-realms" repeatedly figured in both *The Awakening* and *The House of Mirth.* While all novels, in this sense, project "in-between" states for their readers, both Chopin and Wharton place particular emphasis on the temptation and danger of such states in "real life," even while taking pains to heighten the reader's own sense of immersion or suspension in an analogous condition.

Like Chopin, Wharton repeatedly subverts a reader's sense of straightforward progression through narrative time. In *The House of Mirth,* whenever Lily and/or Selden experience the impulse to stop time altogether, the strands of plot begin to split and the direct line of chronological sequence is obscured. Thus, in both novels, strategies of plotting reflect certain nonmimetic aims shared by Chopin and Wharton in projecting a narrated world for readers.

Early in the Bellomont section of *House of Mirth,* as Percy Gryce waits for Lily to accompany him to church, he temporarily loses himself in the pleasures of anticipation, reflecting "agreeably on the strength of character which kept [Lily] true to her early training in surroundings so subversive to religious principles." While nourishing "the hope that Miss Bart might be unaccompanied" (54), Gryce even enjoys the delay. But just when "the coachman seemed to be slowly petrifying on the box and the groom on the doorstep" (54) – that is, when time seems at a total standstill – the ladies' sudden entrance reveals that the clock has not stopped after all ("the precious minutes were flying"; 56) and in a flash "poor Mr Gryce found himself rolling off [to church] between four ladies for whose spiritual welfare he felt not the least concern" (55).

Gryce's delight in anticipation and delay is abruptly subverted. In the meantime – that is, at precisely the same early-morning time – Lily herself undergoes a related process. With the carriage come and gone, the scene shifts to a guest room where Lily still lies in bed. The *scene* shifts, but as far as *time* is concerned we are retracing the very moments during which Gryce waited expectantly for Lily.

Having "risen earlier than usual," fully intending to accompany Gryce to church (55), Lily lies in bed, luxuriating not only in her sense of physical well-being and her pleasurable memories of the night before, but in the certainty that her plot is working and that a secure haven (marriage to Gryce) is right within her grasp. Lying in bed, while the day seems stalled, Lily dwells delightedly in the assurance that she can easily elicit Gryce's marriage proposal – later. However, while Gryce waits for Lily, her own reflections on the events of the previous evening lead her to tremble between bleak visions of a future with Gryce and a still more chilling awareness of the bills on her night-table. With Lily's recollection of those bills, the narrative focus comes back – for the *third* time – to the moment when Sunday morning dawned at Bellomont: "Miss Bart, accordingly, rose the next morning with the most earnest conviction that it was her duty to go to church" (59).

Wharton's sleight of hand is impressive. While only a few moments pass in represented "reality" (Gryce waits, Lily reflects), considerable space in the text is devoted to providing multiple angles on the same brief span of time. Thus, through the circling away from and back over one particular moment, Wharton's handling of the sequence of incident and reverie reproduces quite closely, for the reader, a process repeatedly experienced by the characters: first the sense of time standing still, then the shattering of that illusion. The reader is held in slow motion, in suspension, in a sense of no time passing – not unlike Gryce and Lily themselves. However, once the spell is broken, for both reader and characters, it turns out that something decisive has occurred precisely because time has never really stopped. Lily has missed the coach; Gryce has gone to church without her, and Lily's marriage prospects are significantly reduced.

Wharton's structuring and pacing of narrative incident after the *tableaux vivants* scene reproduces in greater detail such circling away from and back over one limited stretch of time. Here, still more dramatically than on Sunday at Bellomont, a day that begins with the pleasurable denial of reality ends with the shattering of numerous illusions – a shattering at once more definitive and more destructive for Lily than the end of her plans for Percy Gryce.

The passage that renders Lily's awakening the morning after the *tableaux vivants* presents her once again in a state of delightful limbo. Selden has written, asking to see her, and Lily, who "could not bear to mar her mood of luxurious retrospection by an act of definite refusal" (147–8), has agreed to meet him the following day (while telling herself she can easily put him off when the time comes). Lily's state of delicious abstraction from habitual pressures is partly a result of her "luxurious retrospection" (147–8) – the memory of her "culminating moment of . . . triumph" on stage (147). But it is also a result of what we might call "luxurious anticipation" – the pleasure of looking forward to her encounter with Selden (while reserving the right not to *have* it). Lily's taste for suspended moments of this kind is something she shares with Selden himself; it is perhaps the strongest tie that binds them. Immediately after the *tableaux vivants*, for example, although Selden's "first impulse was to seek Miss Bart," he is far from disappointed at failing to find her, because "it would have broken the spell to see her too soon": ". . . his procrastination was not due to any lingering resistance, but to the desire to luxuriate a moment in the sense of complete surrender" (143). Like Lily, Selden finds the sense of surrender particularly "luxurious" when kept short of realization. For him, as for her, delay is a special pleasure in itself. It is also (like anticipation) a pleasure particularly relevant to narrative.[26]

Thus two scenes juxtaposed in the middle of *House of Mirth* not only maximize the pleasures of anticipation and delay for characters and reader, but also underscore the various implications of illusion in life and art. The two scenes in question (Lily at Trenor's house, Selden at Gerty's) thematize the pressure of time running out for Lily while simultaneously deflecting the reader's attention from other aspects of passing time – including the simple fact that the novel's own midpoint has been passed and the end is fast approaching. In the dinner scene between Selden and Gerty, Selden luxuriates in his sense of both anticipation and delay, talking to Gerty of Lily, just to relish the moments until the "surrender" that he thinks is inevitable (162). By dwelling on Selden's idealized image of Lily, while averting the narrative focus from the *real* Lily and her doings at that moment, the text creates a sense of suspended time for both the reader and Selden himself.

No sooner does the text render Selden's misplaced sense of security, however, than it pointedly reemphasizes the relentless movement of time. While he talks expansively of Lily, confident in the future, events occur which transform Selden's sense of reality. When dining with Gerty, he is convinced that he can "separate the woman he knew from the vulgar estimate of her" (162). Even as he revels in this particular certainty, however, Lily is fending off Gus Trenor's aggressive sexuality; therefore, as Selden is walking home toward midnight, he sees Lily silhouetted against Trenor's door, about to get into a cab. It is only at this point that the reader, like Selden, is abruptly returned not only to the reality of Selden's moral cowardice (assuming the worst about Lily), but to the relation between causes and effects, made visible by the passing of time and the recombination of disparate narrative strands.

As in the scene where Gryce waits for Lily while Lily stays in bed, one effect of splitting the strands of a plot is a certain amount of inevitable distortion (or confusion) of linear time from the reader's point of view. While Selden idles at Gerty's, the reader, too, may experience a temporary sense of time standing still, a limbo or deadlock of anticipation matched against delay not unlike Selden's own. All time frames and lines of action recombine, however, when Selden sees Lily emerge from Trenor's door. At that point many illusions are dispelled, for characters and readers alike.

Through Wharton's careful handling of plot, then, both the feeling of time standing still, and the sudden realization of time having passed (two conditions so dangerous for the characters) are reproduced – in a harmless form – for the reader of the text.[27] *The Awakening* tells us at one point that "all sense of reality had gone out of [Edna's] life" (102). To a certain extent, a reader must willingly relinquish his or her hold on reality in order to read fiction at all. A "willing suspension of disbelief" is not the same thing, however, as an unwitting loss of all sense of reality. Thus, whereas Chopin and Wharton write fiction, Edna and Lily are destroyed.

Lily's lack of attention to the shape of her own story, and her unreflecting illusion of time-control, creates a sharp contrast with Wharton's extremely sophisticated understanding of narration and time. Similarly, we can point to the contrast between Edna's longing for a state with no beginning or end and Chopin's own control over beginnings and endings in narrative. As we have seen, however, Chopin (like Wharton) uses her text to implicate her reader in a recurrent sense not only of boundaries and limits but also of timelessness – an in-between state that shares certain qualities with Edna's experience listening to music (especially Chopin!), sailing to Chenière Caminada, or responding to the sea.

At the thematic level, *The Awakening*, like *The House of Mirth*, celebrates the joys of "exaltation" even as it exposes the futility of Edna's wish to sustain (or return to) her "culminating moments" of delight. Thus while Edna is "still under the spell of her infatuation" (54) with Robert several weeks after her own departure from Grand Isle, she repeatedly runs up against proof of time and change: Robert is gone, her sister marries, there are ten tiny new piglets at her mother-in-law's farm (102), and Mme Ratignolle, too, is about to give birth.

During Edna's last encounter with Mlle Reisz, she sits down to read Robert's most recent letter. Anticipating delight, Edna "hold[s the letter] . . . in her hand, while the music penetrated her whole being like an effulgence, warming and brightening the dark places of her soul. It prepared her for joy and exaltation" (80). But when Edna reads of Robert's approaching return, she pulls Mlle Reisz's hands off the keys to get more information. The "joy and exaltation" of aesthetic experience is subverted by urgent expectations in material reality. Like Selden's sudden glimpse of Lily at Trenor's door, Edna's abrupt reentry into a time-bound realm short-circuits the sense of her "spirit set free," the feeling she generally achieves when Mlle Reisz plays the piano. Similarly, toward the end of *The Awakening*, the "intoxication of expectancy" (110) as Edna moves toward sexual union with Robert is interrupted by a knock on the door to request her presence while Mme Ratignolle gives birth.

Pregnancy and birth constitute a kind of natural trope for the notion of time running out. Edna's suicide itself can be seen as a refusal to reenter the cycle of sexuality and birth that makes the presence of "a little new life" inescapable (109). Yet *The Awakening* also projects an entirely different, one could say more primal, image of mother and child. Despite the text's social critique of "mother-women" (10), the figure of mother and child – and of pregnancy itself – is, throughout *The Awakening*, one more vehicle for the idea of merger, the fluid symbiosis or fusion so "seductive" to Edna, and so threatening to the possibility of "emergence." Not surprisingly, Lily's final drift toward death in *House of Mirth* is also accompanied by the image of a mother and baby – rocking, intertwined, and interdependent. In the course of *House of Mirth*, Lily repeatedly longs for the shelter and darkness associated with a mother's arms (157).[28]

Both *The Awakening* and *The House of Mirth* are pervaded by a concern with modes of exaltation and fusion that ultimately make emergence impossible for the protagonists (though they are nonetheless, in themselves, a source of unique satisfactions). Unlike Edna and Lily, of course, both writers and readers can "emerge" from the chaos that constitutes the beginning "of a [fictional] world, especially." Different narrative structures, to be sure, implicate readers in different modes of immersion and emergence. But the start of every story involves a bid for connection between narrator and reader; and the end of every text involves loosening that bond, separation, and finally silence. Thus, in a sense, immersion and separation are always – inevitably – an issue for writers. Perhaps this is one reason why both male and female writers so commonly use birth motifs as a figure for the act of writing itself.

Many reading theorists stress the peculiar phenomenological status of the act of reading. Reading fiction in particular is an unusual condition that allows one, as reader, to be both oneself and someone else at the same time – to experience (as Dorrit Cohn puts it) "what writers and readers know least in life: how another mind thinks, how another body feels . . . ."[29] To read fiction is to experience (a bounded and temporary) sense of merger – such merger as, in Edna and Lily's experience, cannot be sustained in "reality."

The authors who created Edna and Lily as vehicles for exploring issues in their own experience of both life and art were effectively separated from their fictional heroines by the simple fact of having written these stories. It is not only that the authors master the time-bound medium of narrative, while the protagonists engage in a losing race with time and either refuse narrative altogether (Lily) or are threatened with dissolution by it (Edna); it is also that, for Chopin and Wharton, the control and order indispensible to aesthetic experience – what Wharton calls "precision in ecstacy" (*BG* 170) – becomes a source of satisfaction, not of fear.

A spirit "set free" through music or art cannot dwell in "exaltation" forever. If Chopin's or Wharton's narratives may be seen as ontological "borderlands," their own sense of absorption or merger in the writing of fiction is given free rein only within limits that enhance rather than undermine their capacity to project illusion by mastering plot, controlling narrative time, articulating a storytelling voice in language. It is precisely through their heightened consciousness of the limits inherent in magic realms that these writers are able to create such realms for both their characters and their readers.

Unlike Edna telling her story to the doctor, or Lily in the *tableaux vivants*, Chopin and Wharton sustain an awareness of the distinctions between fiction and reality, self and art and audience. At a certain point in *The Awakening*, Edna visits the Ratignolles and recoils from their relentless domesticity. "If ever the fusion of two human beings into one has been accomplished on this sphere it was surely in their union" (56). Such fusion ("on this sphere") is not to be envied, certainly not by Edna (or Chopin). But insofar as reading and writing enable one to fuse without fusing, to merge safely with another ("on this sphere"), Chopin and Wharton solve at least some of their protagonists' problems through authorship – representing otherness "without ceasing to be [themselves]."

NOTES

1 Martin, p. 26. Cf. Showalter ("Tradition and the Female Talent"), p. 48; Gilmore, p. 80. On Lily's "inability to speak for herself," see Showalter ("Death of the Lady"), pp. 142, 145. Cf. Fetterley passim.
2 It is ironic in this context that whereas *The House of Mirth* became a best-seller and put Wharton on the literary map, *The Awakening* virtually put an end to Chopin's career. (See Martin, pp. 8–10; Showalter ["Tradition and the Female Talent"], pp. 33–4; Kaplan, pp. 67–8.) But my main focus is the symbolic, not the social, effects of narration.
3 *A Backward Glance*, p. 223; cf. pp. 144, 217. Further references in the text are to this edition.
4 Chopin, *The Awakening*, p. 63. Further references in the text are to this edition.
5 On this much discussed scene, see Hochman, Steiner, Michaels, Seltzer.
6 The naturalist connection is rarely emphasized, perhaps partially obscured by the emphasis on Chopin and Wharton as trailbreakers in women's fiction. See Showalter ("Tradition and the Female Talent"), pp. 34–5. *The House of Mirth* is more often set in the "naturalist" context than *The Awakening* (see Kaplan, Michaels, Mitchell, Seltzer). Other generic models that could be noted are not directly relevant to the present argument. Wharton can, of course, be situated in the "novel of manners" tradition (see Lindberg); while *The Awakening* is often discussed in the romantic or transcendentalist context (see Balkman, Leary).
7 See Kaplan, pp. 69–74. Cf. Showalter ("Tradition and the Female Talent"), pp. 34–5, 44; Martin, p. 26; Gilbert, pp. 15, 29, 30–2.
8 See Norris, *Literary Criticism*, p. 13.
9 Dreiser, *Sister Carrie*, p. 244.
10 The pair of strolling lovers, the woman in black, the various birds, the sea itself – these attributes of *The Awakening* have received considerable attention. See

Showalter ("Tradition and the Female Talent") on the text's "impressionistic rhythm of epiphany and mood" (43); Cf. Gilmore, pp. 80–1; Jones, p. 169; Horner and Zlosnik, p. 53.

11 Wharton, *The House of Mirth*, p. 236. Further references in the text are to this edition.

12 On Lily's rejection of plot see Bauer, pp. 124–5. Cf. Showalter ("Death of the Lady"), pp. 142–3, 154.

13 Controversy over Edna's experience has raged since the book first appeared (to hostile reviews). Subsequently neglected for decades, its rediscovery in the fifties has generated a wide array of readings. For a view of Edna's development that stresses Edna's "evolution from romantic fantasies of fusion with another person to self-definition and self-reliance," see Showalter ("Tradition and the Female Talent"), p. 33. Cf. Fryer, pp. 257–8.

14 On the narrator's tendency to "distance . . . herself from Edna" see Jones, p. 165.

15 This concern of Edna's (and Chopin's) anticipates both Virginia Woolf's rendering of women's experience in *A Room of One's Own* and a central issue in much current feminist theory. For discussions of *The Awakening* in terms of "women's time," see Jones, pp. 157–8; Toth, pp. 275–6. Cf. Kristeva ("Women's Time"), pp. 187, 190–2, 207, and passim. In Kristeva's psychoanalytic theory, the unrecoverable unity of mother and child becomes the source of poetic language. On Kristeva's distinction between the "symbolic" mode and the "prelinguistic" ("semiotic") mode, see Kristeva (*Revolution*).

16 Many critics engage Edna's and Lily's search for a form beyond time, space, and social reality. See Horner and Zlosnik, pp. 7, 24; Bauer, pp. 145, 148; White, p. 102; Fryer, pp. 257–8. On Lily's inability "to imagine existing in another element," see Horner and Zlosnik, p. 24; cf. Bauer, pp. 124–5. I am suggesting that, unlike Edna and Lily, Chopin and Wharton find "another element" for existence in and through writing.

17 James, "Ivan Turgenieff," pp. 174–5.

18 Norris, *Literary Criticism*, p. 55.

19 Edith Wharton, *The Writing of Fiction*, p. 91.

20 Chopin has harsh words for fiction that is not "seductive enough" to immerse a reader totally. Of *Jude the Obscure*, Chopin writes: "you will just keep on munching a cream chocolate or wondering if the postman has gone by or if there is coal on the furnace" (*Complete Works*, p. 714).

21 For systematic examinations of narrative time, see Gennette, Rimmon-Kenan, Sternberg. In general, narratological approaches to temporal ordering have not engaged questions of gender.

22 That is, the scrubwoman selling letters to Lily, Rosedale meeting Lily leaving Selden's house in chapter 1, Selden glimpsing Lily leaving Gus Trenor's house near midnight, Bertha banishing Lily from the yacht, and so on.

23 See Schweitzer, pp. 163–4, 185; Cf. Fryer, pp. 257–8.

24 On the reading experience as a ground of temporary merger between "self" and "other," see Bakhtin, p. 315; Poulet, p. 56; Iser, p. 293; Jacobus, p. 37.

25 In Jacobus's "other 'medium'" the self is temporarily "dissolved into writing" (37). Cf. Showalter (*New Feminist Criticism*), p. 262; Jehlen, p. 585.

26 On delay, anticipation, and narrative time, see Gennette, Rimmon-Kenan, Sternberg.
27 It may be relevant, in this context, that during the composition of *House of Mirth,* Wharton herself was (for the first time) subject to a writing deadline.
28 Cf. pp. 101, 176, 184, and note 15.
29 Cohn, pp. 5–6.

WORKS CITED

Bakhtin, M. M. *The Dialogic Imagination.* Edited by Michael Holquist. Austin: University of Texas Press, 1981.

Balkman, Elizabeth. "*The Awakening,* Kate Chopin's 'Endlessly Rocking' Cycle." *Ball State University Forum* 20 (1979): 53–8.

Bauer, Dale M. *Feminist Dialogics: A Theory of Failed Community.* Albany: State University of New York Press, 1988.

Chopin, Kate. *The Awakening.* New York: W. W. Norton, 1976.

The Complete Works. Edited by Per Seyersted. Baton Rouge: Louisiana State University Press, 1969.

"Elizabeth Stark's One Story." In *The Awakening and Selected Stories.* New York: Penguin, 1986.

Cohn, Dorrit. *Transparent Minds.* Princeton, N.J.: Princeton University Press, 1978.

Dimock, Wai-Chee. "Debasing Exchange: Edith Wharton's *House of Mirth.*" In *Edith Wharton: Modern Critical Views,* edited by Harold Bloom, pp. 123–37. New York: Chelsea, 1986.

Dreiser, Theodore. *Sister Carrie.* New York: W. W. Norton, 1970.

Fetterley, Judith. "The Temptation to Be a Beautiful Object: Double Standard and Double Bind in *The House of Mirth.*" *Studies in American Fiction* 5 (1977): 199–211.

Fryer, Judith. *The Faces of Eve: Women in the Nineteenth-Century Novel,* New York: Oxford University Press, 1976.

Genette, Gerard. *Narrative Discourse.* Translated by Jane E. Lewin. Ithaca, N.Y.: Cornell University Press, 1980.

Gilbert, Sandra. "Introduction" to *The Awakening.* New York: Penguin, 1986.

Gilmore, Michael T. "Revolt Against Nature: The Problematic Modernism of *The Awakening.*" In Martin, *New Essays,* pp. 59–88.

Hochman, Barbara. "The Rewards of Representation: Edith Wharton, Lily Bart, and the Writer/Reader Interchange." *Novel* 24 (1991): 147–61.

Horner, Avril, and Zlosnik, Sue. *Landscapes of Desire.* New York: Harvester, 1990.

Iser, Wolfgang. *The Implied Reader.* Baltimore and London: The Johns Hopkins University Press, 1974.

Jacobus, Mary. *Reading Woman.* New York: Columbia University Press, 1986.

James, Henry. "Ivan Turgenieff" (1874). Reprinted in *Theory of Fiction: Henry James,* edited by James E. Miller, Jr. Lincoln and London: University of Nebraska Press, 1972.

Jehlen, Myra. "Archimedes and the Paradox of Feminist Criticism." *Signs* 6 (1981): 575–601.

Jones, Ann Goodwyn. *Tomorrow Is Another Day: The Woman Writer in the South 1859–1936*. Baton Rouge: Louisiana State University Press, 1981.
Kaplan, Amy. *The Social Construction of American Realism*. Chicago: University of Chicago Press, 1988.
Kristeva, Julia. *Revolution in Poetic Language*. Translated by Margaret Waller. New York: Columbia University Press, 1984.
"Women's Time." In *The Kristeva Reader,* edited by Toni Moi. New York: Columbia University Press, 1986.
Leary, Lewis. *Southern Excursion: Essays on Mark Twain and Others*. Baton Rouge: Louisiana State University Press, 1971.
Lindberg, Gary. *Edith Wharton and the Novel of Manners*. Charlottesville: University Press of Virginia, 1975.
Martin, Wendy. "Introduction," *New Essays on The Awakening*, pp. 1–32. New York: Cambridge University Press, 1988.
Michaels, Walter Benn. *The Gold Standard and the Logic of Naturalism*. Berkeley and Los Angeles: University of California Press, 1987.
Mitchell, Lee Clark. *Determined Fictions*. New York: Columbia University Press, 1989.
Norris, Frank. *The Literary Criticism of Frank Norris*. Edited by Donald Pizer. New York: Russell and Russell, 1976.
Poulet, Georges. "Phenomenology of Reading." *New Literary History* 1 (1969): 53–68.
Rimmon-Kenan, Shlomith. *Narrative Fiction*. London and New York: Methuen, 1983.
Schweitzer, Ivy. "Maternal Discourse and the Romance of Self-Possession." *Boundary 2* 17 (1990): 161–86.
Seltzer, Mark. *Bodies and Machines*. New York: Routledge, 1992.
Showalter, Elaine. "The Death of Lady (Novelist): Wharton's *House of Mirth*." In *Edith Wharton: Modern Critical Views,* edited by Harold Bloom, pp. 139–54. New York: Chelsea, 1986.
The New Feminist Criticism: Essays on Women, Literature and Theory. London and New York: Pantheon, 1985.
"Tradition and the Female Talent: *The Awakening* as a Solitary Book." In Martin, *New Essays,* pp. 33–57.
Steiner, Wendy. "The Causes of Effect: Edith Wharton and the Economics of Ekphrasis." *Poetics Today* 10 (1989): 279–97.
Sternberg, Meir. *Expositional Modes and Temporal Ordering in Fiction*. Baltimore and London: The Johns Hopkins University Press, 1978.
Toth, Emily. "Timely and Timeless: The Treatment of Time in *The Awakening*." *Southern Studies* 16 (1977): 271–6.
Wharton Edith. *A Backward Glance*. New York: Scribner's, 1964.
The House of Mirth. In *Novels*. New York: Library of America, 1985.
The Letters of Edith Wharton. Edited by R. W. B. Lewis and Nancy Lewis. New York: Scribner's, 1988.
The Writing of Fiction. New York: Scribner's, 1925.
White, Robert. "*The Awakening*." *Mosaic* 17 (1984): 97–110.

IO

JACQUELINE TAVERNIER-COURBIN

The Call of the Wild and *The Jungle*: Jack London's and Upton Sinclair's Animal and Human Jungles

Both leading American realists, both dedicated and militant socialists, Jack London and Upton Sinclair were nevertheless completely different in temperament and philosophy of life. Although they appreciated each other's works, they only met twice, in circumstances not entirely favorable for the development of a friendship. Whereas London hailed the publication of Sinclair's *The Jungle* with generous praise, thus propelling the book and its author toward international fame,[1] Sinclair was less generous in his appraisal of London, basing his criticism not on the work but on the man. Voicing his own deep-set puritanical nature, he damned London for such sins as smoking, drinking, enjoying sex, resigning from the Socialist party, and making too much money.[2] As Charmian London commented, Sinclair's misapprehensions were partly due to his lack of personal acquaintance with London and to his never having seen him sober,[3] both their meetings having taken place in New York where London was seldom on his best behavior. It is unfortunate that Sinclair did not accept London's invitation to visit him at his Glen Ellen ranch in California, since it would have been his only opportunity to see him at work, sober and in his own surroundings. But London's invitation was expressed in his typically direct way, a language which Sinclair found easy to misinterpret:

> Why not plan for you and your wife to run up and visit us at this time. It is a dandy place to work; if you wish you can stay in your own room and have your meals sent in to you and work twenty-four hours out of the twenty-four. . . .
> You and I ought to have some "straight from the shoulder" talk with each other. It is coming to you, it may be coming to me. It may illuminate one or the other or both of us.[4]

Sinclair refused London's invitation because George Sterling had told him that Jack had become rude, domineering, and would allow no one to argue with him.[5] Sinclair was perhaps unaware that Sterling was a lively and inventive gossip who resented Jack and Charmian's withdrawal from the close companionship they had shared for a long time, and who gossiped to London about his visits with the Sinclairs:

> I've just put in a week with the Sinclairs . . . where I walked, chopped wood and gathered apples and nuts ad lib., about paying for my keep, I guess.
> Upton is something fierce, but his wife is adorable. He'd not let me whistle in the house, and if I left a door open he felt the draft and put up a howl.[6]

Although both Sinclair and London rebelled at man's cruelty and felt deeply for the downtrodden and the poor, they were never friends and went about improving the world in different ways. Disappointed by the Socialist party's inaction and the mediocrity of its leaders, and convinced that it would go nowhere because Americans prefer democratic to revolutionary methods, London felt that he could reach more people through his work than through political action[7] and devoted his considerable energies to his writing and to developing and improving his ranch, striving to restore the land to its former richness before the destructive advent of the American pioneer. The betterment of agricultural conditions was his other social dream, and he became one of the first dedicated environmentalists. Sinclair, on the other hand, remained politically active into his sixties.

Both writers were effective muckrakers, but London always subordinated that activity to the novelist's craft, whereas Sinclair did the opposite. London's propagandistic works include didactic sociological essays; a book-length report of his firsthand observations in the East End of London, *The People of the Abyss;* and fictional works which both exposed social injustice and cruelty and aimed at reform, such as *The Star Rover* which revealed the horrors of the straitjacket in American prisons and was instrumental in bringing about the abrogation of the law allowing its use in 1913. However, neither his storytelling nor his character development suffered from London's desire to arouse public awareness. Indeed, while much of his fiction is the vehicle for a message, the message is seldom an assault upon the reader. Novels such as *Martin Eden* and *The Sea Wolf,* intended as pleas against individualism, were interpreted as exalting it, which depressed and angered London. Nonetheless, this misunderstanding was an indirect and unwitting tribute to his talent, for both are powerful novels dramatizing such lifelike protagonists that the message gets lost. Martin Eden and Wolf Larsen embody individualism with such passion, intelligence, romance, and lust for life that one cannot but identify with them.

The immediate success of *The Call of the Wild,* which catapulted London onto the international scene, and the praise lavished upon it by critics, surprised London, who knew that the book was different from other dog stories but was unaware that he had written a brilliant human allegory.[8] Begun as a normal dog story meant to redeem the species from a previous story, "Bâtard," which had dramatized a dog-made-devil by a sadistic master, *The Call of the Wild* "got away" from London and turned out to be far more of "a shot in the dark" than he could possibly have imagined. What he did realize clearly, however, was the therapeutic value of writing the book. Sitting down to it soon after his return from England in 1902, he indirectly expressed his violent reaction against the human jungle he had known in the East End of London; life in a natural jungle seemed an enviable situation by contrast.

Like other American realists of the late nineteenth century, both London and, to a lesser extent, Sinclair were influenced by Emile Zola, and both *The Call of the Wild* and *The Jungle* share characteristics of the naturalistic novel as defined in *The Experimental Novel*. Interest in contemporary French literature was a striking feature of cultural life in the United States during the last decade of the nineteenth century, and Zola's popularity is evidenced by the numerous translations of his works[9] and by the fact that even novels he had not written were published under his name.[10] But American publishers exploited to the utmost the deeply rooted Puritan idea that French literature is essentially wicked, turning Zola's terse titles into melodramatic ones.[11] London had twenty-two of Zola's novels in his personal library, with dates of publication ranging back to the 1880s. He was apparently reading *Germinal* as early as his oyster-pirating days on the sloop *Reindeer,* and he mentions Zola both in *A Son of the Sun* and in *Mutiny on the Elsinore*. He also owned numerous books by other French and American realists, but it is unclear whether he had read *The Experimental Novel,* which became available in English in 1893, as he seems not to mention it anywhere. However, it is clear that his conception of fiction coincided closely with Zola's.

Like Zola, who wanted the naturalistic novel to be a documentary work based solidly on physical reality, London took the gathering of documentary evidence seriously and would go to great lengths to gather data for a story. Wanting to write an American version of his own *People of the Abyss,* he intended to find "some hell-hole of a prison, and have [himself] arrested and sent to it."[12] While he was researching the book, he lived for seven weeks the life of the poorest among the workers and vagrants in the East End of London. He slept and ate in sordid hellholes where people had to wait in line for six or more hours before being admitted, where bunks were slept in continuously in shifts of eight hours, and where one had to break twelve hundred pounds of stone or empty the garbage of hospitals, thus being exposed to contagious diseases, to pay for a night's filthy bed. He saw the ugliest aspects of death and the most miserable ones. After seven weeks of such a life, London emerged from the East End scarred but with a well-documented book which is a violent indictment of a society which allows men to be reduced to a level of existence below that of animals. Before undertaking a new story, London would also carefully research his topic, collecting newspaper clippings and articles, magazines and books, and keeping files for future use on every topic of interest. For instance, over fifteen years, he accumulated a file containing twenty-eight newspaper articles on prison life which he used in writing *The Star Rover,* thus supplementing Ed Morrell's personal memories of San Quentin with other factual data. Indeed, although, at times, it deals with science fiction and astral projection, London's fiction is firmly grounded in reality and based on human documents, usually satisfying the requirements of logic and known scientific data.

Influenced in particular by his reading of Darwin and Spencer, London believed in evolution and determinism, the influence of heredity and of the milieu, as evidenced by much of his work and the abundant notes he left behind.[13] But these beliefs were tempered by a deep love of humanity and a loathing for the cruelty that often characterizes man's treatment of animals and other men. London's accurate descriptions of the inhumanity of man is not a gloating over blood and knuckles, as so many critics have claimed, but an expression of his abhorrence of cruelty and his belief that the best way to expose it is to describe it unemotionally and accurately. Indeed, both Zola and London believed that the novel should neither preach nor satirize but only dramatize life objectively, never drawing conclusions, because the conclusions are implicit in the material. Both also intended the novel to be a powerful social tool but felt that an accurate and objective picture of society and mankind, presented with clinical detachment, is more effective than a compassionate dramatization of man's misery. London made his point clear in a vibrant defense of Kipling's methods and the apparent heartlessness of his descriptions – "The color of tragedy is red. Must the artist also paint the watery tears and wan-faced grief?"[14] – and in his review of Maxim Gorky's *Foma Gordyeeff*:

> One lays the book down sick at heart – sick for life with all its "lyings and its lusts." But it is a healthy book. So fearful is its portrayal of social disease, so ruthless its stripping of the painted charm from vice, that its tendency cannot but be strongly for good. It is a goad, to prick sleeping human consciences awake and drive them into the battle for humanity.[15]

Much like other American realists, however, London had problems with Zola's credo which held that morality should be no more relevant to literature than to science. London was no prude, but he well knew that American readers would not tolerate a frank portrayal of love from an American writer. Although he suggests passionate love in his stories and novels, he never describes it as such, and it only manifests itself in its results: the extent of the lover's sacrifices for the loved one. But he never describes physical contact between human beings in any detail.

The Call of the Wild does not dramatize directly the social problems of the day but focuses on the 1897 Gold Rush, including a vivid portrayal of Klondike types as embodied by the four sets of masters who in turn own Buck: initially, the essentially fair and efficient government couriers François and Perrault, and later the "Scotch half-breed" in charge of the mail train, who along with the other drivers is also just, despite harsh circumstances, and who respects the dogs and spares them what suffering he can. The last two sets of masters Buck works under are dramatically opposite: first, the self-indulgent, ignorant, greedy, and hypocritical Mercedes, Charles, and Hal, who have no respect for the dogs and are made to stand for the worst of the "chekakos"; then John Thornton, the ideal master, "[who] saw to the welfare of his [dogs] as if they were his own children, because he could not help it."[16] Clearly, London cannot dramatize through the eyes of a dog all, or even most, of the social reality of a Klondike invaded by a quarter-million gold hunters, of whom only a scant fifty thousand made it to Dawson City and the North. What he could do was make the human characters he portrayed widely representative of Klondike types he knew and had heard of – types who recur frequently in his other stories of the North.

London's documentation was extensive, as he spent the best part of a year taking part in the Gold Rush, leaving San Francisco on 25 July 1897 and eventually floating down the Yukon, scurvy-ridden, on a raft the following spring. London's party made the trip from Dyea Beach to the Stewart River, where they settled for the winter, in two months, arriving on October 9, four days before the river was traditionally supposed to freeze up, and taking possession of a cabin on an island between the mouth of the Stewart River and the mouth of Henderson Creek. Jack toiled with the rest, daily increasing the load he was packing, until he was proud to pack as well as the Indians, carrying a hundred pounds to the load on good trails and seventy-five pounds on bad ones.[17] Since his outfit weighed a thousand pounds, he carried every load for one mile and came back for the next, thus walking nineteen miles for every mile of progression if he carried ten loads, and twenty-nine miles if he carried fifteen loads. Their route took them over the Chilkoot Pass to Lake Linderman, where they constructed a boat between 9 and 21 September. Jack's skill in handling small boats allowed them to make their way through Lakes Linderman, Bennet, Tagish, and Marsh before entering Fifty Mile River, which narrowed into two dangerous rapids: Box Canyon and White Horse rapids. The river trip from Lake Linderman took them a little less than three weeks, and they decided to make camp on Upper Island, a wise choice, as Dawson was crowded and there was the threat of food shortage.

After staking eight claims, they made their way downriver by boat to Dawson, where London spent six weeks, during which he observed the gold city. It was on 5 November, the day Dawson woke to find the Yukon frozen, that London filed his claim at the gold-records office for his gold strike on Henderson Creek, eighteen days after he first arrived in the city. London spent a great deal of time in Dawson's saloons during these few weeks, often in conversation with some veteran sourdough or noted town character. It was also in such bars that sourdoughs were famous for gambling away their fortunes. If *The Call of the Wild* contains only two saloon scenes (the scene at Circle City in which Buck attacks "Black Burton" and the one in the Eldorado Saloon in Dawson as a result of which Buck is made to pull a sled loaded with a thousand pounds of flour), many of London's stories of the North dramatize the drinking, talking, gambling, and dancing he had witnessed and the places, saloons, restaurants, Opera House, or commercial stores he had frequented. The only aspect of life he avoided describing was prostitution, which was rampant. In fact, dance-hall girls are always treated kindly and gallantly in London's Klondike fiction, often dramatized as kinder human beings than their more respectable sisters: "Butterflies, bits of light and song and laughter, dancing, dancing down the last tail-reach of hell."[18]

Those weeks in Dawson netted London many tales, and the raw frontier town appears often in his stories; but it was during the winter in camp that he came to know the Alaska of the sourdoughs and Indians. Aside from reading *The Origin of Species* and Milton's *Paradise Lost,* which he had taken with him up north, and swapping books with his companions, London's favorite recreation was talking and arguing. Eagerly he questioned the old-timers, listening avidly to their adventures until a picture of Alaska in trail-breaking days grew in his mind. The camp offered a cross-section of the new life that was pulsating through the North. Among the men who most impressed London was Louis Savard, a generally silent French Canadian who provided the inspiration for Louis Savoy in *The Son of the Wolf* and for characteristics of both François and Perrault in *The Call of the Wild,* while Nig, Louis's lovable sled dog who cleverly evaded work, probably became "That Spot" and, according to Joan London, one of Buck's companions. Emil Jensen, who was fifteen years older than London, and whom London greatly admired, became the model for Malemute Kid, London's central and idealized figure in *The Son of the Wolf* and *The God of His Fathers,* as well as for John Thornton.

How much personal experience London had with Northland dogs is difficult to determine. There were many dogs around, and he probably saw some of the best husky teams in the area, as the main trail ran near his cabin, and witnessed more than one prize dog put through the test of breaking a heavily laden sled out of the ice. He also knew well two "outsiders" – Newfoundlands and Saint Bernards – who learned to hold their own on Split-up Island: Louis Savard's Nig and especially Louis Bond's Jack, a cross between a Saint Bernard and a Scotch Collie, whom London greatly admired and whose qualities he used in Buck's characterization:

> Yes, Buck is based upon your dog at Dawson. And of course Judge Miller's place was Judge Bond's – even to the cement swimming tank & the artesian well. And don't you remember that your father was attending a meeting of the fruit-growers Association the night I visited you, and Louis was organizing an athletic club – all of which events figured with Buck if I remember correctly.[19]

What information London did not have he gathered from his reading, in particular Egerton R. Young's *My Dogs in the Northland,* published late in 1902, a few months before London started writing *Call of the Wild.* He probably learned much about the handling and behavior of sled dogs from this book, and several of the dogs in the novel resemble some of Young's dogs: "Young's Jack, a St. Bernard, has some of Buck's feelings of responsibility; Cuffy, a Newfoundland, is not unlike the feminine Curly; the one-eyed husky lead dog Voyageur may have contributed to the portrayal of unsociable, one-eyed Sol-leks; the behavior of Young's Rover, who constantly licks the wounds of other dogs in the team, may have suggested the role of doctor dog assumed by Skeet."[20] Although plagiarism would occasionally be charged against London, his use of such sources was generally a borrowing of technical data that affected neither plot, tone, theme, nor symbolism. He had visited the territory, he knew what he was describing, he had observed and experienced much, and such secondhand data was used to fill the gaps of his knowledge and provide realistic detail and a feeling of authenticity.

However, although *The Call of the Wild* is well documented, it is not crammed with factual data, for London did not believe in providing details that might detract from the "thrust and go" of his story. In his otherwise laudatory review of *The Octopus,* London complained of Norris's passion for documentary detail. As far as London was concerned, no one cared "whether Hooven's meat safe be square or oblong; whether it be lined with wire screen or mosquito netting; whether it be hung to the branches of an oak tree or to the ridgepole of the barn; whether, in fact, Hooven has a meat safe or not."[21] Indeed, he described his own art as "idealized realism" – an art that did not shy away from reality, even in its ugliest aspects, but attempted to grasp the true romance of things at the same time – and always defended his own fiction when attacked by critics who reproached him for giving insufficient detail:

> When I have drawn a picture in a few strokes, he would spoil it by putting in the multitude of details I have left out. . . . His trouble is that he does not see with a pictorial eye. He merely looks upon a scene and sees every bit of it; but he does not see the true picture in that scene, a picture which can be thrown upon a canvas by eliminating a great mass of things that spoil the composition, that obfuscate the true beautiful lines of it.[22]

The influence of the milieu and heredity, the concept of the survival of the fittest, and adaptation as the key to survival are of overwhelming importance in *The Call of the Wild,* which dramatizes the concept of devolution – the return of a civilized being to the primitive when his environment itself has changed from one of mellow civilization to one of brutality where the only law is eat or be eaten, kill or be killed. Until he is kidnapped, Buck lives the life of a sated aristocrat on Judge Miller's estate. His education into the harsh realities of an unprotected life begins shortly after he is abducted and endures a two-day-and-night train journey during which he is vilely treated and neither eats nor drinks. After changing hands a number of times, and in a fever of pain and rage, Buck meets the man in the red sweater, who provides the first step of his initiation into the wild: the dog breaker. Buck had never been struck with a club in his life, but again and again, with each new charge, he is brought crushingly to the ground by a vicious blow of the club. Although his rage knows no bounds and although he is a large, powerful dog, he is no match for a man who is "no slouch at dog-breakin'" and knows how to handle a club efficiently. The man in the red sweater finishes Buck off with a blow directly on the nose and a final "shrewd blow" that knocks him unconscious. Buck thus learns his first lesson: a man with a club is a master to be obeyed, though not necessarily placated. "That club was a revelation. It was his introduction to the reign of primitive law, and he met the introduction half-way" (32). Buck, however, retains his dignity and never fawns on his masters. They are stronger than he; therefore he obeys them. Having seen a dog that would neither obey nor conciliate killed in the struggle for mastery makes the alternatives clear to him: to obey, to conciliate, or to die; and Buck is above all a survivor. He knows he is beaten, but his spirit is never broken.

Buck's next lesson takes place on Dyea beach when Curly, whom he has befriended, is killed by the huskies when she makes friendly advances to one of them. In two minutes, she is literally torn to pieces. "So that was the way. No fair play. Once down, that was the end of you. Well [Buck] would see to it that he never went down" (45). This traumatic lesson often returns to haunt his sleep. There seems to be only one law in this new world, which both men and beasts obey – the law of club and fang – and, like Dave and Sol-leks, one has to learn to give nothing, ask for nothing, and expect nothing.

Adapting to a new environment also entails learning other lessons, not only simple lessons such as digging a sleeping hole in the snow or eating fast, but also lessons involving major moral changes. Buck learns to steal, and London makes it clear that his first theft marks him as fit to survive in the hostile Northland environment: "It marked his adaptability, his capacity to adjust himself to changing conditions, the lack of which would have meant swift and terrible death. It marked, further, the decay or going to pieces of his moral nature, a vain thing and a handicap in the ruthless struggle for existence" (59). London comments with some irony that, while living on Judge Miller's estate, Buck would have died for a moral principle, such as the defense of the Judge's riding whip, "but [that] the completeness of his decivilization was now evidenced by his ability to flee from the defense of a moral consideration and so save his hide" (60). Among other moral qualities Buck sheds are his sense of fair play and mercy, values reserved for gentler climates. In the northern wilds, survival is the only goal, and ruthlessness the only way to survive. Thus, Buck learns through experience and proves that he is eminently adaptable and fit. His body also adapts well to the new demands of the environment: he loses his fastidiousness, grows impervious to pain, achieves an internal as well as an external economy, making the most of whatever comes his way; his senses develop to an incredible acuteness, and forgotten instincts come to life in him.

Heredity also plays an important role in his survival:

And not only did he learn by experience, but instincts long dead became alive again. The domesticated generations fell from him. In vague ways he remembered back to the youth of the breed, to the time the wild dogs ranged in packs through the primeval forest and killed their meat as they ran it down. It was no task for him to learn to fight with cut and slash and the quick wolf snap. In this manner had fought forgotten ancestors. They quickened the old life within him, and the old tricks which they had stamped into the heredity of the breed were his tricks. They came to him without effort or discovery, as though they had been his always.   (62)

The basic instinct which comes to life in Buck is the instinct to kill. He progresses quickly, beginning with small game, and eventually kills men. The instinct to kill is common to all predators; man himself has not completely lost it and indulges it when he goes shooting or hunting. However, for Buck, the killing is infinitely more intimate, as it is not carried out by proxy through a bullet: "He was ranging at the head of the pack, running the wild thing down, the living meat, to kill with his own teeth and wash his muzzle to the eyes in warm blood" (90). The hunt of the snowshoe rabbit marks the awakening of Buck's desire to kill, and he immediately challenges Spitz to a fight, which he wins largely because the knowledge of ancestral fighting techniques becomes his instantly:

As they circled about, snarling, ears laid back, keenly watchful for the advantage, the scene came to Buck with a sense of familiarity. He seemed to remember it all – the white woods, and earth, and moonlight, and the thrill of battle. . . . To Buck it was nothing new or strange, this scene of old time. It was as though it had always been, the wonted way of things.   (93)

After defeating Spitz, and while the pack closes in on his crippled enemy, "Buck stood and looked on, the successful champion, the dominant primordial beast who had made his kill and found it good" (99). Buck has indeed come of age, and, although his education is not finished, he has proven that he is one of the fit.

Once Buck has proven himself on the hereditary and environmental levels and has reverted to instinctual patterns of behavior, his life with a new master, John Thornton, suddenly becomes more mellow, and he has an opportunity to relax his vigilance. But Buck cannot return to his old self, for he has learned only too well the lessons of the wild – that one should never forego an advantage or draw back from a fight one has started, that mercy is misunderstood for fear or weakness, and that such misunderstanding may lead to death. He has gained knowledge from the depth of time, and such knowledge cannot be forgotten once it has become a conscious part of the self. Thus, life with John Thornton, which could, in other circumstances, have heralded a return to the tame, is merely an interval in Buck's evolution, and the call of the wild keeps on summoning him until he has returned fully to the life of his ancestors and become a part of nature.

In the last stages of Buck's devolution, London's handling of the theme of heredity becomes increasingly mythical and archetypal. London understood clearly that Buck's progress in adapting to his environment was in fact a regression into his instinctive past, what Jung would call his "collective unconscious":

> His development (or retrogression) was rapid. . . . And when, on the still, cold nights, he pointed his nose at a star and howled long and wolflike, it was his ancestors, dead and dust, pointing nose at star and howling down through the centuries and through him. And his cadences were their cadences, the cadences which voiced their woes and what to them was the meaning of the stillness, and the cold, and the dark.   (61)

Clearly, London could not have been aware of the extent to which his dramatization of Buck's return to the wild exemplifies C. G. Jung's theories of the unconscious. Nevertheless, Buck offers a perfect harmonization of Jung's progression and regression principles. Because he must adapt to a primitive environment, the hard-won values of the conscious and the vitality and power of the unconscious are no longer at war, and adaptation to his environment involves adopting a new set of values, which enhances rather than thwarts the vitality of his unconscious.

It is the emergence of his collective unconscious added to his physical power and intelligence which allows Buck to survive. This collective unconscious warns him of danger and gives him the tools and techniques necessary to defeat his adversaries. His instant recognition of what might be a trap is a clear instance of behavior controlled by instinctive knowledge arising from the collective unconscious:

> The snow walls pressed him on every side, and a great surge of fear swept through him – the fear of the wild thing for the trap. It was a token that he was harking back through his own life to the lives of his forebears; for he was a civilized dog, an unduly civilized dog, and of his own experience knew no trap and so could not of himself fear it.   (51–2)

Buck's newly discovered ability to bide his time "with a patience that [is] nothing less than primitive" (80) is also evidence of his collective unconscious, and is characteristic of predators whose only hope to eat and survive resides in their ability to lie in wait until their potential victim or foe is at a disadvantage and vulnerable to attack.

Throughout most of the book, Buck's persona and shadow are in equilibrium. He fulfills a social role where work is all-important, and, at the same time, he is in tune with his instincts. Indeed, he is now more fully alive than he ever was on Judge Miller's ranch:

> There is an ecstasy that marks the summit of life, and beyond which life cannot rise. And such is the paradox of living, this ecstasy comes when one is most alive, and it comes as a complete forgetfulness that one is alive. . . . and it came to Buck, leading the pack, sounding the wolf cry, straining after the food that was alive and that fled before him through the moonlight. He was sounding the deeps of his nature, and of the parts of his nature that were deeper than he, going back into the womb of Time. He was mastered by the sheer surging of life, the tidal wave of being, the perfect joy of each separate muscle, joint, and sinew in that it was everything that was not death, that it was aglow and rampant, expressing itself in movement, flying exultantly under the stars and over the face of dead matter that did not move. (91)

Buck had lived a life of quiet happiness in California, which was ruled by his civilized, good-dog persona. In the Northland, after his shadow has been awakened, he lives intensely every aspect of life, be it pain, joy, love, hatred, or work. In fact, he discovers passion, which is a manifestation of the shadow.

The third stage of Buck's evolution consists in the shedding of his new sled-dog persona to adopt a third and final one: a mythical or archetypal persona that becomes the very embodiment of his shadow, as his earlier dog-persona recedes into his personal unconscious. As the "blood longing" grows stronger in him, Buck fights larger and larger prey and begins more and more to resemble his wild brothers, transforming himself in the secrecy of the forest into a thing of the wild, "stealing along softly, cat-footed, a passing shadow that appeared and disappeared among the shadows" (210). Buck kills a large black bear and a huge bull-moose which he stalks and worries for four days before finally pulling him down, with the "dogged, tireless, persistent" patience of the wild "when it hunts its living food" (212). Then, out of despair and anger over the murder of John Thornton, Buck attacks and kills men – the Yeehats who have massacred Thornton's party – kills them in spite of the law of club and fang. His last ties with mankind broken, Buck is now free to join and lead a pack of wolves and live the life of the wild to the fullest, thus becoming the very embodiment of his shadow, as well as a God-image symbolizing the perfect integration of the self: "When the long winter nights come on and wolves follow their meat into the lower valleys, he may be seen running at the head of the pack through the pale moonlight or glimmering borealis, leaping gigantic above his fellows, his great throat a-bellow as he sings a song of the younger world, which is the song of the pack" (228–31).

From the standpoints of objectivity, amorality, and rejection of social taboos, *The Call of the Wild* is naturalistic by default, for Buck's gorgeous coat of fur allowed London to deal uninhibitedly with themes he would otherwise have shunned. Indeed, many painful and shocking scenes are described objectively. The potentially heart-rending scene in which Buck is beaten by the man in the red sweater is rendered in detail but with no expression of sympathy or pity. London does not dwell on Buck's pain, but merely describes accurately what the man does to him and how Buck reacts. The fight between Buck and Spitz, the stalking and killing of the bull-moose, and Buck's standing off the wolf pack are all scenes which London handles unemotionally, never indulging in expressions of horror or pity. He even indicates with remarkable simplicity the economy-of-pain principle upon which the moose herd functions: "it was not the life of the herd, or of the young bulls, that was threatened. The life of only one member was demanded, which was a remoter interest in their lives, and in the end they were content to pay the toll" (213). Pain, suffering, death, London can describe objectively. Love is another matter; but, again, Buck's furry nature frees London from having to wax romantic. Although he describes Buck's passionate devotion to John Thornton in abstract terms, he never allows Buck to lose his dignity and fawn upon his master as the other dogs do. The various instances when Buck proves his love for his master, whether by attempting to jump over a chasm (which would have led to certain death), by attacking Black Burton, by risking his own life repeatedly in the rapids to save Thornton's, or by pulling a sleigh loaded with a thousand pounds of flour, are always described with great economy of emotion. London merely describes Buck's actions – love in action, not as an emotion. What expression of feeling London does dramatize is on Thornton's part. Indeed, the men are awed by the lengths to which Buck will carry his devotion, and Thornton is the one who expresses his love for Buck after the latter has won his bet for him.

The amoral stance of the novel was an easy one for London to assume, because the perfect logic of Buck's reversion to the wild is easily acceptable in an animal. It would be more difficult to accept in a human being, especially by London's early-twentieth-century audience. Many of the themes London dramatizes easily in *The Call of the Wild* are present but transformed in his other fiction, where he never condones loss of moral principles for his two-legged characters. In fact, in his stories of the North, human survival demands virtues such as courage, integrity, and brotherhood. Like dogs, men must change both physically and morally, as only the strong survive; but they must change for the better morally as well as physically, substituting "unselfishness, forbearance, and tolerance" for the courtesies of ordinary life. Those who fail usually die a useless and shameful death after having lived without dignity, such as the protagonists of "In a Far Country" and the miserably incompetent Mercedes, Hal, and Charles in *The Call of the Wild,* who neither "toil hard, suffer sore, [nor] remain sweet of speech and kindly" (141), and who embody the antithesis of what man should be in the northern wilderness. Unlike Buck, London's ideal heroes, such as Malemute Kid and John Thornton, have not lost their moral nature.

Despite this basic difference between London's dramatization of men and animals, many scenes in *The Call of the Wild* have their parallels in his other fiction of the North. Buck's blood lust and the enjoyment he experiences in fighting a worthy opponent is paralleled, for instance, by Scruff Mackenzie's fight in "The Son of the Wolf": "At first he felt compassion for his enemy; but this fled before the primal instinct of life, which in turn gave way to the lust of slaughter. The ten thousand years of culture fell from him, and he was a cave-dweller, doing battle for his female."[23] Buck's stalking of the bull-moose, and the way he prevents the poor animal from getting food, drink, or rest, reminds one of Thomas Stevens's victimization of the mammoth in "A Relic of the Pliocene," and of the more gripping "Law of Life" and "Love of Life." For both men and dogs, imagination can make for survival when all else is equal: it allows Buck to win his fight with Spitz, when both dogs are equally matched; and the lack of it causes the death of the man in "To Build a Fire." Patience and imagination have nothing to do with great physical strength or moral character; but for both men and dogs their absence often leads to death. Indeed, in London's northern wilderness, a man's world and a dog's world have much in common, and both are ruled by naturalistic laws; but in the "dog stories" London could go further, for he was not hindered by the moral requirements of his audience, and perhaps of his own nature. He could never quite handle human protagonists with the same amoral, objective stance.

That Sir Arthur Conan Doyle should have called Upton Sinclair the "Zola of America"[24] is ironic, as no American realist of the time was further removed from Zola's conception of fiction. Sinclair, in fact, glibly dismissed the importance of Zola's work and indeed that of all the great French writers. After beginning an elementary course in French at Columbia University with a class of freshmen and sophomores, and staying long enough to "get the pronunciation and the elements of grammar," he felt that in six weeks he could read French with reasonable fluency and read, presumably in the original, all the classics known to Americans: "all of Corneille, Racine and Molière; some of Rousseau and Voltaire; a sampling of Bossuet and Chateaubriand; the whole of Musset and Daudet, Hugo and Flaubert; about half of Balzac and Zola, and enough of Maupassant and Gautier *to be thankful that [he] had not come upon this kind of literature until [he] was to some extent mature, with a good hard shell of Puritanism to protect [him] against the black magic of the modern Babylon.*"[25] Despite Sinclair's self-proclaimed genius, one cannot but wonder how much of this writing he understood, given his skimpy knowledge of the language. Moreover, his own deep-set puritan prejudices and his neuroticism colored his reading of every author, French or other, and accounts for his complete and self-congratulatory dismissal of a major body of great world classics on moralistic grounds.

Published three years after *The People of the Abyss* and clearly influenced by London's earlier reporting, *The Jungle* documents in fictional form the revolting conditions of work and life in Chicago's meat-packing industry. Unfortunately, in this as well as many of his other works, Sinclair tends to assault the reader with the message he wants to carry, subordinating plot, character development, and verisimilitude to propaganda.[26] In Sinclair's own words, *The Jungle* was misread: he had "aimed at the public's heart, and by accident [had] hit it in the stomach."[27] Not really accidental, the misreading was caused by the vividness of his descriptions of the stomach-turning conditions of work in the Chicago meat-packing plants, the deceitful and unsanitary practices of the meat industry as a whole, and, at the same time, by the presence of characters who are not lifelike and a plot that loses credibility in the last third of the novel. The sympathy and pity one initially experiences eventually give way to exasperation, as Sinclair manipulates his protagonist out of character for socialistic purposes.

By 1904, Sinclair had become a member of the Socialist Party of America and a reader of *The Appeal to Reason,* a weekly populistic-socialistic journal, contributing in September and October 1904 a series of three articles on an unsuccessful strike of the Chicago meat-packers.[28] Just as John Steinbeck's "Their Blood Is Strong" provided the seed for *The Grapes of Wrath,* so these articles were largely the inspiration for *The Jungle*; and, as early as October 1904, Sinclair was proposing to London's editor, George P. Brett of Macmillan, a new novel which would "set forth the breaking of human hearts by a system which exploits the labor of men and women for profit."[29] The project was eventually staked by Macmillan and Fred D. Warren, editor of *The Appeal,* in the amount of five hundred dollars each, and Sinclair left for Chicago.

For seven weeks Sinclair lived among the "wage slaves of the Beef Trust," sitting at night in the homes of the workers, foreign-born and native, listening to their stories, and making notes of everything. In the daytime he would wander about the yards and his friends would show him around. He was not much better dressed than the workers and found that by carrying a dinner-pail he could be inconspicuous and go anywhere. At the end of a month or more, he knew the story he meant to tell, but he had no characters until, on a Sunday afternoon, he saw a wedding party going into the back room of a saloon. He followed and watched. He also talked to many people – including lawyers, doctors, policemen, politicians, and real-estate agents – to complete his research, eating at the University Settlement to check his data against the opinions "of men and women who were giving their lives to this neighborhood."[30]

Although Sinclair did not immerse himself in the Chicago stockyards as deeply as London had in the Klondike or the East End of London, remaining a spectator rather than a participant, he still gathered much documentation and got a feel for the life of the wage-slaves of Chicago. The information was clearly accurate; as a result of the uproar that followed the publication of the novel by Doubleday, Page and Company in 1906, President Roosevelt launched an investigation of the sanitary conditions in the Chicago meatpacking plants which essentially confirmed every abuse charged in *The Jungle,* with the exception of men's falling into vats and being rendered into pure-leaf lard. According to Sinclair, "There had been several cases, but always the packers had seen to it that the widows were returned to the old country."[31]

Sinclair also included in the book much of his own experience with cold and poverty. Although belonging to a genteel Southern family, Sinclair's parents had never prospered and, with the passing of years, moved from cheap boardinghouses to cheaper ones, always trying to keep up appearances, and always failing. The contrasts among the social classes, which became Sinclair's favorite theme, was a reality of his early life, when he would visit well-to-do relatives: "one night [he] would be sleeping on a vermin-ridden sofa in a lodging-house, and the next night under the silken coverlets of a fashionable home."[32] This schizophrenic upbringing took its toll on Sinclair, who desperately needed to support himself, and later his family, but had inherited too lofty a self-image to stoop to any form of menial labor to make his and the lives of those close to him more bearable. His first wife, Meta, is probably the person who suffered most from his refusal to hold a job, for she was not a natural ascetic and wanted a little beauty and joy in her life. Moreover, Sinclair's asceticism was not exclusively economic, having much to do with his own puritanical fears of beauty, joy, and love, even in their most innocent forms. The scenes of hunger, illness, and cold in *The Jungle* were inspired by Sinclair's own experiences, in particular the winter of 1903, which he spent in a small, cold, drafty cabin in the New Jersey woods near Princeton while writing *Manassas* and living with his wife and baby on thirty dollars a month. Inevitably, sickness came, and Meta's troubles were diagnosed as "womb trouble" – as Ona's would be in *The Jungle*. Like Ona, Meta bought patent medicines – which cured nothing but masked the pain with alcohol, opium, or some other stimulant – paying as much as a dollar for a bottle of "Lydia Pinkham's Vegetable Compound." Conditions were so dreadful that Meta even contemplated suicide, Sinclair's awakening one night to find her sitting in bed with a revolver in her hand. She suffered infinitely more from their poverty than her husband, for the choice of life-style had not been hers, and eventually their comfortless and often loveless marital life ended in divorce.

When Sinclair indicated that he had attempted in *The Jungle* to "put the contents of Shelley into the form of Zola,"[33] not realizing that his political idealism was doomed to destroy his naturalism, he could only have had in mind Zola's emphasis on detailed and accurate descriptions of the milieu. Indeed, *The Jungle* is an excellent documentary novel. The living conditions of the workers of Packingtown are mercilessly dissected. The rooming houses are appalling; when it rains, the streets become rivers full of stinking green water deep enough for a tall man to wade in up to the waist and for a two-year-old child to drown; "Bubbly Creek," an arm of the Chicago River where the packing-houses empty their drainage, is constantly in motion, "as if huge fish were feeding in it,"[34] because the grease and chemicals poured into it undergo strange transformations, and bubbles of carbonic acid rise to the surface and burst, making rings two or three feet wide. Chickens feed on it and the packers gather the surface filth to make lard. In the winter, they cut the surface ice of the creek and sell it in the city. The houses are built without sewers, the drainage of a generation sitting in cesspools beneath them. The workers are surrounded by endless vistas of ugly and dirty little wooden buildings, foul smells ("an elemental odor, raw and crude. . . . rich, almost rancid, sensual and strong" [25]), thick, black, oily smoke, and an elemental sound made of "the distant lowing of ten thousand cattle, the distant grunting of ten thousand swine" (26).

Not only do the workers live in a sewer of germs and bacteria, but everything they eat is adulterated: tea, coffee, sugar, flour, and milk are doctored with chemicals such as formaldehyde: sausage bought in America is not the nutritious food the emigrants had eaten a great deal of in Lithuania. Its color created by chemicals, its smoky flavor a result of more chemicals, and its contents of potato flour and spoilt meat, the stink of which has been removed by yet more chemicals, "it has no more food value than so much wood" (113), when it is not actually lethal. Sinclair's horrifying descriptions of the processing of meat struck a responding chord in the reading public. Sympathize as they might with the plight of the workers, the thought of the unspeakable mixtures they were buying under the fancy names of "boneless hams," "California hams," "head cheese," or "smoked sausage" was a direct hit to the readers' stomachs and pocket books.

> There was never the least attention paid to what was cut up for sausage; there would come all the way back from Europe old sausage that had been rejected, and that was moldy and white – it would be dosed with borax and glycerine, and dumped into the hoppers, and made over again for home consumption. There would be meat that had tumbled out on the floor, in the dirt and sawdust, where the workers had tramped and spit countless billions of consumption germs. There would be meat stored in great piles in rooms . . . and thousands of rats would race about on it. . . . These rats were nuisances, and the packers would put poisoned bread for them; they would die, and then rats, bread, and meat would go into the hoppers together. (131)

The processing of hams was not much better, spoilt hams being pickled and colored chemically to hide the smell and taste. Government inspectors, paid to screen hogs' carcasses for tuberculosis, would enter into conversation and let a dozen carcasses go by without feeling the glands of the neck, while explaining the deadly nature of ptomaine. The condemned meat industry was a particular horror. Inspectors were paid merely to make sure that diseased meat was kept in the state. Thus, carcasses of tubercular steers, containing deadly poison, were sold in the city. "There was said to be two thousand dollars a week hush money from the tubercular steers alone; and as much again from the hogs which had died of cholera on the trains, and which you might see any day being loaded into boxcars and hauled away to a place called Globe, in Indiana, where they made a fancy grade of lard" (93).

> There were cattle which had been fed on "whiskey-malt," the refuse of the breweries, and had become what the men called "steerly" – which means covered with boils. It was a nasty job killing these, for when you plunged your knife into them they would burst and splash foul-smelling stuff into your face. . . . It was stuff such as this that made the "embalmed beef" that had

killed several times as many United States soldiers as all the bullets of the Spaniards; only the army beef, besides, was not fresh canned, it was old stuff that had been lying for years in the cellars.   (94)[35]

Small wonder that the miserable fate of the workers turned out to be of remoter interest to Sinclair's readers than their realization of the contaminated food they were eating, and that the public outcry following the book's publication, despite angry disclaimers on the part of the packers and a vicious press war, led directly to the passing of the Meat Inspection Bill on 26 May 1906 and of the Pure Food and Drug Bill, which had been stalled in Congress for months, in June 1906. Even after the passing of these bills, Americans did not regain their appetite for processed meat for decades.

Sinclair's descriptions of dehumanizing working conditions in the meat-packing plants are just as powerful, but met largely with reader indifference. The law of supply and demand governs everything and the workers are mercilessly exploited. If they arrive at work a minute late, they are docked an hour's pay; if they arrive several minutes late, they lose their job and have to join the hungry crowd at the packing-house's gate (19). When there is little work, the packers keep the workers waiting most of the day without pay in twenty degrees-below-zero temperature in the winter or sweltering heat with an overpowering stench in the summer. Then, "speeding-up" begins late in the afternoon, when the packers have bought the day's cattle on their own terms (85–6). "Speeding-up," the general practice, brings about crippling and deadly accidents, for which the packers never assume responsibility.

> On the killing beds you were apt to be covered with blood, and it would freeze solid; if you leaned against a pillar you would freeze to that, and if you put your hand upon the blade of a knife, you would run a chance of leaving your skin on it. . . . Also the air would be full of steam, from the hot water and the hot blood, so that you could not see five feet before you; and then, with men rushing about at the speed they kept up on the killing beds, and all with butcher knives, like razors, in their hands – well, it was to be counted a wonder that there were not more men slaughtered than cattle.   (79)

Sinclair's descriptions of the workers' injuries are as repulsive as those of meat processing: pickle-room workers and wool-pluckers have their fingers eaten off by acid one by one; butchers', boners', and trimmers' hands are mere lumps of flesh; stamping-machine workers have parts of their hands chopped off; fertilizer men's skins are soaked with phosphates that cannot be washed off, killing them in a few years and making it impossible to stay close to them without gasping.

Such descriptions are the most vital aspect of the book and remain more vivid in the readers' minds than the characters. If heredity plays no part in the novel, the influence of the milieu does, as no one can remain physically and mentally immune from such misery. Alcoholism is, for many, a natural consequence of unbearable living conditions; prostitution and corruption often appear as the only means of survival: "nobody rose in Packingtown by doing good work . . . if you met a man who was rising in Packingtown, you met a knave" (59). The poor graft off each other; votes are bought many times over by opposing parties; police, courts of law, and city hall are on the packers' payroll; acts of kindness are rare and come from the lowest and poorest. Like London's Buck, Jurgis and his family learn that this is an inimical world where one can give nothing, expect nothing, and ask for nothing: "It was a war of each against all, and the devil take the hindmost. You did not give feasts to other people, you waited for them to give feasts to you. You went about with your soul full of suspicion and hatred. You understood that you were environed by hostile powers that were trying to get your money. . . ." (73).

Moral integrity and traditions are the natural casualties of such an environment, as Jurgis discovers during his wedding, when his guests do not honor the *veselija* and leave the newlyweds to pay for the expenses of the feast. Sentiments die from lack of expression. Indeed, it is difficult to express tenderness when one is constantly dead tired, cold, and hungry. But jealousy and blind rage do not die along with Jurgis's ability to express love, and, unfortunately, these are the very emotions he cannot afford to indulge, as the logical consequences of his attack on Connor inexorably make clear: the poor cannot afford to live by the same moral principles as the bourgeoisie. Moral and social rules, when not adapted to actual circumstances, become destructive. This theme, which reminds one of Stephen Crane's "Maggie: A Girl of the Streets," where a drunken, vicious hag of a mother drives Maggie away from their hovel of a "home" on moral principles, thereby ensuring her eventual suicide, is summarized by Marija: "When people are starving . . . and they have anything with a price, they ought to sell it, I say. I guess you realize it now when it's too late. Ona could have taken care of us all, in the beginning" (281). Marija, who becomes a prostitute when there are no other means of survival, keeps the rest of the family alive and sends the children to school. Jurgis's moral indignation, or rather insane jealousy, brings about the death of his wife through starvation, the loss of their house, and incredible hardship for the whole family, including the death of his only son. The women in the novel seem to bow more easily to the requirements of a brutal environment, understanding, like Buck, that the defense of moral considerations has little place in the jungle. Jurgis, too, is eventually ready to relinquish his moral integrity when it serves his interest and becomes a criminal, a strike breaker, a boss taking graft, and a corrupt political agitator.

Sinclair's characters are hardly believable at times for several reasons, in particular, because he gives them a North American rather than a European mentality. In actual fact, the likelihood of a family of poor European immigrants buying a house a little more than a week after arriving in America and sinking all their savings into it against the advice of those who have more experience, when they have many mouths to feed and only some of the adults have neither secure nor well-paid jobs, is almost inconceivable. Sinclair compounds the improbability by having them take out a large mortgage on the house and buy their furniture on credit, when the very concept of credit was, to say the least, disreputable in Europe until recently, especially among the poor. Thus, the premise for plot and characterization is flawed, especially as Sinclair does not draw Jurgis as being either stupid or unconventional, but as merely stubborn. Letting women close the deal on a house purchase would also have been inconceivable for a European peasant, and even more so when he could not understand the language or read the legal documents. Such people were above all survivors, who had fought hardship for centuries and hung onto their money for dear life, suspicious of others' motivations – a fact to which Sinclair merely pays lip service: "Still, they were peasant people, and they hung on to their money by instinct" (48). Even a reader unfamiliar with the European mentality cannot help questioning Jurgis's stubborn disregard of the advice of friends who have been in America longer than he, and the speed and gullibility with which he makes such important decisions.

Furthermore, too many catastrophes happen to Jurgis and his family to allow the reader to identify with them fully. Sinclair clearly telescoped all the woes he had witnessed in many workingmen's families into the lot of a single family, with little regard for credibility. But, because he pushed too hard, divesting his characters of resourcefulness and vitality and depriving them of control, he processed them into trapped animals or mindless cogs, thus arousing the reader's sympathy only for a time. In fact, animal and mechanical imagery abounds, none perhaps more powerful than the slaughtered hogs simile (35–6). Zola wanted characters to be individuals in their own right as well as largely representative of their social class, and he knew better than to make one single man or family bear the cross of the cumulative mistakes and pains of their group. In a humorless analog to Voltaire's *Candide, everything* goes wrong for Jurgis, and his life knows no relief or unpredictable and joyful occasions. Indeed, the true may not always be believable, and, in Frank Norris's words, fiction is what *seems* real, not what *is* real – a fact Sinclair disregarded when he decided to stack the deck of Jurgis's miseries. Even though such a relentless succession of disasters is possible in life, it is too much for a reader to accept in fiction. From the moment the family sets foot in America, they are robbed by almost everyone they encounter; when it should have provided a tidy nest-egg, the wedding feast leaves them over a hundred dollars in debt; they are thoroughly swindled in the purchase of their house, and eventually lose it and all the money they put into it; old Antanas dies of blood poisoning after saltpeter has eaten through his boots and feet; young Stanislovas is eaten alive by rats in a basement and little Antanas is drowned in the street; Marija and Jurgis lose their jobs because of accidents and because they are headstrong, and Marija eventually turns to prostitution and drugs; Ona is terrorized into prostituting herself to keep her job, loses it after Jurgis beats up her boss, then, at eighteen, dies in childbirth of starvation and cold.

When catastrophes are not brought about by fate, Jurgis brings them upon himself by willfully disregarding the advice of those who have more experience or by acting on violent impulses without stopping to think about the logical consequences of his actions. Although this is clearly Sinclair's attempt to dramatize the "beast in man" in naturalistic fashion, the reader is unprepared for this suddenly violent and irrational aspect of Jurgis's character. Indeed, Jurgis, whom Sinclair describes as a big, strong man, appears as meek as a lamb, responding to every new problem with "I will work harder" – until he discovers that Connor has blackmailed Ona into his bed and yields to blind rage and violence:

> To Jurgis this man's whole presence reeked of the crime he had committed; the touch of his body was madness to him – it set every nerve atremble, it aroused all the demons in his soul. It had worked its will upon Ona, this great beast – and now he had it, he had it! It was his turn now! Things swam blood before him, and he screamed aloud in his fury, lifting his victim and smashing his head upon the floor. . . . In a flash he had bent down and sunk his teeth into the man's cheek; and when they tore him away he was dripping with blood, and little ribbons of skin were hanging in his mouth. (152)

What takes the reader aback here is not the animal nature of the reaction, which is magnificently rendered, but its unexpectedness, as Sinclair has cautiously avoided mentioning Jurgis's physical nature up to now and avoids it again until his second attack on Connor.

Sinclair had never come to terms with the animal nature of man in his own life and avoided dramatizing it in his fiction except when absolutely necessary for plot development. There is no satisfying brawling or physical release of tension in *The Jungle.* There is little fun, dancing, or loving except during the wedding feast. There is no ecstasy of being, no passionate love or will to live, no sensual pleasure – only a desperate and dumb endurance arising from dulled senses. An aura of puritanism also pervades the book, manifest in the exaggerated reaction of Ona when she confesses Connor's sexual blackmail and in the short scene when Jurgis has a sexual encounter after Ona's death: "he went upstairs into a room with her, and the wild beast rose up within him and screamed as it has screamed in the jungle from the dawn of time" (212–13). There are definite overtones of Jack London here, but it is anomalous to find London's atavistic language in the context of a commonplace sexual act. Although he had known and chosen want, Sinclair never really belonged to the world of the poor and the manual workers, and watched it from the outside with horror. London, who had lived in that world during his youth and known most of its facets, could give a more balanced and intimate picture of it, which did not exclude the simple joys of life.

After the remarkable unity of the first section of *The Jungle,* with its climax in little Antanas's death, and the emotional intensity of the relentless suffering of Jurgis and his family, which transcends the relative weakness of the characterization and leaves one emotionally drained, the reader is almost relieved to be able to dissociate his sympathies from Jurgis in the remainder of the novel, where Sinclair tries to make him into a thinker. After the death of his wife and son, and having abandoned the rest of the family to probable starvation, Jurgis is offered a hand by a farmer who needs help in the fields, including a decent salary and board with plentiful food – all of which should be welcome to a man in his situation. Instead, Jurgis turns the offer down contemptuously because the work will not last past November, never considering that he would be better off facing the winter in good physical shape and with over two hundred dollars saved than with nothing at all, or the pitiful fifteen dollars he manages to save before going back to Chicago after a spring and summer of tramping and occasional work. From a disciplined work-beast, Jurgis turns overnight into a pseudosocial critic, and Sinclair's approving commentary – "Jurgis was beginning to think for himself nowadays" (209) – leaves the reader baffled. From that moment on, Jurgis becomes a puppet in his creator's hands – a puppet in whose fate the reader quickly loses interest, because he is no longer convincing.

Sinclair was aware that the ending of the novel was weak and blamed it on lack of money: "never have I been able to write a single thing as I would have liked to write it, because of money. Either I was dead broke and had to rush it; . . . Think of my having to ruin *The Jungle* with an ending so pitifully inadequate, because we were actually without money for food."³⁶ This rationalization of the second and third sections of the novel is disingenuous, for it is preaching that weakens the ending, as well as the attempt to put Jurgis through a long series of jobs that comprise a Cook's tour of the manual workers' world, the political world, and the underworld. Worse, when Jurgis becomes a socialist, everything starts going well for him and he finds a compassionate and understanding employer. Had Sinclair ended *The Jungle* with chapter 21 and the climax of little Antanas's death, the novel, as an allegory of victimization, would have had a unity of theme and effect infinitely more powerful, without alienating the reader by belaboring themes already dramatized or by presenting socialism as a universal and miraculous panacea. Lack of money did not force Sinclair to ruin the ending of *The Jungle*; what did were his inability to leave well-enough alone and trust his readers to draw their own conclusions from the material presented, as well as his compulsive need to preach.

The natural and the urban jungles dramatized in these two novels have much in common. Both attest to the utmost survival skills, endurance, and the ability to overcome; and both are unforgiving of errors and unsparing of the weak. However, in the magnificent human allegory *The Call of the Wild*, natural instincts and animal nature are in harmony with the background, whereas in *The Jungle* they are self-destructive when pitted against the powerful industrial machinery of the stockyards. But the difference resides less in the indulging of instinctual urges than in the intelligent/unintelligent, imaginative/unimaginative, use of those instincts. Buck knows better than to pick a fight with Spitz before he can win it and uses all the forces he can master to weaken his enemy, exhibiting the infinite and elemental patience of the wild when survival is at stake. Jurgis, on the other hand, shows neither imagination nor patience in adapting to the world of the stockyards and, later, in taking vengeance on Connor. As a result, he remains an underdog despite his physical strength and hard work, and punishes himself and those he loves rather than Connor, who escapes with a few superficial wounds. Half equipped, Jurgis is lost between the animal and human worlds, never recognizing that to survive in a modern urban jungle one needs to exercise the same skills that enabled primitive man to survive. Buck is a hero with whom the reader can identify with exhilaration; Jurgis is a victim of his character and milieu whom the reader fears to recognize in himself, and therefore pities.

The major difference between these two jungles, however, is the presence or absence of beauty. However cruel, the natural jungle is beautiful and logical, while the man-made jungle is revolting and illogical. In the North, everything is gloriously pure and frozen. The beauty of the landscape and of Buck are breathtakingly rendered by London's lyrical prose. His depiction of an instinctual behavior perfectly suited to the environment, of emotionally satisfying immanent justice, of a joy in life shared by the most simple and complex organisms, and of a simple and primal relationship between life and death all testify that, with a few qualifications, London accepted the animal basis of human existence, and even reveled in it. In contrast, the setting of the human jungle is repulsive. Work in the stockyards is brutal; animal instincts are misused or missing, thus bringing about destruction; love of life and beauty are absent; and human feelings are deadened by drudgery and suffering. The social jungle is also irrational in its advocacy of virtues that bring about destruction and its condemnation of vices, such as corruption and prostitution, which allow for survival. Sinclair, unlike London, rejected man's animal nature and therefore only dimly perceived that survival, in both a complex human jungle and an amoral animal one, requires finely tuned animal instincts. But both the white and frozen northern wilderness with its redeeming purity and the urban world of pain, misery, and dumb endurance continue to exert a strong fascination as metaphors of man's animal past and present.

NOTES

1 See, in particular, Upton Sinclair's letter to Joan London, 13 August 1937 in the Huntington Library, referring to London's review of *The Jungle* in the *Appeal to Reason* as a great service and as the beginning of his literary success; London's review of *The Jungle* in the *New York Evening Journal*, 8 August 1906; and Sinclair's acknowledgment in *Mammonart* that if *The Jungle* went "all over the world, it was Jack London's push that started it." (Pasadena, Calif.: Upton Sinclair, 1924), p. 372.

2 See *Mammonart*, pp. 363–72.

3 Charmian London's letter to Upton Sinclair, 20 September 1918, the Huntington Library.

4 Jack London to Upton Sinclair, 18 August 1916, in *The Letters of Jack London*, ed. Earle Labor, Robert C. Leitz, and I. Milo Shepard (Stanford, Calif.: Stanford University Press, 1988), p. 1564.

5 See letters from Upton Sinclair to Joan London, 3 and 9 August 1937, the Huntington Library.

6 George Sterling to Jack London, 13 November 1914, the Huntington Library.

7 See Ernest Untermann's letter to Joan London, 8 April 1938, the Huntington

Library. A fellow socialist and close friend of London's, Untermann attempted to explain London's socialist beliefs to London's daughter, who was researching her father's life for her book *Jack London and His Times,* in three important letters dated 11 and 22 January, and 8 April 1938. Unfortunately, Joan London largely ignored Untermann's explanations.

8 See Joan London, *Jack London and His Times* (Seattle and London: University of Washington Press, 1968), p. 252.

9 See "Translations of Zola in the United States Prior to 1900," *Modern Language Notes,* 55 (1940): 521.

10 This happened at least twice: *Emile Zola's First Love Story,* published by Jewett and Buchanan (Chicago, 1895) and *The Two Duchesses,* published by F. Tousey's *Brookside Library* (New York, 1884).

11 See, for instance, *la Fortune des Rougons,* translated as *The Girl in Scarlet* and *Wedded in Death; Madeleine Férat,* translated as *Driven to Her Doom* and *The Finger of Fate; Thérèse Raquin,* translated as *Haunted by the Specter of a Murdered Man;* and *la Conquête de Plassans,* translated as *The Abbé and His Court, A Fatal Conquest,* and *Buried in the Ashes of a Ruined Home.*

12 Manuscript JL437, the Huntington Library.

13 See, for instance, Jack London to Cloudesley Johns, 23 June 1899, in *Letters,* p. 89.

14 "These Bones Shall Rise Again," *The Reader,* June 1903; collected in *Revolution and Other Essays* (1910) and reprinted in *No Mentor But Myself,* ed. D. L. Walker (Port Washington, N.Y.: Kennikat, 1979), p. 71.

15 *Impressions,* November 1901; collected in *Revolution and Other Essays* and reprinted in *No Mentor But Myself,* pp. 40–1.

16 Jack London, *The Call of the Wild* (New York: Grosset and Dunlap, 1909), p. 163. Further references will be to this edition.

17 *Letters,* p. 11.

18 Jack London, *A Daughter of the Snows* (Philadelphia: J. B. Lippincott Co., 1902), p. 117.

19 Jack London to Marshall Bond, 17 December 1903, in *Letters,* p. 399.

20 See *Jack London and the Klondike: The Genesis of an American Writer* (San Marino, Calif.: The Huntington Library, 1972), pp. 240–1.

21 Jack London, "Review of *The Octopus,*" *Impressions* (June 1901); reprinted in *No Mentor But Myself,* p. 35.

22 Letter to Anna Strunsky, 20 December 1902, in *Letters,* pp. 328–9.

23 *The Son of the Wolf* (London: Arco Publications, 1962), p. 46.

24 Upton Sinclair, *My Life in Letters* (Columbia: University of Missouri Press, 1960), p. 174.

25 Upton Sinclair, *American Outpost: A Book of Reminiscences* (Pasadena, Calif.: Upton Sinclair, 1932), p. 88. My italics.

26 Sinclair believed that "*Art is a representation of life, modified by the personality of the artist, for the purpose of modifying other personalities, inciting them to changes of feeling, belief and action*" and that "*Great art is produced when propaganda of vitality and importance is put across with technical competence in terms of the art selected. . . . Art is play, to the extent that it is instinctive; it is propaganda when it becomes mature and conscious*" (*Mammonart,* pp. 10, 20).

27 Upton Sinclair in *Cosmopolitan Magazine* (October, 1906).
28 "You Have Lost the Strike! And Now What Are You Going to Do About It?" 17 September 1904, p. 1; "The Spirit That Wins," 24 September 1904, p. 3; and "Farmers of America, Unite!" 15 October 1904, pp. 2–3.
29 Upton Sinclair, *The Appeal to Reason*, 11 February 1905, p. 1.
30 *American Outpost,* p. 154.
31 Ibid., p. 169.
32 *The Autobiography of Upton Sinclair* (New York: Harcourt, Brace & World, 1962); quoted in Jon A. Yoder, *Upton Sinclair* (New York: Frederick Ungar, 1975), p. 19.
33 "What Life Means to Me," *Cosmopolitan* 41 (1906): 594.
34 Upton Sinclair, *The Jungle* (Urbana and Chicago: University of Illinois Press, 1988), p. 92. James R. Barrett's excellent introduction and notes provide much useful background information, documenting the one-sidedness of Sinclair's description of Packingtown.
35 General Nelson Miller estimated that three thousand soldiers had died of "embalmed" beef during the Spanish-American War. "But although he had collected the evidence and was prepared to produce two thousand witnesses, he could not find anyone in Congress who wished to open this particular can of worms" (Yoder, *Upton Sinclair,* p. 41). See also the *New York Times,* 5 June 1906, p. 2, col. 7.
36 Upton Sinclair to Mr. and Mrs. Gaylord Wilshire, 28 June 1906; quoted in Howard H. Quint, "Upton Sinclair's Quest for Artistic Independence – 1909," *American Literature* 29 (1957–8): 196.

I I

KENNETH W. WARREN

Troubled Black Humanity in *The Souls of Black Folk* and *The Autobiography of an Ex-Colored Man*

Once I thought my grandfather incapable of thoughts about humanity, but I was wrong. Why should an old slave use such a phrase as, "This and this or this has made me more human," as I did in my arena speech? Hell, he never had any doubts about his humanity – that was left to his "free" offspring. He accepted his humanity.

Ralph Ellison, *Invisible Man*

These ruminations by the protagonist of Ralph Ellison's *Invisible Man* are paradoxical. Chattel slavery in the United States was a system calculated to impress on black and white alike the inferiority and brutishness of black people, and yet in the memory of Ellison's narrator, his enslaved grandfather could emerge as more human than a young, intelligent black man of the twentieth century. Certainly it is true that the horrors of slavery were not felt uniformly and unceasingly by the enslaved, and that black resistance to the physical and psychological dimensions of bondage was endemic. In the words of Lawrence Levine, "Slave music, slave religion, slave folk beliefs – the entire sacred world of the black slaves – created the necessary space between the slaves and their owners and were the means of preventing legal slavery from becoming spiritual slavery" (80). But however effectively blacks managed to nurture their sense of humanity while in bondage, it seems curious that these same people and their descendants would experience that humanity more tenuously under freedom than they had under slavery.

Levine attempts to unravel the paradox by suggesting that, "although it happened neither suddenly nor completely, the sacred world view so central to black slaves was to be shattered in the twentieth century" (158) by the effects of literacy on an oral culture, the migrations of black people from the countryside to the city, and the limited but real increase in economic opportunities for some African Americans. With the shattering of this worldview, the prejudices and stereotypes that had been kept at bay during slavery were presumably able to penetrate and infiltrate black self-consciousness in an unprecedented way, apparently resulting in the onset of what W. E. B. Du

Bois termed "double-consciousness" – that "sense of always looking at one's self through the eyes of others" (364). Freedom, then, was a gain, but also, from the standpoint of black psychic self-sufficiency, a loss. And the prospect of this loss left Du Bois fearful that "the ideals of [black] people . . . with their simple beauty and weird inspiration, [would] suddenly sink to a question of cash and a lust for gold" (418–19).

Du Bois's reckoning of the spiritual losses for black folk that seemed to have accompanied emancipation, however, was politically pointed. The world that Du Bois saw as threatened was not merely the spiritual realm of the untutored and unlettered. In Du Bois's view, it had been the black teacher as much as the black preacher who, during Reconstruction, had held the flame of black idealism aloft. The missionary spirit of Reconstruction had "put thirty thousand black teachers in the South," and it was they who had "wiped out the illiteracy of the majority of the black people of the land, and they made Tuskegee possible" (430). Training his critical sights on Booker T. Washington's program for black advancement, in which vocational and industrial education had elbowed aside broadly humanistic endeavors, Du Bois was making it clear that a sense of spiritual loss and a diminution of black humanity had not followed emancipation as if by some law of physics. Rather, the experiences of ex-slaves were made legible as deracination and loss through concerted efforts to deny ex-slaves full entry into the American polity and to undo the political, social, and educational gains of Reconstruction. Part of my task in taking up W. E. B. Du Bois's *The Souls of Black Folk* and James Weldon Johnson's *The Autobiography of an Ex-Colored Man* is to reflect on a literary "coming to terms" with the growing sense of doubtful black humanity during the post-Emancipation era and to see that doubt as a sensitive and sophisticated registering of the intensifying resistance to racial democracy in the United States from emancipation through the early twentieth century. To paraphrase C. L. R. James's remarks from another context, it was "the creative power, the democratic desires, the expansion of human personality" of emancipation that "called forth the violence, the atrocities" of the state to repress democracy (156–7). Taken together, Du Bois's *Souls* and Johnson's *Ex-Colored Man* chart the expansion and contraction of human personality during this nation's first profound assault on the color line.

I

Although *Souls* clearly stands as a landmark in the cultural history of the United States, it is a text that is best seen in the light cast by some of its immediate predecessors as well as its contemporaries. The early 1890s, for example, found Anna Julia Cooper, in *A Voice From the South*, lamenting the failure of putatively liberal whites to take into account *"the Black man's personality."* Continuing her lament, Cooper went on to remark white Americans' unwillingness to grant

> respect, if I may so express it, to [the black man's] manhood or deferring at all to his conceptions of the need of his people. When colored persons have been employed it was too often as machines or as manikins. There has been no disposition, generally, to get to the black man's ideal or to let his individuality work by its own gravity, as it were. A conference of earnest Christian men have met at regular intervals for some years past to discuss the best methods of promoting the welfare and the development of colored people in this country. Yet, strange as it may seem, they have never invited a colored man or even intimated that one would be welcome to take part in their deliberations. Their remedial contrivances are purely theoretical or empirical, therefore, and the whole machinery devoid of soul. (37)

As bodies devoid of personality, black Americans emerge as little more than marginally successful attempts to impersonate human beings. As part of a soulless machinery, the black American is projected into a growing consensus that the resolution of social problems is better achieved through calculation and experimentation than through consultation and negotiation.

Of course, any discussion of impersonation had to presume some shared sense of what constituted the human, and Cooper's observations are helpful here. To be human is to be presumed to have the capacity to speak knowledgeably on one's own behalf. It is to be invited into the synod as something more than the object of inquiry. In censuring both the "theoretical" and the "empirical," Cooper further indicates that to be human is to be presumed to be in possession of something incalculable, something beyond the reach of science, which is precisely what a manikin is not. As a model used for anatomical exhibitions and demonstrations of surgical procedures the manikin was the human body made available to science; it was the body by measurement and calculation. And to the extent that *manikin* also meant "little man," "dwarf," or "pygmy," the black man as manikin was a man who had not yet, and might not ever, achieve his full stature as a human being. The convergence of the biological and the anthropological in the word *manikin* indexes the growing sway of social Darwinism that underwrote the notion of the human not as something divinely bequeathed but as something attained only after centuries of struggle.

The black man, in Cooper's estimation, had been dwarfed by circumstance: "We are the heirs of a past which was not our fathers' moulding . . .

and it is no fault of [the Negro's] that he finds himself to-day the inheritor of a manhood and womanhood impoverished and debased by two centuries and more of compression and degradation"; and unless efforts were made immediately, the "weaknesses and malformations, which to-day are attributable to a vicious schoolmaster and a pernicious system, will a century hence be rightly regarded as proofs of innate corruptness and radical incurability" (28).

What is, of course, disturbing in Cooper's words is the belief that at some specifiable point in the future it will be "right" to view invidious differences in human populations as innate rather than conditioned. Prompting this disturbance in Cooper's thought is the crisis of the moment of emancipation in which it suddenly becomes empirically possible to hold blacks responsible for their condition. Cooper laments that the black woman had not been allowed to speak. But once having spoken as the representative voice of black women, Cooper cannot attribute further shortcomings in black populations solely to her having been denied the opportunity to speak. Having centered her diagnosis of black oppression in the enforced silence of black women, she must necessarily reassess the accuracy of her diagnosis if the social and political degradation of black populations continues in the wake of her having delivered her utterance.

Cooper's problem does not merely result from the fact that the effectiveness of an utterance depends on the quality of response it evokes, and that there were few, if any, white Americans capable of accepting the full import of her challenge to the white racial hierarchy. What Cooper's dilemma also points up is the way in which modern democratic movements inevitably up the ante on the minimal tangible and intangible requirements necessary to experience our humanity fully. And in thus upping the ante, these movements expand the number of points at which it becomes possible to feel our humanity as diminished. This experience is far from uniform, however. What appears necessary from one angle feels extravagant from another. So that at a time when less than 0.2 percent of the nation's population availed themselves of a college education, a cadre of black scholars confronted the daunting task of presenting as a necessity that which many of their fellow citizens still regarded as an extravagance. And perhaps because Cooper's voice had not achieved the effect it so desired, W. E. B. Du Bois, the most famous writer on black education to come in her wake, would, despite his capacity to draw numerous poignant examples of the desire of black women for higher education, put forth the making of man as the most pressing task for black and white America.

II

Prefacing his reflections on black education with a quatrain from Edward FitzGerald's translation of Omar Khayyam's "The Rubaiyat" and four bars of music from the black spiritual "March On," W. E. B. Du Bois opens "Of the Training of Black Men," the sixth chapter of *The Souls of Black Folk,* with a passage whose rhetorical cadences recall in various ways the opening chapters of Genesis from the King James version of the Bible. There is in these paragraphs a reliance upon the imagery of waters, an account of human origins, and an effective use of repetition. In a chapter that concludes with the famous paragraph celebrating a possible high cultural transcendence of racial segregation ("I sit with Shakespeare and he winces not . . ."), and with an invocation of the Children of Israel's wanderings through the wilderness, the introductory paragraphs help effect a transit from Genesis to Exodus and beyond. Du Bois writes:

> From the shimmering swirl of waters where many, many thoughts ago the slave-ship first saw the square tower of Jamestown, have flowed down to our day three streams of thinking: one swollen from the larger world here and overseas, saying, the multiplying of human wants in culture-lands calls for the world-wide cooperation of men in satisfying them. Hence arises a new human unity, pulling the ends of earth nearer, and all men, black, yellow, and white. The larger humanity strives to feel in this contact of living Nations and sleeping hordes a thrill of new life in the world, crying, "If the contact of Life and Sleep be Death, shame on such Life." To be sure, behind this thought lurks the afterthought of force and dominion, – the making of brown men to delve when the temptation of beads and red calico cloys.
>
> The second thought streaming from the death-ship and the curving river is the thought of the older South, – the sincere and passionate belief that somewhere between men and cattle, God created a *tertium quid,* and called it a Negro, – a clownish, simple creature, at times even lovable within its limitations, but straitly foreordained to walk within the Veil. To be sure, behind the thought lurks the afterthought, – some of them with favoring chance might become men, but in sheer self-defence we dare not let them, and we build about them walls so high, and hang between them and the light a veil so thick, that they shall not even think of breaking through.
>
> And last of all there trickles down that third and darker thought, – the thought of the things themselves, the confused, half-conscious mutter of men who are black and whitened, crying "Liberty, Freedom, Opportunity – vouchsafe to us, O boastful World, the chance of living men!" To be sure, behind the thought lurks the afterthought, – suppose, after all, the World is right, and we

are less than men? Suppose this mad impulse within is all wrong, some mock mirage from the untrue?

So here we stand among thought of human unity, even through conquest and slavery; the inferiority of black men, even if forced by fraud; a shriek in the night for the freedom of men who themselves are not yet sure of their right to demand it. This is the tangle of thought and afterthought wherein we are called to solve the problem of training men for life. (424–5)

This rhetorical alternation of thought and afterthought, of idealism and materialism, invokes the larger structure of *Souls of Black Folk,* in which Du Bois's thoughts on the black and white worlds are literally framed by a "Forethought" and an "After-Thought." And while the twofold oscillation from thought to afterthought in chapter 6 seems to correlate somewhat imperfectly with the structure of a text divided into three parts – forethought, thought, and afterthought – the fit is fairly exact: the introductory forethought works to establish Du Bois's *Souls* as the thoughts of a thing itself ("need I add that I who speak here am bone of the bone and flesh of the flesh of them that live within the Veil? [360]). The body of the text, then, stands as thought, and the afterthought corresponds to the three afterthoughts of chapter 6.

Each of the first three paragraphs traces a stream of thought, each stream in turn bedeviled by its own countercurrent: afterthought follows, interrupts, perhaps even overtakes thought, so that the anaphoras introducing each afterthought provide a kind of troublesome refrain – domination, segregation, and self-doubt have been the recurring features of the intersection of white and black worlds. And while the representation of history as thought points up Du Bois's idealism, each thought is located within the political and economic history of the West; culture itself is producing the material needs that drive European and U.S. imperialism.

These paragraphs register the troubling fact that cooperation and domination seem equally suited to fulfilling the wants of Western societies. The first paragraph, particularly, confronts a conceptual difficulty in construing blacks as being fully human and not yet quite human, as they are still engaged in the process of developing their humanity. This difficulty was the false dilemma of the Reconstruction era. If the freedmen were indeed men they should not need help beyond the removal of the impediments of slavery; if more help than this was required, then perhaps the freedmen were not indeed men. In his narrative Du Bois efficiently resolves this difficulty by employing the common metaphoric substitution of sleep for death. The world's darker people are represented in a figure that would become a commonplace in referring to the potential of nations that had not yet reached the state of Western "civilization." They are merely sleeping – human but not yet active. Those nations already wakened were clearly advantaged relative to the slumbering hordes, but to take advantage of the sleeping was truly deplorable.

In the passage, however, the white world is not figured as wakened nations but as the "living Nations." The confrontation between white and darker worlds, then, is represented by an imperfect opposition in which life is opposed to sleep rather than death. The world's darker folk should awaken into life; should they wake merely to die, that death is to be understood as a detour rather than an inevitable outcome.

In drawing out these metaphors, the epigraph from "The Rubaiyat" hovers meaningfully over this first paragraph – indeed, over the entire chapter and book as well:

> Why, if the Soul can fling the Dust aside,
> And naked on the Air of Heaven ride,
>   Were't not a Shame – were't not a Shame for him
> In this clay carcase crippled to abide?

Khayyam's words present human existence as the soul's confinement, the soul's release being a relinquishing of individual particularity. The poem attempts to assuage the Victorian era's spiritual doubt by suggesting that, although there can be no eternal cognizance of our individuality, there can be something like eternity. In fact, two stanzas after the one printed by Du Bois, Khayyam rebukes the fear that the earth will see our "like no more" and that "The Eternal Saki from that Bowl has poured / Millions of Bubbles like us, and will pour." The message conveyed is that we must learn not to grieve what we cannot escape, but strive rather to take whatever consolation this life offers.

Paralleling "The Rubaiyat's" consolatory ethos are the more somber moments of Du Bois's survey of the black South. At these moments, for Du Bois, the human body of death merges uncomfortably with black racial identity, and toward the end of the chapter Du Bois seems almost to be paraphrasing the Khayyam verse: "And to themselves in these the days that try their souls, the chance to soar in the dim blue air above the smoke is to their finer spirits boon and guerdon for what they lose on earth by being black" (438). The souls or finer spirits of black folk are imprisoned in earthly black bodies. The heavenly "dim blue air" in this case, however, is not a return to the impersonal eternal, but a recommitment to the black liberal arts college. These colleges, as described in the course of this chapter, were politically progressive institutions but, equally significant, were also places of consolation where individuals could gain a moment of respite from the burden of being black in a white world. Indeed, in Du Bois's estimation, the world of higher education was the place where he "finally proved to my entire satisfaction that my race forms but slight impediment between men and kindred souls" (quoted in Lewis, 145). What is celebrated here is not being black, but the moment in which one does not have to feel intensely the limitations of blackness at the turn of the century.

The extent to which the inebriate melancholy of Khayyam's poem informs the whole of *Souls* is an open question. In FitzGerald's translation, the image of the veil – a key trope in Du Bois's text – appears in stanzas 32, 34, and 47 (Du Bois quotes stanza 44). And in stanza 65 the wise sayings of scholars and prophets, "Are all but Stories, which, awoke from Sleep, / They told their comrades, and to Sleep returned." Worth stressing, however, is the way that the Rubaiyat's exquisite drama of consolation and doubt are echoed by Du Bois's text – it, too, may be a story told in the brief moment of waking from an extended sleep to which he will soon return. The historical moment of democratic vision that Du Bois saw in the Reconstruction era and testified to in *Souls* may have been as fleeting as a waking dream.

The thought of the old South, which the second paragraph of chapter 6 takes up, describes the social and political strictures within which Du Bois's vision of black education takes shape and which threaten to make that vision a mere dream. On one side is popular culture. The image of African Americans as "clownish, simple creature[s]" derives straight from both the minstrel stage, with its burnt-cork performances, and from the school of plantation fiction as represented by such writers as Thomas Nelson Page, whom Du Bois singles out in the second chapter of *Souls* as an author whose vision ought to be argued with. On the other side, as expressed in the afterthought of the second paragraph, is the legal machinery of Jim Crow that Southern states had set in motion during the 1890s – the "walls so high" and "veil so thick" enveloping black populations.

Over and against the legal and cultural barriers of racism stands the thought of black people – "the thought of the things themselves." Du Bois's purposely paradoxical phrasing captures both the contradictions of the white South in the second paragraph and the anxieties of the black South in the third. Although the ideology underpinning slavery and white supremacy required that whites regard blacks as things, in day-to-day interactions across the color line there could not help but be some acknowledgment that these "things" were indeed people with whom one had to talk, reason, argue, and even discipline. Southern jurisprudence under slavery reflected these ambivalences; and nationally, from the Constitution's "three-fifth compromise" through the U.S. Supreme Court's *Plessy* v. *Ferguson* decision in 1896, the American legal system had been called upon to reiterate how black individuals could be at once human and yet something less than fully human. And though blacks actively contested their definition as "things," the hegemonic sway of such ideals as the self-made man – one of Frederick Douglass's most popular lectures was on this topic – was such that in the face of the obvious barriers created by Jim Crow, it was still possible to wonder whether black insufficiencies were somehow internal and immutable (McFeely, 298).

The resistant feature of black thought is first expressed in chapter 6 in the snippet from the jubilee, "March On," which Du Bois employs as the chapter's second epigraph. As Du Bois would assert in the final chapter of *Souls*, he had found the most poignant expression of the thought of black people in the black spirituals and jubilees, which constituted "the articulate message of the slave to the world" (538). And though Du Bois did not reprint the lyrics for these songs in the chapter headings, Eric Sundquist's recent discussion of *Souls* argues persuasively for the importance of the spirituals' "lyrics, which Du Bois does not reproduce" (493). The words that accompany the musical epigraph are:

> Way o-ver in the E-gypt land,
> You shall gain the vic-to-ry,
> Way o-ver in the E-gypt land,
> You shall gain the day.
> (Sundquist, 502)

Rightly drawing attention to the lyrics' "martial" quality, Sundquist observes that "March On" was for slaves a "song of hope, even of controlled militancy; for the free men and women of the post-Reconstruction South, it was adamantly a song of demand and of resistance to the lures of simple materialism and, by the same token, the Washingtonian philosophy of manual training" (503).

But throughout *Souls,* and in chapter 6 particularly, Du Bois's allegorical use of the book of Exodus was as sobering as it was inspirational. By the turn of the century the spiritual and its references to victory in Egypt were paying homage to past achievements and past hopes. The "black and whitened" folk of the post-Emancipation era were yet wandering in the wilderness of segregation, disfranchisement, and terror, having escaped Pharaoh's bonds of legal servitude. Specifically for Du Bois, these were the years in which the Tuskegee model of Booker T. Washington had become an educational juggernaut. The afterthought of the third paragraph, questioning the "mad impulse" that had prompted the attempt to secure for black scholars the life of the mind, recalled the wandering Israelites' misery and despair as well as the temptation that led them to construct for themselves idols of gold. Further complicating Du Bois's invocation of the wanderings in the wilderness was the active resistance to black progress on the part of white southerners in the post-Emancipation era. It was as if Pharaoh and his chariots had somehow escaped death in the Red Sea and were pursuing their quarry through the wilderness. Thus, as he concludes chapter 6 with his image of a high cultural utopia above the veil of racism, Du Bois and black Americans, standing in the position of Moses whose death has already been foretold, address not God but the nation, wondering, "Is this the life you grudge us, O knightly America? Is this the life you long to change into the dull red hideousness of Georgia? Are you so afraid lest peering from this high Pisgah, between Philistine and Amalekite, we sight the Promised Land?" (438). Although the resonances are clearly metaphoric, the high Pisgah was also specifically Atlanta University, where Du Bois had come in the late 1890s to teach and conduct research, a school that "stood angular and handsome on the highest of the hills cradling the ungainly new railroad city" and espoused Arnoldian ideals in its curriculum (Lewis, 213). Du Bois's promised land lay in promulgating the merits of institutions like Atlanta University; but more than that, it lay in the possibility of securing a vision of a broader black humanity, a vision that would transform the "dull red hideousness of Georgia" into something truly wonderful.

III

When the protagonist of James Weldon Johnson's 1912 novel *The Autobiography of an Ex-Colored Man* first arrives in Atlanta intent on attending Du Bois's Atlanta University, that larger transformation has not as yet taken place. Confronting the eager student is "a big, dull, red town," and Johnson's protagonist goes on to attribute his depressed state of mind to the quality of the landscape:

> This dull red colour of that part of the South I was then seeing had much, I think, to do with the extreme depression of my spirits – no public squares, no fountains, dingy streetcars, and, with the exception of three or four principal thoroughfares, unpaved streets. It was raining when I arrived and some of the unpaved streets were absolutely impassable. Wheels sank to the hubs in red mire, and I actually stood for an hour and watched four or five men work to save a mule, which had stepped into a deep sink, from drowning, or, rather, suffocating in the mud. (52–3)

The wheels of progress are literally stuck in the mud in the red, Georgia clay. And the spectacle of the suffocating mule, seen retrospectively through the lens of Zora Neale Hurston's evocative elucidations of mules as folkloric figures of black folk, reinforces the sense that it is the black population itself which is sinking into the mire of Georgia. The university, however, stood out by contrast: "here the red hills had been terraced and covered with green grass; clean gravel walks, well shaded, led up to the buildings; indeed it was a little bit of New England transplanted" (60). Rousing a Du Boisian echo, Atlanta University is presented as a monument to the success of the Reconstruction spirit. Unable as yet to exert any sway over the surrounding landscape, the school has at least created itself as an oasis in an inhospitable desert. Significantly, however, Johnson's narrative constructs a plot that detours his protagonist around this "little bit of New England."

This detour is the first road not taken by the protagonist in a novel that chronicles what might be called the failure of a man to become a man. The prefix "ex" extends not only to the protagonist's skin color but to his human status as well. The son of a light-skinned black woman and a white father, who only appears momentarily in his life, Johnson's musically talented narrator embarks on a picaresque journey through blackness, whose pathos derives from a sense that its dimensions may have been epic rather than journalistic. For after having sensed the immense cultural power latent in black music and dance – not only the Sorrow Songs but ragtime and the cakewalk as well – Johnson's ex-colored man ends up passing for a white man whose ideals have been supplanted by the business of moneymaking. Cast in the form of a confession, Johnson's novel seems, when taken as a whole, to endorse Du Bois's contentions that for blacks to be fully human they must not forsake higher cultural ideals in favor of material success.

Embedded within Johnson's narrative, however, is the lurking afterthought from chapter 6 of *Souls* – the making of a man into less than a man. The emergence of this afterthought is decisive in the ex-colored man's life. Having spoken of and embarked upon his enterprise to derive classical musical compositions from black folk materials, the ex-colored man appears to have found his life's mission. As he makes his way through the South collecting materials, however, he stumbles upon a lynching that breaks in on his consciousness, and on the narrative, with frightening speed. Compelled by curiosity and fear to witness the scene of Southern mob violence, the narrator asks the reader, "Have you ever witnessed the transformation of human beings into savage beasts? Nothing can be more terrible" (186). By using the plural, the narrator introduces the lynching as if it were going to serve as a figure for the dehumanization of the perpetrators, the "fierce, determined men . . . blond, tall, and lean, with ragged moustache and beard, and glittering grey eyes" (187). Instead, however, the narration takes a curious turn, with the focus falling on the victim: "There he stood, a man only in form and stature, every sign of degeneracy stamped upon his countenance. His eyes were dull and vacant, indicating not a single ray of thought. Evidently the realization of his fearful fate had robbed him of whatever reasoning power he had ever possessed. He was too stunned and stupefied even to tremble" (186–7). Bereft of thought, reason, and emotion, the nameless victim is at best a manikin, brought back to voice only by the unimaginable pain of the flames that burn his body into "blackened bones" and "charred fragments." By contrast, the "determined men" remain human despite their brutality: "Some of the crowd yelled and cheered, others seemed appalled at what they had done, and there were those who turned away sickened at the sight" (187).

The narrative's curious turn to a dehumanization of the victim rather than the perpetrators is part of an overall strategy by which we are led to judge both the narrator's and the nation's moral deficiencies. The narrator, of course, chooses to pass for white rather than cast his lot with the black race. He bolts from the plot of Exodus for a role in a Horatio Alger story. Before doing so, however, he elucidates the outdated aesthetic that enables the North to indulge the white South: "Looked at from a certain point of view, [Southern whites] are picturesque. If one will put oneself in a romantic frame of mind, one can admire their notions of chivalry and bravery and justice. . . . So can an ordinary peace-loving citizen sit by a comfortable fire and read with enjoyment of the bloody deeds of pirates and the fierce brutality of vikings" (189). By focusing on the brutalization of the mob's victim, however, the novel performs a crucial act of demystification and deromanticization. The scene as depicted lacks any pathos whatsoever; it is the site of humiliation and horror.

Yet something else is at work here as well. The narrative's participation in the dehumanization of the mob's black victim is prefigured by a question that is asked in Paris by a man from Luxembourg before the narrator's return to his homeland: "Did they really burn a man alive in the United States?" (136). The narrator's and Johnson's travels through Western democracies set a stage on which the inability to respond in the negative to the man from Luxembourg is not merely an indictment of the United States but a veiled contempt for black Americans. The routine expectation of bodily security by an expanding number of citizens in Western democracies does not always work unequivocally to expand the points of sympathetic contact with those who cannot lay claim to similar expectations. To the extent that such benefits as bodily security can be experienced as birthrights, they can also be experienced not as rights that states confer upon individuals but as benefits that individuals enjoy by virtue of their refusal to countenance anything less. The growing enjoyment of liberty in still imperfect liberal democratic societies manifests itself as an expansion of opportunities for individuals to experience their good fortune and security as deriving from individual will and agency, rather than from collective activity.

By way of example, one can contrast Johnson's description of the successful lynching of the unnamed man in his narrative to the unsuccessful attempt in Twain's *The Adventures of Huckleberry Finn* to lynch a white man, Colonel Sherburn, for the murder of Boggs. In that narrative, too, the gathering of the mob is at first a horrible thing. Huck observes that "They swarmed up the street towards Sherburn's house, a-whooping and yelling and raging like Injuns, and everything had to clear the way or get run over and tromped to mush, and it was awful to see" (124). But in Twain's narrative, it is the mob and not the would-be victim that is unmanned as Colonel Sherburn spews his contempt on the crowd:

> "The idea of *you* lynching anybody! It's amusing. The idea of you thinking you had pluck enough to lynch a *man*! Because you're brave enough to tar and feather poor friendless cast-out women that come along here, did that make you think you had grit enough to lay your hands on a *man*? Why, a *man's* safe in the hands of ten thousand of your kind – as long as it's day-time and you're not behind him." (125)

The essential cowardice of the mob sets off the individual masculine heroism of Sherburn. The double-barreled shotgun he wields is not portrayed as the equalizer but as an accoutrement of manhood. It is men who effectively wield guns, and not guns that make men. In contrast to Johnson's victim, Twain's *man* simply refuses to be lynched.

To be sure, what I have deemed the narrative's complicity in the dehumanization of the lynched man is not, strictly speaking, Johnson's. Well into the 1920s Johnson worked indefatigably if not successfully to secure passage of anti-lynching legislation, under the assumption that the bodily security of black populations could only be assured by impressing upon whites that they could not with impunity act against alleged black criminals. Johnson's only novel serves, in some respects, as an imaginative brief in these efforts. Perhaps banking on the reader's tendency to identify with the first-person voice, Johnson hoped to make all the more remarkable the narrator's conclusion that he had erred gravely in giving up his black identity. That someone would come to see black identity as preferable to white identity even in the face of Southern and Northern horrors was a remarkable achievement.

More remarkable is the narrative's displacement of social scandal. The ex-colored man's confession reveals that he has transgressed the South's most sacred moral code. Legally a black man, he has married and produced children with a white woman. He is, through his own words, a candidate for the fate of the unnamed lynched man whose demise he unfortunately witnesses. And yet when the narrator remarks upon his "impulse which forces the un-found-out criminal to take somebody into his confidence," what he seems most driven by is not his sexual transgression of the color line but his racial apostasy. In fact, the narrator de-realizes the sexual transgression by suggesting that he had "never really been a Negro" (210). And though he worries that his confession may indeed compromise his children, he reserves his deepest emotion for his failure to join "that small but gallant band of coloured men who war publicly fighting the cause of their race." In comparison to them, he "feel[s] small and selfish. I am an ordinarily successful white man who has made a little money. They are men who are making history and a race" (211).

The diminished stature of the white man who could have been black stands as a testament to Johnson's facility with narrative plot, but also to the marvelous transformation in thinking about race that Du Bois's work made possible. The grandeur of black achievement constitutes the afterthought of the ex-colored man's economic achievement, an apparent reversal of Du Bois's rhetorical strategy, but only apparent in that it nonetheless remains true to the spirit of *The Souls of Black Folk* and its preference for the humane over the merely economic. Johnson's narrator in fact praises Du Bois's book as an attempt "to give the country something new and unknown, in depicting the life, the ambitions, the struggles, and the passions of those of their race who are striving to break the narrow limits of traditions" (168). And yet, in a somewhat ironic reversal of *Souls, The Autobiography of an Ex-Colored Man* concludes by making Booker T. Washington the exemplar of the "earnestness and faith" of black folk (211). The harsh critique of Washington in Du Bois's work is muted in Johnson's novel in favor of a romanticization of black enterprise as a whole. The narrator's failed matriculation at Atlanta University looms large, here. He is, though white, a race man without any particular intraracial allegiance. He can endorse the black race disinterestedly and from a distance sufficient enough to romanticize the racial mission as a whole. The result of this romanticization, though Johnson did not intend it as such, constitutes perhaps the ex-colored man's worst crime. For by enabling a reading of Washington and Du

Bois that would highlight their points of agreement rather than disagreement, a man without color paradoxically used color to mask the historical conflicts that had made his marvelous narrative possible.

WORKS CITED

Cooper, Anna Julia. *A Voice from the South*. New York: Oxford University Press, 1988.

Du Bois, W. E. B., *The Souls of Black Folk* in *Writings*, pp. 357–552. New York: Library of America, 1986.

Ellison, Ralph. *Invisible Man*. New York: Vintage, 1980.

Genovese, Eugene. *Roll, Jordan, Roll: The World the Slaves Made*. New York: Vintage, 1974.

James, C. L. R. "Dialectical Materialism and the Fate of Humanity." In *The C. L. R. James Reader*. Edited by Anna Grimshaw, pp. 153–89. New York: Blackwell, 1992.

Johnson, James Weldon. *The Autobiography of an Ex-Colored Man*. New York: Vintage, 1989.

Khayyam, Omar [Edward FitzGerald]. *The Rubaiyat*. In *The Norton Anthology of English Literature*, 2:1509–20. 3d ed. Edited by Abrams, Donaldson, et al. New York: Norton, 1974.

Levine, Lawrence. *Black Culture, Black Consciousness: Afro-American Folk Thought from Slavery to Freedom*. New York: Oxford University Press, 1977.

Lewis, David Levering. *W. E. B. Du Bois: Biography of a Race, 1868–1919*. New York: Henry Holt and Co., 1993.

McFeely, William S. *Frederick Douglass*. New York: Norton, 1991.

Sundquist, Eric J. *To Wake the Nations: Race in the Making of American Literature*. Cambridge, Mass.: Harvard University Press, 1993.

Twain, Mark. *The Adventures of Huckleberry Finn*. In *The Norton Anthology of American Literature*, 2:27–213. 3d ed. Edited by Baym, Gottesman, et al. New York: W. W. Norton, 1979.

FURTHER READING

This list is confined to general studies of American realism and naturalism, and to studies of these movements in other countries that cast light on the American phenomenon. Works devoted to one author are not included.

Ahnebrink, Lars. *The Beginnings of Naturalism in American Fiction . . . 1891–1903.* Cambridge, Mass.: Harvard University Press, 1950.

Auerbach, Erich. *Memesis: The Representation of Reality in Western Literature.* Princeton, N.J.: Princeton University Press, 1953.

Baguley, David. *Naturalist Fiction: The Entropic Vision.* Cambridge: Cambridge University Press, 1990.

Becker, George J., ed. *Documents of Modern Literary Realism.* Princeton, N.J.: Princeton University Press, 1963.

Realism in Modern Literature. New York: Ungar, 1980.

Bell, Michael Davitt. *The Problem of American Realism: Studies in the Cultural History of a Literary Idea.* Chicago: University of Chicago Press, 1993.

Berthoff, Warner. *The Ferment of Realism: American Literature, 1884–1919.* New York: Free Press, 1965.

Block, Haskell M. *Naturalistic Triptych: The Fictive and the Real in Zola, Mann, and Dreiser.* New York: Random House, 1970.

Borus, Daniel H. *Writing Realism: Howells, James, and Norris in the Mass Market.* Chapel Hill: University of North Carolina Press, 1989.

Bowron, Bernard R., Jr. "Realism in America." *Comparative Literature* 3 (1951): 268–85.

Cady, Edwin H. *The Light of Common Day: Realism in American Fiction.* Bloomington: Indiana University Press, 1971.

Cargill, Oscar. *Intellectual America: Ideas on the March.* New York: Macmillan, 1941.

Carter, Everett. *Howells and the Age of Realism.* Philadelphia: Lippincott, 1954.

Chase, Richard. *The American Novel and Its Tradition.* Garden City, N.Y.: Doubleday Anchor, 1957.

Chevrel, Yves. *Le Naturalisme.* Paris: Presses Universitaires de France, 1982.

Conder, John J. *Naturalism in American Fiction: The Classic Phase.* Lexington: University Press of Kentucky, 1984.

Cowley, Malcolm. "'Not Men': A Natural History of American Naturalism." *Kenyon Review* 9 (1947): 414–35. Reprinted in *Evolutionary Thought in America,* ed. Stow Persons. New Haven and London: Yale University Press, 1950.

Ellmann, Richard, and Feidelson, Charles, Jr., eds. *The Modern Tradition: Backgrounds of Modern Literature*. New York: Oxford University Press, 1965.

Falk, Robert. "The Literary Criticism of the Genteel Decades, 1870–1900." In *The Development of American Literary Criticism*, ed. Floyd Stovall. Chapel Hill: University of North Carolina Press, 1955.

"The Rise of Realism, 1871–1891." In *Transitions in American Literary History*, ed. H. H. Clark. Durham, N.C.: Duke University Press, 1953.

The Victorian Mode in American Fiction, 1865–1885. East Lansing: Michigan State University Press, 1965.

Figg, Robert M. "Naturalism as a Literary Form." *Georgia Review* 18 (1964): 308–16.

Furst, Lilian R., and Skrine, Peter N. *Naturalism*. London: Methuen, 1971.

Geismar, Maxwell. *Rebels and Ancestors: The American Novel, 1890–1915*. Boston: Houghton Mifflin, 1953.

Graham, Philip. "Naturalism in America: A Status Report." *Studies in American Fiction* 10 (1982): 1–16.

Habegger, Alfred. *Gender, Fantasy, and Realism in American Literature*. New York: Columbia University Press, 1982.

Hakutani, Yoshinobu, and Fried, Lewis, eds. *American Literary Naturalism: A Reassessment*. Heidelberg: Carl Winter, 1975.

Hicks, Granville. *The Great Tradition: An Interpretation of American Literature Since the Civil War*. New York: Macmillan, 1933.

Hirsh, John C. "Realism Renewed." *Journal of American Studies* 25 (1991): 235–43.

Hoffman, Frederick J. "From Document to Symbol: Zola and American Naturalism." *Revue des Langues Vivantes*, U.S. Bicentennial Issue (1976): 203–12.

Hook, Andrew. *American Literature in Context III, 1865–1900*. London: Methuen, 1983.

Howard, June. *Form and History in American Literary Naturalism*. Chapel Hill: University of North Carolina Press, 1985.

Kaminsky, Alice. "On Literary Realism." In *The Theory of the Novel: New Essays*, ed. John Halperin. New York: Oxford University Press, 1974.

Kaplan, Amy. *The Social Construction of American Realism*. Chicago: University of Chicago Press, 1988.

Kaplan, Harold. *Power and Order: Henry Adams and the Naturalist Tradition in American Fiction*. Chicago: University of Chicago Press, 1981.

Kazin, Alfred. *On Native Grounds: An Interpretation of Modern American Prose Literature*. New York: Reynal & Hitchcock, 1942.

Kolb, Harold H., Jr. *The Illusion of Life: American Realism as a Literary Form*. Charlottesville: University Press of Virginia, 1969.

Levin, Harry. *The Gates of Horn: A Study of Five French Realists*. New York: Oxford University Press, 1963.

"What Is Realism?" In *Contexts of Criticism*. Cambridge, Mass.: Harvard University Press, 1957.

Lukács, Georg. "Narrate or Describe? A Preliminary Discussion of Naturalism and Formalism." In *Writer and Critic and Other Essays*, ed. Arthur D. Kahn. London: Martin Press, 1970.

Studies in European Realism. London: Hillway, 1950.

McKay, Janet H. *Narration and Discourse in American Realistic Fiction.* Philadelphia: University of Pennsylvania Press, 1982.

Martin, Jay. *Harvests of Change: American Literature, 1865–1914.* Englewood Cliffs, N.J.: Prentice-Hall, 1967.

Martin, Ronald E. *American Literature and the Universe of Force.* Durham, N.C.: Duke University Press, 1981.

Michaels, Walter Benn. *The Gold Standard and the Logic of Naturalism: American Literature at the Turn of the Century.* Berkeley and Los Angeles: University of California Press, 1987.

Mitchell, Lee Clark. *Determined Fictions: American Literary Naturalism.* New York: Columbia University Press, 1989.

Parrington, Vernon Louis. *The Beginnings of Critical Realism in America, 1860–1920.* Vol. 3 of *Main Currents in American Thought.* New York: Harcourt, Brace, 1930.

Pizer, Donald. *Realism and Naturalism in Nineteenth-Century American Literature.* Rev. ed. Carbondale: Southern Illinois University Press, 1984.

The Theory and Practice of American Literary Naturalism: Selected Essays and Reviews. Carbondale: Southern Illinois University Press, 1993.

Twentieth-Century American Literary Naturalism: An Interpretation. Carbondale: Southern Illinois University Press, 1982.

Pizer, Donald, and Harbert, Earl, eds. *American Realists and Naturalists.* Vol. 12 of *Dictionary of Literary Biography.* Detroit: Gale Research, 1982.

Rahv, Philip. "Notes on the Decline of Naturalism." *Image and Idea.* Norfolk, Conn.: New Directions, 1949.

Seltzer, Mark. *Bodies and Machines.* New York: Routledge, 1992.

Stromberg, Roland N., ed. *Realism, Naturalism, and Symbolism: Modes of Thought and Expression in Europe.* New York: Walker, 1968.

Sundquist, Eric J., ed. *American Realism: New Essays.* Baltimore: Johns Hopkins University Press, 1982.

Taylor, Gordon O. *The Passages of Thought: Psychological Representation in the American Novel, 1870–1900.* New York: Oxford University Press, 1969.

Thorp, Willard. *American Writing in the Twentieth Century.* Cambridge, Mass.: Harvard University Press, 1960.

Trachtenberg, Alan. *The Incorporation of America: Culture and Society in the Gilded Age.* New York: Hill and Wang, 1982.

Trilling, Lionel. "Reality in America." *The Liberal Imagination.* New York: Viking, 1950.

Walcutt, Charles C. *American Literary Naturalism, A Divided Stream.* Minneapolis: University of Minnesota Press, 1956.

Wellek, René. "The Concept of Realism in Literary Scholarship." *Concepts of Criticism.* New Haven and London: Yale University Press, 1963.

Wilson, Christopher P. *The Labor of Words: Literary Professionalism in the Progressive Era.* Athens: University of Georgia Press, 1985.

Ziff, Larzer. *The American 1890s.* New York: Viking, 1966.

INDEX

Cambridge Companions to Literature

Printed in the United States
1268800003B/129